Legal Stories

Legal Stories

Narrative-Based Property Development in the Modern Copyright Era

GREGORY STEIRER

University of Michigan Press
Ann Arbor

Published in the United States of America by the
University of Michigan Press
Printed and bound by CPI Group (UK) Ltd, Croydon, CR0 4YY

First published July 2024

A CIP catalog record for this book is available from the British Library.

Library of Congress Cataloging-in-Publication Data

Names: Steirer, Gregory, author. | Michigan Publishing (University of Michigan), publisher.
Title: Legal stories : narrative-based property development in the modern copyright era / Gregory Steirer.
Description: Ann Arbor : University of Michigan Press, 2024. | Includes bibliographical references (pages 269–290) and index.
Identifiers: LCCN 2024002469 (print) | LCCN 2024002470 (ebook) | ISBN 9780472076826 (hardcover) | ISBN 9780472221714 (ebook)
Subjects: LCSH: Copyright—Fictitious characters—United States. | Copyright—United States. | Intellectual property—United States. | Fiction—Authorship—Law and legislation—United States.
Classification: LCC KF3020 .S74 2024 (print) | LCC KF3020 (ebook) | DDC 346.7304/82—dc23/eng/20240205
LC record available at https://lccn.loc.gov/2024002469
LC ebook record available at https://lccn.loc.gov/2024002470

Cover illustration: “Untitled,” by Kate Altman.

For Robert M. Ring

Contents

Digital materials related to this title can be found on the Fulcrum platform via the following citable URL: https://doi.org/10.3998/mpub.11537357

Illustrations

Table

Figures

Acknowledgments

When I first began work in 2012 on the project that eventually became *Legal Stories*, I had no idea what a massive undertaking it would be—nor just how much help it would require to pull off. Over the ten-plus years spent working on it, I have been assisted by a vast number of people, including colleagues, students, entertainment-industry professionals, lawyers, fiction-writers, fans of the properties I examined, editors, friends, and family members; numerous institutions and archives; the United States government, in the form of a year-long National Endowment of the Humanities fellowship; and even a few animals. So many helped in so many ways that it is impossible to acknowledge them all here by name. But to all of you, I am immensely grateful.

A few individuals and institutions deserve special recognition for the outsized—and I suspect often undeserved—degree of resources, advice, and encouragement they contributed to this project. To Jennifer Holt and Michael Curtin, I cannot express enough how much your mentorship has mattered to me. There is no way that *Legal Stories* would have gotten off the ground without you. Thanks also to all the scholars involved with the Connected Viewing Initiative of the Media Industries Project at the Carsey-Wolf Center at the University of California Santa Barbara: Michael and Jen, and also Joshua Braun, Abigail De Kosnik, Elizabeth Evans, Nitin Govil, Daniel Herbert, Anikó Imre, Melanie Kohnen, Aynne Kokas, Amanda Lotz, Paul McDonald, Elissa Nelson, Matthew Thomas Payne, Karen Petruska, Kevin Sanson, Louisa Stein,

Sharon Strover, Chuck Tryon, Ethan Tussey, and Patrick Vonderau. I can think of no better introduction to the field of media industry studies than to have gotten to work alongside you all in collaboration with Warner Bros. Home Entertainment. Special thanks also to Russell Arons, Anuraj Goonetilleke, Dave Miller, and Daniel Ornstein.

To Alisa Perren, I'm still not sure what induced you to take me on as a research partner a decade ago, but I am ever grateful. Thinking and talking through our research for *The American Comic Book Industry and Hollywood* proved invaluable to the development of *Legal Stories*. Your curiosity and sense of humor have helped make scholarly work feel worthwhile—as have the innumerable meals, phone calls, emails, and interviews we've shared since I began this project.

Thank you to my colleagues at Dickinson College, especially those in the Department of English who read drafts of this book's chapters: Sheela Jane Menon, Wendy Moffat, Siobhan Phillips, and Claire Seiler. You have supported this project unconditionally from the get-go, even as it strayed from traditional literary scholarship. A number of students helped with this project: Max Abramson, Logan Cort, Amanda Sowah, Melissa Sturges, and Genevieve Veres. Thank you for the work you did—and for suffering through endless Conan histories and copyright case law. Thank you also Kate Altman for your brilliant, beautiful cover design.

Thank you to Doug Edlin, Kathryn Heard, and Aletheia Allen for helping me think through the challenge of accessing old case files. Thank you as well to Brett Service, at the Warner Bros. Archives at the University of Southern California; Robert Beebe, at the National Archives at Kansas City; and Sabrina Sondhi, at the H. Laddie Montague, Jr. Law Library at Dickinson Law, for going above and beyond to help me gain access to archival material for this project. I am also grateful to Chris Karr and Ken Quattro for providing me with access to hard-to-find legal files and to Paul Marchegiani and Brent LaBarge for taking the time to chat with me about present-day intellectual property law.

Thank you to Matthew Goldmark, Matthew Thomas Payne, and Kevin Sanson for threading the needle through this crazy academic career alongside me. You've influenced this project in more ways than you know, and I can't imagine having found the stamina to complete it without your friendships. Thanks too to Courtney Brannon Donoghue, Hollis Griffin, John Kneisley, Ross Melnick, Mary Naydan, Samuel Portelance, and Kristen Warner for helping me recognize what makes research worthwhile.

Thank you to the National Endowment for the Humanities, which supported this project with a substantial fellowship while it was in its early stages. Thanks also to my editors at the University of Michigan Press: Mary Francis and Sara Cohen. I am grateful for the support you have provided this project and all the help you've given in seeing it published. Thanks also to Annie Carter, Kevin Rennells, and Mark Scott.

To my mom and to Robert Ring, thank you for your inexhaustible encouragement, and for the mountainous piles of books in which I live. Thank you Ronni Rosenstein for always believing in me, and for giving me a space to write: substantial portions of these chapters were first drafted on your dining room table. Matthew Colville, I'm grateful for your generosity in talking comics and movies with me, playing video games (or sometimes reenacting them with me in real-life), and collaborating with me in various kinds of mischief-making.

Thank you Keith Witham for living alongside this project—and all of the books and movies and photocopies of old legal files it entailed—for so many, many years. Thank you as well for introducing me to Bruno Latour, for always politely listening to my never-ending stream of epiphanies, and for your endless empathy and support.

To Azazel, you were there at this project's beginning, walking across the keyboard as I typed or sleeping on my lap as I read through legal treatises. I wish you were here to see the completed book—and to stretch out upon a copy in the sun upon my desk. To Lyra and June and Maverick and Moo, and to Cody, thank you for keeping me company as I wrote and for the many study breaks we took together. To Winnie, at my feet as I write this, thank you for the love and sense of purpose you brought at this project's end.

And thanks, finally, to Jake, who lay beside me for hours at a time as I wrote and researched and who, at the completion of each workday, journeyed outside with me to visit neighbors, go to the park, or walk in sweeping circles the streets of our neighborhood. With you at my side, the world felt so full of promise that every walk seemed the beginning of a grand new story that the two of us would write together. Thank you for the year you spent with me while I finished this manuscript. I miss you.

Introduction

This is a book about stories. Specifically, it is about big, multitext stories that develop over years, across multiple media, and under the hands of diverse authors and managers. Contemporary scholars and entertainment professionals refer to such stories with a variety of terms, including *narrative franchise, transmedia storytelling, story world, IP* (an abbreviation for *intellectual property*), and *adaptation.*[1] Today, such stories are among the most popular and profitable in the world and are managed by some of the United States' largest entertainment and technology companies. Under the names of Star Wars, Harry Potter, The Walking Dead, Halo, and The Marvel Cinematic Universe (to list just a few), they have become a ubiquitous feature—or perhaps even the paradigmatic form—of twenty-first-century media and popular entertainment.[2] If the nineteenth century belonged to the novel, and the twentieth to film (and television), then the twenty-first, at least so far, might be said to belong to the narrative franchise.

During the historical period with which this book is concerned, however, the franchise was in its infancy. Between 1909 and 1978, big, multitext, multimedia, multiauthor stories existed, sort of, but they were created, managed, and consumed very differently from today. With few exceptions, they also tended not to be the mammoth money- and attention-generators that they have been this century. Major media companies did not endeavor to produce them, nor until the very end of this period would they have recognized them as a distinct category of narrative product. Partly for these reasons, the period lacked a specialized vocabulary to refer to them. What we call *franchises*, *transmedia*, and *IP* were not called much of anything before 1978. The texts of which they consisted were instead identified and treated as the same kind of property that constituted any narrative product. Indeed, the texts and their underlying assets were often referred to as *literary* property, even when they originated in visual media such as film and television.

In tracing the history of such property before it was important enough to producers and consumers to be given a name, this book demonstrates how the meaning and form of narrative-based property at any given time is integrally bound up with the letter and practice of intellectual property law at that time. In other words, the reason big, multitext, multimedia, multiauthor stories were created, managed, and consumed differently before 1978 is because the legal principles pertaining to narrative-based property before 1978 reflect a different set of values, expectations, and basic ontological premises from the laws of today. Legally speaking, a story was a different kind of property from what it is now.

This is not to say that the law is all-determining or that it operates in some top-down manner to dictate how authors and other creative professionals think about storytelling. To the contrary, the law is also in many ways a product of authors' and creative professionals' own values, expectations, and basic ontological premises. As one set of values changes—the law's or creators'—so does the other's; but with the two so "imbricated" or "constitutively entangled" (to borrow the language of organizational scholarship and the sociology of science and technology) that it is often impossible to tell on which side the change originated.[3] *Legal Stories* traces this entanglement to tell the story of how modern multitext, multimedia, multiauthor storytelling functioned (and did not function) as a legal-industrial object. Drawing inspiration from Bruno Latour's work mapping the connections between different domains of knowledge,[4] the book offers a dual history of literary property development and copyright law in the United States, beginning in 1909 and ending a couple years after the passage of the Copyright Act of 1976—a period that I call, for reasons explained in the following section, *the modern copyright era*. To tell this story, the book provides case studies of legal disputes involving six important properties created and developed during this time: Sam Spade and the Maltese Falcon, the Cthulhu Mythos, the Katzenjammer Kids, Barney Google and his horse Sparkplug, Superman, and Conan the Barbarian.

Such franchise-like literary property is, however, not the only kind of story this book is about. *Legal Stories* also takes as its subject matter the stories we tell about intellectual property law itself. How do we understand this branch of law to work and how do we relay it working? And who exactly is the *we* who does this understanding and relaying? Inspired by the scholarly field of law and society and adopting the epistemology of actor-network theory, this book takes a broad and inclusive approach to answering these questions, locating the production of legal knowledge not just in the black-letter law of judicial opinions and congressional statutes, nor the briefs, books, and law review articles produced by lawyers, but also in the everyday practices and productions of laymen: authors, editors, readers, fans, and heirs. It treats legal knowledge as a practice, both institutionalized and highly discursive, developed—by disputants, as well as their counsel and the judges that decide their cases—through research, argument, experimentation, improvisation, and often by accident or even mistake. In keeping with normative legal theory, legal decisions, both in and out of court, are revealed to hinge on logical reasoning and analogy—but not exclusively. They are also shown to hinge on a number of other factors: the resources available to disputants; the moral values of the disputants and their judges; the cognitive costs of committing to an argument, belief, or understanding (and/or of admitting one is wrong); the communication skills of those involved in the dispute, as well as their personalities and temperaments; and even the aesthetic features of the literary properties being fought over.

Because of its attention to these nonnormative factors, the history of copyright law presented in *Legal Stories* is rather different from the histories of copyright law presented elsewhere. Although drawing upon many of the same statutes and case law as other scholarly histories, this book presents a vision of the law as stumbling, accident-prone, and susceptible to contingency; a law with myriad inputs and outputs beyond judicial opinions and statutes; a law that takes place as often outside the courtroom as inside; and a law shaped and practiced as much by laymen as lawyers. The case studies draw upon archival material—trial transcripts, letters, briefs, contracts, even (in chapter 2) a legal team's research notes—to present a grounds-eye picture of how the law operates—and at times evolves—in practice. For all its diversity and idiosyncrasy, however, the law as represented in these pages is also relatively stable. It constitutes, in its basic premises and statutory requirements, a distinct period, which, though continuing to evolve at the edges, does not undergo radical change until after the implementation of a new copyright act in 1978.

Before I discuss this period in greater detail, a brief introduction to the book's term for big, multitext, multimedia, multiauthor stories is in order. I refer to these stories, and the assets of which they are comprised, as *narrative-based property*. Rather than rely on already existing terms, originally developed to describe changes to media in the twenty-first century, this book primarily relies upon this new term, largely devoid of scholarly connotation. The goal in doing so is to defamiliarize the book's research object and thereby make more easily visible the actions—legal, managerial, and aesthetic—by which that object was given form over the course of the modern copyright era. A narrative-based property can be defined as a fictional text, a collection of such texts, and/or the assets that originate in such texts, the use of which is believed by legal actors, rightly or wrongly, to be constrained in some fashion (by statute, contract, morality, etc.), to have financial value, and to be alienable. This is a broad and somewhat amorphous definition, which might seem to encompass most (though not all) works of fiction. At first glance, it might even seem to apply to a much larger set of works than do the terms *franchise*, *transmedia*, or *IP*. As the rest of this book should make clear, however, such a broad and amorphous definition accurately reflects how legal, creative, and managerial actors understood and developed fictional texts during the modern copyright era.

It is also important to note that this book focuses solely on *narrative-based* property. It does not consider copyright law as it applies to other kinds of intellectual property, such as music, which developed under a very different legal-industrial logic. Nor does it consider patent law, except as it intersects with copyright law (specifically in reference to consumer goods based on cartoon characters)[5], nor state laws protecting mere ideas.[6] Trademark law is discussed, but—as the history provided by the book demonstrates (and as chapter 4 explains in detail)—trademark law played a minimal role in the management of narrative-based property during the modern copyright era.[7] A history of intellectual property law that puts music or patent law at its heart would likely be quite different from the history offered here—and may even require a different approach to periodization.

The Modern Copyright Era: 1909–1978

The roughly seventy-year period that serves as the subject of this book begins with the implementation of the Copyright Act of 1909 (in 1909) and ends with the implementation of the Copyright Act of 1976 (in 1978). As noted above, this was an unusually stable period of time for copyright law at the legislative level. With respect to statute, the law remained, in nearly all its important features, the same in 1977 as it was in late 1909. As a result, the vast majority of significant legal developments (at least with respect to narrative-based property) took place via case law produced by judges—what legal scholars usually refer to as the *common law.* Unlike in some other countries (particularly those with a system of civil law), the U.S. common-law system is adversarial, meaning that judges cannot create law *ex nihilo*; rather, they produce law as part of the process of adjudicating disputes between at least two distinct parties. The evolution of common law thus follows a process that is logically distinct from legislative lawmaking and is often slow, winding, and marked (by design) with a tendency toward path dependency, which can impede its ability to respond on its own to changing technical, industrial, and social conditions.

Because there was minimal legislative action between 1909 and 1976, and because the 1909 Act was even in 1909 already in important respects old-fashioned, judges—prompted by industrial actors—were forced during this time to make the law "serviceable" through their rulings, creating what legal scholar Jessica Litman has called "the common law of statutory copyright."[8] The period in which this common law reigned is radically different, at the legal level, from the periods preceding and following it. As Litman explains:

> The common law of statutory copyright possessed a number of strengths and some unsurprising weaknesses. Like many bodies of judge-made law, the common law doctrines were often inconsistent and contradictory, not only among courts but within courts; not only among lines of cases, but within lines of cases. The law was riddled with analytically indefensible distinctions, impractical definitions, and wholesale distortion of statutory language. It was nonetheless a magnificent edifice.[9]

It was also, as *Legal Stories* demonstrates, largely functional. Industrial actors of all kinds—both highly capitalized companies and individual creators—were able to work with and under it, albeit not always without difficulty. Sometimes they did so by developing managerial and contractual practices that rendered common law decisions irrelevant. At other times, they managed to induce, through legal battle, the common law to evolve in ways that served their respective interests.

Whether one assesses the common law of statutory copyright positively or negatively, however, one fact is undeniable: with the Copyright Act of 1976, Congress reclaimed its function as lawmaker, substantially transforming how copyright law worked and rendering whole swathes of the common law irrelevant for future creators. Barbara Ringer, the register of copyrights from 1973 to 1980, described the Act in radical terms:

> [T]he New Act is not a "general revision" in the same sense that the 1909 Act was, *i.e.* a bringing together of scattered statutory provisions with relatively few changes or innovations. The New Act is rather a completely new copyright statute, intended to deal with a whole range of problems undreamed of by the drafters of the 1909 Act. Even more important, the new statute makes a number of fundamental changes in the American copyright system, including some so profound that they may mark a shift in direction of the very philosophy of copyright itself.[10]

Indeed, copyright worked so differently before 1978 from how it did after 1978 that it is impossible to treat the two as part of the same legal regime except when speaking at a very high degree of generality. This is not to say that the new law did not preserve aspects of the old (it did quite explicitly, for example, for works that were created before 1978[11]), but rather that if one is interested in the process of historical change—both with respect to the law and to the management of narrative-based property—then the intellectual-property regime inaugurated by the Act of 1976 must be taken as a clear break from the regime that preceded it.

Of course, the regime of 1909–1978 differs from what came next not solely because of the changes wrought by the new statute. After 1978, significant technological, industrial, and cultural changes occurred as well, and these had a profound impact on intellectual property law and the entertainment businesses dependent on narrative-based property. Such changes include the widescale profusion of software and software licenses, the emergence of the Internet, the establishment of multiple modes of digital distribution (piracy, electronic sell-through, streaming, etc.), the mainstreaming of fan/geek culture, and the disabling of traditional gatekeeping via platforms for user-generated content. These developments have created much work for courts and legislators, who continue today to struggle with how best to accommodate (or in some cases inhibit) them via intellectual property law, but they have also changed how narrative-based property is understood by creators, companies, and consumers.

As for the earlier historical boundary point, one might argue that the Copyright Act of 1909 represents more of a continuance than a break from the Act that preceded it (the Copyright Act of 1870). Although true, the scope and speed of technological, industrial, and cultural change within the entertainment industry during the first eight decades of the twentieth century render this period a different legal and business environment from that of the century preceding it. Silent film, sound film, comic strips, comic books, radio, television, animation, pulp magazines, and paperbacks did not exist until the twentieth century (or, for a few of these media, the very last years of the nineteenth), and with them came radical changes to the economics of authorship, the business models of entertainment companies, and the everyday practices of popular cultural consumption.[12] The period of 1909–1978 thus represents a legal regime distinct in important ways, some of them even, as Ringer suggested, "philosophical," from that of the periods both following *and* preceding it. I call this regime *the modern copyright regime.*

Unfortunately, the word *modern* has quite a diverse range of uses in legal scholarship, with some scholars employing it merely as a synonym for *present-day* or *contemporary*. Others, such as Pamela Samuelson, associate *modern* copyright law with the implementation of the first (English) copyright statute, the Statute of Queen Anne, passed in 1710; in this schema, the English Stationers' Guild's earlier regulatory regime represents "pre-modern" copyright law.[13] Complicating the word's meaning further still are the varied national histories to which different scholars apply it. Brad Sherman and Lionel Bently, for example, in *The Making of Modern Intellectual Property Law,* have argued that "modern intellectual property law" as "a separate and distinct area of law replete with its own logic and grammar," emerged in Britain around 1850 and was ultimately codified by statute in 1911.[14] Scholars of Chinese intellectual property law, by contrast, identify "modern" copyright law with the late-twentieth and early-twenty-first centuries.[15]

In naming the period of 1909–1978 *the modern copyright era* in the context of U.S. law, I have followed the lead of legal scholars Ron Gard and Elizabeth Townsend Gard, who argue that the Copyright Act of 1909 was built on "modernist" assumptions focusing "on the object, rather than on the value of the object."[16] By this they mean that the Act was organized around protecting individual texts, such as a single poem or book, created by singular authors, instead of (and sometimes in ways that undermined) the uses that the text's owners or licensees wished to put the text. This left American copyright law, Gard and Gard claim, ill-suited for many of the cultural and industrial developments of the twentieth century.[17] What copyright law most needed, they suggest, was a "reorientation toward the concept of circulation,"[18] especially as cultural modernism came to an end in the 1970s. Their approach to copyright periodization provides a useful framework for studying the development (or lack thereof) of the law, and it has proven to be well-supported empirically by the case studies that make up *Legal Stories*, which often demonstrate the importance of modernist values in both the workings of the law and in the management of narrative-based property.

The question of what to label the period notwithstanding, my assertion that U.S. copyright law worked differently before and after 1978 is by no means novel. Indeed, that the law changed fundamentally via the Act of 1976 is a basic knowledge point in both legal practice and legal scholarship. It is also well understood by rightsholders whose copyrighted works originated before the Act was implemented. That said, the period has been surprisingly understudied (at least with respect to narrative-based property) as a distinct legal regime and/or period of property production. The vast majority of law review articles (or essays in law-related journals) on copyright or IP law published over the last two decades frame themselves around the concerns of twenty-first-century law, while more historically inflected work has tended to focus on American copyright's first century or on its history as a whole, stretching from a variety of origin points (including that of common law copyright) to the present day.[19] More surprising still, there exists not a single work of book-length scholarship focusing on legal issues pertaining to narrative-based property in the period preceding 1978. The closest is Dorothy Howell's ahead-of-its-time treatise, *Intellectual Properties and the Protection of Fictional Characters*, which, in part because it was published in 1990, devotes considerable attention to pre-1978 case law.[20]

Legal Stories focuses on this period instead of an earlier or later period because many of the twenty-first century's most valuable narrative-based properties (excepting those originating in the video game industry) emerged during the modern copyright era. Mickey Mouse, Superman, Batman, Spider-Man, Peanuts, Tarzan, Perry Mason, Star Trek, Star Wars, and countless other American properties were created between 1909 and 1978, as well as numerous British properties (James Bond and Lord of the Rings, to name just two) whose success is partly owed to their exploitation in the United States during this period. Despite the apparent problems with a legal regime founded on modernist values, the regime seems to have worked well enough to give rise to long-lasting, globally cherished properties. How did it do so and what might it have to teach us about the legal needs of narrative-based property development today? Because these properties have been so long lasting, it is also important to recognize that the past is, in important respects, the present. Despite the significant changes to copyright law introduced by the Copyright Act of 1976, earlier contracts, earlier case law, and earlier conditions of production have all continued to inform how properties have been managed after 1978. If one wants to understand a given narrative-based property today (or, for that matter, a given law or legal practice), it is helpful to understand how and why it emerged as it did.

I have tried in the chapters that follow to accurately convey the state of knowledge (or confusion) as it existed during the period about which I write. To do so, I rely primarily on primary source documents: law review articles, legal textbooks, case law, memoirs, guild publications, and other textual documents that were written and published during the period itself. I have adopted this approach for two reasons. First, in keeping with the tenets of actor-network theory, I have sought to produce an account of discursive formations as produced by historical actors in response to the challenges, opportunities, and uncertainties that they themselves faced. Rather than see the production of modern narrative-based properties retrospectively, from a twenty-first-century perspective, I have endeavored as much as possible to see such production as the properties' creators, managers, fans, and legal advisors did. Second, much present-day legal scholarship on intellectual property has, for good reason, aims and concerns that are far afield from those of actors in the modern copyright era. Some key features of the modern era, such as indivisibility (discussed in chapter 1), are considered historical relics and, as such, rarely figure into contemporary discussions of intellectual property law at all, especially in relation to narrative-based property. Likewise, many of the most pressing intellectual-property concerns of today—such as trademark dilution, legal immunity for Internet platforms, or what constitutes transformation under the doctrine of fair use—were barely on the radars of modern-copyright-era actors. My emphasis on historical discourse and historical knowledge does not mean that *Legal Stories* ignores more recent scholarship where relevant. Such scholarship features significantly in the introductory framing provided at the start of each chapter and in discussions of the broader historical significance of the different legal principles I analyze. In the case studies themselves, however, I have tried, like other works of media history, to privilege primary historical sources.

Actor-Network Theory

Actor-network theory (ANT) is an approach to sociological research that advocates treating complex, socially significant objects as assemblages comprised of a myriad of human and non-human actors.[21] It takes big, important things that social science typically treats as singular and self-evident, such as a law or an author, and demonstrates how these things are actually multiple and interdependent. For a law to function as a law, for example, all sorts of human beings (judges, lawyers, paralegals, law review editors, textbook writers, publishers, monitoring agents, those whom the law affects, etc.) must continually perform actions that communicate, interpret, and enact the law. And to perform these actions, they need the help of a tremendous number of tools and artifacts, including printers, photocopiers, books (including books of case law), phones, file cabinets, shipping trucks, office buildings, courthouses, etc.—things that ANT calls "non-human actors," since such things don't just facilitate human actions but actively determine their form and meaning.[22] Scholarship that employs an ANT framework proceeds by tracing the interactions of these various human and non-human actors—a task that, much like the "thick description" of traditional ethnography,[23] depends heavily upon slow, detailed storytelling.

Both the research conducted for this book and the form the book's chapters ultimately took was heavily influenced by ANT. In keeping with ANT's epistemological framework, *Legal Stories* avoids hypostasizing complex objects, such as a story world, a dispute, a law, or a lawsuit, preferring to represent such objects as assemblages given form by multiple actors (human and non-human) interacting over time. Instead of leaping from a statute, a judicial opinion, or a contract to conclusions as to what a law did, how a dispute was resolved, or what rights the different parties held, it traces out the slow and often twisting processes by which legal knowledge and legal action were given shape. The chapters thus practice what Bruno Latour at one point called "slowciology,"[24] wherein the costs of moving from point to point must continually be paid and—as he puts it in a cringe-inducing simile—the "ANT-scholar has to trudge like an ant, carrying the heavy gear in order to generate even the tiniest connection."[25]

That said, *Legal Stories* differs from other ANT work in one important regard: it is a work of history, relying upon archival research, and not a work of ethnography. Since the 1980s, ANT's biggest impact has been on the discipline of sociology (particularly in science and technology studies), where it has introduced new ways of thinking about and conducting ethnographic research. In disciplines less reliant upon ethnography, such as media studies and legal studies, ANT has had a much smaller impact[26]—and in the discipline of history, it has so far had almost no impact whatsoever.[27] *Legal Stories* hopes to help change this by demonstrating how ANT can be productively employed outside of ethnographic contexts and, in particular, on historical research projects. This book provides an example of how an ANT-inflected history rooted in archival research might work, and how such an approach can prove useful when dealing with copyright law, narrative-based property, and other hybrid, legal-aesthetic objects.

Chapter Overviews

Legal Stories consists of five main chapters, each of which is oriented around one or two legal principles, plus a short concluding chapter. For all but chapter 1, each chapter begins, after a short introduction, with a detailed description of the principles it is addressing. This description is followed by case studies of one or more narrative-based properties. The case studies attend carefully to the narratological and aesthetic dimensions of the properties, but each ultimately revolves around disputes of a legal kind that concerned the properties. The stories the chapters tell are thus as much legal histories as they are textual or managerial histories. Indeed, the book as a whole aims to demonstrate that these three kinds of history—legal, textual, and managerial—are one and the same, and that to bracket off (for example) the legal in favor of the textual is to mistake how textual development usually took place during the modern copyright era.

For better and worse, the legal principles the book examines, like the narrative-based properties it explores, do not lend themselves to a strict chronological ordering. The idea-expression dichotomy (discussed in chapter 2), for example, functioned concurrently—and indeed interacted with—the principle of authorial genius (discussed in chapter 3) during the entire modern copyright era. Each of the properties also developed and changed over multiple decades (with most continuing to develop today), which means there is little benefit in ordering them temporally, for example, by their initial creation or publication dates. What I have done instead is ordered the chapters by way of increasing legal complexity, with chapter 1 focusing on the most basic of copyright legal principles, familiarity with which is assumed by all subsequent chapters. The chapters thus work cumulatively, with each chapter building upon and occasionally referencing the legal principles presented in earlier chapters. Although I have tried to write the book so that one might jump around in one's reading without getting lost, it is intended to be read in order, so that, for example, chapter 2's exploration of whether fictional characters are protected by copyright can be later complicated by chapter 4's examination of how case law approached the same question with respect to comic and cartoon characters.

Chapter 1 differs from subsequent chapters in that it does not contain a case study. Instead, it introduces two very basic legal principles, which, though mostly irrelevant to present-day copyright law, fundamentally defined this earlier era: *short copyright duration* and *copyright formalities.* Offering detailed analyses of registration and deposit requirements and copyright indivisibility as examples of the latter, the chapter illustrates how the two principles functioned as the foundational infrastructure of the modern copyright era, influencing the behavior of creators, businesspersons, lawyers, and judges in sometimes predictable and sometimes unpredictable fashion. Because the two principles were fundamental to the development of narrative-based property, virtually every copyright dispute occurring during the modern copyright era revolved around them to some extent—including those taken up in subsequent chapters. In addition to being the first part of the book's description of the modern copyright era, this chapter thus also functions as an introduction to the chapters that follow.

Chapter 2 offers a detailed account of *Warner Bros. Pictures v. Columbia Broadcasting System* (or what has come to be called "the Sam Spade case") and the modern-copyright-era legal principles of *the idea-expression dichotomy* and *iterative textual derivation.* A precedent-setting case often seen today as erroneously decided, *Warner Bros. Pictures v. Columbia Broadcasting System* concerned the rights to the fictional detective who serves as the main protagonist of the novel and film titled *The Maltese Falcon.* The chapter provides detailed descriptions of the two legal principles, one formal and the other informal, demonstrating how they functioned together to shape what narrative-based property looked like during the modern copyright era. It traces Dashiell Hammett's career as an author and what I call an *IP entrepreneur.* And it explains the genesis of the legal dispute and the particular structure it took in court(s). The majority of the chapter, however, is devoted to providing an account of how the legal principles played out in the actual legal battle. Drawing upon papers held at the Warner Bros. Archive at the University of Southern California, I describe how lawyers for Warner Bros. developed, argued, and ultimately lost their case—and thereby demonstrate why the Ninth Circuit's opinion was not—as most contemporary legal scholars view it—faulty. In addition to illustrating how fictional characters were understood by legal actors during the modern copyright era, the chapter aims to serve as a definitive account of *Warner Bros. Pictures v. Columbia Broadcasting System.*

Chapter 3 examines H. P. Lovecraft's Cthulhu Mythos, an unusual property that by the standards of formal copyright law would probably not have constituted bona fide "property" during the modern copyright era. Despite the lack of protection a court would have likely given it, however, it nevertheless functioned, both semantically and legally, like a property from its creation in the 1920s until the 1970s. This chapter demonstrates how the legal principle of *authorial genius* made this possible. More specifically, the chapter reveals how Lovecraft himself served, both during and after his life, as the primary semantic and legal fulcrum of the property. Tracing the property's development from its creation in the 1920s by Lovecraft and the Lovecraft Circle to its "loss" of copyright protection in the 1970s after decades of clever management by Lovecraft's friend and posthumous publisher, August Derleth, the chapter shows how narrative-based properties can depend as much—if not more—on informal legal rights than formal. Drawing in part upon Lovecraft's published letters and on the papers of August Derleth held by the Wisconsin Historical Society, the chapter illustrates how authors, fans, editors, managers, and other stakeholders who lacked legal training applied their own understandings of the law to interact with, develop, and/or protect a property—in ways inconsistent with formal law but nevertheless with frequent success.

Chapter 4 takes up a long recognized (and frequently criticized) quirk of U.S. common law: the law seemingly grants greater protection under copyright to cartoon characters (a term used at the time to refer to characters originating in comic strips, comic books, and animated film) than it does characters associated with other media. The chapter provides an explanation for this quirk. Drawing upon both general legal history and three influential cases involving cartoon characters, I argue that, in dealing with such characters, legal actors (both formal and informal) imported principles into copyright law that one would today recognize as more properly belonging to unfair competition and trademark law. They did so, in part, because the principles of *unfair competition* and *trademark law* were not understood during most of the modern copyright era as being applicable to narrative-based property except in a very limited sense. Whereas the other chapters introduce and explain the key legal principles of the modern copyright regime, in this chapter the emphasis is on the *absence* of a legal principle and the effects its absence had on the regime. The chapter employs case files for *Star Co. v. Press Publishing Co.* (held at the Smithsonian Archives of American Art) and *King Features v. Fleischer* and *Detective Comics v. Bruns* (both held at the National Archives at Kansas City) in order to provide a general picture of how cartoon characters were understood and treated by authors, publishers, and toy manufacturers—as well as lawyers and judges—during the modern copyright era. The case files also serve, however, to demonstrate the way the common law can be shaped (as it was on this issue) by arbitrary and contingent aspects of formal disputes: the skill of counsel, the precedent that is deemed controlling, the language of an opinion, the temperament of a judge, even the personal conduct of a party to the suit. In keeping with some of the conclusions of legal realism and law and society research, it thus presents the common law as a kind of knowledge production uniquely influenced—for better and worse—by *stare decisis* (i.e., precedent).

Chapter 5 focuses on the development of the Conan the Barbarian property. One of the first recognizable fantasy properties, Conan originated in the fiction of Robert E. Howard in the 1930s and, through careful, clever, and lucky management, developed into a narrative-based property that still functions as such today, despite most of the original stories having many years ago entered the public domain. Indeed, of all the properties examined in this book save for Superman (the disputed subject of *Detective Comics v. Bruns Publications*, discussed in chapter 4), the Conan property has come to most resemble those of twenty-first-century media franchises and transmedia storytelling. Thanks in part to the principle of *informal contracting*, however, for a substantial portion of its history the property was in serious danger of disintegrating. Drawing in part on the archives of L. Sprague and Catherine Crook de Camp, held at the Harry Ransom Center at the University of Texas Austin, this chapter reconstructs this history and demonstrates how informal contracting was both a threat to the property's long-term success and, paradoxically, directly responsible for this success. The history as presented here also serves as a kind of culmination of the chapters that preceded it: all of the legal principles presented previously in the book play important roles in the account I provide of the Conan property. The chapter thus serves as an example of a holistic, multicausal legal history of a narrative-based property.

The book's coda briefly turns toward the changes to narrative-based property development wrought, first, by the Copyright Act of 1976, and then by a series of other legal, technological, and cultural changes. It asks, in effect, what comes after the modern copyright era, and it provides a provisional sketch of how such a question might be answered. Offering up the examples of three post-1978 legal principles—*transformative use*, *trademark law*, and the *safe harbor provision*—it provides a speculative periodization of intellectual property law after 1978, proposing a *post-modern copyright era* stretching from 1978 to 1998, followed by a *trademark era*, stretching from 1995 to the present.

As stated earlier, *Legal Stories* is, at its heart, a book about stories. It investigates the processes by which stories and their unique assets were transformed into narrative-based property during the modern copyright era. Put simply, the book asks how such property came to be recognized, however imperfectly, by the law. In this regard, the "legal stories" indicated by the book's title are stories that relevant historical actors—including creators, lawyers, judges, and fans—believed to have a claim to protection under copyright law as a special kind of property. But the book is also concerned with a different kind of "legal story": the kind that people tell about the law. As the case studies reveal, the human beings involved with narrative-based property were constantly crafting stories to make sense of the law and to persuade others that this sense was correct. Indeed, U.S. law actively requires such storytelling, and formal disputes are almost always, to some degree, a battle between storytellers. *Legal Stories* pays careful attention to the ways that important instances of such storytelling worked (or failed to work) during the modern copyright era.

There is yet, however, one additional sense of "legal story" meant by this book's title: the stories about narrative-based property and copyright law that *Legal Stories* itself tells. Informed by the principles of law-and-society scholarship and the epistemology of actor-network theory, and taking the form of scholarly accounts of the law, these stories are still, at their heart, stories, and like all stories they have been inspired by a myriad of other tales, many of them relayed to me in speech or writing by fans of the properties the book examines. I am grateful to these fans, without whom *Legal Stories* could not have been written. Indeed, in addition to sharing with me their stories, some of these fans provided me access to legal material that was otherwise unavailable to the public. I hope that these and other readers find pleasure in the stories this book contains, and that the book's stories, like the stories from which it was made, go on to inspire future stories—by writers of fiction, lawyers, scholars, and other kinds of storyteller.

CHAPTER 1

The Modern Copyright Era's Foundational Legal Infrastructure

Short Copyright Duration and Copyright Formalities

In this brief introductory chapter, I describe two interrelated principles of the modern copyright era—*short copyright duration* and *copyright formalities*—that were so stable and so unyielding that they are best understood as the modern copyright regime's foundational infrastructure. Statutory creations that neither judges nor private contracts could undo, the two principles functioned for creators and property managers as a set of concrete requirements and limitations, which more often than not impeded these actors' abilities to develop and manage long-lasting narrative-based properties. Both constituting and deriving from an assemblage of nonnegotiable, usually unforgiving, and often arcane rules, these principles are much like those associated today with a federal income tax or electoral voting system: clear in purpose and never taken for granted but with inner workings that are often difficult to understand. This is not to say that legal actors did not sometimes seek to use the rules to their advantage or, as we will see in subsequent chapters, ignore them outright (and hope not to get caught doing so). But the principles themselves—and their vital importance to narrative-based property development during this period—were never seriously questioned.

Because the principles of short copyright duration and copyright formalities constitute the foundational infrastructure of the modern copyright era, virtually every copyright dispute occurring during the period on which this book focuses revolves around them to some extent. A basic familiarity with these principles is thus essential for fully understanding the case studies provided in subsequent chapters. In addition to being the first part of the book's description of the modern copyright era, this chapter is thus also intended to serve as a propaedeutic for the chapters that follow. Perhaps in a book on twenty-first-century copyright law, such a propaedeutic would not be necessary, as readers might be expected to have some basic, if vague, knowledge of how long a copyright lasts and in what manner a copyright is secured and enforced. Except for copyright law historians (or aging industrial actors), however, few readers of this book are likely to possess such knowledge for the years between 1909 and 1978. Indeed, as this chapter demonstrates, the principles governing the length of copyright, the process of registration, and the meaning of a license during these years are so different from those governing these things today that the two older principles alone might be sufficient reason for characterizing the period as its own distinct legal regime.

Duration of Copyright

Although contemporary advocates of copyright reform regularly characterize the history of U.S. copyright law in terms of what they call "copyright creep" or "copyright maximalism" (by which is meant the gradual but steady lengthening of the duration of protection), for most of the twentieth century the period of protection granted by U.S. copyright law was significantly shorter than that of most other nations.[1] From 1909 to the 1960s, at which time a series of one-, two-, and three-year extensions were authorized by Congress while it worked to develop and pass a new copyright statute, the United States granted published works a total of fifty-six years of protection, split into two successive terms of twenty-eight years each.[2] That this is lower than the period of protection provided by other countries can be demonstrated by reviewing, in table 1, the findings of early copyright scholar Augustine Birrell, who surveyed the copyright terms of eleven nations just before the end of the nineteenth century.[3]

A more extensive survey, conducted by the U.S. Register of Copyrights in 1903 produced similar results: the period of protection granted in the United States was found to be exceptionally brief.[4] In addition, the United States was idiosyncratic in its division of the protection into two terms and its assignment of a fixed duration, unrelated to the length

TABLE 1. Duration of Copyright by Nation in 1899

Nation	Duration of Copyright
Brazil	life of author + 10 years
Britain	life of author + 7 years or 42 years from first publication (whichever is longer)
Chile	life of author + 5 years
France	life of author + 50 years
Germany	life of author + 30 years
Guatemala	perpetual
Italy	life of author or 40 years (whichever is longer), followed by a second period of 40 years in which rights are subject to a compulsory license
Mexico	perpetual
Peru	life of author + 20 years
Spain	life of author + 80 years
Venezuela	perpetual

of the author's life. Although a few countries offered perpetual copyrights, the Register concluded in 1903 that "[t]he life of the author and a term of fifty years after his death is perhaps the most generally approved period of protection."[5]

As the two studies demonstrate, the total period of protection available in the United States during most of the twentieth century was significantly shorter than that offered by most other nations *at the end of the nineteenth century*. Beginning in the 1920s, a plethora of bills were introduced in one or both houses of Congress that would have extended—either as their main goal or as incidental to another goal—the duration of copyright. Some never had hearings, most were never voted upon, and none were passed into law. What hearings there were suggest that, with the exception of the broadcasting industry, virtually all stakeholders—and it would seem most lawmakers—were in favor of a longer period of protection. However, because the relatively straightforward problem of duration was always attached to more complicated legislative problems (such as what constitutes publication or how copyrights in musical works should be governed), Congress proved unable to make progress on it.[6] As the century proceeded and the rest of the world gradually adopted the Berne Convention's recommended minimum of life of the author plus fifty years (with the United Kingdom adopting it in 1911 and Germany in 1934), the United States' two short, fixed periods continued to fall even further out of sync with international norms.[7]

Even more extraordinary, this international comparison, based as it is on written statutes alone, attributes to the United States a much longer period of protection during these years than most U.S. rightsholders ever received. In practice, the vast majority of rightsholders received only one twenty-eight-year-term of protection, for most simply failed to apply for the second term. An exhaustive study of copyright renewals undertaken by the U.S. Copyright Office in 1960 found that for each year between 1910 and 1959 between 85.3 and 97 percent of eligible copyrighted works were not renewed.[8] The reasons that copyrights were so rarely renewed are, as we will see in some of the chapters that follow, multiple. Renewals could be complicated and arduous, and they hinged upon precise timing: an application for renewal had to be submitted in the year prior to the expiration of the first term of protection—no earlier and no later. Failure to file at the correct time, no matter what the reason, forfeited the right to a second term of protection. Renewals also hinged upon precise records: one needed to know the title of the work as it had been originally registered, the name of the person or company registered as rightsholder, and the original year of registration. Because titles frequently changed, rights were sometimes transferred without recordation of the assignment, and records were not always kept by authors and publishers (who did not have easy access to photocopiers until the 1960s), this information was often not readily available to rightsholders, who in any case were often simply unaware that renewals might be coming due.

Further contributing to the problem was the fact that the different media industries, as well as different actors within the different industries, were inconsistent in their handling of renewals: sometimes an agent was responsible, sometimes a publisher, sometimes a lawyer, and sometimes the author him- or herself. If the responsible individual shirked his or her duty, misunderstood that duty, or (as sometimes happened) grew ill or died when the duty required execution, the one-year renewal window assured that the rightsholder would almost certainly lose the copyright. Although best-selling authors of prose fiction, who worked with top publishing houses, were unlikely to accidentally forsake second copyright terms, such lapses were not unheard of even for famous literary works, especially if they came up for renewal after the author's death.[9] Statute dictated that when the original author was no longer living, renewal rights automatically passed to the surviving spouse and/or the author's children—who often knew little of the details of a work's history and nothing at all of copyright law. Making things even more complicated, the renewal right itself (as opposed to the actual copyright protection it secured) was nontransferable—at least, according to the letter of the law—which meant that in cases where a third party, such as a publisher or film studio, had acquired a work from its original author, the third party was unable to file for the renewal on its own behalf.[10] As we will see in subsequent chapters, so complicated and unforgiving was the renewal process that even when a deceased author's family had recourse to a literary executor, the executor often lacked sufficient information about a work's history and/or the intricacies of copyright law to properly execute renewals.

With the Copyright Act of 1976, the United States finally joined the rest of the world in revising its period of protection to a single term lasting the life of the author plus fifty years. For anonymous/pseudonymous works and works made for hire, protection would last seventy-five years from publication or one hundred years from creation (whichever came first). Under the new regime, renewals and the problems that accompanied them were a thing of the past—except, that is, for works created prior to 1978 that were still in their first twenty-eight-year term of protection.[11] Because renewals remained necessary to secure copyright protection for these works for a second term (extended, by this point, to forty-seven years), such works were, in effect, condemned to remain more in than out of the modern copyright regime, with its complex and rarely met renewal demands. At least, they were for a little while; in 1992, Congress amended the Act of 1976 to make renewal automatic for those works still under their first period of protection—i.e., works first registered between 1964 and 1977. For works created after 1978, the Copyright Act of 1976 (slightly modified in 1998 by the Copyright Term Extension Act[12]) ensured a single, long period of protection that did not depend upon renewal or even—as we will see below—registration.

Copyright Formalities

The term *copyright formalities* refers to the specific actions and procedures required by law as a condition of securing whatever rights, protections, or benefits a copyright statute grants. In the context of U.S. copyright law before 1978, such formalities included registration, recordation of transfer, deposit of published works with the copyright office or Library of Congress, notice (i.e., marking of published copies with information about copyright ownership), and application for renewal. In theory, formalities ensured that information as to the ownership and duration of a copyrighted work was publicly accessible. Because complying with them involved nontrivial expense in time, labor, and money, formalities also forced authors to approach copyright as an economic question: was the protection in each case worth the expense? Since the answer was presumably sometimes "no," a formalized copyright regime thus ostensibly resulted in a larger, richer public domain than would otherwise be the case. These supposed benefits, however, typically came at a tremendous cost: an author or business partner's failure to observe the requisite procedures could have serious negative consequences, up to and including the forfeiture of a work's copyright protection or the inability to secure it in the first place.

As the word *formality* might suggest, the mandated actions required during the modern copyright era were often seen by authors and licensees as burdensome and overly technical—a set of arbitrary hurdles to be cleared in order to secure and maintain copyright.[13] They were also, by the beginning of the twentieth century, a peculiarity of the United States copyright regime, most other nations having more-or-less phased out formalities during the preceding century.[14] Taken as a whole, the U.S. regime before 1978 was heavily "formalized," with a complex array of intertwined technical stipulations governing copyright. It was possible—as we will see in the following chapters—for an author or proprietor to fail to observe these stipulations without fatal results, but usually only if they managed to stay out of court. Especially in the early decades of the twentieth century, courts were unforgiving when it came to copyright formalities: an author's failure to observe them would almost always result in the invalidation of copyright. Toward the middle of the century, courts gradually came to adopt a more relaxed approach to some (but not all) of the formalities. For a variety of reasons, however, courts' relaxation of the rules tended to result in more confusion, not less. Right up until the Copyright Act of 1976, rightsholders and would-be rightsholders thus tended to persist in attempting to observe all of the formalities regardless of the common law's ostensible position on them.

The rules regarding copyright renewal described earlier represent one example of how complicated formalities could be before 1978. But they arguably misrepresent the modern copyright regime as simpler and more predictable than it actually was, since courts did little to modify how renewal worked until right before the Act of 1976 went into effect. Better examples of the complex interplay between statute, judicial ruling, and industrial practice can be found by briefly examining, first, the joint requirement of registration and deposit[15] and, second, the principle of indivisibility.

REGISTRATION AND DEPOSIT

Under the extraordinarily strict rules of the International Copyright Act of 1891, copyright was dependent upon the deposit of two copies of the published work at the Library of Congress "not later than the day of the publication thereof."[16] Recognizing that such a requirement was unduly demanding, Congress eventually relaxed it through the Copyright Act of 1909, which required that published works merely be "promptly deposited."[17] But how much time, authors, lawyers, and judges were forced to wonder, was meant by "promptly"? In the decades following the Act, courts gradually came to interpret the word "promptly" quite broadly, eventually holding in *Washingtonian Publishing Co. v. Pearson* (1939) that registration and deposit could take place any time after publication.[18] According to the letter of U.S. Supreme Court Justice James Clark McReynolds's opinion for the majority, registration and deposit, although required to maintain legal action for copyright infringement, could even be completed *after* the alleged infringement had taken place: "mere delay will not destroy the right to sue."[19] This was ostensibly a radical deformalizing of one aspect of the U.S. regime. An author might now legally adopt a wait-and-see attitude with respect to registration and deposit, forgoing them until he or she had reason to file suit.

Although in theory the Supreme Court's ruling in *Washingtonian* thus effectively divorced copyright from the formality of registration and deposit, in practice rightsholders continued to treat registration and deposit as mandatory procedures. A study undertaken by the Copyright Office in 1956, for example, found that 95.03 percent of registrations/deposits occurred within six months of publication.[20] Indeed, in the research I conducted for the case studies that serve as the subject of this book's subsequent chapters, I came across no instance of a rightsholder deliberately delaying—or even considering delaying—registration and deposit. As the Library of Congress Advisory Committee on Copyright Registration and Deposit (ACCORD) recounted in a 1993 report, "After 1939 there was uneasiness, inertia, and traditional lawyer's conservatism; people kept on registering and depositing, and there seemed to be a reluctance to accept the Supreme Court's decision at face value."[21] Although uneasiness and inertia no doubt offer some explanation for the industry's adherence to the formality, in truth these likely played less of a role than the fact that the copyright system as a whole still incentivized registration and deposit: the dual act remained a precondition for renewals and transfers as well as the ability to file suit.

But there were two other important reasons for the practice's persistence through the remainder of the era. First, many industry stakeholders were simply unaware of the common law's shift. Copyright manuals and guidebooks (which rarely reported common law developments anyway) continued to represent "prompt" registration and deposit as necessary for establishing copyright, and the Copyright Office's own literature continued to speak of such actions as mandatory.[22] Second, registration and deposit had been so extensively routinized, and over such a long period of time, within the entertainment industry, that industry transactions—particularly those involving subsidiary rights and licensing—could not take place effectively without them. For the film industry in particular, an administratively recognized chain of title was often considered essential when purchasing rights in a preexisting literary work. Despite all the complexity of the registration process, industrial actors had thus come to rely upon the record it produced as an essential proof of ownership. And indeed, even today, close to half a century after the Copyright Act of 1976 formally abolished the requirement of deposit as a condition of copyright, most professionalized and/or corporate authors continue to register and deposit near the date of publication.[23]

COPYRIGHT INDIVISIBILITY

In part because the principle of indivisibility has been almost completely forgotten by present-day legal practitioners and scholars—and in part because no country other than the United States has ever had anything like it—twenty-first-century discussions of the history and/or concept of copyright formalities invariably ignore it. Like the more traditionally recognized formalities, however, the principle posed serious administrative impediments both to securing and exercising the rights associated with copyright. Indeed, for the first half of the twentieth century, no aspect of U.S. copyright law caused as much confusion and consternation within the entertainment industry as the principle of copyright indivisibility.

Sometimes referred to—usually in a disparaging sense—as "judge-made law," the principle of indivisibility had its roots in the language of the Copyright Act of 1909, which, though not expressly stating that a copyright could not be divided up among different owners, is intelligible only if such a proscription is assumed. As legal scholar Harry Henn explained in a 1955 piece for the *Cornell Law Review*, the various requirements of the Act appear to require that copyright proprietorship be exclusively singular, i.e., indivisible:

> It is the copyright proprietor who secures and registers the claim to copyright and deposits the copies; whose name must appear in the copyright notice; who renews the copyright in stated situations; who reserves ad interim copyright; who is entitled to damages, profits or statutory damages in case of infringement; whose signature is necessary to the assignment, grant, or mortgage of the copyright; whose consent is necessary to the production of a copyrightable new version of the copyrighted work; from whom or under whose authority the first authorized edition of the work must issue; who has several functions under the compulsory licensing provisions applicable to musical compositions; who is liable to a $100 fine for failure to deposit copies of the copyrighted work on demand; and who may be required before a permanent injunction is granted to reimburse innocent infringers where the copyright notice has been omitted from a particular copy or copies by accident or mistake.[24]

The principle of indivisibility meant that, excepting joint ownership (in which two or more parties own the same copyright and are subject, as partners, to a single set of the above requirements), there could only be one legal holder of any single copyright in a work. The copyright could not be divided up, as it frequently is today, into a bundle of separate rights—the film rights to a comic book, for example, or the first publication rights to a piece of short prose fiction—that could be sold or transferred to multiple parties. Any assignment made by the copyright holder of less than the entire copyright was typically held by courts to be a license rather than an actual assignment of any legal right.

Although the distinction between *assignment* and *license* might at first sound merely semantic, it had two serious implications for creators and their business partners.[25] First, under the modern copyright regime, a licensee had no standing to enforce any of the rights guaranteed by copyright; only the actual copyright holder had such standing. As a result, if someone infringed upon a particular right—for example, by creating an unauthorized film version of a novel—the holder of that right could not bring suit to enjoin the authorized production unless she was the registered owner of the copyright in its entirety. Had she merely licensed the film right, she was out of luck. A partial assignment of rights by the copyright holder was thus, as Abraham Kaminstein concluded in a 1957 study of indivisibility undertaken for Congress, in reality no more than "a contract not to sue the licensee" for violating one of the copyright holder's exclusive rights.[26] Or, as Morris Cohn put it in a 1954 study of film and television rights, "In strict contemplation of law, such an instrument purporting to convey less than the whole, actually *conveys* nothing, that is, no interest in the work itself."[27] Because a licensee thus technically had no rights in the underlying work, even if the license she acquired was exclusive and perpetual, she was forced to entreat the actual rightsholder to bring suit on her behalf in instances where an unauthorized third party infringed upon the rights granted her by the license.

The requirement that the actual rightsholder initiate legal proceedings was rooted in a legitimate worry that, without such a restriction, multiple actions might be taken against the same single act of infringement. But the requirement involved a host of problems for licensees, the simplest of which were added legal costs and delays, and the most serious an inability to bring suit at all (especially when the original rightsholder had died or—if a company—gone out of business). To get around this problem, a sophisticated licensee might insert a clause into the license giving it both the right to act as attorney for the copyright holder and to join the copyright holder as plaintiff or defendant in cases where the licensed rights were infringed. As we will see in the next chapter, however, such a workaround was not without risks of its own.

Despite the serious problems indivisibility posed to the conveyance and exercise of the different rights associated with copyright, these problems were arguably of less importance than the additional burden the principle placed upon the execution of copyright registration and notice. Specifically, the Act of 1909 required that registration be made and notice be given in the rightsholder's name, not a licensee's name. Failure to observe this requirement would, under a strict reading of the statute, result in invalidation of the copyright. Although one might assume that providing the correct name for these purposes was a relatively simple endeavor, it in fact proved extremely challenging for publishers to get right, in part because it was sometimes impossible to determine whom a court would hold to be the technical rightsholder when assignments and licenses were involved (as they nearly always were). Indeed, the complexity caused by the interaction of rules pertaining to indivisibility, registration, and notice was so extreme that no one—neither author, businessman, nor lawyer—could confidently predict what the law actually required during this era.

By way of example, let us take the Second Circuit's decision in *Dam v. Kirk La Shelle Co.* (1910), the first appeals court ruling to hinge upon the validity of copyright registration under the doctrine of indivisibility.[28] The case involved a story written by Henry Dam titled "The Transmogrification of Dan," which had been sold to a literary magazine named *The Smart Set* and subsequently published in the magazine's September 1901 issue. As was standard business practice in the periodical industry for much of the twentieth century, the publisher, Ess Ess Publishing Company, obtained a single collective copyright for the entire issue rather than individual copyrights for each work the issue contained. After the story was published, the defendant, the Kirk La Shelle Company, devised a play titled "The Heir to the Hoorah," which Dam alleged was an unauthorized dramatization of his story. Dam sued for copyright infringement but before doing so arranged—in keeping with the doctrine of indivisibility—that Ess Ess Publishing Company formally transfer to him the copyright in his story. In both his original bill and in an affidavit taken for the district court trial, however, Dam stated that he had sold the publisher only serial publication rights, reserving all other rights to himself. Seizing on this statement of facts, the defendant argued that because Dam had not sold the publisher the entire copyright, the sale constituted only a license, and, as a result, the story had not been covered under the publisher's copyright for the issue, since the law does not allow a licensee to copyright a work in the licensee's name, let alone a partial right in a work. In other words, by the defendant's logic, "The Heir to the Hoorah" did not constitute an infringement because the work on which it had been based had never been correctly copyrighted. The trial court flatly disagreed and found for Dam. The appeals court, however, held that the defendant was correct as to the question of law: had Dam sold only first serial rights, the magazine's copyright would not have been valid, and Dam's story would be part of the public domain. But to everyone's surprise the court also held that *both parties* were incorrect regarding the facts of the case: despite Dam's statement to the contrary, the court held that he *had* in fact sold Ess Ess Publishing Company the entire copyright in the story, thus rendering the magazine's copyright—and, by extension, that of the story—valid.

Beyond its significance in establishing precedent, the decision is noteworthy in three regards. First, it serves as an extreme though not necessarily atypical example of the degree to which the common law tended to disregard or ignore customary trade practices in the entertainment industry during the first half of the twentieth century. Indeed,

Judge Walter Noyes's opinion goes so far as to set forth a requirement of law practices that would be difficult—and potentially even injurious—for creators and their business partners to implement. As lawyer Franklin Laskin complained in the *Yale Law Review*, the ruling "meant that if an author wanted to protect the other rights he must give them all away; but if he tried to reserve them he would not be protected."[29] Second, the appeals court's ruling on the question of facts (a privilege usually restricted to that of the original trial court) demonstrates how indivisibility had rendered conformity to the law something of a crapshoot. If judges might revise the facts of a case on the fly so that the case better fits the strictures of the law as they perceive it, then industrial actors had no way of ensuring that their actions would mean what they intended them to mean. Finally, although the specific trade practices at issue in the case pertained primarily to the periodical industry, which was dependent on collective copyright registration in a way other industries were not, they nevertheless had enormous implications for the rest of the entertainment industry. For most of the modern copyright era, periodicals were not only the largest conveyer of copyrighted material in the United States, but they were also the initial place of publication for the vast majority of narrative-based properties. If a copyright for a story appearing in a periodical were found to be invalid under the principle of indivisibility, any subsequent assignment or license (such as film rights or book rights) would thus be rendered worthless.

Whereas most aspects of modern copyright law had their detractors, indivisibility was unique in that nearly every stakeholder deplored it. That the doctrine nevertheless persisted until it was officially abrogated by the Copyright Act of 1976 demonstrates, again, how sclerotic the legislative process can be. But it also reveals how slow the common law could sometimes be in responding to the needs of the entertainment industry. For most of the twentieth century, the industry was therefore stuck with indivisibility, and industrial actors tended to respond to it in three ways. First, authors organized. The Authors' League of America—the first national organization to support the rights of authors and the precursor to both the Dramatists Guild of America and the Screenwriters Guild of America—was expressly created in 1913, as executive committee member and general counsel Arthur Train explained, "to combat the pernicious and destructive effect of Damm *vs.* LaShelle" [sic].[30] (That the precursor to today's entertainment industry guilds and unions originated in response to the injustice of common law rather than that of employment and contracting practices is a fascinating—and often ignored—aspect of these institutions' histories). Second, industrial actors of all kinds—but especially writers and film producers—pressured legislators to change the law.[31] Lawmakers were largely sympathetic, and up until the Act of 1976 numerous bills were proposed in congress that sought to institute copyright divisibility.[32] All failed to pass, however, due to provisions unrelated to indivisibility.

Finally, and perhaps most importantly, companies simply ignored the law. As lawyer Robert Burton put it in a 1951 lecture delivered to the Federal Bar Association of New York, New Jersey, and Connecticut, "I think it a fair enough proposition for present purposes to state that a copyright is *industrially* divisible," even if it were not *legally* so.[33] Indeed, creators and their business partners could hardly have presumed otherwise, as the problems posed by indivisibility could not have been solved without radical, systematic change in both business practice and industrial structure. Attempting to adhere to the principle was even something of a fool's errand: after all, courts themselves applied the doctrine unpredictably, sometimes even ignoring it altogether.[34] When it was applied to deny standing the results were frustrating but rarely fatal: a plaintiff was usually given the opportunity to amend the suit by bringing on the original rightsholder or by acquiring the copyright in full. The risk of a court ruling that an author or publisher had, because of indivisibility, failed to properly secure or maintain the copyright, on the other hand, was potentially quite serious; however, it too could be safely ignored in the majority of business transactions. This is because—even had the common law's logic been clear and predictable in this regard—third parties had no practical way of ascertaining whether an author or publisher had actually adhered to it. Adherence hinged upon the details of contractual arrangements, which, unless made an issue in court, were private. Industrial actors in their everyday transactions thus had no option except to assume that the law had been followed, nor would they have benefitted in any way—except in extremely rare instances—from ascertaining that it had not been. The rules governing copyright validity under indivisibility were, in this sense, not just "judge-made law" but "defense-made law," as they were only ever invoked as a form of post hoc defense against copyright infringement.

With the passage of the Copyright Act of 1976, the principle of copyright indivisibility was finally abolished. Section 201 (d)(1) of the new law authorized the transfer of partial rights in a protected work, while (d)(2) extended to all rightsholders the ability to initiate legal actions: "The owner of any particular exclusive right is entitled, to the extent of that right, to all of the protection and remedies accorded to the copyright owner by this title."[35] Whether or not this section of the law also resolved the problems indivisibility posed to notice and registration is unanswerable, for these problems were rendered irrelevant by an even more dramatic change in the United State's copyright regime: the abrogation of formalities altogether.

With the Act of 1976, the United States finally joined the rest of the world in making copyright automatic. As legal scholar Christopher Sprigman (2004) explains, the nation "moved from a 'conditional' copyright system that premised the existence and continuation of copyright on compliance with formalities to an 'unconditional' system in which a reduced set of voluntary formalities play only a minor role."[36] Although such a move had long been sought by most of the entertainment industry (and many lawmakers) for the increased simplicity, reduced friction in dealmaking, and overall lower costs it would bring, the removal of formalities was also necessary for the United States to become (finally) a party to the Berne Convention for the Protection of Literary and Artistic Works, an international treaty requiring that all member nations recognize the copyrights of citizens from other member nations. The 1908 revision to the Convention mandated the automatic vesting of international copyright while also forbidding the employment of formalities as a condition of granting or enforcing copyrights on works by foreign authors.[37] To be sure, in the years immediately following the Act of 1976, the United States' new, "unconditional" system remained—and has continued to remain—more conditional than that of most other Berne parties. Copyright registration, for example, is still a prerequisite for bringing suit for U.S. works (but not foreign works; and the registration can occur post-infringement). But the underlying metaphysics or ontology of the U.S. system now resembles that of the rest of the world, with copyrights, in practice, functioning more like naturally occurring property rights than statutorily conditional monopolies.

Conclusion

In this chapter, I have provided a bird's-eye view of two principles that are constitutive of the legal regime this book attributes to the seventy-year period of time referred to as the modern copyright era: short copyright duration and copyright formalities. These are, of course, not the only principles that define the regime; and the rest of this book is devoted to examining others. The two principles described here, however, are unique in that they are statutory creations: they exist and exert a strong influence on creators, businesspersons, lawyers, and judges for the fundamental reason that the Copyright Act of 1909 says they do. We might thus call them legal infrastructure, albeit a particularly "dumb," as in silent or disinterested, kind. This is to say that short copyright duration and copyright formalities functioned during the modern copyright era more as brute regulatory facts than as purposive architecture. They were, in the eyes of most stakeholders, many of whom looked enviously at the copyright systems of other nations, less the *means* of developing and managing narrative-based properties than they were (pointless) *impediments* to doing so.

The principles examined in the following chapters, each by way of one or more micro-level case studies, are more ambiguous in this regard. Neither dumb nor disinterested, they are closer to what present-day technologists and media studies scholars typically mean by the term *infrastructure*: the behind-the-scenes architecture necessary for doing things.[38] And yet, unlike pipes or labor guilds or statutory laws (all regularly recognized as infrastructure), the principles explored in the following chapters, as we well see, have an immateriality to them—as well as an often ambiguous provenance—that makes them harder to recognize and account for than other infrastructure. They are also, with respect to the creation and management of narrative-based property, subtly malleable: able to be bent and shaped and even momentarily reconfigured by creators and their business partners without losing their underlying forms. What they are powerless to do, however, and what makes them logically secondary to the legal principles examined in this chapter, is ignore or deny the brute requirements of statute: that formalities be observed and that copyright last for what was, from a global perspective, a relatively short period of time.

CHAPTER 2

"Only the Chessman in the Game of Telling the Story"

Warner Bros. Pictures v. CBS, the Idea-Expression Dichotomy, and the Principle of Iterative Textual Derivation

How does copyright law understand fictional characters as a distinct form of intellectual property? What protections does the law provide creators and owners of fictional works against unauthorized use of the characters that appear in those works? And how does the law distinguish between trade in the rights to fictional works and trade in the rights to fictional characters? Does the former necessarily, and thus simultaneously, constitute the latter?

Such questions, difficult as they may be to answer, would nevertheless strike a twenty-first-century lawyer, publisher, or writer of fiction as more or less intelligible. Much of our present-day entertainment economy revolves around complex, multimedia, multifirm uses of fictional characters as distinct from fictional works. Alongside the writers, actors, and other talent that have long constituted entertainment companies' primary production input, we now routinely place characters as well, sometimes even assessing a company's competitive advantage by counting the number of characters they "own."[1] Indeed, the very idea of a narrative franchise takes for granted that characters constitute an independent form of protectable property. For these reasons, questions of the kind I have asked above have been regularly taken up by lawyers and laymen alike over the past few decades, in law review articles, courts of law, blogs, how-to guides, and even fan discussion threads.

By contrast, until *Warner Bros. Pictures v. Columbia Broadcasting System (CBS)* was heard by the Ninth Circuit in 1954 (and even for many years afterwards), a twentieth-century lawyer, publisher, or writer of fiction would have struggled to make sense of these questions.[2] Not only would our imaginary auditor likely object that the questions involve a misunderstanding of how copyright works, he or she would also probably reject them as irrelevant to how the business of entertainment is actually conducted. Perhaps, if feeling generous, our auditor might even suggest that what these questions are trying to ask (albeit not very clearly) is about the unauthorized *copying* (i.e., imitating) of characters—a subject of legal questioning that, although lacking easy answers, was familiar to most lawyers and interested laypersons during the first half of the twentieth century and which received considerable attention in legal, professional, and even popular forums during that time. The subject of characters *as* property, on the other hand, was discussed by almost no one.

This chapter has a number of aims, the first—and perhaps simplest—is to explain why the questions with which it opens, so legible to us today, would have been illegible a century ago. Accordingly, in the chapter's first section below, I introduce two legal principles of the modern copyright regime that are essential for understanding the legal status and narrative function of fictional characters during this era: *the idea-expression dichotomy* and *iterative textual derivation*. For simplicity's sake, I call the first a *formal* legal principle and the second an *informal* legal principle, with the distinction indicating the different loci of my analyses: appellate court decisions for the first and actual business practices and lay discourse for the second. As we will see, the distinction will end up proving artificial, with the formal and informal in reality being messily interwoven, but it is a useful starting point.

In bringing these legal principles together, the chapter provides a new way of approaching the complex question of what a character *is* in a legal sense—i.e., as a kind of property. Although everyday parlance, business speak, and humanistic scholarship commonly refer to characters as intellectual property, the exact substance of such property is difficult to identify when abstracted from the texts in which it is embodied. In legal studies, there has been a great deal of work over the last thirty years interrogating the legal constitution of a fictional character.[3] Very little of it, however, focuses expressly on what legally constituted a character between 1909 and 1978—a period in which legal and managerial thinking on this subject was quite different from today. One of these differences lies in the integral connection judges and media makers saw between character and narrative. Today, in part because of the growth of trademark protection for characters (discussed in chapter 4), characters are commonly imagined as ontological entities exceeding or easily separable from the stories in which they appear. This was not the case before 1978. In demonstrating why, the chapter also contributes to the larger scholarly conversation on narrative franchises by showing how narrative story worlds that lack seriality (a quality usually considered essential for contemporary narrative franchises or transmedia) can—and once routinely did—function nevertheless as franchises or transmedia.

More narrowly, this chapter seeks to provide a definitive account of *Warner Bros. Pictures v. CBS*—often referred to today as "the Sam Spade case"—the ruling of which I argue hinges upon the recognition and application by the court of the idea-expression dichotomy and the principle of iterative textual derivation. The decision should thus be seen as representative of—and "in sync" with—how narrative-based property was legally understood and governed during the modern copyright era. If this sounds like a defense or rehabilitation of the decision, that is deliberate, for history has been extremely unkind to Judge Albert Lee Stephens's opinion for the Ninth Circuit. Twenty-first-century casebooks on copyright law, introductory textbooks, and systematic treatises frequently omit the case from their contents,[4] while those that include it tend to frame the court's reasoning as confused or erroneous.[5] Contributors to law reviews routinely disparage the opinion[6]—a tradition dating back to Edward Brylawski's scathing 1974 piece for the *Bulletin of the Copyright Society of the U.S.A.*[7]—or disparage it by proxy, summarizing the opinion and its significance via surveys of the disparagement it has received elsewhere.[8] Even judges themselves have denounced the opinion, with Richard Posner, for example, declaring for the Seventh Circuit in a 2004 opinion on the "copyrightability" of fictional characters that *Warner Bros. Pictures v. CBS* "is wrong."[9] Although norms and pressures associated with the practice of law (an enterprise that is usually concerned with the contexts and concerns of the present or future) have encouraged lawyers and judges to discard the decision in this manner, doing so, I argue, has distorted our understanding of how IP law worked and what a narrative-based property consisted of for much of the twentieth century.

In order to rehabilitate the decision, this chapter approaches it in a manner that is slightly uncharacteristic of traditional legal studies and sociolegal approaches to case law. Although it devotes some attention to the letter of the appellate court opinion, the analysis presented in this chapter relies on neither close reading nor analogical reasoning; nor, for obvious reasons, does it employ social science research methods, such as surveys or interviews. What it offers instead is threefold. First, it provides the aforementioned historical explications of the two relevant legal principles, one formal (and thus in keeping with doctrinal legal scholarship) and one informal (and thus out of keeping). Second, it provides specific historical context for the lawsuit in the form of a reconstruction of defendant Dashiell Hammett's work as what I call an "IP entrepreneur" and his business relationships with the other parties to the lawsuit. Finally, it reconstructs how the legal dispute actually played out in practice: across multiple courtrooms, with multiple parties, represented by different lawyers, who put forth multiple arguments and pursued multiple strategies for persuading the judge(s) and winning the case(s). To reconstruct the dispute in this fashion, the chapter relies on an extraordinary archive: material collected and produced by Warner Bros.'s legal team during the course of the suits and preserved in the Warner Bros. Archive at the University of Southern California Cinematic Arts Library. This material includes *formal* case file documents, such as briefs, transcripts, and exhibitions—but also a kind of document that is much rarer and that we might call, using the language of doctrinal legal studies, *informal*: notes, letters, drafts, and marginalia produced by Warner Bros.'s legal team as they gathered facts, conducted research, developed their strategy, and argued in court.

In addition to serving the chapter's goal of reconstructing *Warner Bros. Pictures v. CBS*, the use of the chapter's employment of the archival material serves an important epistemological aim in drawing attention to the kind of work that is regularly left out of the stories we tell about lawsuits and legal disputes: *the work of knowledge production*. The Warner Bros. material helpfully renders visible what is one of the primary tasks of every lawsuit: the generation of knowledge within the specific, bounded context of the dispute. This knowledge is what lawyers are producing over the many hours they (and their assistants) spend "putting together" or "building" a case for court. And this knowledge is what formal legal proceedings themselves are intended to produce, as judges are tasked with developing—through the assistance of testimonies, briefs, oral arguments, research conducted by themselves or their clerks, etc.—their own knowledge of the facts, context, and law, with lawyers competing to shape this knowledge in whatever ways most benefit their clients.[10] Judicial opinions, though the result of this process of knowledge production, are commonly treated as logically divorced from it, the products of rational deliberation or ideologically motivated reasoning. This chapter aims to show what is wrong with this approach, and why scholars of franchises, transmedia, and intellectual property might often be better served by crafting the stories we tell about legal disputes in ways that account for the processes through which the knowledge contained in opinions is produced. This is not to say that every legal story need incorporate the kind of archival material consulted here, but merely that the production of knowledge—even (and especially) when it is messy, stuttering, or inconclusive—should play a key role in the construction of our narratives. For the production of such knowledge requires *work,* and this is the work of a lawsuit.

Finally, this chapter has one more goal, and that is to provide new context, new information, and hopefully new pleasure for the myriad of Hammett and *Maltese Falcon* fans around the world today. Indeed, this chapter could not have been written without the work of these fans, who have created bibliographies, published histories and biographies, and reproduced archival material (a special thank you to Richard Layman for the treasure trove that is *Discovering the Maltese Falcon and Sam Spade*). These fans have helped me appreciate both Hammett and Spade as vital, still relevant: characters, if you will, that, though born almost a century ago, continue to live on in our works and our imaginations.

The Idea-Expression Dichotomy and Iterative Textual Derivation

Let us begin, as a lawyer would begin, with the formal legal principle: what lawyers call *the idea-expression dichotomy.* Since copyright's inception with the Statute of Anne in 1709, one of the law's fundamental tenets has been that the protection it grants creative works covers only the actual words or images by which the work is made manifest. The ideas represented by such words or images receive, by contrast, no protection; they belong to the public. This distinction has its origin in the fact that when copyright was first instituted in eighteenth-century Britain the only medium it governed was print, and the only aspect of print it protected was the actual manuscript (or "copy"). In the United States, this approach to copyright lasted well into the nineteenth century, where it served as the legal basis for the Pennsylvania Circuit Court's famous ruling in *Stowe v. Thomas* that an unlicensed translation of the novel *Uncle Tom's Cabin* did not constitute an infringement of the original author's copyright:

> The claim of literary property . . . cannot be in the ideas, sentiments, or the creations of the imagination of the poet or novelist as dissevered from the language, idiom, style, or the outward semblance and exhibition of them. His exclusive property in the creation of his mind, cannot be vested in the author as abstractions, but only in the concrete form he has given them, and the language in which he has clothed them. When he has sold his book, the only property which he reserves to himself, or which the law gives to him, is the exclusive right to multiply the copies of that particular combination of characters [i.e., printed marks] which exhibits to the eyes of another the ideas intended to be conveyed. This is what the law terms copy, or copyright.[11]

New statutes gradually carved out exceptions to the principle (the rights of translation and dramatization, for example, were created in 1870 and film rights in 1912), but the underlying distinction remained operative into the beginning of the twentieth century.[12]

During the first decades of the 1900s, however, courts increasingly struggled to square these exceptions with the logic that underlays the idea-expression dichotomy—and thus copyright itself. The problem facing courts was, in part, a result of the rapid expansion in new technologies, such as film and sound recording, and the new business practices that developed around them. But the problem was also a product of the United States' approach to law making, which—then and now—foists upon courts the responsibility for reconciling with common law whatever new laws are passed by Congress. The granting of dramatization rights via the Copyright Act of 1870, for example, suggested logically that copyright in a work of fiction protected something more than the "concrete form" in which the story was expressed. But what was this something more if not the ideas themselves? The statute is silent on this question, leaving it to judges to work out an answer. For a while, courts floundered, sometimes even punting the issue. In the famous "*Ben Hur* case" (concerning an unauthorized film dramatization of a novel), for instance, the U.S. Supreme Court acknowledged the problem while abdicating its responsibility to solve it:

> It is suggested that to extend the copyright to a case like this is to extend it to the ideas as distinguished from the words in which these ideas are clothed. But there is no attempt to make a monopoly of the ideas expressed. The law confines itself to a particular, cognate and well known form of reproduction [i.e., dramatization]. If to that extent a grant of monopoly is thought a proper way to secure the right to the writings this court cannot say that Congress was wrong.[13]

To the plaintiff's objection that the Second Circuit had, in its earlier ruling, undermined the idea-expression dichotomy by granting protection to a novel's un-"clothed" ideas, the Supreme Court responded in this passage not by correcting the plaintiff's logic but by asserting its refusal to second-guess Congress. That the Court recognized its reply for the hedge it was is suggested by Judge Oliver Wendell Holme's remarkably ambivalent language, employing both the conditional tense ("If . . . is thought") and a litotes ("this court cannot say that Congress was wrong").

By the end of the 1920s, however, what would eventually become the common law's new approach to the idea-expression dichotomy had begun to emerge: expression would constitute not merely the actual language in which ideas were conveyed but also the unique sequence or arrangement of these ideas—that is, the ideas' relationships with each other—within the protected work. Judge Learned Hand, for example, in the precedent-setting *Nichols v. Universal Pictures Co.* (concerning whether a film had plagiarized the plot of a play), premised his reasoning upon a conception of the protected work as an organic form:

> Upon any work . . . a great number of patterns of increasing generality will fit equally well, as more and more of the incident is left out. The last may perhaps be no more than the most general statement of what the play is about, and at times might consist only of its title; but there is a point in this series of abstractions where they are no longer protected, since otherwise the playwright could prevent the use of his "ideas," to which, apart from their expression, his property is never extended. . . . Nobody has ever been able to fix that boundary, and nobody ever can. In some cases the question has been treated as though it were analogous to lifting a portion out of the copyrighted work . . . ; but the analogy is not a good one, because, though the skeleton is a part of the body, it pervades and supports the whole. In such cases we are rather concerned with the line between expression and what is expressed.[14]

Like that of a human (or animal) body, the protected work, in Hand's construction here, becomes more than a collection of parts; it becomes a unified whole. And as the work is given life in this manner, the ontology underlying the common law's traditional approach to idea and expression becomes reversed. Whereas the expression was previously understood as an arbitrary instantiation of an independently existing idea (the "clothing" in which an idea is dressed), Hand's metaphor proposes that the law now see—at least sometimes, in some cases—the idea as the *product* of the expression.[15] Inseparable from the language in which it is manifest, and existing not before but after (or perhaps alongside) the work, the idea becomes "what is expressed."

To be sure, my reading of Hand makes more, logically, of the metaphor he uses than might the reading of a harried lawyer or judge in the early twentieth century. But our early-twentieth-century reader would, like me, find him or herself forced to wrestle with the logic of Hand's decision, for not only is it difficult to parse, it also—on the face of it—seems to provide little guidance for deciding an actual dispute. Future lawyers would attempt to resolve these problems by operationalizing (and vastly simplifying) Hand's reasoning into an analytical procedure that has come to be called the "abstraction test."[16] For our purposes, however, the fact that Hand's attempted revision of the idea-expression dichotomy via the concept of organic form is difficult to understand and apply is precisely what is important about it. As the entertainment industry grew larger and more complex and courts increasingly found themselves asked to police the "boundary" between idea and expression, the hard rule that had once governed the distinction became soft, its application a kind of art. In a decision three decades after *Nichols v. Universal Pictures Co.*, Judge Hand would even conclude that "no principle can be stated as to when an imitator has gone beyond copying the 'idea,' and has borrowed its 'expression.'"[17]

That the rule was soft, however, did not mean that it had no value. It worked, in fact, well enough for the vast majority of business proceedings in the entertainment industry during the modern copyright era. Very few of these raised difficult questions over the "boundaries" between idea and expression—nor was it in the interest of established players in the industry to do so. Besides, Hand's basic approach to the dichotomy made a kind of intuitive and generalizable sense: a work, taken as a whole, was protectable; the parts and/or ideas that comprised the whole, when separated from each other and employed in conjunction with other ideas, were not. Up until *Warner Bros. Pictures v. CBS*—and for at least a decade after it—the rule thus not only worked fairly predictably in court, it also corresponded almost perfectly to our second, informal legal principle: what I call *iterative textual derivation.*

Admittedly, my neologism fails to capture how early-twentieth-century creative professionals actually spoke about the logic underlying the practices they employed to create what the law today names *derivative works*; but this is a necessary failure, for creative professionals in fact rarely spoke or wrote about such logic at all. Today, textual derivation, referred to more generally as *adaptation,* is taken for granted as a highly intentional and reflective practice, involving complex questions of form, interpretation, and reception. College students take courses on adaptation, trade associations hold panels on translating "source material" from one medium to another, humanities and social science scholars publish research in the journal *Adaptation,* and creative professionals regularly speak—in trade interviews, at fan conventions, and on social media—of the perils and pleasures of adapting characters, storylines, and fictional worlds for new entertainment offerings. No such activities—nor their historical analogues—took place during the modern copyright era; nor did *derivative work* or *adaptation* figure as key concepts in the discourse of lawyers and judges until near its end. The Copyright Act of 1976 would define *derivative work* as "a work based upon one or more preexisting works"[18] and include as examples "a translation, musical arrangement, dramatization, fictionalization, motion picture version, sound recording, art reproduction, abridgment, condensation, or any other form in which a work may be recast, transformed, or adapted,"[19] but the Copyright Act of 1909 does not include the term at all and employs the words *adapt* or *adaptation* only in the context of musical compositions.[20] The terms' lack of importance is similarly reflected in copyright guidebooks, which—through at least the 1960s—rarely use either term at all, let alone mark them as important via chapter titles, section headings, or index entries. This is not to say that adaptation was not an important practice within the early entertainment industry nor that it was approached haphazardly. Far from it. But there existed no reflectively articulated theory of this practice. Adaptation and textual derivation took place on the fly or, to borrow cognitive ethnographer Edwin Hutchins's term, "in the wild": as a creative, largely context-driven process for generating one text from another.[21]

Despite the untheorized and somewhat improvisatory nature of this process, however, both the general approach to textual derivation and the narratological type of derivative work it produced remained remarkably consistent across media during the modern copyright era. Indeed, with rare (and often idiosyncratic) exception, U.S. creative professionals appear to have employed only a single model of textual derivation. Today, creative professionals have numerous models to choose from, including what I call the *sequential* (where each new text serves as the originary source for another, as in many twenty-first-century film and novel sequels) the *rhizomatic* (where each new text can serve as the originary source for multiple others, as in late-twentieth- and twenty-first-century comic book universes), and the *biblical* (where a single, often unpublished text serves as the originary source for multiple, potentially unrelated others, as in some twenty-first-century gaming franchises). But before the 1960s, the only model much in evidence is the *iterative*. In iterative textual derivation, the derivative work is a kind of reproduction: the new text duplicates the narrative of the original. The task of the producer of the derivate work is to iterate by making alterations that differentiate the new text from the original without disrupting its underlying identity with that original—what Judge Hand might have described as putting new flesh on old bones. Although involving difficult problems at the level of both form and narrative (especially when translating across media), the fundamental goal is that of narratological *reproduction*, not transformation or expansion—a fact that perhaps explains why the task of adaptation did not generate in this period the discursive reflection and conceptual explication that it does today.

Let me be clear: that the goal of adaptation in the modern copyright era was narratological reproduction does not mean that derivative works were expected to slavishly imitate every detail of their progenitors, but rather that the derivatives tended to function as iterations of the original, reproducing the narratological arrangements of the ur-texts' core components (characters, setting, style, and basic plot) with only minimal and relatively superficial alterations. A Sherlock Holmes or Tarzan film, for example, would be produced as an iteration of—and not an extension to or continuation of—the original Arthur Conan Doyle or Edgar Rice Burroughs story from which the film right derived. This iterative approach to textual production governed not only formally licensed textual derivations in new media (via films, for example, or radio shows) but also derivations produced by the original text's author in the same medium as the original text (as was most common in print fiction and novels). A new Doc Savage story by Lester Dent (under the pen name Kenneth Robeson), for example, would proceed identically to the Lester Dent Doc Savage story that preceded it: the name of the villain might change and the setting be transformed from a jungle to a desert, but the narrative as a whole remained the same. Characters were not spun-off, transformed or further "developed" except in superficial manners associated with generic tropes (particularly: marriage, pregnancy, and parenthood) that typically had little impact on the characters outside the specific texts in which the tropes occurred as plot points. Whatever "story world" might be said to inhere in the whole of the resulting texts was a fundamentally static one, wherein the same characters, encountering the same kinds of circumstances, forever took the same kinds of actions in order to achieve the same kinds of outcomes. Umberto Eco, in his famous 1972 review of the Superman comic strip, thus concluded that the series narratives of contemporary popular culture exhibited a unique form of textual amnesia, forever forgetting what occurred in earlier texts, and thereby evoking what he described as an "ever-continuing present."[22]

The entertainment industry's iterative approach to textual derivation in the modern copyright era is reflected not only in the actual entertainment products the industry produced but also in the documents industrial actors created and employed to manage textual rights. For most "franchises," contracts and company records treated the original ur-text as the property itself; they thus made no mention of ostensibly separable characters, settings, or other narratological or aesthetic features associated with that text. Let us take, as an example, the "Story Digest" forms employed by Warner Bros. between the 1930s and 1950s to keep track of relevant rights information for stories it had acquired. These single-page forms each contain six sections labeled "Title," "Picture Title," "Rights," "Copyright in Name of," "Assignments," and "Purchase Data and Remarks," which appear in descending order on the page (save for the "Picture Title" section, which occupies a small column to the right of the "Title" section). As the Story Digest associated with *The Maltese Falcon* demonstrates, the forms treat the original copyrighted text (the name and author of which occupy the "Title" section) as the primary contractual unit. The "Rights" it catalogues are rights to the text as a whole, expressed as the rights to use the story in other media: "silent," "talking," "radio-television," "stage and dramatic," "music," and "fictionalization." No mention is made—nor is there space to mention it—of rights to characters, settings, plot-points, and so forth. The minimal space provided in the "Picture Title" section for listing basic information pertaining to completed motion picture adaptations seems to also reflect the administrative expectation that a single acquired text would not give rise to more than one or two film versions. To accommodate all three film versions of *The Maltese Falcon*, the employee who updated the Maltese Falcon's Story Digest form was forced to add the 1941 film by hand in tiny letters. The assumption of the Story Digest form and forms like it was that adaptation was an iterative process, involving the reproduction of a specific text in other media but not that text's extension, expansion, or narratological transformation.

That the industry relied on iteration does not mean that textual derivations—particularly those occurring across media—did not sometimes differ significantly from the texts on which they were based. Hollywood studios, for example, sometimes altered key details of a licensed text in the process of adapting it for film. Some alterations were necessitated by budgetary, technological, and regulatory limitations. Others were an effect of Hollywood studios' practice of buying up story rights prophylactically in order to protect themselves from being sued for producing films that made use of (typically unprotectable) story ideas found in preexisting texts. In these cases, the film versions were never meant to be adaptations at all, a fact that licensors tended to understand.

When a film adaptation shared a title, character, or author credit with the text on which it was based, however, the licensor and licensee typically had an informal understanding that the adaptation's story would not depart too much from that of the original—unless the contract stipulated otherwise. As Louis Frohlich and Charles Schwartz's *The Law of Motion Pictures* (a 1918 treatise consulted by Warner Bros.'s lawyers in preparation for *Warner Bros. Pictures v. CBS*) suggests, this understanding was often based upon assumptions about common law:

> The literary product of an author or playwright is a thing jealously watched by him, and one in which the common law gives him certain well-defined rights, even where he has parted title with the work. These rights may not be violated even by one who purchases the product of the author; and it often becomes a serious question to determine just how far a producer may go in making changes in the work without invading the rights of the author or playwright.[23]

Courts were rarely asked to answer this question, but Judge Clark Knox's 1922 opinion for *Curwood v. Affiliated Distributors* suggests that they would require that adaptations exhibit at least some fidelity to the texts on which they were contractually based:

> I take it that, while scenery, action, and characters may be added to an original story, and even supplant subordinate portions thereof, there is an obligation upon the elaborator to retain and give appropriate

> expression to the theme, thought, and main action of that which was originally written. . . . [E]laboration of a story means something other than that the same should be discarded, and its title and authorship applied to a wholly dissimilar tale.[24]

Accordingly, studios usually took care to ensure that film adaptations did not depart too radically from the original texts without the licensee's authorization. When radical changes were deemed necessary, studios often sought to protect themselves by obscuring the film's affiliation with the licensed property: changing the film's title, renaming characters, altering the setting, and substantially changing the storyline. The resulting film thus constituted (in twenty-first-century terms) not the elaboration of a preexisting franchise but the constitution of a new one altogether (though with potential legal ties to the former). One of pulp author Frederick Nebel's popular MacBride and Kennedy stories, for example, was adapted in this manner by Warner Bros., which changed it from a buddy crime-fighting story into a romantic comedy film series (with light detective elements) centering around a blonde reporter named Torchy Blaine.

For the most part, however, the properties that we today would recognize as early franchises remained largely faithful to the basic details of the original texts from which they derived. This reflects the fact that texts and the narratives of which they consisted were considered property under copyright law and were therefore tradable; individual characters, specific plot points, and settings, however, were not. To trade in narrative property in the modern copyright era thus meant to trade in the rights to texts *qua* unified expressions; and though these rights could be—and often were—treated by the entertainment industry as distinct and divisible (into film rights, for example, or television rights), the individual components and ideas that comprised the texts (what today might be called its narrative "assets") were not.

Because the idea-expression dichotomy and the principal of iterative textual derivation were so central to the workings of the early entertainment industry, stakeholders had little reason to think much about the protectability of fictional characters. The industry's practice of iteratively reproducing whole works of fiction meant that, for the overwhelming majority of business transactions, the question of whether characters were separately protectable under copyright law was not only irrelevant but almost nonsensical. The question was thus rarely raised in copyright manuals or guild publications before *Warner Bros. Pictures v. CBS*; and besides that lawsuit, not one copyright suit alleging unauthorized use of a character in an original work of fiction appears to have been filed before the 1970s. The issue of protection for fictional characters is also given no direct address in the thousand-plus total pages of the thirty-one studies commissioned by the Congressional Judiciary Committee as part of a holistic review of U.S. copyright law in the 1950s; nor was the idea-expression dichotomy itself deemed controversial enough to have been given concerted attention via a devoted study.

In the odd instances where stakeholders did consider the issue, they inevitably concluded that characters were not by themselves protectable. M. A. Mills, for example, in a 1913 essay for *The Bulletin of the Authors' League of America*, observed succinctly that the Authors' League was "forced to the conclusion that inasmuch as an ideal or fictitious character must come within the general term, mental conception, the interpretation of the Copyright Law . . . establishes beyond controversy that no exclusive claim [pertaining to a character] may be maintained."[25] Early circuit court decisions regarding Nick Carter detective stories and Buster Brown comic strips seemed to deny characters trademark protection as well.[26] Even as late as the 1950s, the general view within the industry was that, as a matter of law—and except in regards to merchandise licensing (which was usually treated under unfair competition law) and cartoon or comic book characters (which gave rise to their own distinct case law, which I discuss in chapter 4)—fictional characters inherently belonged to the public. As A. K. Berle and L. Sprague de Camp reasoned in their 1959 layman's guide to intellectual property law, "Cartoons and continued stories may be copyrighted, but a single copyright covers only a particular set of pictures or a particular script. It is not possible to copyright fictitious or fanciful characters or settings, used in such stories or cartoons, so as to keep others from imitating them."[27]

Dashiell Hammett, IP Entrepreneur

Of the many early-twentieth-century American authors of crime and detective fiction, none—save perhaps Raymond Chandler—is as well-remembered today as Samuel Dashiell Hammett: author of *The Maltese Falcon*, supposed inventor of the "hard-boiled" detective genre, alcoholic and serial adulterer, not-so-secret lover of the playwright Lillian Hellman, and (depending upon your political persuasion) communist activist or martyr to liberal democracy. Indeed, today Hammett, always remembered as larger than life, has even become something of a narrative franchise himself, as subsequent authors have continually resurrected and reimagined him for their own creative projects, in the process building up around him what film scholar William Mooney has called a "mythology."[28] Unlike most of Hammett's contemporaries—some of whom, such as Erle Stanley Gardner and Cornell Woolrich, were at least his equals in influence and literary success—Hammett has been the subject of a seemingly never-ending stream of biographies, starting with Richard Layman's *Shadow Man: The Life of Dashiell Hammett* in 1981 and continuing into the twenty-first century with Jo Hammett's *Dashiell Hammett: A Daughter Remembers* and, most recently, Nathan Ward's *The Lost Detective: Becoming Dashiell Hammett.* Over this same period, Hammett has been a popular subject of literary scholarship, which, across journal articles, book chapters, and a surprising number of single-author monographs,[29] has focused as much on Hammett's biography and psychology as it has his fiction. Hammett has also featured as the fictional protagonist of multiple novels—including William Nolan's *The Black Mask Murders,* Owen Fitzstephen's *Hammett Unwritten,* and Sam Toperoff's *Lillian & Dash: A Novel*—as well as one high-profile film, Wim Wender's succinctly titled *Hammett.* For decades, Hammett has even been the subject of a San Francisco sightseeing tour;[30] and today travelers can choose from two different Hammett-themed guidebooks to the Northern California city where Hammett briefly lived.[31]

That the work of scholars, novelists, and tour guides (among others) has rendered Hammett more myth than man matters to us here because the mythology they have collectively produced has its origins in Hammett's work as a creator, licensor, and salesman of intellectual property—what I call "an IP entrepreneur." Indeed, the mythology is in many ways his own invention, although it has depended upon numerous individuals, operating both during his life and after his death, to make it stick. A talented writer of fiction, shrewd businessman, and unusually sophisticated reader of the law, Hammett also recognized the advantage he could gain as a writer from having a wild, romantic backstory. Starting near the very beginning of his career, he thus relied strategically upon the perception that he was an unruly genius—more like the action-oriented, ethically ambiguous, and slightly dangerous heroes of his fiction than a professional author. As we will see, at key moments the value of his intellectual property—and even the determination of who owned parts of it—depended as much upon the persona he maintained as it did his creative talent and business acumen.

Before I proceed with the history of Hammett's work as an IP entrepreneur, however, it is worth briefly unpacking what I mean by this term and why I prefer it, in Hammett's case, to the words *author* and *writer.* In twenty-first-century business and lay usage, the word *entrepreneur* refers to a person who takes on the financial risks associated with owning and running a business, especially (as the *Oxford English Dictionary* tells us) when that person "sets up" or is the founder of said business.[32] By this definition, entrepreneurs are distinguished from other businesspersons by having invested their own capital in the businesses they manage. From the perspective of economics, we might also say (drawing particularly on the work of Israel Kirzner[33]) that the entrepreneur discovers unrealized profit opportunities and, by orchestrating the material, financial, and social interactions necessary to realize them, teaches other market participants how to see them.

Neither of the above definitions reflects how we traditionally think of authors and writers, professions that are typically framed in terms of imagination, creativity, genius, craft, and prestige. But authors and writers, at least when not working for hire, can be said to become entrepreneurs in the first sense after they have completed (or sometimes in anticipation of their completing) a literary or artistic work, which, once copyrighted, becomes a special form of capital that must be actively managed—today we would say *exploited*—via the sale and/or licensing of the specific rights associated with it in order to generate profit.[34] Many, perhaps even most, authors rely on someone else—a publisher, an agent, a business manager—to manage their property in this sense. But some, like Hammett, take on this task themselves. Indeed, for a few, the task of exploiting the copyrighted property comes to dominate and define the author's creative labor to such an extent that it supplants the writing or authoring of new property altogether. When this happens, as it did with Hammett, the author's economic function much more closely resembles that of the business entrepreneur in the economist's sense than it does that of a creator in the humanistic sense: instead of endeavoring to produce literary or artistic works, he or she endeavors to produce contractual relationships for the exploitation of underutilized or undervalued assets. To fully understand Hammett's career—and the legal dispute over the rights to fictional private eye Sam Spade—we thus need to see Hammett as much as an entrepreneur of intellectual property, an IP entrepreneur, as we do a literary author.

Hammett's first success as an author and IP entrepreneur came in the 1920s, with his creation of an unnamed series detective typically referred to in editorial copy as the "Op" or "the Continental Op." Part of a new wave of realistic, action-oriented detective fiction appearing initially in the pulp magazine *Black Mask,* the Op stories—like nearly all detective fiction at the time—were stand alone, iterative works, with few repeated characters, no persistent plot threads, and almost no textual memory. Although quite a number of literary scholars have argued that this fiction—usually labeled "hard-boiled"—was the first to shift the focus of the detective genre from plot to character,[35] the Op stories, featuring a hero who lacks a name, family, intimate relations, interiority, long-term goals, and even the most rudimentary back story, demonstrate how little "character" in the late-twentieth-century sense mattered here. Much more important were the fiction's wry, laconic tone, fast pace, emphasis on action (typically of a violent kind), and pessimistic—or, if one prefers, realist—worldview. Between 1923 and 1929, the Op appeared in twenty-eight stories, two of them novel length (and thus serialized across multiple *Black Mask* issues). By 1928, the book rights to the two novel-length stories, *The Cleansing of Poisonville* and *The Dain Curse* had been acquired by the publisher Alfred A. Knopf, Inc., under a three-book contract negotiated directly with Hammett, which—as was typical of a writer's first contract with a major publishing house—granted Hammett a royalty but no advance, a 75 percent cut of future sales of motion picture rights, and a 50 percent cut of broadcast and stage rights. As was also typical, the contract stipulated that copyrights for the works would be secured in Knopf's name (a contractual practice that would have significant import later).[36]

Within a year after the publication in 1930 of Hammett's third novel, *The Maltese Falcon,* Hammett had left behind the world of pulp fiction (notwithstanding the serialization of his third and fourth novels in *Black Mask*) and become an elite and well-remunerated literary celebrity, regularly feted by Hollywood studios, which routinely licensed his work and hired him on as a screenwriter. In abandoning the pulps, Hammett likewise abandoned the series detective: with each new novel, he introduced a new protagonist and social milieu. These included Sam Spade, a tough but ethical private eye operating in San Francisco in *The Maltese Falcon;* racketeer Ned Beaumont, a handsome "fixer" for a political boss in a small, unnamed city in *The Glass Key;* stolid parolee Brazil, recently returned home to his country house in the novella *Woman in the Dark;* and Nick Charles, a retired private eye and heavy drinker living in New York City with his beautiful, wealthy wife Nora in *The Thin Man.* All four works were praised for their realism and their sparse, witty prose style, and all four were made into successful films in the 1930s—the first two by Warner Bros., the third by RKO, and the fourth by MGM.

Essential to Hammett's success was not simply the quality of his fiction—although it was roundly regarded as excellent—but also the impression, carefully cultivated by Hammett since his earliest days as a pulp writer, that his protagonists were all thinly veiled versions of himself. Having worked briefly as an operative for Pinkerton's National Detective Service in the years immediately preceding and following World War I, Hammett routinely emphasized, in a variety of forums, the real-world basis of his detective fiction. Hammett's "From the Memoirs of a Private Detective," originally published in the March 1923 issue of *Smart Set*, for example, offered a slew of epigrammatic reflections on the detective trade, most of them cast in the first-person and with an almost boasting (albeit sometimes sardonic) tone: "I know a man who will forge the impressions of any set of fingers in the world for $50," for instance, and, "Of all the men embezzling from their employers with whom I have had contact, I can't remember a dozen who smoked, drank, or had any of the vices in which bonding companies are so interested."[37]

How much on-the-street detective work Hammett actually experienced during his time at Pinkerton's is impossible to determine (scholars and biographers have struggled to substantiate most of his claims), but editors, marketers, and interviewers happily took him at his word, even sometimes expanding on his claims. *True Detective* introduced the author of "Who Killed Bob Teal?" (one of Hammett's only Op tales published outside *Black Mask*) as an employee of the (non-existent) Continental Detective Agency where Hammett's fictional character worked.[38] *Black Mask* likewise advertised the first installment of *The Dain Curse* by falsely asserting that "Mr. Hammett was formerly head of a large detective agency. He knows how a detective works and he tells it in this interesting story. . . ."[39] Numerous other examples could be supplied, up to even the present day, and the novels themselves encouraged these kind of pseudo-biographical associations.[40] *The Maltese Falcon*'s Sam Spade shares, after all, the same first name as Hammett and is described in language that could almost describe Hammett as well:

> Samuel Spade's jaw was long and bony, his chin a jutting v under the more flexible v of his mouth. His nostrils curved back to make another, smaller, v. His yellow-grey eyes were horizontal. The v *motif* was picked up again by thickish brows rising outward from twin creases above a hooked nose, and his pale brown hair grew down—

> from high flat temples—in a point on his forehead. He looked rather pleasantly like a blond satan.[41]

Nor did the day-to-day details of Nick Charles's life as an aging, drink-happy person of means in *The Thin Man* appear all that different from that of Hammett's at the time of the novel's publication, a fact underscored by the use of Hammett's picture on the dust jacket—*not* as a photo of the author on the back flap (a practice that was, in any case, quite rare in the 1930s) but as a photo of (ostensibly) Nick Charles himself.

With the publication of *The Thin Man* at the end of 1933, Hammett ceased writing prose fiction and began devoting most of his energy and attention to IP entrepreneurship, banking off his own celebrity to help exploit the fictional works he had previously created. Although his work had been routinely licensed and adapted by film studios since the publication of *Red Harvest* in 1929, Hammett's first major success with Hollywood did not come until 1934, when MGM released its version of *The Thin Man*, starring William Powell and Myrna Loy. The film's extraordinary success at the box office persuaded MGM to acquire from Hammett both the rights to a second film—eventually titled *After the Thin Man*—and an original story for it. After this film also proved a tremendous success, MGM purchased the rights to *The Thin Man* outright from Hammett and his publisher for $40,000, leaving only the print publication rights and radio rights behind.[42] By the time the third Thin Man film, *Another Thin Man* (also based on an originally commissioned story by Hammett), had left theaters in 1939, MGM was clearly in possession of one of the hottest film properties in Hollywood—and Hammett himself was widely seen by those in the entertainment industry as a hot commodity.[43]

Leveraging his association with both the *Thin Man* films and Warner Bros.'s third *Maltese Falcon* adaptation (starring Humphrey Bogart and released to critical acclaim in 1941), Hammett moved into radio licensing in the 1940s. A popular radio series based around the Nick and Nora characters launched on NBC as *The Adventures of the Thin Man* in 1941 and ran through 1950, periodically switching networks. *The Adventures of Sam Spade* began its six-year run in 1946, moving from ABC to NBC to, finally, CBS. And *The Fat Man*, which followed the detective work of a corpulent private eye seemingly based upon the overweight antagonist of *The Maltese Falcon*, premiered in 1946 on ABC, where it remained until 1951 (Universal also released a film version of *The Fat Man* in 1951). Although these shows sometimes used Hammett's name on the air and occasionally based their plots on short stories he had written, Hammett had no direct involvement with them beyond the initial pitching process and licensing negotiations.

As the 1940s drew to end, Hammett had started drumming up interest for a broadcast series (either for radio or television) based upon his early Continental Ops stories, had entered initial discussions with the New York newspaper *The Mirror* for a Sam Spade comic strip, and had begun, as he explained in a letter to his oldest daughter, reviewing his past work for other licensable property: "I've a couple of other radio or television ideas—based on characters invented in the dim past—in more or less formative stages."[44] By the end of 1951, however, the radio shows had gone off the air, the deals dried up, and Hammett's property become, in practice, worthless. The abrupt reversal of fortune was a consequence of Hammett's refusal to testify in a 1951 case related to the activities of a supposedly communist political group. For this refusal, he was found in contempt of court, imprisoned in a West Virginia jail, subsequently investigated by the House Un-American Activities Committee, and effectively blacklisted within the entertainment industry.

In the late 1940s, however, Hammett's properties were still of significant value, and Warner Bros., riding high off the success of their 1941 version of *The Maltese Falcon*, saw considerable potential in the further exploitation of its rights in the novel, which included not only film rights but also radio and television rights. Indeed, the radio rights alone were proving to be lucrative for the studio, with at least five licensed radio adaptations of the novel (some of them featuring Bogart reprising his role as Sam Spade) broadcast before 1950.[45]

Despite the obvious value of the radio rights they possessed, however, Warner Bros., still at this time conceiving of itself almost exclusively as a film company, took little initiative in engaging with or even monitoring the burgeoning radio market, save as a marketing tool for its films and stars. This explains the studio's obliviousness to Hammett's own licensing activities with respect to the character of Sam Spade. Chancing to hear a December 1947 episode of *Suspense* on CBS titled "The Kandy Tooth" that featured Spade, a Warner Bros. employee alerted the studio's legal department, which, after reviewing its files and finding no license had been granted for this airing, directed the studio's outside counsel, Gordon Files (of Freston & Files) to send letters alleging copyright infringement to the show's producer, sponsor, and network. Not having yet done much research into the episode or the conditions of its production, Warner Bros. and their lawyers assumed, in keeping with the norm of iterative textual production, that Sam Spade's inclusion as a character in the "The Kandy Tooth" meant that the radio show was an unauthorized adaptation of *The Maltese Falcon.* Only after Files had sent the legal threats and after the alleged infringers had responded, denying Warner Bros.'s allegation, did Warner Bros. realize that the *Suspense* episode was not a standalone adaptation at all but rather a rebroadcast of two episodes of *The Adventures of Sam Spade,* a popular series produced by the Regis Radio Corporation that had been airing on CBS since 1946.[46] Nor did the studio realize until months after it had filed suit in a California federal court against everyone involved in the radio show except Hammett that Hammett had formally licensed the character of Sam Spade to Regis in 1945 and had been receiving a $400 per episode royalty.[47] Upon grasping his involvement—not through any fact-finding of its own but through the details of a separate suit filed by Hammett against Warner Bros. in New York (which we will examine below)—Warner Bros. amended its suit to include Hammett as a defendant.[48] And so began what legal treatises refer to as *Warner Bros. Pictures v. CBS,* or sometimes simply "the Sam Spade case."

The Sam Spade Case

Although sometimes characterized, usually disparagingly, as a mere dispute over the meaning of a contractual clause (i.e., what constituted radio rights in *The Maltese Falcon*), the fundamental issues around which the Sam Spade case revolved were in fact much more far-reaching, reflecting an unresolved question at the heart of the modern copyright regime regarding the legal protection of fictional characters. As described above, most stakeholders at the time believed, even if they could not point specifically to the idea-expression dichotomy as the reason, that fictional characters could not themselves be copyrighted. In practice, however, the principle of iterative textual derivation had meant that stakeholders also believed that characters were, for all intents and purposes, protected anyway, since any text featuring a preexisting character was almost certain to involve substantial imitation of the original text in which the character appeared—and the original text *could* be copyrighted. Because unauthorized use of an uncopyrightable character could thus have been treated as unauthorized use of a copyrighted story, such use was, as noted earlier, extraordinarily rare. But what if an author (perhaps enterprising, perhaps conniving) broke with these assumptions and sold to a licensee (perhaps brazen, perhaps gullible) the radio rights to a character itself—not to the work in which the character originated, the radio rights to which the author no longer possessed? And what if (to press the question further) the work in which the character originated did not appear to lend itself to iterative derivation anyway, so that further use of the character was unlikely to require much from the original text beyond the character's name, appearance, and profession? For the first time, a U.S. judge would be forced to say explicitly whether a character by itself could or could not be protected by copyright and to square his answer with both the letter of the law (statute and common law) and the customs of the entertainment industry. These, in a nutshell, are the circumstances surrounding the Sam Spade case, and they explain why industry professionals (particularly studio executives) paid particularly close attention to the outcome.

WHERE AND WHO

Let me begin my account of the lawsuit with answers to what might initially appear to be two of the simplest questions one could ask about it: in what court did it take place and who were the parties involved? Virtually every published account of the dispute situates it solely within the Southern District of California. The vast majority of these accounts discuss it exclusively in terms of the 1954 opinion of the Ninth Circuit Court of Appeals, leaving the lower California district court proceedings (which lasted from mid-1948 through the end of 1951 and in which a hefty portion of the relevant facts were generated) unmentioned though presumably implied. There is, as any practicing lawyer will explain, good reason for situating the case in such a way: if one's primary concern is the precedent the dispute produced and if one understands precedents (as most lawyers and judges do) as rules abstracted from appellate opinions, then the only court "battle" that matters is the one that took place in the Ninth Circuit Court of Appeals. But if we want to understand how the law worked in practice in this dispute, and how the different parties understood and interacted with it, then we must extend the boundaries of the dispute so that it comprises, alongside the proceedings of the Ninth Circuit appellate court, not only that of the California district court, but also that of district and appellate courts in the Second Circuit, where another case, *Hammett v. Warner Bros. Pictures*, was fought.[49]

As in other complex civil suits, where ostensibly separate cases are often integrally bound up with each other, *Hammett v. Warner Bros.*

Pictures cannot be cleanly separated from *Warner Bros. Pictures v. CBS*. Indeed, the former exists in this case only because of the latter: Warner Bros., filing suit in California before it had accurately understood the basic facts pertaining to its complaint, neglected to include Hammett as one of the alleged infringers. When Hammett heard news of the suit and relayed it to Leonard Zissu, his New York lawyer, Zissu immediately spotted in Warner Bros.'s oversight an opportunity. Within a month of Warner Bros.'s filing, Zissu had filed his own suit in the Southern District of New York, seeking from that court a "declaration that under the terms of the agreement of 1930 Warner Brothers [sic] has no rights in the name and character 'Sam Spade' except in its use thereof in connection with the story 'The Maltese Falcon.'"[50] Had Hammett been a party to the California case, the New York suit would have been rejected out of hand, but because Hammett was not, Zissu reasoned that the fundamental legal issue underlying the dispute could be quickly resolved via the last-minute adjudicative prophylactic of a declaratory judgment—which Zissu wagered a New York judge could be convinced to grant in their favor. Although taken by surprise, Warner Bros. was not slow to respond: after being served the summons, it quickly amended its California suit by naming Hammett as one of the defendants. The primary legal question facing the New York judge thereby became one of legal procedure: which case involving Hammett as a party—the New York or the California—came first and thus had legal priority? If the former, the New York court would be free to rule and thus could consider the legal questions regarding property rights in fictional characters. If the latter, the New York court would be barred from ruling, lest it interfere with the California case. Because Hammett did not become a party to the California case until *after* the New York case had been initiated, there was no obviously correct answer. The judge, weighing the arguments of both sides, decided that the California case had priority and so dismissed Hammett's complaint without addressing the question regarding copyright.[51] A month later, a Court of Appeals for the Second Circuit affirmed.[52]

Although Hammett technically lost *Hammett v. Warner Bros. Pictures*, the case had a tremendous influence on *Warner Bros. Pictures v. CBS*. Its most obvious and immediate effect, of course, was the bringing on of Hammett as a party in the California case. Perhaps Warner Bros. would have eventually sued him anyway, but Hammett's Second Circuit suit unquestionably hastened his formal involvement in the California trial, and from the moment he became involved, the framework by which the legal questions would need to be fought there changed. What Warner Bros. had initially perceived as a clear-cut case of copyright infringement became, because of Hammett's inclusion (and the work of his lawyer), an almost metaphysical contest over the origin and scope of an author's rights in the fictional characters he created. In this respect, *Hammett v. Warner Bros. Pictures* set the terms of the Ninth Circuit case, with the arguments presented by both sides in the former (at least those pertaining to Hammett's rights) serving as prototypes for those that would be employed in the latter. A careful comparison of both cases reveals even a kind of path dependency, whereby the specific framework of the Second Circuit case (film studio versus author over the rights to one of the author's ideas) came to determine that of the originally quite different Ninth Circuit case (film studio versus radio show over the copying of a story).

At an even more basic level, we should also see the New York case as an essential step in the work of knowledge production undertaken by the parties' lawyers. All of the knowledge generated during the New York trial, including not only the facts of the dispute but also the previous case law that was presumed relevant, was carried forward by the two parties' lawyers into *Warner Bros. Pictures v. CBS.* The more accurate answer thus to *where* (i.e., in which court) the Sam Spade case took place must be multiple: the U.S. District Court for the Southern District of New York, the Court of Appeals for the Second Circuit, the U.S. District Court in the Southern District of California, the Court of Appeals for the Ninth Circuit, and—if we stray from the norms of traditional legal historiography (but not those of lawyers' billing practices)—the U.S. Supreme Court as well, which, though it did not hear the case, did provide a kind of virtual venue for the parties' last battle, fought through documents submitted to the Court in attempts to convince it that the case should or should not be reviewed.

With the *where* question satisfactorily answered, let us turn now to the *who* question: Who were the parties involved in the case? Inspired no doubt by the simplicity of the appellate opinion's abbreviated title, most scholarly accounts frame *Warner Bros. Pictures v. CBS* as a bilateral contest, with *Warner Bros.* on one side and Hammett and the companies associated with the Sam Spade radio show on the other. But to understand fully the case—and its relevance to narrative-based property during the modern copyright era—we need to see it instead in quadrilateral terms. In one corner, we have a jumble of stakeholders, all accused of copyright infringement and unfair competition by Warner Bros., and all represented in court by the same counsel, Clarence Runkle of Crider, Runkle & Tilson. These stakeholders included CBS; William Spier (producer and director of the radio program); The Wildroot Company, Inc. (sponsor of the radio program); Regis Radio Corp. (assignee of the radio rights); Batten, Barton, Durstine & Osborn, Inc. (the advertising agency working for Wildroot); and three of the radio program's writers. Although most of these stakeholders had their own individual lawyers in addition to Runkle, their differing interests were made roughly equivalent in court through their collective reliance upon Runkle's representation there.

Although Hammett and the other defendants comprise the same "side" in the case, a proper account of the proceedings requires that we pull them apart, placing Hammett by himself in a separate corner. The necessity of doing so is indicated, at the most superficial level, by Hammett's reliance in court upon his own representation: Leonard Zissu, a brilliant lawyer form New York City with a strong understanding of intellectual property law. Zissu, as we have seen, developed separately his own legal strategy, which he first employed in New York Court in a suit to which the other California defendants were not parties. He (and Hammett) thus entered into the California case with their own already established ideas of how the law worked and what their defense should be. That Hammett brought Zissu into the California court rather than rely on the other defendants' counsel also reflects a fundamental divergence between Hammett's interests and that of his codefendants. A loss at court would have meant for them cancellation of the radio show and payment of damages (a significant portion of which would have been covered by insurance). For Hammett, by contrast, a loss would have stripped him of the underlying rights (whatever they were) he had in Sam Spade, endangered some of his other business dealings, bankrupted him, and opened him up to subsequent lawsuits with respect to the warranties he had provided when he licensed Spade.

The significant extent to which the interests of Hammett and the other defendants were misaligned is in evidence not only in the trial court transcripts, which reveal Runkle and Zissu presenting different arguments to the judge (with Zissu's appearing to be more persuasive), but also in the assessment of Warner Bros.'s own legal team, who, up until a year before the trial court's ruling, were involved in settlement negotiations with the legal representatives of all of the defendants *except* Hammett. As Morris Ebenstein, Warner Bros.'s in-house lawyer assigned to the suit, observed in a letter to Gordon Files, the lawyer representing the studio in court: "I must say that the various moves and movements of the defendants' attorneys toward and away from settlement appear to me as very mysterious. They resemble the moves of a bashful and hesitant lover."[53] Files, in response, blamed the defense's ambivalence on the "different motives" of the various defendants, attributing, for example, to Wildroot and its settlement-seeking lawyer a lack of "particular concern with copyright law," and describing Hammett (in a manner very much in line with how the media had consistently portrayed him) as irrationally stubborn: a "difficult character" who sits defiantly "outside the circle of negotiation."[54] Although settlement appears to have been taken off the table during the subsequent appellate hearing, Hammett's separation from his co-appellees persisted, with Zissu and Runkle submitting to the court separate briefs putting forth incompatible arguments for the protectability of fictional characters.

For all the differences between Hammett and the other defendants, they are, at least, aligned in their basic goal of winning from the judge a particular verdict ("not guilty"). The same cannot be said for our two plaintiffs: Warner Bros. and Alfred A. Knopf, Inc., Hammett's primary publisher. Although nominally both plaintiffs, Warner Bros. and Knopf not only had differing stakes in the case's outcome (with Knopf barely having any stake at all); they also held antithetical conceptions of how the law functioned. Indeed, Knopf was much closer, in terms of both its broader interests and its understanding of the law, to Hammett than it was Warner Bros. That it was nevertheless positioned opposite Hammett as a plaintiff had nothing to do with the facts of the case but was rather the result of what would likely be for many twenty-first-century readers the most obscure of modern-copyright-era legal principles: copyright indivisibility. Copyright indivisibility meant that as a matter of law, a copyright registered in a specific work (such as *The Maltese Falcon* novel) was singular and could not be split up into separate rights, held by separate parties. As described in chapter 1 of this book, the ramifications of this principle were complex and far-reaching and its significance to the modern copyright regime as a whole profound. For our purposes here, however, it is enough to recall that one of the principal's main effects was to bar licensees from bringing suit by themselves for copyright infringement; to file such a suit, a licensee needed the actual copyright holder to serve as plaintiff. With respect to *The Maltese Falcon,* Knopf (in keeping with publishing industry practice in the 1930s) was the registered copyright holder and Warner Bros. a licensee. Warner Bros. was thus forced to execute a contractual provision allowing it to join Knopf to the suit as a "formal party only," with no right to any damages Warner Bros. might recover.[55] Although technically, as a mere formal party, Knopf had virtually no role in any of the courts' proceedings, its involvement as a plaintiff, even a nominal one, nevertheless underscored a significant problem with Warner Bros.'s eventual legal argument (a problem that does not appear to have been lost on any of the California judges): the custom of the publishing industry, of which Knopf was a part, supported Hammett's interpretation of the law and not Warner Bros.'s.

COPYRIGHT AND CUSTOM

That the California judges' opinions in 1951 and 1954 would ultimately revolve around custom (i.e., the accepted though usually unwritten practices of a distinct community) and its intersection with copyright would not have surprised Hammett and his lawyer at the time the suit began in 1948.[56] Both men, well-versed in how the publishing industry worked, understood from the dispute's beginning that the customs of that industry with respect to characters supported their legal position; accordingly, they early on made custom the center of their defense, with the other defendants' lawyers (mostly) eventually following their lead. To Warner Bros.'s legal team, however, the role that custom came to play in the legal battle almost certainly came as a surprise. This is not because the studio's lawyers began the suit believing that publishing custom supported the studio's claims or that custom was irrelevant to the facts at hand; it was rather because they were ignorant of publishing custom altogether. Only as the trial proceeded did they learn (partly through the work of the defendants and partly through their own research) how publishers traditionally handled "rights" in fictional characters.

Based on the documents contained in the Warner Bros. Archives, it is impossible to reconstruct a precise timeline of how this learning proceeded. As is true of most such legal files from this era, the notes, drafts, and even internal correspondence that make up the documents preserved by Warner Bros.'s legal team were repeatedly copied, reused, and annotated by the team throughout the life of the dispute, rendering it often impossible for a researcher like myself to authoritatively date their creation and reception. What is clear, however, is that Warner Bros.'s lawyers engaged primarily in seven different kinds of research during the life of the case:

1. Guided by legal treatises, such as Louis Frohlich and Charles Schwartz's *Law of Motion Pictures,* they conducted a thorough review of case law.[57]
2. They carefully analyzed the language of contracts and correspondence between Warner Bros. and Hammett and/or Knopf.[58]
3. They conducted a comparative close reading of "The Kandy Tooth" with that of *The Maltese Falcon* (the novel) in order to demonstrate that the former was an unauthorized copy of the latter.[59]
4. They reviewed the marketing material Warner Bros. had created for its three *Maltese Falcon*-based films in order to provide evidence in support of a charge of unfair competition/trademark infringement with regard to the name "Sam Spade."[60]
5. They attempted to assemble data demonstrating that *The Maltese Falcon* book sales increased substantially after the release of each film.[61]
6. They conducted a historical survey of character-based literary "series" and attempted to develop a definition of what constituted, legally and aesthetically, a "series."[62]
7. Through conversations with publishers (such as Knopf) and readings of published scholarship, they worked to understand how print publishing—and particularly the publishing of mystery/detective fiction—worked.[63]

The first three of these represent conventional practices in the preparation of a copyright lawsuit, both during the modern copyright era and today, and were most likely begun at the very start of the dispute. The fourth and fifth were borne out of hunches or hypotheses, both of which proved to be either unfounded or impossible to establish adequately; as such, they were abandoned before the completion of the trial. The final two kinds of research were prompted by arguments made by the defense and appear, based upon the files, to have been the most difficult and time-consuming for Warner Bros.'s lawyers to conduct. These final two also appear to be the most sustained, with significant work on them occurring from the time of the initial California trial up to Warner Bros.'s filing of a petition for certiorari with the U.S. Supreme Court. For better or worse (and the trial's outcome suggests worse), Files and Ebenstein relied almost entirely upon other people to do this work. Helen Maloney, a studio reader, did much of it, making phone calls, writing letters and memos, and assembling and writing up summaries of fictional works and scholarship. For what we might call the "synthesis" of Helen's research, Warner Bros. relied upon John T. Winterich, contributing editor of the *Saturday Review*, detective-fiction review columnist, and author of several works on book collecting. The following excerpt from a 1955 memo from Winterich to Ebenstein shortly after the California appellate court ruling provides a sense of how extensive an undertaking this was:

> Herewith master copies (originals) and checked copies (carbons) of PUBLISHING HISTORY and SEQUELS. . . .
>
> Herewith, also, photostats for both PUBLISHING HISTORY and SEQUELS.
>
> In addition, a group of books (property of WBP) which form essential exhibits are between the windows against the west wall of my office, so-called.
>
> In the file cabinets (Mrs. Gould's room) is a big envelops [*sic*] full of scraps, scratch material, etc. This is probably of no use but I hate to throw it away until the show's over.
>
> The only material to come is the two tabulations which Helen Maloney has been working on. These should go with SEQUELS, to which they will form an appendix. . . .
>
> All library books charged to me have been returned. There are other books about which must be returned to various libraries. Helen knows about these.[64]

Although this research was extraordinarily valuable to Warner Bros.'s legal team, which would not have been able to respond to Hammett's argument about custom without it, the knowledge that it generated for Files and Ebenstein also presented a serious problem, for this knowledge suggested rather strongly that Hammett's argument was in fact correct.

What was Hammett's argument about custom? He argued that it had long been the practice of authors of detective fiction to reuse the detective characters they had introduced in one story in "later and different stories" that they wrote.[65] Such a practice, "as old as this form of literature itself," was in fact integral to how detective series fiction traditionally worked.[66] The example he and his lawyer cited most frequently across the multiple trials and hearings was the British writer Sir Arthur Conan Doyle's Sherlock Holmes—a character who appeared across sixty detective novels and short stories between 1887 and 1927—but more contemporary references were also made to S.S. Van Dine's popular detective Philo Vance and Erle Stanley Gardner's crime-sleuthing lawyer Perry Mason (both of whom had, like Spade, also been featured in films). Indeed, Hammett even pointed to his own work with Sam Spade: between 1931 and 1932, he'd reused Spade for three short stories, originally published in magazines but a decade later collected in book form under the title *The Adventures of Sam Spade and Other Stories by Dashiell Hammett*.[67] The "open and notorious custom" of reusing characters meant, Hammett argued, that in any business deal involving rights to an author's work the default assumption was that the author would retain the right to reuse their characters in new stories.[68] In a deposition for the New York trial, Hammett spelled out the implications for Warner Bros.'s complaint:

> In view of this known tendency it would be absurd to suppose that parties bargaining for anything like character, sequel, continuation or other similar rights would not make express provision therefor. And when it is further borne in mind that [Warner Bros.] . . . was a wide and experienced user and dealer in literary properties and prepared the very contract in suit the conclusion is utterly inescapable that no rights in connection with characters were being transferred apart from and beyond the use of characters in connection with the basic story told.[69]

In order to persuade the various judges that the practice of character reuse was universally recognized and accepted within the publishing industry—was, that is, a *custom*—Hammett and Zissu employed two strategies. The first, and most straightforward, was to spend a significant amount of time having witnesses describe for the California judge how the publishing industry and detective genre worked. One of these witnesses, of course, was Hammett. Others were professionals from the industry, including Howard Cady, senior editor at Doubleday and Co., and William White (known professionally as Anthony Boucher), editor of *Magazine of Fantasy and Science Fiction*, writer, and mystery-fiction reviewer. As a means of persuading the trial judge, the strategy seems to have worked. During an exchange with Zissu early in Hammett's testimony, for example, Judge William C. Mathes expressed skepticism about the degree to which the practice of reusing characters was widespread and well-known enough to actually constitute a custom: "It might be a matter of common knowledge if I had judicial knowledge of it and could be able to take judicial notice of it, but I frankly have not read enough literature in this field to know whether it should be a matter of common knowledge."[70] Upon hearing further elaboration and examples, however,

Mathes changed his mind: "Having Mr. Hammett recall it to my mind, I should think it is a matter of common knowledge. Those [Van Dine and Gardner] are the most prominent writers in that field. It is a matter of common knowledge. I should think in their writings they re-use the characters, the main character. Can't that be stipulated?"[71] Here we have a clear-cut example of the trial as the work of knowledge production, and though the knowledge here is quite obviously ends-oriented (i.e., produced in service to Hammett's argument), that does not prevent the judge from coming to treat it as fact. Indeed, in his decision he will even employ the language of Hammett's striking description of the custom as "open and notorious" as if it were his own.[72]

The second strategy Hammett and Zissu employed was to introduce evidence pertaining to a business dealing between Warner Bros. and Hammett that suggested that the studio itself understood and accepted this custom. As Hammett explained in both a deposition for the New York case and in testimony before the judge in the California trial, Warner Bros. contracted with Hammett in January 1931 to write a new Sam Spade story, eventually titled *On the Make*, which the studio hoped to develop into a film featuring the actor William Powell.[73] In exchange for the rights to the finished story, the studio agreed to pay Hammett three installments of $5,000, with the final installment (and subsequent transfer of rights) predicated on the acceptance of the finished story. When Hammett delivered the finished story later that spring, Warner Bros.'s Darryl Zanuck rejected it, complaining in a letter to Hammett's agent that "the finished story . . . has none of the qualifications of 'Maltese Falcon,' although the same character was in both stories. . . . Therefore, we elect to take our loss of money so far advanced to him."[74] Why, Hammett asked, would Warner Bros. have needed to contract with him for a new Sam Spade story if they already owned the rights to the character? "Not only is there no indication of any claim of Sam Spade character rights in the two exhibits," Hammett argued, "but indeed these writings implicitly reveal the character and any new stories featuring that character are matters of independent dealings and rights for myself."[75] How much weight this argument was given by Judge Mathes or (later) the Ninth Circuit appellate judges is impossible to say, as neither mention the 1931 deal in their opinion, but—if accepted as true—it painted a picture of a plaintiff that had been, at best, inconsistent in its own interpretation of what rights it had acquired in *The Maltese Falcon* and thereby put Warner Bros. on the defensive.

Seemingly caught off guard by both the contract and the Zanuck letter, Warner Bros.'s lawyers nevertheless proved able to muster a response that, while not exactly invalidating Hammett's argument, at least introduced doubt over his account of the facts. Although, as demonstrated by the contract introduced into evidence, Jack Warner had indeed arranged with Hammett to write another Sam Spade story, Warner Bros.'s lawyers argued that the story he turned in (*On the Make*) did not in fact contain Sam Spade. Edward Muhl, head of the legal department for Universal Pictures—which eventually bought the script from Warner Bros.—swore in an affidavit that it did not, as did Helen Maloney, the Warner Bros. reader helping with the defense.[76] The character, she alleged, was named "Gene Richmond." No original copies of the script could be located; only versions of the script that had been corrected by Warner Bros., which (unsurprisingly) supported Maloney's contention.[77] What then of Zanuck's letter and its explicit acknowledgment that "the same character was in both stories"? Some clever close reading explained this: "what Zanuck meant was that 'the same character'—i.e., a private detective, 'was in both stories.'"[78]

When it came to the argument about custom, however, Warner Bros. was in serious trouble. The problem, they came to understand, was that Hammett and his witnesses' description of publishing industry practice was correct. Indeed, even Knopf, their own co-plaintiff and the nominal holder of the original copyright in *The Maltese Falcon*, agreed with Hammett. As Knopf's lawyer for the case, Jospeh Karp, explained in in a 1951 letter to Files:

> I have received the impression . . . that you are primarily interested in ascertaining what the attitude of Knopf is with respect to the defendant's contention that there is a custom in the book publishing business for the author of a detective story to retain sequel rights in a detective character contained in a book in which Knopf has acquired exclusive publication rights. Knopf's attorney assures me that publishers do not take the position that once having acquired exclusive publication rights in a detective story, they have exclusive publication rights in the characters of that story. In other words, such exclusive publication rights, according to him, have not been regarded by the publishers as depriving the author from selling publication rights in sequels in which the same characters are used.[79]

Karp's language, carefully but explicitly rejecting Warner Bros.'s suggestion that publishers acquire sequel rights, must have been devastating to

Files and Ebenstein, who by this point had begun to suspect the central role that publishing custom would play in Judge Mathes's ruling.

Despite this serious flaw in their case, Warner Bros. did not give up. Recognizing that they could not argue that the custom did not exist, Files and Ebenstein's first strategy was to argue that the custom's legal foundation had been incorrectly described by the defense, both as it applied to this particular publishing contract and as it applied to the publishing industry as a whole. Their argument, clever albeit tortuous, was that because copyrights to mystery fiction such as *The Maltese Falcon* were in the 1920s and 1930s and sometimes still in the 1950s registered to the publisher, publishers were in these cases the sole owners of the copyright. It followed that when an author wrote a sequel, a publisher was, via an informal (often merely verbal) contract, granting the author the limited right to reuse one or more characters, which remained the property of the publisher.[80] In a nutshell: When Knopf had acquired the copyright to *The Maltese Falcon*, it had acquired all rights to the character of Sam Spade. That Hammett was able to write and publish sequels featuring Spade was only because Knopf had (informally) granted him permission to do so; such permission, however, did not extend to selling character rights to broadcasters.

Warner Bros.'s second strategy was to argue that the publishing custom, even if one disputed the account they offered of its legal foundation, did not in any case apply to this particular dispute. "The customs found," as Files and Ralph Lewis (another lawyer at Freston & Files) wrote flatly in their opening brief for the California appeal, "are irrelevant."[81] Even if the publishing custom worked as Hammett alleged (and Files and Lewis vigorously denied that it did), it had no bearing on entertainment industries other than that of publishing. What *this* dispute involved was rather the customs of the motion picture industry:

> The 1930 contract [between Warner Bros. and Knopf and Hammett] is primarily a transaction with a producer of motion pictures and the field is quite different. A publisher buys a story so that he can print it and sell the book. A motion picture producer buys a story in order to use its components in the creation of a new work in a new medium. The 1930 contract went into detail in making sure that Warner as a picture producer could break up the story and use all of the pieces or any of them from time to time and in any way deemed necessary. To the motion picture producer the story is raw material while to the publisher it is the finished product.[82]

Files and Lewis's argument here was not based on firsthand experience but had been developed out of consultations with film producers, who insisted that they did not purchase rights to published stories but instead to the "raw material" contained within those stories. As one producer, presumably working for Warner Bros., explained to Files in an unsigned letter, "At the time that we buy the material we do not know the part of it we will use . . . We, therefore, acquire the exclusive rights in the dialogue and the plot and the characters, and we reserve to ourselves the exclusive right to use the dialogue and/or the plot and/or the characters in various combinations."[83] "There is," he concluded, making virtually the same argument that Files and Lewis would later make, "therefore, no warrant or support for arguing that some custom in another business . . . affects an actual contract—plus an existing practice—in our business."[84]

As clever as they might at first have seemed, both of Warner Bros.'s strategies suffered serious weaknesses, which ultimately rendered them unpersuasive. The problem with Warner Bros.'s argument about the custom's legal foundation was twofold. First, and most obviously, no one in the publishing industry agreed with the studio's characterization of how the custom worked legally. Indeed, the characterization appears to have been based upon a misunderstanding of what copyright registration in a publisher's name meant. Unlike in the film industry, where copyright registration meant copyright ownership, in the publishing industry, the former did not, in practice, entail the latter. The tradition of publishers, rather than authors, registering copyrights in the books they published (a tradition already fading by the time the case was decided) had merely developed as an efficient solution to the problems posed by copyright formalities and indivisibility; no reputable publisher would ever claim ownership of the underlying copyright. What is more, Warner Bros.'s account of the custom seemed to ignore a basic fact about author-publisher relations that was introduced at trial: authors sometimes change publishers and nevertheless continue to publish books featuring characters they supposedly "sold" to their original publishers.[85] Indeed, Hammett himself did this with Spade, publishing in book form a collection of short stories featuring the character with a publisher other than Knopf. A major problem with Warner Bros.'s first strategy was thus that the account it provided appeared to be empirically false.

But that was not the strategy's only problem, for it also seemed to reject the idea-expression dichotomy by positioning characters themselves—apart from the stories in which they featured—as protectable by copyright. Warner Bros.'s lawyers advanced this argument most transparently in their brief to the Second Circuit Court of Appeals, where, leaning heavily on a rather strained interpretation of Judge Hand's opinion in *Nichols v. Universal Pictures Co.* (discussed earlier in this chapter), they argued for a "fundamental proposition that the copyright in every fictional and dramatic work embraces and protects at least two components, i.e., *component plot* and *component characters*; in short, that the copyright owner will be protected against the copying by others either of *original plot* or of *original characters*."[86] Although Files adopted in subsequent venues less schematizing language, the basic proposition persisted unchanged—as did its obvious weakness in elevating mere ideas (i.e., characters) to the status of protectable property. Neither Runkle nor Zissu and Abraham Marcus—each submitting separate briefs to the Ninth Circuit Court of Appeals—had any difficulty dismantling Warner Bros.'s argument. Characters, both sets of lawyers countered, are not protected by copyright. Succinctly summarizing the case law, Zissu and Marcus explained:

> Such text or expression as fully develops or delineates in detail a character by describing the character or his acts or setting forth his dialogue would be protected against copying as any other text or expression of a copyrighted work. Only that is meant, no more, in saying that a character may be protected under copyright when it is fully developed or delineated in detail.[87]

Lest that suggest that characters are free for the taking by anyone who wishes to use them, the defense proposed that characters are protected as property by other kinds of law. In arguments that anticipated how IP law would evolve after 1978, Runkle describes character rights as "analogous to trade-mark rights," while Zissu and Marcus contended that characters "would be protectible as a matter of common law under a doctrine of or akin to unfair competition."[88] By this argument, the defense was thus able to offer a simpler and more elegant legal basis for trade in characters that was also compatible with the idea-expression dichotomy.

Warner Bros.'s second strategy suffered a different but not unrelated problem: the argument that the customs of the publishing industry did not apply in this dispute depended, unwisely, upon convincing the court to accept and apply the customs of the motion picture industry. Indeed, the primary evidence put forth for the irrelevance of the former was the relevance to the plaintiff of the latter. This was thus a risky argument, for why should the court apply one industry's customs to the dispute and not another's? And were it forced to do so, why—given that the disputed content was a radio broadcast and Hammett a writer of print fiction and given also that the original work from which all the others derived was a novel—would the court choose that of the motion picture industry? Add in the further problem that the motion picture industry's custom, by carving up a story into separable assets (i.e., "raw material") seemed on the face of it to violate the idea-expression dichotomy, and the strategy seemed doomed from the start. For were a judge to formally validate, via his opinion, the motion picture industry's custom (at least as described by the plaintiffs) he would have been rejecting (or, at the appellate level, overturning) almost a century of precedent regarding what was and was not protected by copyright.

Given the serious shortcomings in Warner Bros.'s arguments, one may wonder why the studio's legal team made them in the first place and why they stuck with them so doggedly throughout the life of the dispute, including even their petition to the U.S. Supreme Court for certiorari. First, it is worth remembering that a lawsuit is, among other things, a process of knowledge production, and that the production of knowledge is not just for the purpose of educating the judge but also educating the parties themselves (or at least their lawyers). In this respect, Warner Bros. entered the dispute at a considerable disadvantage, for in contrast to Hammett and Zissu they knew very little about how the publishing industry (or even the radio industry) worked—to say nothing of the relevant facts regarding who had done what in what manner with respect to "The Kandy Tooth." To correct this imbalance, Warner Bros.'s legal team engaged, as we have seen, in a tremendous amount of very rapid learning for themselves. Unfortunately, the development of their case could not wait until such learning was "finished." The team was thus forced to develop, on the fly, avenues of argumentation based on hunches and analogical reasoning, most of which unfortunately proved to be dead ends. Although Files, Ebenstein, and Lewis endeavored to adapt, only so much course correction seems to have been possible once the first hearings (in New York) had introduced the core facts and determined the basic framework for the dispute.

Based on the archival material, it also appears evident that Warner Bros.'s case was—no matter how the studio's lawyers might have decided to approach it—simply not a strong one. As the studio proceeded and its lawyers were forced to face off with Hammett, the weakness of the studio's position became increasingly obvious to them. Indeed, the archival records, albeit in somewhat jumbled fashion, demonstrate the growing recognition by Warner Bros.'s legal team that the suit was Hammett's to lose. Many of the documents contain marginal comments, unattributed but presumably made by Ebenstein, Files, or Lewis, providing commentary or review. A good number of these identify the weaknesses in Warner Bros.'s arguments. For example, in a copy of the opening brief in the appeals case, next to the passage I quoted above wherein Files and Lewis argue on behalf of the motion picture industry's custom, there is the penciled notation, "This's mistake."[89] Next to one of the arguments presenting Warner Bros.'s (empirically false) explanation of publishing industry custom, someone has similarly added the word "Error," underlined twice.[90] Even during the New York case, there is evidence that Warner Bros. had already begun to realize the difficulties they faced in winning their California suit. In a remarkable January 1949 letter from Files to Ebenstein, Files spells out many of the difficulties the suit poses, noting that, "[i]n discussing this case with other lawyers, we have met exactly the same [negative] reaction which you have described. It is apparently very difficult for a layman or for a lawyer to believe that the author of a mystery novel does not have an unlimited right to produce sequels using the principal of characters of his original work."[91]

Why then did Warner Bros. persist with the case so doggedly, even petitioning the U.S. Supreme Court for a hearing? Part of the answer, of course, is that Warner Bros. was wealthy enough to carry on with the lawsuit until it had exhausted all legal possibilities, regardless of its chances of winning. The studio may also have feared that losing might have ramifications for how the motion picture industry functioned (although, admittedly, the risks for potential ramifications became greater with each appeal). Other industry stakeholders shared these fears, especially after the appellate court's ruling. "It is evident that the decision is of significance to our industry," worried the Motion Picture Association in a 1954 letter to members of the Association's copyright committee. "It raises serious problems and creates dangerous possibilities."[92] Warner Bros. thus likely felt pressured or duty-bound to continue its lawsuit.

Upon reading through the archival material, however, one can see also another force at work: what we might call, borrowing from the discipline of psychology, *confirmation bias.* Confirmation bias, as psychology scholar Raymond Nickerson explains, "connotes the seeking or interpreting of evidence in ways that are partial to existing beliefs, expectations, or a hypothesis in hand."[93] Such bias is evident in the overconfidence with which Warner Bros.'s legal team sometimes judged their arguments, as when, for example, Ebenstein noted in a 1950 letter to Files, "I might add, somewhat in the nature of a parenthesis, that I was really impressed by how good our case looks when put down on paper."[94] It is also evident in the way that Warner Bros.'s lawyers, upon losing an argument in court, would double down on it rather than revise or change it. Indeed, with each iteration from the trial to the appeals court to the petition for certiorari, Ebenstein appears all the more certain that his arguments are right—and all the more obstinate in his attribution of error to the court(s) and not to his side's case.[95] Here we see another important but frequently ignored aspect of how legal disputes, even those undertaken by highly trained and well-resourced lawyers, work in practice. Individual understandings of the law are heavy things, hard to move; once established and once reinforced through argumentation and the production of artifacts, such as briefs, their creators can sometimes be loathe to abandon them. Knowledge is often, to borrow the language of institutional theorists Walter Powell and Paul DiMaggio, a "cognitive" sunk cost, and lawyers are no less subject to the irrational biases associated with such costs than are laypersons.[96]

THE VERDICT(S)

Except for its procedural wins in New York, Warner Bros. consistently lost its dispute with Hammett. The California district court, with Judge Mathes presiding, found for Hammett and the other defendants, primarily along contractual lines, and—unsurprisingly—the U.S. Supreme Court rejected Warner Bros.'s request for a hearing. But it was the Ninth Circuit appellate court opinion, authored by Judge Stephens, that represented Warner Bros.'s biggest loss and which would come to draw the ire of future lawyers, judges, and law review contributors.

If this chapter has succeeded in the aim I have set for it, the substance of the appellate court's opinion should seem—contra the claims of its detractors—rational, even inevitable. Hammett, the court concluded, echoing Judge Mathes's opinion, did not convey the rights to his characters or the characters' names in his contract with Warner Bros., nor had Warner Bros. "a large, experienced moving picture producer" really "intended to take" them—for if it had, it would have named them in the contract.[97] "The conclusion that these rights are not within the granting instruments," Judge Stephens explained, "is strongly buttressed by the fact that historically and presently detective fiction writers have and do carry the leading characters with their names and individualisms from one story into succeeding stories"—a practice that Warner Bros. itself had not objected to when, "long after the Falcon agreements," Hammett published additional stories featuring Spade.[98]

Unlike Judge Mathes's opinion, however, Judge Stephens's did not stop here; it proceeded to "consider whether it was ever intended by the copyright statute that characters with their names should be under its protection."[99] Its answer was no. In a densely argued four paragraphs, the court explained its reasoning, which was premised, in a nutshell, on custom: "The practice of writers to compose sequels to stories is old."[100] And although this practice is never mentioned by copyright statute, it would be unreasonable to assume that Congress had wished to restrict it, since the practice accommodates the natural limitations of a creator's genius. "The characters of an author's imagination and the art of his descriptive talent, like a painter's or like a person with his penmanship," Judge Stephens wrote, "are always limited and always fall into limited patterns."[101] Were copyright understood to restrict such a practice, it would thus, by preventing authors from employing these patterns, "effect the very opposite of the statute's purpose which is to encourage the production of the arts."[102] Authors thus have special rights, when it comes to their own creations, to reproduce in sequels characters from previous works, even when the rights to those works have been transferred to someone else.[103]

These rights are not, however, completely unrestricted. An author cannot reproduce exactly the story of a work to which he has parted with the copyright. And it is at least *possible* to imagine a character being so integral to a story that the character could not in any fashion be reused without also reproducing that story—in which case the author would be barred by copyright from reusing the character. But those are the only restrictions. In Judge Stephens's famous (or notorious) words, "It is conceivable that the character really constitutes the story being told, but if the character is only the chessman in the game of telling the story he is not within the area of protection afforded by the copyright."[104] Recognizing that in detective fiction, as in all iterative storytelling, the detective is such a chessman, the court thus concluded that the characters of *The Maltese Falcon*, foremost among them Sam Spade, "were vehicles for the story told, and the vehicles did not go with the sale of the story."[105]

Although, as I detailed at this chapter's beginning, Judge Stephens's opinion has for decades been decried as bad law, with his short disquisition on characters and copyright deemed both illogical and unnecessary for the ruling, the opinion is well in keeping with how intellectual property law was understood to work during the modern copyright regime. His conclusions about character and copyright were not new interpretations of the law; to the contrary, they reflected how narrative industries other than the film industry had long understood and managed copyrighted property. Furthermore, dicta or not, Stephens was compelled to make them by the three legal teams involved in the dispute, whose strategies in the appellate court all revolved around the question as to what kind of legal property a character was. To be sure, Stephens's answer (like that of many IP rulings in the modern copyright era) was almost gnomic in its concision. But the answer was not unwarranted, as it was necessary to settle a point of law raised by the parties themselves. By resituating the opinion in the context of the actual lawsuit, we can also see that the court did not declare characters unprotectable. It merely declared them unprotectable by copyright. Indeed, one might argue that the opinion, by seeming to invalidate copyright as a means of protecting what Warner Bros.'s lawyers called "components" (and what we today call "IP assets"), helped prompt the shift to the IP regime that exists today, wherein trademark and unfair competition law are the primary means of protecting the individual pieces of narrative-based property. Such was, after all, the argument put forth by the defense: characters are akin to trademarks. At the time of the ruling, however, this argument was so far outside everyday understandings of the law that other lawyers, authors, and entertainment professionals—including counsel for film industries—were slow to grasp it and how it might benefit their industries. But grasp it they eventually did.

Conclusion

The account of *Warner Bros. Pictures v. CBS* provided in this chapter focused on the idea-expression dichotomy and the principle of iterative textual derivation. Although the account presents these primarily as *legal* principles, both should be seen, as the chapter as a whole suggests, as managerial and aesthetic principles too. Not just abstract rules or theories, the principles simultaneously emerge from and inform practice: practice by lawyers before a judge and practice by creators and entertainment-industry professionals as they produce and develop narrative-based properties. The first principle might be called *formal*, in that it is codified by judicial ruling, and the second *informal*, in that its nature precludes such codification, but they are both institutionalized through the everyday work of entertainment industry actors: authors and publishers, studios and broadcasters, journalists and lawyers—even, as we will see in the following chapters, readers, viewers, and fans.

As the chapter also suggests, however, these two principles are not the only ones at play in the Sam Spade case. The principle of copyright indivisibility (introduced in the previous chapter) helped shape the form the case took in court. The principles of unfair competition and informal contracting (the subjects of chapters 4 and 5 respectively) also informed the case at multiple points, with the latter even, perhaps, bearing ultimate responsibility for there being a case at all. And the principle of authorial genius (described in the following chapter) had such an impact on all aspects of the case, including even the opinion of Judge Stephens, that this entire chapter could have been written with it—rather than the idea-expression dichotomy and the principal of iterative textual derivation—as its organizing framework. Such is the case of all histories, legal and otherwise, of narrative-based properties: the important causal forces at work in them are multiple.

In emphasizing the idea-expression dichotomy and the principle of textual derivation in this chapter's account of *Warner Bros. Pictures v. CBS*, I have thus not meant to imply that they are all that matters here. I have privileged them in part for the sake of producing a chapter-length history that might be legible both to those with limited experience of the law and those with limited knowledge of the history of narrative-based property production. But I have also privileged them because these two principles are so fundamental to the ontology of narrative-based property development in the modern copyright era that one cannot get very far in the study of properties from this era without a solid understanding of them. Indeed, just as they did in the Sam Spade property recounted here, these two principles exert tremendous influence on the properties that are the focus of subsequent chapters, including that of the next one: H. P. Lovecraft's Cthulhu Mythos.

More broadly, the discussion of the principles contained here also suggests an alternative approach to identifying and evaluating narrative-based properties that may be useful to scholars of transmedia storytelling and narrative franchises: specifically, the iterative as a mode of narrative. Since Henry Jenkins first coined the term *transmedia storytelling* in *Convergence Culture*, his 2006 study of twenty-first-century media change, transmedia scholarship and work on narrative franchises has largely followed his lead in privileging complex, gradually developing narratives with rhizomatic, sequential, and/or biblical structures as the paradigmatic forms of such storytelling.[106] Though the emphasis on such narratives has produced valuable work, this chapter suggests a more inclusive approach to the study of multitext narrative. Its account of Sam Spade can serve to remind us that there are multiple ways of telling stories across texts and media, and that the stories that repeat themselves and forget (or ignore) their own textual histories raise legal, managerial, and narratological issues that are just as complicated, demanding, and (ultimately) interesting as those raised by complex multitext sagas such as *The Matrix* and the Marvel Cinematic Universe. Because the iterative mode of storytelling dominated narrative-based property production and development for the much of the twentieth century, we might also benefit from looking to it—rather than unusual early prototypes of such twenty-first-century sagas—to understand how transmedia storytelling developed historically, as well as the entrepreneurial, managerial, and legal practices that have supported it.

CHAPTER 3

From Yog-Sothery to Property

H. P. Lovecraft and the Making of the Cthulhu Mythos

> "His self had been annihilated; and yet he—if indeed there could, in view of that utter nullity of individual existence, be such a thing as he—was equally aware of being in some inconceivable way a legion of selves. It was as though his body had been suddenly transformed into one of those many-limbed and many-headed effigies sculptured in Indian temples, and he contemplated the aggregation in a bewildered attempt to discern which was the original and which the additions—if indeed (supremely monstrous thought) there were any original as distinguished from other embodiments."
>
> —H. P. Lovecraft and E. Hoffmann Price, "Through the Gates of the Silver Key"

The story from which this chapter's epigraph derives was originally conceived and written by pulp-fiction writer E. Hoffmann Price as a sequel to H. P. Lovecraft's short fantasy tale, "The Silver Key." Subsequently revised and moderately rewritten by Lovecraft himself, Price's story was ultimately submitted as a coauthored piece to the pulp magazine *Weird Tales,* which published it in its July 1934 issue under the title of "Through the Gates of the Silver Key." One of Lovecraft's only coauthored tales, the story is a strange and unwieldy amalgam of literary homage, metaphysical didacticism, and fictional eulogy that describes the proceedings of a meeting held to apportion the estate of the character Randolph Carter, a fictionalized version of Lovecraft who had appeared in a number of Lovecraft's earlier stories and was now, after having been missing from the fictional universe (and from print) for many years, presumed by the impatient lawyer representing his familiar heirs to be dead. Carter's literary executor, Etienne de Marigny, however, is not so sure, and the majority of the story consists of an alternative explanation, offered by a mysterious swami with a "singularly immobile face," of what *really* happened to Carter, whom the swami contends is not dead but has rather learned to move through space and time and inhabit different versions of himself.[1] At the story's climax, Ernest Aspinwall, the lawyer (who is also Carter's cousin)—suspecting the swami to be a fake—grabs at the swami's face, revealing it to be a mask, and upon seeing the horror that lies behind it dies instantaneously of fright. The swami, announcing himself to be an extradimensional iteration of Randolph Carter, then shuffles inhumanly toward a hieroglyphed, coffin-shaped clock set against the wall and disappears inside it. The story ends with a description of Carter's now very confused literary executor, who "scarcely know[s] what to make of the business."[2] Is Carter alive or is he dead? If alive, in what form? And what should be done with his estate?

Although not typically considered part of the Cthulhu Mythos—and never considered one of Lovecraft's better stories—"Through the Gates of the Silver Key" can serve as a useful introduction to the case study at the heart of this chapter: Lovecraft's intellectual property and its development, primarily in the hands of people other than Lovecraft, into the narrative-based property usually referred to as the *Cthulhu Mythos.* As this chapter demonstrates, the history of the Cthulhu Mythos involves many of the same questions and confusions that underlie Price and Lovecraft's story. When, and according to what procedure, should a narrative-based property be alienated from its original author? Does such alienation benefit or inflict harm upon that author's "individual existence"? And what is to be done—and by whom—with the property once its author has passed away? In the story, the swami's ultimate identity is unknown, but if he is, as he claims, Carter himself, he is also very much unlike the Carter his friends remember. He is an alien Carter, conspicuous in his disguise, and seemingly one of many: an aggregation of selves that is all addition and no original. Indeed, the text suggests that the Carter of previous stories, such as the novella *The Dream-Quest of Unknown Kadath,* was himself a mere "embodiment," just one of a "legion of selves." Should the confused literary executor of the modern copyright era respect the wishes of such a "many-limbed" and "many-headed" author? What would it even mean to do so?

More generally, this chapter seeks to shed new light on the principal of authorial genius, long suspected by scholars and commentators of being integral to the ontology of twentieth-century U.S. copyright law despite the principle's ostensible incompatibility with the needs of a rapidly industrializing entertainment industry—and despite its lack of formal codification via statute or case law. Unlike the copyright systems of civil law countries such as France, which have since the nineteenth century explicitly recognized authorial genius (often glossed as "literary personality") as the foundation for a set of inalienable and "noneconomic" rights called moral rights, U.S. statute has rarely recognized genius or personality as having any legal meaning at all.[3] Under a strict black-letter reading of U.S. copyright law, once an author has published her work in the United States, the author's identity as the work's progenitor becomes legally irrelevant (except for the purpose of renewal)—and this is as true today as it was one hundred years ago. As the last chapter's account of *Warner Bros. Pictures v. Columbia Broadcasting System* should suggest, however, U.S. courts during the modern copyright era often acted otherwise, sometimes even basing rulings on what seem to be metaphysical conceptions of the relationship between creator and creation. In doing so, judges were following the lead of the U.S. entertainment industry, which routinely granted authors *informal* rights of various economic and noneconomic kinds.

Assuming the relationship between creator and creation was, in some ways, sacrosanct, stakeholders of all sorts—including publishers, rightsholders, executors, collaborators, would-be licensors, and heirs—routinely factored it into their deal-making, sometimes according creators such as Lovecraft noncontractual rights far beyond what a court would recognize or uphold. In contrast to the "moral rights" that are part of other countries' intellectual property regimes, these informally recognized rights were often treated by stakeholders as intermittently fungible. They might, for example, extend beyond a creator's death and be transferred, in whole or in part, to others as a kind of property, even in the absence of spouses or children who could be seen as having a moral claim to them. This chapter provides, via its case study of the Cthulhu Mythos, an example of how these informal rights worked in practice—and how they could be integral not only to the legal and business development of a narrative-based property but to its aesthetic development as well.

In addition to illustrating how the principle of authorial genius functioned legally during the modern copyright era, the case study that makes up the bulk of this chapter serves three additional purposes. First, and likely to be of special interest to scholars of media authorship, the chapter provides two early examples of the constitution of "unified author figures" for multitext (and eventually transmedia) story worlds. As Suzanne Scott has argued, such story worlds place a "dual emphasis on dispersal and unification," simultaneously "disintegrating" the world's author and "restoring and reaffirming" that individual's significance.[4] In the twenty-first century, the establishment of such author figures by large media corporations, including the Walt Disney Co. and WarnerMedia, has become vitally important to the business of transmedia property development and has often taken the form of a heterosexual, male fan turned professional, such as Kevin Feige, James Gunn, and J. J. Abrams, being elevated into a position of creative (and often managerial) authority. In the example of the Cthulhu Mythos, however, we are not dealing with a large, global corporation's strategic construction of a unified author figure; the process here is, by contrast, local, ad hoc, and more the product of organic growth—and, as we will see, death—than purposive artifice. The author figures of Lovecraft and August Derleth are not the products of corporate coordination, nor do they much resemble the twenty-first-century archetype of the "fanboy auteur." Their semantic function, though similar, is tonally distinct, more that of the sensitive father, self-sacrificing best friend, or even *erastês* (the older lover in a pederastic relationship in ancient Greece) than the all-knowing, "masculinist,"[5] canon-obsessed, and avowedly heterosexual "Author-God"[6] that is the fanboy auteur. Lovecraft and Derleth's mode of story-world "authorship" was also—unlike that of the twenty-first-century media corporation's—poorly reinforced by modern-era copyright law, which was on its own largely incapable of (and uninterested in) supporting the development of multiauthor story worlds of the kind represented by the Cthulhu Mythos. As the case study demonstrates, the formal law was not only useless for maintaining the unity or coherence of a singular story world, it seemed even to encourage a babel-like proliferation of authorial claims to that world. How such a proliferation was nevertheless prevented through the actions of a unified author figure is thus one of the core questions of this chapter. The answer, as the case study demonstrates, lies in the idiosyncrasies of the Mythos itself, including the accidents of its history: the nature of its narrative assets, the personalities of its contributors, the deaths of key participants and the ambiguity of their estates, the inadvertent (or advertent) expiration of key copyrights, and the politics and emotional entanglements of a unique form of literary apprenticeship.

Second, the case study underscores the insufficiency of black-letter legal frameworks for explaining how narrative-based properties from this era were managed legally in practice. To be sure, many media industry scholars and legal scholars (especially those working in the field of law and society) have emphasized the additional importance of customs, norms, and personal relationships on the practice of business.[7] To date, however, scholarship focusing specifically on narrative franchises and story worlds (especially those originating during the modern copyright era) has tended to rely upon black-letter readings of the law as a backdrop to textual analysis and/or production history. The legal history of the Cthulhu Mythos, as the chapter's case study demonstrates, requires a rather different approach. Instead of the kind of formal assertion of rights that we saw in the previous chapter, here we see stakeholders' informal application of formal law. Rights that a court would not recognize were given recognition, actors with no formal claim to a fictional work were treated as owners of that work, and artistic creations that did not constitute legal property were governed as property. Indeed, black-letter readings of the Mythos's history (sometimes attempted by fans) typically conclude that most of the property's narrative "assets" either belonged to the public from the get-go or were very quickly ceded to the public. And yet no one involved with the production of the property believed either of these things; nor is the path the property's development took from the 1930s to the early 1970s compatible with these beliefs. The Cthulhu Mythos thus presents a seemingly paradoxical instance of a narrative property that had little to no protection under U.S. copyright law but nevertheless functioned for almost four decades as though it did. Although in some ways a special case, the history of the Mythos is not *that* special—or at least no more special than most cases are. A substantial portion of narrative-based properties during the modern copyright era were managed legally by nonlegal experts, involved little to no substantive interaction with lawyers, and did not ever require the intervention of a court of law.

Finally, the case study is meant to be an important contribution to the large body of scholarship—both professional and amateur—on H. P. Lovecraft's work and its legacy. Most of this scholarship has focused on the cultural, biographical, philosophical, and textual dimensions of Lovecraft's work rather than its managerial or legal development.[8] What few works exist that have taken up legal issues have struggled to render them legible, in part because of the apparent disconnect between the law on the books and the law as it was, in this case, practiced.[9] This disconnect has been partly responsible for the often vitriolic tenor of (some of) the scholarship, which has not infrequently aimed at "judging" particular actors—primarily writer, publisher, and Mythos manager August Derleth—as untalented, unethical, or immoral. Although I am indebted to previous Lovecraft scholars (especially S. T. Joshi), without whom this chapter would have been near impossible to write, I aim here to provide a new way of thinking about and studying Lovecraft's legacy. The approach to the Cthulhu Mythos I have taken here borrows from what legal scholars such as Debora Threedy have called "legal archaeology" but adapts that method so as to "excavate" a case history that never involved a lawsuit or judicial opinion.[10] Drawing on archival material, some of which is held by the Wisconsin Historical Society, I demonstrate how a series of obscure texts, with only superficial textual linkages, that were written for little money and originally read by few people, were transformed via specific managerial/legal actions into an aesthetically and legally coherent narrative-based property that went on to become one of the most influential of the twentieth century. The history I provide is a history not of the ideas underlying the Mythos but of the processes governing the Mythos's production, distribution, and reception: the legal-managerial architecture or infrastructure upon which the Mythos *qua* property was founded.

This chapter consists of four sections. In the first I describe the principle of authorial genius and explain its impact on the legal, managerial, and aesthetic development of narrative-based properties during the modern copyright era. The remaining three sections trace the history of the Cthulhu Mythos, beginning with its creation by H. P. Lovecraft and the Lovecraft Circle and concluding with its development under August Derleth.

The Principle of Authorial Genius

Beginning with the work of Peter Jaszi and Martha Woodmansee in the early 1990s, critical and humanities-oriented scholarship on copyright has tended to hold as a fundamental axiom that Western copyright law has, since the second half of the eighteenth century, been grounded (for better or worse) in a Romantic conception of literary authorship.[11] Recounting developments in U.S. copyright law between 1880 and 1940, Jaszi and Woodmansee write, "The rhetoric of authorship invoked in this body of law casts authors as individuals of superior talent, or genius, who break with tradition to create something new and unique, in a word, 'original.'"[12] For scholars, this conceit has been especially productive: it has enabled new kinds of scholarly approaches to the study of Romanticism and eighteenth-century cultural production; it has prompted attention to the overlaps and divergences between copyright's aesthetic and economic functions; and it has encouraged new kinds of attacks against contemporary copyright law—both for the law's attribution of authorship to corporations and for its failure to recognize literary invention as a social or collective process.[13] Kathy Bowrey's recent *Copyright, Creativity, Big Media and Cultural Value,* for example, argues that the persisting "Romantic Victorian characterisation of the significance of copyright" is the unfortunate legacy of decades of case law method, legal positivism, and "conventional legal historiography," combined with centuries-old authorial advocacy focusing on "liberal," upwardly mobile author-intellects.[14] Lee Marhsall, by contrast, argues that Romanticism is central to modern capitalism itself and thus an inevitable component of copyright law. "Romanticism and copyright," he claims provocatively, "are both forms of the same social relations."[15] Whatever its origins or inevitability—and whether or not we see it positively or negatively—Romanticism's hold on the U.S. (and U.K.) legal imagination is undeniable, at least for the period with which this book is concerned. From 1909 through 1978, U.S. legislators, judges, and a substantial portion of industrial actors tended to understand creative (i.e., literary or artistic) production in terms of the Romantic principle of authorial genius.

The Romantic principle of authorial genius, originating as it did in eighteenth-century philosophy and literary theory and having since been applied by scholars and critics to a wide variety of contemporary cultural formations, is a particularly diffuse concept, shifting subtly in meaning depending upon the context in which it is employed. Perhaps for this reason, formal definitions of the concepts are usually absent from legal scholarship that employs it.[16] If we bracket off its historical origins and attend primarily to the principle's employment in case law, however, the concept can be defined as comprising three interconnected beliefs about creative production:

1. the practice of production is solitary, i.e., undertaken in each case by a single individual, working by him- or herself;
2. the original ideas underlying a creative work are generated endogenously within the author's own mind or imagination; and
3. there exists a natural and inalienable connection, usually framed in terms of parentage or personality, between an author and the work he or she creates.

This set of beliefs, usually held unconsciously by judges, regularly functioned as an unspoken set of first principles in twentieth-century copyright suits involving authors. The word *genius*, for example, though not appearing at all in the Constitution's copyright clause or in either the Copyright Act of 1790 or 1909, shows up repeatedly without reflection or comment in copyright case opinions from the mid-1800s to the end of the modern copyright era. *Fox Film Corp. v. Doyal* (1932) can serve as a typical example with its gloss of copyright as a protection "given by the public for benefits bestowed by the genius and meditations and skill of individuals."[17]

In some cases, however, judges appear to have been at least somewhat conscious of the Romantic conception of authorship they were employing. Such is the case, for example, in *Burrow-Giles Lithographic Company v. Sarony* (1884), which involved the question of copyright protection for photographs. In an opinion frequently cited in subsequent copyright cases, Supreme Court Judge Samuel Miller proffered a series of reflections on the meaning of authorship so as to support a figuring of copyright as "the exclusive right of a man to the product of his own genius."[18] Identical logic underlay Oliver Wendell Holmes's opinion for the court in *Bleistein v. Donaldson Lithographing Company* (1903), another frequently cited Supreme Court copyright case, this time involving chromolithographic circus advertisements. Defining a work of art as "the personal reaction of an individual upon nature," Holmes proceeded to ground copyright on the concept of personality. "Personality always contains something unique," he asserted. "It expresses its singularity even in handwriting, and a very modest grade of art has in it something irreducible, which is one man's alone. That something he may copyright unless there is a restriction in the words of the act."[19] The rather unintuitive results of these cases—that a photograph (widely seen at the time as a merely mechanical means of reproduction) and an advertising poster were each held to be the unique artistic expression of a singular personality—demonstrates just how deeply rooted the conception of Romantic genius was in U.S. legal thinking; even in cases where it seemed to poorly fit the work in question, judges proved unable to relinquish or replace it.[20]

Critics of the U.S. copyright system have sometimes argued that twentieth-century judges' dependence upon the concept of genius represents a failure of U.S. common law to adapt to the changing realities of creative production under late capitalism. Even if the formal law's thinking about authorship, these critics charge, was appropriate for eighteenth- and nineteenth-century publishing practices (a point that has been itself much disputed), it does not accurately reflect the way creative production takes place in the twentieth and twenty-first centuries.[21] Peter Jaszi, for example, has influentially argued that "the law's engagement with (or failure to engage) the realities of contemporary polyvocal writing practice—which increasingly is collective, corporate, and collaborative"—has resulted in an inability for the law to understand or even perceive at all how contemporary creative production takes place.[22] I am sympathetic to the intellectual spirit driving these critiques but find them too beholden, methodologically, to the "high theory" that prompted them (for most, work associated with Michel Foucault and Jacques Derrida) and thus overly simplistic or flat-out wrong in their empirical description of twentieth-century creative production. As legal scholar Justin Hughes has similarly objected, "the [empirical] case for this new descriptive account of the world has not been made (and it will be difficult to make)."[23] Indeed, the historical research I have conducted for this book suggests that for much of the twentieth century, the law's Romantic approach to creative production was well aligned with that of industrial practice, at least in the narrative industries.[24]

When dealing with original creative works, especially published works of print fiction, industrial actors at all levels—even those who were involved in so-called polyvocal production—as well as significant portions of the public itself, tended to see these works as expressions of individual authors' own geniuses and, as such, intrinsically linked to the authors' minds and personalities. Early examples of what we might now call "literary franchises" were thus widely seen as ontologically identical with the author who originally produced them: Arthur Conan Doyle's Sherlock Holmes stories, L. Frank Baum's Oz stories, Edgar Rice Burroughs's Tarzan stories, a host of now unremembered properties such as Burt Standish's Frank Merriwell stories—and (as we will see in the following chapter) virtually all of the original comic strip properties.[25] Indeed, this perspective was so pervasive that copyright proprietors sometimes endeavored to keep an original author involved in a narrative-based property even after the author had formally parted with all of his or her rights. In the case of Superman, for example, Detective Comics, after acquiring the rights to the character through an unusually unambiguous contract, not only kept the character's creators Jerry Siegel (writer) and Joe Shuster (artist) in charge of the comic book and comic strip's production for almost a decade (up until the two were drafted into the U.S. army), they also for many years emphasized the pair's role as creators through a variety of paratexts. For example, a full page from *Superman* no. 1 (1939) (which began as a book reprinting/repackaging stories from the *Superman* comic strip) features large color pictures of Siegel and Shuster while entreating readers in bold font highlighted in bright yellow to "Meet the creators of the one and only SUPERMAN—America's Greatest Adventure Strip!"[26] Smaller text below offers brief biographies and commentary on the pictures and, through its use of pronouns, subtly attributes the character to the creators, not the publisher. The photograph of Seigel, for instance, is described as follows: "Here is Jerry Siegel at his typewriter, thinking up his next thrilling adventure of SUPERMAN."[27] To be sure, Detective Comics may have emphasized Siegel's and Shuster's identities as creators via paretexts like this one in order to keep the two men happy and avoid a lawsuit; but just as important was the publisher's belief during the comic book character's early years that the commercial magic of Superman was a product of Siegel's and Shuster's geniuses and might thus vanish without them. As Ian Gordon's careful study of the authors' early relationship with Detective Comics suggests, such a belief, though perhaps overblown, was probably not incorrect.[28]

Even the film industry—the least Romantically organized segment of the entertainment industry during the modern copyright era—was not immune to the belief in artistic genius. Film studios regularly wooed celebrated novelists, not just by licensing their work but also by purchasing story ideas from them or hiring them on as screenwriters.[29] The assumption in many cases was that the novelists' creative magic was not the product of craft or training but was intrinsic to their unique, authorial personalities; a studio could thus tap into it simply by bringing the personality to bear on a film's scenario or screenplay. When a Hollywood adaptation of a work of print fiction was successful, Romantic ideology also helped the studios understand (and thus seek to replicate) its success. As film scholar Richard Fine explains, studios tended to court the authors of the source material on which such adaptations were based, offering to pay generously for story ideas or employ them as screenwriters, even when the authors had no hand in the adaptations beyond the mere licensing of the film rights.[30] Although the writer-studio working relationships that Romantic ideology helped spawn rarely justified the ideology's underlying assumptions (see especially the Hollywood misadventures of Dashiell Hammett, F. Scott Fitzgerald, and William Faulkner), the practice continued until the demise of the classical Hollywood studio system.[31]

With respect to *filmmakers,* however, the film industry was more conflicted, in part because of the "Fordist," factory-style dimensions of studio production during the first half of the twentieth century,[32] and in part because films, unlike books, were transparently collective productions to which singular authorship was difficult to assign. Until forced to do so by the combined effects of the breakdown of the classical Hollywood studio system and the rise of Hollywood guilds, studios thus resisted acknowledging filmmakers as authors of the studios' films. As a result, some filmmakers sought such recognition—and the rights that might stem from it—in a court of law.[33] As Peter Decherney has recounted, "the majority of U.S. cases involving the potential for moral rights have involved films and filmmakers," rather than creators in other industries.[34] Decherney's careful historical account places responsibility for this imbalance on conflicting international norms unique to film, as well as medium-specific technological change, such as the rise of television. That such suits occurred much less often in other media industries, however, can also be explained by the fact that recognition of authorial genius—and with it something resembling moral rights—had long been quasi-institutionalized within America's early-twentieth-century print industries. Until a wave of mergers reshaped it in the 1960s, for example, the U.S. book publishing industry, like the U.K.'s, employed what historians have sometimes called a "gentlemanly" system of social dealing, which implicitly recognized and often (though not always) tried to accommodate values associated with moral rights in a way that the film industry, with its capitalist and corporatized business structure, was never capable of.[35] The print industry was thus able to minimize and, when necessary, internally adjudicate moral-rights conflicts without recourse to a court of law.[36]

The early treatment of filmmakers notwithstanding, during the modern copyright era recognition of authorial genius was, in many respects, integrally bound up with the customs and practice of large swathes of the entertainment industry. Although under the formal letter of the law authors were entitled to no rights beyond those provided by copyright law, they were often treated informally, in practice, as though they were—even sometimes in Hollywood. Attribution (except in the pre-Guild film industry) was routinely given; widowed spouses and heirs were sometimes provided for; and film, radio, and television licensors often (though not always) endeavored to secure the original authors' blessings for the changes they made in the work of adaptation. In some instances, publishers and licensors even treated works as copyrighted despite knowing the copyright had expired. The Sherlock Holmes property provides one famous example of this; we will encounter another example in chapter 5.[37]

So pervasive was the industrial institutionalization of authorial genius that it sometimes even found itself recognized formally by a court of law. In *Warner Bros. Pictures v. Columbia Broadcasting System*, as we saw in chapter 2, the district court based its finding for author Dashiell Hammett on the customary treatment of authors by the publishing industry beyond (it would seem) what was strictly required by copyright law. In *Esquire, Inc. v. Varga Enterprises, Inc.* (1948)—to give another example—the court ruled that an artist who parted with copyrights in his paintings could not be found guilty of copyright violation for subsequently producing very similar paintings because, the court concluded, an artist cannot fairly be alienated from the specific "type of art" he has "in his mind."[38] Such legal rulings were, admittedly, unusual. Still, the widescale recognition, albeit usually informal, of authorial genius explains why few stakeholders during the modern copyright era saw a need to advocate for a special category of intellectual property rights (i.e., a "moral right") that would secure such recognition formally. Organizations such as the Author's League devoted their energy instead to other goals, such as combatting the doctrine of copyright indivisibility or advocating for standardized contracts and minimum basic agreements.

Certainly, business practices recognizing authorial genius or personality seem far afield from what present-day legal scholars would call moral rights. And, for sure, such practices, despite the benefits they provide creators, do not constitute formal legal rights under black-letter law. But as the case study offered in this chapter demonstrates, the lack of a formal legal right does not necessarily mean that the protections such a right would provide do not exist; there may be other means (customs, institutions, collective bargaining agreements—even ideologies) by which such protections are secured. Indeed, one might argue that the formal *legal* concept of moral rights is predicated upon the assumption that a copyright regime, when left to its own devices, would naturally *fail* to recognize and protect genius. Although such a regime might characterize that of the late twentieth and early twenty-first centuries (though there is, it seems to me, ample evidence to argue the opposite), it does not characterize that of the earlier period with which this book is concerned.

Lovecraft's Communal Yog-Sothery: The Cthulhu Mythos before 1937

Compared to most successful professional writers working between 1910 and 1940 (or for that matter today in the early twenty-first century), H. P. Lovecraft was highly atypical in his approach to literary production. For starters, he was a slow and infrequent writer of fiction. Despite having little family money and earning virtually all his income through sales of stories to pulp magazines, he wrote relatively few stories during his lifetime, and of these managed to sell only about half—thirty-seven sales in total, all but seven of which were made to the same magazine: *Weird Tales.* That he sold so few stories was in part because he relied primarily upon just one publishing venue (itself a risky and unusual professional practice) and because he was resistant to producing fiction that fit that venue's requirements with respect to action, style, and length. In this, and in his slow, meditative approach to writing, Lovecraft was resolutely anticommercial, and to the end of his life proved unable to reconcile the craft of literary production as he understood it with the exigencies of commercial publishing.

Somewhat ironically, however, Lovecraft was also a long-practicing—albeit severely underpaid—"ghostwriter," who provided copy editing, revision, and full-scale writing services to a small assortment of amateur and professional writers, including celebrity magician Harry Houdini. Of the ninety-four surviving stories now credited to Lovecraft as author, an astonishing twenty-five were originally published or submitted for publication under another individual's name.[39] For many of these, Lovecraft was paid remarkably little. For "The Curse of Yig," a short story that, as Lovecraft noted in a letter to Clark Ashton Smith, "is well-nigh a piece of original composition on my part," Lovecraft charged only $17.50—little more than ten percent of the amount its credited author, Zealia Bishop, received from *Weird Tales* for the publishing rights.[40] Although it has never been unusual for a modern fiction writer to take on occasional ghostwriting jobs during the early phases of his or her career, few professional writers in the 1920s and 1930s devoted as much energy to them and charged as little for them as did Lovecraft.

There is no doubt that Lovecraft's ghostwriting was a contributing factor to his low literary output, but in the final analysis another of Lovecraft's authorial idiosyncrasies appears to have played an even more important role: Lovecraft kept up for most of his life an almost inconceivably high rate of letter-writing. As estimated by Lovecraft's first biographer, L. Sprague de Camp, Lovecraft wrote eight to ten letters a day, most of which were between four and eight hand-written pages long, with some stretching over sixty pages in length.[41] The surviving correspondence (estimated by S. T. Joshi to consist of ten thousand letters) has often been judged a literary treasure in itself, and Lovecraft's letter writing, as we will see, played a key role in the development of the Cthulhu Mythos; nevertheless, Lovecraft's epistolary practice—like his anticommercialism and extensive, underpriced ghostwriting—was wildly out of sync with the demands of a professional writing career.[42] De Camp accordingly describes Lovecraft's career as "a horror story of another kind—a cautionary tale showing how not to be a writing man."[43] And although this seems unsympathetic, it is true that Lovecraft, unable (or unwilling) to produce and/or sell much of his own fiction and thus unable to generate sustained interest among book publishers and film producers, spent much of his adult life in near-poverty, subsisting on a diet of mostly canned food, which many believe to have been partly responsible for his death of intestinal cancer at the age of only forty-six.[44] If judged at the time of his death in 1937, Lovecraft's career would have by any standard—no matter how sympathetic—been almost certainly considered a failure.

Today, however, excluding those works that have been lost or destroyed, nearly everything Lovecraft has written exists in print or, in the case of his copious correspondence, is forthcoming, much of it in annotated, illustrated, slip-cased, and limited-edition formats. As a preliminary categorization, we can divide this corpus into two different kinds of text, each serving a different function for the reader: first, there are the stories, and second, there is what I will call Lovecraftiana. The aesthetic experience provided by the first inheres, at least potentially, within the texts themselves; a reader need know nothing of their author to engage with and appreciate them. By contrast, the experience provided by the second (in which I place Lovecraft's occasional essays, most of his poetry, and a good deal of his correspondence) is heavily dependent upon the reader possessing knowledge of and/or interest in Lovecraft himself and/or his "genius," i.e., his personality and biography. For the most part, Lovecraftiana are a posthumous construction—neither the texts that comprise them nor the knowledge and interest needed to engage with them would have been available to general readers during Lovecraft's lifetime.

As the history of the Mythos will quickly demonstrate, however, the distinction between *story* and *Lovecraftiana*, so clear in theory, has always been in practice rather muddy. For an invested community of early readers, many of whom became writers themselves, Lovecraft's fiction was treated, upon first publication (if not earlier), as Lovecraftiana as much, if not more, than it was treated as story. Although only a very small portion of *Weird Tales*'s readers approached Lovecraft's work this way, after Lovecraft's death their approach would gradually become the primary way by which his fiction was read. This tendency to read story as biography and vice versa reflects the unusual means by which Lovecraft's Cthulhu Mythos was produced, disseminated, and managed posthumously as property.

What is the Cthulhu Mythos? The Mythos depends upon a collection of underlying narrative features that readers since at least the late 1920s have found both coherent and easily recognizable. If we abstract from the stories themselves and ignore questions of production and reception history—thereby treating the Mythos as an independent thing in itself—the Mythos can be defined in terms of a limited set of what a twenty-first-century media company would call "IP assets."[45] These include the following:

1. a quasi-pantheon of demons, Gods, and alien intelligences, mostly possessing strange-sounding names, such as Cthulhu, Yog-Sothoth, Shub-Niggurath, and Yig;
2. a number of imaginary occult books, the most well-known of which is the *Necronomicon,* and a library (the Miskatonic University Library) in which copies are sometimes housed;
3. a series of imaginary places, including a set of New England towns (Arkham, Innsmouth, Dunwich), a mythical plateau in Asia (Leng), and an assortment of alien dimensions/planets (Yuggoth, R'lyeh, Yith, etc.); and
4. a myriad of made-up anthropological, sociological, and historical detail, including languages such as Aklo; historical figures such as "the mad Arab," Abdul Alhazred; human cults, such as the Esoteric Order of Dagon; monstrous races, such as the mi-go; etc.

To these four types of narrative asset should also be added three storytelling principles or comportments:

5. a commitment to what S. T. Joshi and others have called "cosmicism," by which is usually meant the suggestion of alien and/or extra-human frames of reference (moral, aesthetic, epistemological, etc.)[46];

6. a concern with issues of inheritance and descent, sometimes expressed in genealogical/ethnological terms, sometimes in social/material terms; and
7. a predilection for self-contained, original stories that neither refer to/build upon each other nor iteratively reproduce each other.

As an abstracted delineation of what the Mythos *was* during Lovecraft's lifetime, the above list provides a useful introduction to the property and already gestures to some of the property's peculiarities (the absence, for instance, of main characters among its assets). The list proves useless, however, in understanding how the Mythos came to be. How were the narrative assets it describes originally created? And how did they come to be associated with each other? The very cleanness of the list also risks obscuring the profound messiness of the Mythos's actual development process, in part by suggesting that the Mythos existed as a kind of ideal or a priori form, providing Lovecraft a model to employ when sitting down to write the actual stories. Although many twenty-first-century narrative properties *do* function in such a manner (often through the help of story or IP "bibles"), nothing could be further from the truth with respect to Lovecraft and the Cthulhu Mythos. As we will see, the Mythos's development during Lovecraft's lifetime was accidental, improvisational—and, for Lovecraft the anticommercial writer, largely beside the point. This was not because the concept of a horror-genre or science-fiction literary franchise was inconceivable at this time (Lovecraft was well aware, for example, of Seabury Quinn's Jules de Grandin property, which had been regularly featured in *Weird Tales*), but rather because, with few exceptions, Lovecraft's primary concern as an author was writing aesthetically effective, literary-quality fiction, not creating a marketable franchise. As author and editor Lin Carter succinctly put it in his 1976 *Lovecraft: A Look Behind the Cthulhu Mythos*, "The fact of the matter is that Lovecraft was not deliberately writing a series of mythos stories—he was just writing stories."[47]

The development of the Mythos is thus unusual in that it was driven less by Lovecraft himself than it was *his readers*, a number of whom were (or quickly became) writers themselves. Deriving from Lovecraft's work a model of the Mythos similar to that represented by the list I provided above, these readers/writers contributed to the Mythos's development not only by publishing their own Mythos stories but also by privately elaborating on the Mythos via regular correspondence with Lovecraft and each other. Even during Lovecraft's lifetime, the Mythos was thus quite literally a communal production, with a large number of Lovecraft's associates, most of whom were published alongside him in *Weird Tales,* producing the stories through which the property became manifest. These include Robert Bloch, August Derleth, Robert E. Howard, Henry Kuttner, Frank Belknap Long, and Clark Ashton Smith. Surprisingly, however, the communal production of the property did not result in the erasure or dilution of the Mythos's identification with Lovecraft; rather, the unique form that this production took functioned paradoxically to strengthen Lovecraft's authorial association with the property while simultaneously disorganizing and dispersing control of it.

Let us take, as an example of how this mode of production worked, Robert Bloch's involvement with the Mythos. Best known today for his authorship of the novel *Psycho* (famously adapted for film by Alfred Hitchcock), Bloch wrote hundreds of short stories, numerous screenplays, and close to thirty-five novels before his death at age seventy-seven in 1994. When he began corresponding with Lovecraft in 1933, however, he was only sixteen years old: "a half-fledged teenage nonentity," as Bloch retrospectively described himself.[48] Having recently discovered Lovecraft's work in *Weird Tales* and eager to read the stories that had been published before he had started reading the magazine, Bloch sent Lovecraft a brief letter, care of *Weird Tales,* inquiring where he could locate the author's earlier work. To Bloch's astonishment, Lovecraft responded with a handwritten letter of close to one thousand words, listing all of his written fiction, offering to lend Bloch copies of his stories, and asking Bloch whether he could see any of the sixteen-year-old's own literary efforts.[49] An intimate correspondence quickly developed, in which the two men traded photographs, lent each other manuscripts, described the goings on of their daily lives, and discussed a range of topics, including world events, motion pictures, weird fiction, and the craft of writing.

From the beginning of their correspondence, Lovecraft also endeavored to connect Bloch with the other fans and writers with whom the older author corresponded (what is referred to today as the "Lovecraft Circle"[50]). In his second letter to Bloch, Lovecraft shared the addresses for Frank Belknap Long and Clark Ashton Smith; and in his eighth letter, he provided Bloch with the names and addresses of eight additional correspondents, along with a detailed description (ranging from thirty-five to one-hundred-fifty words in length) for each of them.[51] At various points, he also sent Bloch photographs of several of these correspondents.[52] Not only did Lovecraft encourage Bloch to get in touch with these men, he wrote to them of Bloch as well. A month or so after sending Bloch the address of Robert Barlow, for example, Lovecraft wrote to Barlow suggesting he write to Bloch:

> If you are interested in dramatics or humorous dialogue you ought to get in touch with a new correspondent of mine—a 16-year-old kid named Robert Bloch, 620 East Knapp St., Milwaukee, Wis., who has written & presented many school shows, & is now ambitiously attempting to promote a semi-professional minstrel organization. Incidentally—this youth is an extremely clever artist, & has executed some astonishingly good drawings in the manner of Clark Ashton Smith.[53]

Thanks to such encouragement, Bloch began corresponding with other members of the Lovecraft Circle, and the resulting sense of community seemed to further inspire Bloch and contribute to his developing sense of himself as an author. Clark Ashton Smith's artwork, for example, encouraged Bloch to try his own hand at weird illustration; and August Derleth's harsh criticism helped him learn how to revise and respond to critique. Following Lovecraft's example, Bloch also encouraged one of his own correspondents, Henry Kuttner (who also became an early writer of Cthulhu Mythos fiction), to begin writing to Lovecraft. Steeped in the milieu of the Lovecraft Circle, Bloch's writing ability developed quickly, and in July of 1934 the teenager made his first sale to *Weird Tales*: a short story (read in draft form by Lovecraft and possibly also Derleth) employing a number of Mythos assets and titled "The Secret of the Tomb."

Given the nature of Bloch and Lovecraft's relationship, the fact that Bloch's early fiction borrowed heavily from Lovecraft's should not be surprising. "Lacking a style of my own," Bloch recalls in his biography, "I imitated HPL's; devoid of original concepts, my sketchy plots were, to put it charitably, derivative."[54] What is more surprising is how little Lovecraft tried to control or manage this borrowing. Lovecraft's letters provided praise, encouragement, and rather gentle constructive criticism, but at no point exhibited a sense of proprietorship over his story ideas or narrative assets. As Bloch remembered in an interview conducted many years later: "He merely praised what I did, and if he made any criticisms they were always couched as suggestions and largely that was factual matters."[55] Far from claiming ownership over his ideas, Lovecraft, in fact, treated the Gods, places, and books he invented playfully, sprinkling silly references throughout the letters (e.g., "This contraption [a fountain pen] of mine still works like a charm—though Cthulhu knows how long it will last"[56]) and referring to his correspondents with made-up, Mythos-sounding names. Bloch himself was first Bho-Blôk, then Ludvig, and once even "O Ludvig, Brooder on the Outer Void."[57] Only once, early in their correspondence, did Lovecraft provide Bloch with significant instruction regarding the use of Mythos assets, and even this instruction is framed gently in terms of education rather than command:

> Oh—one more thing. I see you have Grey read the *Necronomicon* through in a single night—which is incompatible with its supposed *length* as established in tales already in print. You will perhaps recall my citing a very high page number is [*sic*] in "The Dunwich Horror." Accordingly I am calling Grey's copy "fragmentary." Also—you give [Robert E.] Howard's von Junzt the praenomen of *Conrad*, whereas at least one printed allusion (which I put in a story I ghost-wrote for a revision client!) establishes it as *Friedrich*. Howard himself, amusingly enough, did not give von Junzt a first name so far as I know. (Am I mistaken?) Before I forget it, let me enclose (please return) a skeletonic history of the imaginary *Necronomicon* which I prepared for myself in order to avoid self-contradictions in future tales.[58]

To Bloch's use of the Mythos assets (as well as Bloch's creation of new assets), Lovecraft otherwise responded with pleasure and encouragement. Earlier in the letter just quoted, for example, Lovecraft comments on Bloch's borrowing of the city of Leng as follows: "'The Blasphemy Beneath' is very vivid & colorful, & forms an admirable atmospheric study. I marvel that I never guessed Leng's direful secret before!"[59] Bloch's invention of Ludvig Prinn and his book *Mysteries of the Worm* is likewise welcomed enthusiastically by Lovecraft:

> Your allusion makes me very anxious to see Herr Prinn's "Mysteries of the Worm," & I have applied for a copy at the Miskatonic Library in Arkham. If I ever get around to original writing again you may find Ludvig & his hellish volume figuring in some yarn of mine. Nothing like giving these lurking horrors publicity![60]

Lovecraft would subsequently employ this book in his own fiction via its Latinized title *De Vermis Mysteriis,* along with another of Bloch's creations (often miscredited to Derleth because it plays on Derleth's name) the Comte d'Erlette's *Cultes des Goules.*

During Lovecraft's lifetime, Bloch sold to *Weird Tales* approximately a dozen stories that drew upon Mythos assets, many of which provided additional background material for the God Nyalthrotep and the history of his worship on Earth. The most famous of these, "The Shambler of the Stars," is worth examining here in more detail, as it serves as a striking example of how the Mythos's communal production process worked simultaneously to reaffirm Lovecraft's authorial identification with the property while dispersing control of it. Begun sometime in the second half of 1934, "Shambler" appears to have been read by Lovecraft in early draft form in October or early November of that year. The older author offered suggestions in the draft's margin and encouraged Bloch to keep working on it.[61] Bloch did, and by the time it was published, "Shambler" had evolved into a tale that was in no small part about the process of literary inheritance.

In the tale, an unnamed narrator, after having some small success selling "stereotyped, ephemeral" stories to magazines but wishing to write one day "a real work of art," begins a correspondence with a "mystic dreamer in New England," from whom he learns of ancient books such as the *Necronomicon* and the *Book of Eibon*.[62] Believing occult knowledge necessary for the great work he wishes to write, the narrator begins "a widespread postal campaign" with an assortment of people whose contact information had been given him by his New England friend.[63] "Angered that their secret should be thus unveiled by a prying stranger," however, the correspondents are "unfriendly" in their responses, and the narrator is forced to continue his search alone.[64] Eventually, he discovers at an old bookstore a copy of Prinn's *Mysteries of the Worm*. Bringing the book to his friend in Providence, Rhode Island, the narrator watches, paralyzed with fright, as his mentor reads aloud from the book a spell and is subsequently broken in half and drained of blood by an invisible monster.

As the above summary should make evident, "Shambler" draws heavily upon Bloch's own experience of literary apprenticeship, and the story's New England dreamer is obviously meant to be Lovecraft, whose real-world home was Providence, Rhode Island. Today, the story lends itself rather well to an allegorical reading, with Derleth or Donald Wandrei representing the unfriendly correspondents, and with Lovecraft's selfless and possibly self-sabotaging devotion to people like Bloch mirrored in the dreamer's death. At the time Bloch wrote the story, however, he intended it to function as a kind of comic homage to Lovecraft, and this is exactly how Lovecraft took it.

Before it could be published, however, Farnsworth Wright, the editor of *Weird Tales*, insisted that Bloch obtain Lovecraft's permission to use Lovecraft as a character in the story. Lovecraft was surprised and a good deal amused by Wright's concern, and promptly provided Bloch with the necessary permission in the form of a fictionally notarized document bearing the signatures of Mythos characters Abdul Alhazred, Friedrich von Junzt, Gaspar du Nord, and the Tcho-Tcho Lama of Leng:

> This is to certify that Robert Bloch, Esq., of Milwaukee, Wisconsin, U.S.A.—reincarnation of Mijnheer Ludvig Prinn, author of DE VERMIS MYSTERIIS—is fully authorised to portray, murder, annihilate, disintegrate, transfigure, metamorphose, or otherwise manhandle the undersigned in the tale entitled THE SHAMBLER FROM THE STARS.[65]

Satisfied, Wright accepted the story, publishing it in the April 1935 issue of the pulp magazine.

Readers of *Weird Tales* appear not only to have liked "Shambler" but also to have recognized its intended function as an homage to Lovecraft. In the letters page of the November 1935 issue, a reader even suggested that "Mr. Lovecraft return the compliment, and dedicate a story to the author."[66] Lovecraft promptly did so, and in its December 1936 issue, *Weird Tales* published "The Haunter in the Dark," a Mythos tale in which the narrator from "Shambler," now revealed to be a writer and painter from Milwaukee named "Robert Blake," returns to Providence, taking a room in a Georgian house that, as Bloch notes in his biography, "bore more than a passing resemblance to Lovecraft's own."[67] Unwittingly releasing an alien monster who murders in darkness, Blake is eventually killed by it during a freak power outage. As clues to his death, he leaves behind only a series of cryptic jottings in his journal, one of which contains Bloch's real-world address: "My name is Blake—Robert Harrison Blake of 620 East Knapp Street, Milwaukee, Wisconsin. . . . I am on this planet. . . ."[68] As printed in *Weird Tales*, the story also begins with a parenthetical note: "(Dedicated to Robert Bloch)." The story ultimately proved to be Lovecraft's last. A few months after its publication, Lovecraft passed away.

The example of Bloch's early involvement with Lovecraft and the Cthulhu Mythos demonstrates how communal production of the Mythos worked. For those early writers whose fiction participated in the Mythos, Lovecraft regularly served the role of mentor, with the Mythos functioning as a means of connecting him, literally through letters, with other writers. Not all of these writers were as young or inexperienced as Bloch (though many were), but all came to rely upon Lovecraft and the letters he wrote them for inspiration, validation, and a sense of literary community. In this respect, the Mythos was more a means of communal participation than it was a set of preestablished narrative assets to be used in telling stories. Accordingly, neither Lovecraft nor the other Mythos writers tended to treat these assets seriously or with a sense of proprietorship. Led by Lovecraft himself, who generously encouraged his correspondents to employ the assets as they wished, communal production of the Mythos often worked in practice to de-systematize rather than codify the property.

This does not mean, however, that the Lovecraft Circle's use of these assets can be dismissed as "play activity,"[69] a "game,"[70] or a "fictional jape";[71] for although a sense of humor often accompanied their use, the writers' employment of the assets functioned quite seriously as a means of documenting textually the authors' connections to Lovecraft and each other. We should thus understand, for example, Lovecraft's quick incorporation of Bloch's *Mysteries of the Worm* into his own stories only secondarily as a means of expanding or further cementing the Mythos; for Lovecraft—and indeed for Bloch as well—the act of asset borrowing was more importantly an act of friendship and intimacy. The Mythos's shared story world or mythology was thus in part an after-effect of the Lovecraft Circle's communal interaction via writing. Which is also to say that the *provenance* of the Mythos's assets was often more important to the Lovecraft Circle than whatever narrative "content" they conveyed. In this respect, the assets functioned not as intimations of textual continuity or a trans-textual story world but as textual markers of literary community and friendship. And nowhere is such marking clearer than in the Mythos writers' occasional transformation of Lovecraft the friend and author into Lovecraft the fictional character and property asset, for in stories such as Bloch's "Shambler" the Lovecraft Circle's semiprivate signaling of friendship becomes, via Lovecraft's representation as a character, a *public* declaration of friendship, community, and literary inheritance.

Wright's objection to Bloch's fictional exsanguination of Lovecraft in "The Shambler" should likewise be understood as taking place within this framework of friendship and literary community. Observing that Wright had many years earlier let Frank Belknap Long kill off a fictional version of himself (that time, a character who was actually *named* Howard Lovecraft), Lovecraft was perplexed by Wright's objection to Bloch's story, and seemed to see it as a form of meddling.[72] But the circumstances surrounding Long's story were different: when Long submitted "The Space-Eaters" to *Weird Tales* in 1928, he was already an established writer and one whom Wright knew to be a close friend of Lovecraft.[73] Wright could thus assume that Long's use of Lovecraft as a character was occurring within the bounds of the two authors' friendship. Bloch, however, was relatively unknown to Wright in 1935. Wright's insistence that the young author obtain Lovecraft's permission was thus a means for Wright, who controlled what was until near the end of Lovecraft's life the only publishing venue for weird fiction, of recognizing and protecting Lovecraft's authorial status and genius and thereby supporting and even contributing to the Mythos's intimate form of collective production.

There is yet another quirk to the development of the early Cthulhu Mythos, for not only was the Mythos a literal collective production, developed by a group of Lovecraft's friends, it was also a metaphorical collective production, which Lovecraft, like the swami of "Through the Gates of the Silver Key," elaborated from behind the authorial masks of others, namely his ghost-writing clients.[74] If we exclude the writing and editing work that Lovecraft did out of friendship—both for the members of the Lovecraft Circle and for his wife, Sonia Greene—we are left with twenty-two stories to which Lovecraft contributed in some significant fashion but for which he received no authorship credit at initial publication. Fourteen of these stories were undertaken after the completion of "The Call of Cthulhu" (usually seen as the first "real" Mythos story) in 1926, and of these, ten contain Mythos assets. The extent of Lovecraft's contribution to these stories varies (and is not always clearly ascertainable), in some cases appearing to be little more than the kind of light editing he provided Bloch, while for others consisting of as much as the entire plot and all of the prose. In every story in which Mythos assets appear, however, they were almost certainly put there by Lovecraft. In some of them, such as Hazel Heald's "Winged Death" or Adolphe de Castro's "The Electric Executioner," the assets have little narrative importance and amount to a few brief references. In others, however, such as Hazel Heald's "The Horror in the Museum" and Zealia Bishop's "The Mound," the assets are an integral part of the story and are extensively incorporated.

There are two common explanations for Lovecraft's use of Mythos assets in his ghostwriting (or "revision") work. First, we might see—as numerous fans and critics have seen and continue to see—the Mythos as an inseparable component of Lovecraft's unique authorial genius.[75] From this perspective, the Mythos naturally incorporated itself into everything Lovecraft wrote, and Lovecraft would have had to work, so to speak, against himself in order to keep the Mythos out of his fiction. If this is true, we would expect to find that the greater the extent of Lovecraft's contribution to a ghostwritten story, the more integral is that story's use of Mythos assets. And, indeed, that is exactly what we find, with stories like "The Mound" (which Lovecraft appears to have written largely from scratch) making much greater use of assets than stories like Wilfred B. Talman's "Two Black Bottles" (which in fact makes no use of Mythos assets, and to which S. T. Joshi estimates Lovecraft contributed "no more than 30%").[76]

Alternately, we might understand Lovecraft's incorporation of Mythos assets into his ghostwriting work as a means of providing the Mythos a false historical authenticity. Robert M. Price, for example, has suggested that Lovecraft "regularly included in ghost-written stories allusions to Cthulhu, Azathoth, et al., to create the effect of wide citation by many authors, something . . . Lovecraft thought gave his artificial mythology a greater ring of genuineness."[77] From this perspective, ghost-written stories like de Castro's "The Last Test" and Bishop's "The Mound" were deliberate attempts by Lovecraft to disown the Mythos, so that it might function—as Greek mythology and ancient Egyptian religion seem to function today—as an ancient, authorless, and thus historically authentic "mythos" or mythology. As Lovecraft explained in a 1930 letter to Robert E. Howard (who had noted the use of Mythos assets in a tale by de Castro): "I think it is rather good fun to have this artificial mythology given an air of verisimilitude by wide citation."[78] Although this explanation gels somewhat poorly with the previous explanation, as it suggests a conscious deliberateness rather out of keeping with the concept of Romantic genius, both explanations have, with different degrees of explicitness, come to underlie how fans and critics understand Lovecraft's deployment of Mythos assets in his ghost writing.

I wish to offer, however, a third explanation here, one that frames Lovecraft's employment of the Mythos in his ghostwriting as a kind of authorial signaling, similar in form (if not necessarily in function) to the communal marking effected by the Lovecraft Circle's incorporation of Mythos assets into their own fiction. To be sure, Lovecraft took on ghostwriting jobs because he desperately needed income—although they also may have served (just as the letter-writing may have served) as a means of enabling him to *write* free from the pressure of producing great literature. He was nevertheless proud of most of the resulting stories, and by including Mythos assets within them he was able to maintain a subtle authorial claim on them: marking them, so to speak, as his, and thereby signaling his authorship of them to his friends in the Lovecraft Circle (and to astute *Weird Tales* readers). Indeed, Lovecraft regularly pointed out his ghostwriting in letters, and in doing so often underscored—however modestly—the signaling function of the Mythos assets. In the 1930 letter to Howard referenced in the previous paragraph, for example, Lovecraft's goal of "verisimilitude by wide citation" is coupled with a coy claim of proprietorship:

> The reason for its [the Cthulhu Mythos's] echoes in Dr. de Castro's work is that the latter gentleman is a revision-client of mine—into whose tales I have stuck these glancing references for sheer fun. If any other clients of mine get work placed in W.T. [*Weird Tales*], you will perhaps find a still-wider spread of the cult of Azathoth, Cthulhu, and the Great Old Ones![79]

Far from suggesting story world development or what transmedia scholars sometimes call narrative expansion, the "spread of the cult" (with "cult" curiously in the singular here) describes merely the expansion of Lovecraft's publishing success.[80] *If you see the Mythos turn up in stories by people other than me or my friends,* Lovecraft effectively instructs Howard, *I likely put it there.* That this peculiar form of signaling ultimately functioned much as Lovecraft intended can be demonstrated by the fact that we today credit the ghostwritten stories to Lovecraft and regularly include them in anthologies of his work. Had Lovecraft neither included Mythos assets in these stories nor discussed them in correspondence with friends, we may never have known that Lovecraft authored them.

With regards to Lovecraft's ghostwriting, it is also worth noting briefly that his use of Mythos assets is heavily gendered, with the stories that make the most significant use of the Mythos having been written for women: Hazel Heald and Zealia Bishop. The complex character of Lovecraft's relationship to women is well beyond the scope of this chapter—and indeed demands more serious attention than it has yet received by scholars. That Lovecraft exploited his position as a ghostwriter to write himself (and the Mythos) *over* or *into* the work of these women—thus marking their stories all the more explicitly as his—cannot be dismissed as a possibility, although it is almost certainly an oversimplification of the dynamics at play. Had ownership or control been Lovecraft's goal, for instance, he would have been much better off undertaking the work as a coauthor (as he did, for instance, with Price's "Through the Gates of the Silver Key"). Because he did not do so, Head and Bishop received most of the benefits of authorship, including not only the lion's share of the profit and the underlying copyrights in the work but also—in the case of Bishop—an eventual book deal with Arkham House for the stories Lovecraft had written.[81] Despite the complex gender dynamics at play (which stem also from the highly gendered construction of American weird fiction as a genre), the ghostwriting Lovecraft did for female clients thus seems to be colored by the same mix of authorial marking and generous disowning that characterized his treatment of his male friends in the Lovecraft Circle.

As the above discussions of the Mythos's collaborative production and of Lovecraft's ghostwriting demonstrate, the Cthulhu Mythos during Lovecraft's lifetime was a strange form of narrative-based property, freely taken by and given away to others and yet in important ways still "belonging" to Lovecraft himself. Although not every reader knew about the production processes that gave rise to the Mythos, these processes exerted a tremendous influence on the form the Mythos stories took. Indeed, the stories' playful and anti-systematic use of assets, their standalone yet non-iterative structure, and their fascination with inheritance and genealogy were all heavily determined by the Mythos's unique mode of production. But what, a careful reader might be wondering at this point, would a formal reading of U.S. copyright law have made of this mode of production? Within the framework of the modern copyright regime, would a court of law have recognized the Cthulhu Mythos itself as intellectual property?

The answer is almost certainly *no,* albeit with an important qualification. Modern copyright law's tendency to subject literary property to the idea-expression dichotomy (discussed in the previous chapter) means that the Mythos assets themselves would have almost certainly received no legal protection from courts. Judges would have understood the underlying copyright in any Mythos story to pertain only to the story as a whole and not to the discrete, separable components (characters, places, monsters, books) from which the story was made. Claims that the Mythos components themselves should constitute intellectual property would have been unlikely to be taken seriously by a court—but even if they were, a lawyer would have faced the problem of having to demonstrate satisfactorily that the assets had any substance to begin with, given their often superficial and/or deliberately vague employment within the stories. What exactly, for example, *is* Azathoth? And is "Ludvig Prinn" a character, an inside joke, or merely a form of citation? Although courts would probably not have viewed communal use of an asset as dispositive with respect to the asset's protectability, the fact that the Mythos writers themselves treated Mythos assets as freely usable, without the need for permission or license, would have almost certainly encouraged a court to do likewise.[82] Given the complex production and publication history of Mythos stories, treating the assets otherwise would have resulted in what we might fairly call a rights quagmire, since ownership of the copyrights in the underlying stories in which each asset first appeared was so widely distributed, with the stories' authors owning some of them, Lovecraft's ghostwriting clients others, and *Weird Tales* (which sometimes purchased all rights to a story) still others; while those first published in fanzines often had no copyright at all.

Still further complicating the question of the Mythos's status under the modern copyright regime is the substantial amount of informal contracting employed by those involved in the property's development. Like many other magazines (and as explored in more detail in chapter 5), *Weird Tales* relied almost exclusively on incomplete contracts expressed in casual language: rights were often not discussed or enumerated, policies regarding copyright formalities were nonexistent, payment was made after publication, and check legends often served as ostensible contracts. Both the magazine itself and many of the Mythos writers (including Lovecraft) also relied much more heavily on individual memory than careful recordkeeping—a tendency that, as we will see, created significant difficulties for the property after Lovecraft's death.

Given the legal and industrial considerations laid out above, the Cthulhu Mythos as it existed during Lovecraft's lifetime could fairly be called, at least by the standards of twenty-first-century IP, a legal mess. Based upon vaguely defined discrete narrative assets rather than unified textual expressions, the property appears to have strayed too far from what copyright deemed protectable for a court to have enjoined or punished "unauthorized" use of it. Worse still, informal contracting ensured that whatever rights to the Mythos a court may have been willing to recognize would have been difficult and in some cases perhaps even impossible to sort out. Especially in comparison with twenty-first-century narrative-based properties, the Cthulhu Mythos thus appears to have lacked the qualities necessary to be considered a property at all.

Such a perspective, however, is misleading, for, as the history of the Mythos demonstrates, the Mythos developed during Lovecraft's lifetime in a manner that was coherent and consistent, legally untroubled, and, not least of all, satisfactory to everyone involved with it, including publishers, writers, and readers. Which is to say that the Mythos functioned successfully as a narrative-based property, even if we can confidently conclude that a court would probably not have recognized it as such. Indeed, the hypothetical game I have played in the above paragraphs of asking how a court *would have* viewed the property is not only anachronistic but also irrelevant, for not only did no one bring such questions to court by way of a lawsuit, but no one appears even to have considered doing so. So long as Lovecraft was alive, readers, authors, and publishers understood the property, in every way that mattered to them at the time—and despite the borrowing of assets by Lovecraft's friends and ghost-writing clients—to be Lovecraft's.

That they did so demonstrates the importance during the modern copyright era of the principle of authorial genius, which encouraged industrial actors to consider the creator of an artistic work to be its natural or intrinsic owner. Certainly, the informal rights accompanying Lovecraft's "natural" ownership of the Cthulhu Mythos were never explicitly spelled out—and were even perhaps so context-dependent as to render spelling out impossible; but those who interacted with the property in a professional context recognized them, and these natural rights functioned to regulate and organize development of the Mythos. In one telling instance, Farnsworth Wright, in his capacity as editor of *Weird Tales,* even rejected "The Horror from the Lake," a piece of Mythos fiction written by the young August Derleth on account of the younger writer's heavy borrowing from Lovecraft's fiction (Wright did not know at the time that Derleth was a friend of Lovecraft). As Wright explained in an unusually long rejection letter, as a tremendous admirer of Lovecraft he simply could not allow another writer to employ assets taken from Lovecraft's fiction in the explicit manner that Derleth had done, which was "unfair to Lovecraft."[83] Given that *Weird Tales* was at the time the only venue for such fiction, Wright's editorial policy functioned in effect to enforce, under the principle of "fairness"—and even potentially against Lovecraft's own wishes—Lovecraft's authorial right to his own creations.[84] Wright was no doubt exceptional in the power he wielded as editor over the Mythos, but his understanding of Lovecraft as the Mythos's natural proprietor was widely shared by others. Indeed, not only did *Weird Tales* never publish a Mythos story during Lovecraft's lifetime that was not written by a member of the Lovecraft Circle, but also (as far as we know from archival evidence) the magazine appears never even to have received a submission of a Mythos story during that period from anyone outside the Circle.

Despite Lovecraft's importance, however, the Mythos was also, in many respects, not his at all, but a property that belonged to his community. During Lovecraft's lifetime, as many Mythos stories were published by fans-turned-friends as were published by Lovecraft himself; and although these friends usually retained the publication and media rights to their own stories, the assets they introduced or developed within them were, as we saw above, meant to be freely utilized by other members of the Lovecraft Circle. Because this usage was otherwise unrestricted and uncontrolled, the assets thus often struck early readers (as they continue to strike readers today) as existing in and of themselves, bound by a logic that exceeds and constrains the intentions of whomever employs them. In this, the Mythos assets often have a peculiarly twenty-first-century feel, more like those of the contemporary Marvel Comics universe (for example) than that of modern-copyright-era properties such as Burroughs's Tarzan stories or Hal Foster's Prince Valiant.

Functioning simultaneously as the property of Lovecraft and his community, the Mythos thus developed in such a way that it effectively harmonized two seemingly incompatible principles of the modern copyright era: authorial genius (and the quasi-moral rights associated with it) and the idea-expression dichotomy (with the "parts" of the expression being free for others to use). Borrowing the language of physics, we might even understand the Mythos as having achieved a unique form of semantic/industrial equilibrium, with Lovecraft as genius exerting a centripetal or centralizing force on the property and the Lovecraft Circle's free use of the assets exerting a corresponding centrifugal or dispersing force. But however we envision it, the harmonization of the two principles was also inherently precarious, as it depended upon both the Lovecraft's Circle's continuous recognition of Lovecraft's authorial rights and Lovecraft's own continuous rejection of those same rights. Were one of these to cease, the property would risk falling apart. Rejection of Lovecraft's authorial rights would result in competing and uncoordinated use of the property's assets, thereby endangering its semantic coherence; while a concerted attempt by Lovecraft to enforce these rights and claim ownership of his creations would likely bring the property's development to a halt. After Lovecraft's death in 1937, one or both of these outcomes thus seemed inevitable, as the transformation of Lovecraft's work from a living expression of its author's genius into a literary "estate," to be managed by an assigned executor seemed certain to end the delicate balancing of interests upon which the property depended. That neither outcome ultimately occurred—and that the Mythos qua narrative-based property ended up functioning after Lovecraft's death much as it did during Lovecraft's lifetime—is thus remarkable, and is in large part the direct result of the managerial efforts of one particular member of the Lovecraft Circle: August Derleth.

"Instructions in Case of Decease": Lovecraft's Literary Estate

When Lovecraft died in early 1937, the will he left behind was nearly a quarter of a century old and made no direct mention of his literary work. Under its terms, his family's lawyer, Albert Baker, was named the will's executor and the entirety of Lovecraft's property was left to his surviving aunt, Annie Gamwell, a seventy-year-old widow with no children or surviving siblings of her own.[85] Shortly before his death, however, Lovecraft attempted to amend his will so that it better reflected both his interests as a writer and the many intimate relationships he had formed over the previous twenty years by writing out for his aunt a set of new instructions for the handling of his estate.[86] Originally untitled, the document is today referred to by way of the identifying label Lovecraft had written on the envelope in which he had placed the document for safekeeping: "Instructions in Case of Decease."[87] These "Instructions" named Robert Barlow, a nineteen-year-old member of the Lovecraft Circle, as Lovecraft's "literary executor," and left most of the author's "books, pictures, curios, and other articles" to his friends and correspondents. First choice of this property was to go to Barlow and second choice to Clark Ashton Smith; whatever remained was then to be divvied up, as interests warranted, among the thirty-six friends whose names and addresses Lovecraft listed in the document.[88]

At first glance, Lovecraft's choice of Barlow as literary executor may seem strange. Other members of the Lovecraft Circle had much greater knowledge of the professional publishing world—and many, such as Frank Long, had known Lovecraft significantly longer than Barlow had. Lovecraft's relationship with Barlow, however, had been an extraordinarily close and intimate one, and during the last years of Lovecraft's life the two men had devoted significant time to each other, with Lovecraft, in the summer of 1934, even spending a month with Barlow at the teenager's home in Florida.[89] Barlow, for his part, cared deeply for Lovecraft and, having yet no career or family of his own, was in a position that enabled him to spend substantial time and energy on behalf of Lovecraft and his work. While Lovecraft was alive, for example, Barlow had typed copies of a number of the handwritten and often tattered manuscripts that represented Lovecraft's only copies of much of his fiction. He had also worked with Lovecraft to assemble and prepare for publication Lovecraft's sonnet sequence, *Fungi from Yuggoth.* At the time of Lovecraft's death, Barlow thus probably possessed more detailed knowledge of the author's literary output than anyone else in the Circle. Such knowledge would have served Barlow well as Lovecraft's executor, since Lovecraft himself left behind no reliable documentation spelling out what specifically constituted his literary estate (i.e., the names of the stories, the locations of the manuscripts, the publication histories, and the statuses of the relevant publishing rights). In assigning Barlow control of his work, however, Lovecraft had also likely been thinking as much about Barlow's future as he had that of his own legacy, and, given Barlow's longstanding interest in starting a small publishing press of his own, Lovecraft no doubt imagined that Barlow himself would undertake publishing at least some of his surviving work.[90]

As for the "legality" of Lovecraft's "Instructions," the few Lovecraft scholars to have taken up consideration of the document have argued that, because of its informal language and lack of witnesses, it had no real legal authority.[91] The question of the document's legality, however, should be resolved not by asking how a hypothetical court might treat the "Instructions" but rather by examining how the relevant stakeholders themselves treated it. In this regard, the primary stakeholder that mattered, Annie Gamwell, treated "The Instructions" as a legitimate addendum to the will—at least at first. Recognizing that the "Instructions" represented her nephew's wishes, on March 26, 1937, she formalized Barlow's role as literary executor by signing a contract that granted Barlow control of Lovecraft's writings for the purpose of publishing them (with all but 3 percent of the gross receipts earned by doing so to be paid to Gamwell).[92] In observance of the "Instructions," she also allowed Barlow to remove a number of Lovecraft's books and manuscripts from the house she had shared with her nephew. During the following year, however, she appears to have regretted doing both of these things, and—under the prompting of Donald Wandrei, August Derleth, and Baker in his role as the will's executor—acquiesced as Wandrei and Derleth effectively supplanted Barlow as Lovecraft's literary executors. Although the contract she had signed with Barlow was never formally terminated—and Barlow's rights to Lovecraft's work were in subsequent years sometimes nominally recognized—Barlow informed Baker on October 12, 1938, that he "would stand aside voluntarily in favour of Mr. Derleth's superior [publishing] opportunities."[93]

The events that led to Gamwell's change of mind have been the subject of some controversy, although most scholars that have considered the issue agree that Gamwell herself had no strong opinion one way or the other with respect to Barlow.[94] The letters that exist between Gamwell and Derleth support this view and suggest that Gamwell, finding herself overwhelmed by the handling of the will, increasingly deferred to both Baker and Derleth. "I admit I am rather falling down on the job," she wrote in the fall of 1938, "for I am very wearied with thinking + thinking + have felt I could only live along on the surface awhile + hiding my head in the sand."[95] According to letters between Barlow and Baker, Baker's objection to Barlow appears to have been based on a misunderstanding, fueled in part by Derleth (with whom the lawyer was in conversation via letter), but also resulting from the fact that Gamwell had apparently failed to inform him of Lovecraft's "Instructions."[96] Whatever the cause, after Barlow promised not to interfere with Derleth's publishing plans, Baker ceased to involve himself with Lovecraft's literary estate. "I do not see why I as Executor [of the will] am further interested," he explained in an apologetic letter to Barlow, "as my desire was to avoid possible conflict between two or more persons exercising literary executorship and to preserve any substantial rights of the Estate, for the benefit of Mrs. Gamwell."[97] For their part, Derleth and Wandrei appear to have been less concerned with Gamwell's financial interests than they were with Lovecraft's legacy as a writer, which they believed—rightly or wrongly—to be in safer hands with the two of them than with Barlow. Having begun to plan a volume of Lovecraft's fiction almost as soon as Lovecraft had died, they also feared having to modify these plans or cede control of them to another person.[98] Accordingly, they endeavored to convince Gamwell that Barlow had taken advantage of her and that the contract she had signed with him should be set aside.[99]

For the purposes of this chapter, the ethicality of Derleth and Wandrei's efforts to supplant Barlow as Lovecraft's literary executor is irrelevant; what matters is rather what these efforts reveal about the fate of the Lovecraft Circle—and that unique mode of communal production that it had enabled—in the years immediately following Lovecraft's death. In Lovecraft's absence, self-interest, often expressing itself in the form of competing claims to Lovecraft's legacy, quickly came to dominate and thereby dissolve the complex web of relationships that Lovecraft had fostered among his friends and on which the Cthulhu Mythos had previously depended. The fate of Lovecraft's "Instructions" is telling in this regard, for though the document is nominally a set of rules for the distribution of his property, it is also a declaration of community—with the long list of names and addresses that make up most of the document even resembling the lists of potential friends and interlocutors that Lovecraft had provided to young writers such as Bloch. That the "Instructions" were ultimately disregarded by Lovecraft's friends and family reflects in part the inherent difficulty involved in formulating and executing a will whose primary beneficiary is a community of individuals; but it also reflects the degree to which the Lovecraft Circle's sense of community depended, somewhat paradoxically, upon Lovecraft's authority. Without Lovecraft there to "enforce" that community, the Circle rapidly split apart into factions, with a small coterie of older writers (organized around Wandrei) either attacking the younger members or merely ignoring them outright.

Barlow received the worst of this, and, given how much Lovecraft had cared for him and how difficult a life Barlow ultimately had (he committed suicide in 1951 at the age of thirty-three), the harsh manner in which Wandrei, Derleth, Clark Ashton Smith, and others discussed and treated him seems unduly cruel.[100] That Barlow nevertheless continued to assist these men in their publishing efforts, and to do so despite receiving almost no recognition or reward, suggests that, in this respect at least, he put the interests of Lovecraft's legacy above his own. Indeed, because these older Circle members disliked Barlow, the important role he played in preserving Lovecraft's writing (which included depositing a trove of material at Brown University's John Hay Library) remained obscured for many years and his memory subjected to continued abuse even decades after his death. Peter Ruber, for example, described him in the introduction to *Arkham's Masters of Horror* in 2000 as "a rabid fan obsessed with a compulsion to possess Lovecraft's manuscripts and books, and whose behavior can best be explained by a psychiatrist."[101] Such was the legacy Barlow had earned from participating in the Lovecraft Circle, and it is only recently—and thanks to the work of scholars such as S. T. Joshi and David Schultz—that the legacy has been revised.

No member of the Lovecraft Circle was treated as harshly after Lovecraft's death as Barlow; younger members of the Circle were, however, not infrequently viewed by some older members as interlopers or outsiders. Robert Bloch and Henry Kuttner were, for example, regarded with suspicion by a group of older members. Howard Wandrei even reported to Derleth in March of 1937 that "the whole gang" believed a story recently published in *Weird Tales* by "Block" and titled "The Mannikin" had in fact been written by Lovecraft.[102] Derleth, having known and corresponded with Bloch, conveyed his skepticism to Wandrei, but to no avail. Wandrei cited Barlow as proof, claiming that Barlow had access to the manuscripts and had confirmed to him that Lovecraft had written *all* of Bloch's Mythos stories (as well as Kuttner and Heald's) save for "a maximum of ten lines to a story."[103] When that still did not convince Derleth, Wandrei resorted to second-hand insults, sharing, for example, that Frank Long, thought Derleth "off his nut" for doubting that "The Mannikin" was written by Lovecraft—and for not recognizing Bloch as a liar.[104] Unsurprisingly, Bloch and Kuttner (who remained friends for life) subsequently came to have minimal interaction with other members of the Circle.

As the Lovecraft Circle began to dissolve, Derleth, with Donald Wandrei's assistance, assumed the role of Lovecraft's literary executor. Within less than a week after Lovecraft's death and days before Barlow had even learned of Lovecraft's "Instructions," Derleth took it upon himself to begin initial negotiations with *Weird Tales* over book rights for Lovecraft's fiction.[105] Starting in April 1937, he also began selling to *Weird Tales* (and eventually *Fantastic*) serial rights to Lovecraft's poems and fiction.[106] For his part, Wandrei, excited by the prospect of publishing a book of Lovecraft's letters, began contacting members of the Lovecraft Circle and requesting that they send him whatever letters they still possessed.[107] Their main focus, however, was the assemblage of a book manuscript representing Lovecraft's best fiction. With significant help from Barlow, the manuscript was finished by mid-1938, at which time Wandrei began shopping it around professional publishing houses in New York.[108] After Scribner's, Doubleday-Doran, and Simon & Schuster had all rejected it, Derleth and Wandrei concluded that they would need to publish it themselves, and on August 30, 1939, the two men signed a contract creating the publishing house they eventually called Arkham House.[109] Four months later, Arkham House published Lovecraft's first book of fiction, *The Outsider and Others,* in an edition of 1,268 copies.[110] Over the next decade, Arkham House would publish four other books of Lovecraft's work, as well as numerous books of other authors' weird fiction and poetry.

From the beginning of their work as Lovecraft's literary executors, Derleth and Wandrei were largely improvising with respect to intellectual property law. For one, they remained uncertain of the legal status of the rights to Lovecraft's previously published fiction. When Derleth first informed *Weird Tales* of his plan to assemble this fiction in book form, Farnsworth Wright indicated that the magazine had a claim to the book rights for the stories the magazine had already published. "We shall be glad to waive our royalty rights in any books of HPL's work," Wright explained, "provided that we receive assurances that the royalties will go to Mrs Gamwell."[111] Lovecraft, however, had intimated to Derleth in a number of letters that he had not sold anything except serial rights to *Weird Tales* for his later stories.[112] Frank Long told Howard Wandrei (who in turn told Derleth) that Lovecraft had retained book rights for all work published after 1931, while Barlow reportedly asserted that Lovecraft kept all rights after 1926.[113] Because Lovecraft and *Weird Tales* relied upon informal contracting, and because Lovecraft—and likely *Weird Tales* as well—kept no clear records of Lovecraft's rights, the exact status of who owned what rights to Lovecraft's stories was impossible to determine. Derleth and Donald Wandrei were thus forced to act as though the rights were simply unencumbered and Lovecraft's work free for them to publish. So long as all potential rightsholders agreed that any profit resulting from such publication should go, out of respect to Lovecraft's authorship, to his aunt, there was little risk that Derleth and Wandrei's exercise of these rights would be contested. As Wandrei explained to Derleth in a worried exchange over the stories' copyrights, the issue was probably irrelevant, for no one's interest would be served by challenging their rights to publish *The Outsider.*[114]

A bigger problem for Derleth and Donald Wandrei—at least in the long term—was that they were uncertain as to when Lovecraft's published stories had been copyrighted or if some of them had even been copyrighted at all. Lacking the time, money, and presumably knowhow required to exercise a series of complex copyright searches through the U.S. Copyright Office, Wandrei instead relied upon a list of stories and dates that Lovecraft himself had assembled. Wandrei recognized that doing so was likely to produce errors (in part because the magazine cover dates Lovecraft recorded did not correspond with actual publication/copyright dates) and that such errors might, under the laws governing proper copyright notice, end up invalidating the copyrights altogether; but beyond double-checking *Weird Tales*' own copyright notices Wandrei could think of no alternative.[115] Wandrei—who seemed to better understand intellectual property law than Derleth (no doubt partly because Wandrei's father was a lawyer)—also understood that copyright law's principle of indivisibility required the original publishers of Lovecraft's stories (which had registered them for copyrights in their own names) to reassign the copyrights for these stories to Arkham House—even if the original publishers had already exhausted their rights to them.[116] Despite this knowledge, neither Wandrei nor Derleth broached the question of reassignment with any of Lovecraft's former publishers until well after *The Outsider* had been published.[117] That they did not do so might in part be because the process is complex and time-consuming; but a more likely reason for their omission is that requesting copyright reassignments would have almost certainly upset the delicate balance of interests that allowed Arkham House to use the rights without ever having to determine who exactly owned what parts of them.

These problems were simultaneously complicated and simplified by Gamwell's death in January 1941. Gamwell's will left to Derleth and Donald Wandrei whatever royalties were due her for *The Outsider and Others*; the rest of her estate was to be divided equally between her cousins, Ethel Morrish and Edna Lewis, with Edna Lewis named as executor.[118] No mention was made of the rights to Lovecraft's writing. Technically, Gamwell's death meant that the informal contracting arrangement she had made with Derleth—which had allowed him to act on her behalf with respect to Lovecraft's work—was no longer valid. As Wandrei explained in a March 11, 1941, letter to Derleth, with Gamwell's estate passing to her cousins, Arkham House appeared no longer to have the legal right to publish most of Lovecraft's work.[119] Although new arrangements could have been negotiated with Gamwell's heirs, such negotiations would likely have been difficult, as the informal arrangement the men had secured with Gamwell had been based upon a kind of second-order intimacy between the parties, based on their mutual love for Lovecraft, which saw the two men effectively *donating* their work as agents and publishers so as to provide financially for Lovecraft's aunt. With Gamwell's death, the justification for this arrangement vanished, since Gamwell's cousins had barely known Lovecraft or his work. Equally problematic was the fact that the new rightsholders likely knew little or nothing about U.S. copyright law and the basic industrial practices around which publishing revolved. Contracting with Gamwell's heirs would thus likely have been complicated, time-consuming, and expensive.

The heirs' ignorance also meant, however, that if Derleth and Wandrei simply continued to act *as though* they themselves had legal authority over Lovecraft's writing, no one was likely to know that they did not. Ignoring the heirs also promised to make rights management simpler: with a legal rightsholder no longer in the picture, the two men would no longer need to obtain permission to publish or sell Lovecraft's work, nor would they need to give up the profit they generated from doing so. Although the heirs—or some other interested party—might eventually find out and object, Wandrei reasoned that the small amount of money involved meant that the likelihood of anyone doing so in a court of law was slim.[120] Ultimately, Wandrei and Derleth chose to follow this strategy, saying nothing to the heirs, and quietly instructing editors such as Dorothy McIlwraith at *Weird Tales* to remit payment to Derleth after Gamwell's death.[121]

Similar reasoning likely also informed Derleth's inaction regarding the copyright renewals for Lovecraft's fiction, which began coming due in 1950. Under the letter of the law, only a surviving spouse, child, or (if neither of these existed) next of kin could legally claim a renewal. Lovecraft scholar George Wetzel has thus suspected that Derleth did not renew the copyrights because the law did not allow him to do so.[122] By the 1950s, however, most courts would probably have accepted a renewal application filed by a third party on behalf of a legal claimant as valid—indeed, many of Derleth's own publishers filed such applications on his behalf. That Derleth neither applied for renewals for Lovecraft's work nor informed Gamwell's heirs that *they* needed to do so thus suggests that he believed Arkham House's interests would be better served by allowing the copyrights to expire. Renewing them risked stripping Arkham House of control over Lovecraft's work, in part because a renewal functioned legally to "reset" the rights to the renewed work, negating any contractual encumbrances that preexisted the renewal. Renewing the copyrights would thus not only have caused Gamwell's heirs to learn that they owned Lovecraft's work; it would also have enabled the heirs to freely license the rights to this work or to hire an agent to do so for them. Arkham House would have almost certainly ended up much worse off as a result. Derleth would henceforth have had to pay the heirs for publishing rights (making Arkham House uneconomical), and he would no longer have been able to exercise control over how Lovecraft's work was utilized by other writers and publishers. In either case—the copyrights being renewed or left to expire—Derleth would have ended up with no legal authority to exercise control over Lovecraft's work. Because Arkham House technically had no legal authority over Lovecraft's work even before the renewals were due, however, letting them expire was the safer path, as the likelihood of anyone learning that they expired was minimal. Derleth thus chose to do nothing regarding the renewals, and Arkham House continued for over two decades as the presumed and de facto legal owner of Lovecraft's work, even as much of this work technically (that is, according to the letter of formal U.S. copyright law) entered the public domain.

In recent decades, Derleth's control of Lovecraft's work has been the subject of much criticism by fans and scholars, and the means by which Derleth achieved this control has been regularly cast as underhanded or unethical.[123] Some have taken in particular the lack of a formal contract granting Arkham House rights as evidence that its founders overstepped the bounds of both propriety and the law. When one attempts rigorously to apply the letter of copyright law to the history of the estate—as Wetzel did in "Copyright Problems of the Lovecraft Literary Estate"—one can in fact hardly conclude otherwise, as Derleth's handling of the rights to Lovecraft's work appears to jive very poorly with the formal requirements of the law. As the account I have offered above should demonstrate, however, a rigorous application of U.S. copyright law was never the goal of anyone involved with the estate. The informal arrangements made between stakeholders in the years immediately following Lovecraft's death were designed not to fulfill the law's formal requirements but rather to achieve the publication of Lovecraft's work after his death. Derleth's arrangement with Gamwell achieved this result by creating a single, unencumbered "rightsholder" for Lovecraft's work: Arkham House. The fact that Arkham House was able to continue to occupy this role even after Gamwell's death indicates both the industrial necessity that such a "rightsholder" exist (especially from the perspective of other media companies, who increasingly wished to license Lovecraft's work) and the lack of interest or incentive for other potential stakeholders to either assume this role or to challenge the presumptions (many of them out of sync with statute and common law) on which it depended.

The Cthulhu Mythos under August Derleth, 1937–1971

With one important exception, the Lovecraft Circle stopped producing Cthulhu Mythos fiction within a few years of Lovecraft's death. Stories utilizing Mythos assets continued to be published by Circle members in *Weird Tales* and *Strange Stories* through the early 1940s, but most of these stories had been started years earlier, while Lovecraft was still living. With Lovecraft dead—and the Circle's center left empty—the production of Mythos fiction lost much of its purpose for former Circle members, who gradually turned to other styles and genres of writing or left the weird-fiction/science-fiction scene entirely. As the production of Mythos fiction diminished, the property became textually frozen, so that by the 1950s readers and fans tended to see it more as a coherently structured narrative system in the vein of Edgar Rice Burrough's Barsoom property than as an organic product of communal improvisation. In part, they did so because the Mythos as they encountered it, inhering primarily in work completed between the mid-1920s and late 1930s, seemed a decades-old and thus long since "finished" storytelling project. But the more significant cause of this shift in perspective was the systematizing practices of Arkham House itself, which in the decades after Lovecraft's death effectively transformed the Mythos from a relatively open, communal project into a single-authored set of static assets and storytelling comportments.

Arkham House, which Derleth ran mostly by himself after Donald Wandrei was drafted into the U.S. Army in 1942, effected this transformation in two ways. First, it used editorial apparatuses or "paratexts"—forewords, glossaries, and supplemental essays—in order to systematize and (as critics such as S. T. Joshi would later charge) simplify the Mythos. The most famous of these paratexts is what has come to be called the "black magic quotation," a single-sentence summary of the Mythos supposedly authored by Lovecraft, which Derleth (and others) regularly reproduced in Arkham House books:

> All my stories, unconnected as they may be, are based on the fundamental lore or legend that this world was inhabited at one time by another race who, in practicing black magic, lost their foothold and were expelled, yet live on outside ever ready to take possession of this earth again.[124]

I will leave aside here the tortuous history of this quotation, which is now widely believed to be spurious; the important point is rather that the quotation worked to reframe the Cthulhu Mythos, under the authority of its author, as a long-running cosmic battle between a *bad* "black-magic"-using race (which Derleth variously called "the Great Old Ones" and the "Ancient Ones") and a *good* race (the "Elder Gods") that occasionally intervened by "expelling" the former from earth.[125] As Derleth explained it to Arkham House readers, the Mythos represented "the primal struggle between good and evil" and was thus "essentially similar to the Christian Mythos, especially relating to the expulsion of Satan from Eden and Satan's lasting power of evil."[126] As Derleth must have recognized, Lovecraft's individual stories provide rather weak support for such a Manichaean narrative: they are too idiosyncratic in their thematic interests and story structures and are largely uninterested in moral systems, Christian or otherwise. From the perspective of narrative-based property management, however, the good-versus-evil framework served a useful systematizing function, offering readers a simple—even familiar—means of reading the stories (which in fact often have very little to do with each other) as parts of a singular, coherent saga.

Glossaries and textual histories provided Derleth with another paratextual means of systematizing the Cthulhu Mythos. In 1942, as Arkham House was still developing a regular publishing program, Derleth discovered in a fanzine called *The Acolyte* what appeared to be the first published attempt to compile and define all of the "settings & dramatic entities" that had appeared in Mythos fiction.[127] Grasping the value of such a work (what today's IP manager would call a property "bible"), Derleth contacted the author, a young science-fiction fan named Francis Laney, and offered to help him revise and expand it for publication in Arkham House's second book of Lovecraft's work. Published as "The Cthulhu Mythos: A Glossary," Laney's piece identifies five types of what we might today call assets but which the piece calls narrative "forms" or "names" (neither Laney's essay nor Derleth's introduction is quite sure what to call them) that constitute the Mythos: deities, prehuman races, geographical place-names, "mythical books of black magic and forbidden knowledge," and, finally, a "miscellaneous" category, which includes "unclassifiable signs and tokens."[128] The exact impact of Laney's glossary on readers is difficult to trace—in part because, as the "black magic quotation" indicates, it was merely one part of a broader systematizing program. The glossary nevertheless seems to have inspired readers and writers to approach Lovecraft's work from a similar systematizing perspective. Future science-fiction and fantasy writer Fritz Lieber, Jr., for example, provided a textual history of the fictional Miskatonic University for Arkham House's third book of Lovecraft's work, *Something about Cats*.[129] Science-fiction and fantasy writer (and future Conan *pasticheur*) Lin Carter—to give one more example—produced a series of glossary-like works, the first two of which, "H. P. Lovecraft: The Books" and "H. P. Lovecraft: The Gods," were published (along with a glossary-like "Addendum" by Tom Cockroft) in Arkham House's fourth book of Lovecraft's work, *The Shuttered Room & Other Pieces*.[130]

In addition to employing editorial apparatuses to systematize and simplify the Mythos, Derleth frequently used them to de-emphasize the communal production process upon which the Mythos had originally depended, positioning the Mythos instead as the singular product of Lovecraft's own authorial genius. In some cases, Derleth did so explicitly via his publications' front matter. He asserted, for example, in *Beyond the*

Wall of Sleep that the Mythos was primarily the product of Lovecraft's own imagination, and that it had been "well on the way to precise and conclusive development when Lovecraft's death interrupted his work."[131] Elsewhere, he cast the involvement of other writers in terms of a top-down or hierarchical model of property production: "When at last he [Lovecraft] began consciously to construct the pantheon, he invited some of his fellow writers to add to it."[132] In keeping with this vision of a hierarchically constructed property, Derleth organized the existing Mythos stories by way of a "canon," the "primary stories" of which (he explained in *The Trail of Cthulhu*) were "thirteen in number," all by Lovecraft.[133]

To be sure, Derleth did not deny the existence of Cthulhu fiction by other writers; in fact, he published much of it during Arkham House's first two decades. Until the 1960s, however, he rarely identified it as such. Of the five collections of Circle writers' short stories published in the late 1940s, only Derleth's own collection, *Something Near,* alerts readers (in this particular case via the dustjacket) that the book contains Mythos stories.[134] Although by the 1960s Derleth began applying the "Cthulhu" tag more liberally, his construal of the Mythos as fundamentally belonging to Lovecraft remained unchanged. On the dustjacket to Long's *Rim of the Unknown,* for example, Derleth even falsely described Long as "one of the six individuals designated by Lovecraft at his death with exclusive permission to make use of his Cthulhu mythos . . . for literary purposes."[135]

Derleth's "editorializing" played a key role in reshaping the Cthulhu Mythos after Lovecraft's death, but it was not the only method employed by Arkham House to do so: of equal importance was Arkham House's overall publishing program, which tended in practice to frame Lovecraft's fiction as the product of his unique authorial genius. In the first three decades of Arkham House's existence, Derleth published nineteen volumes authored by Lovecraft—an average of approximately two books every three years. This figure does not include the many other Arkham House books that discussed Lovecraft or contained work he had written—publications including Bishop's *The Curse of Yig* (containing the essay "H. P. Lovecraft: A Pupil's View"), Robert E. Howard's *Skull-Face and Others* (opening with an essay by Lovecraft), and Derleth's own *Some Notes on H. P. Lovecraft.* In order to maintain this publishing schedule, Arkham House relied upon what I earlier named Lovecraftiana: fragments, juvenilia, working notes, and letters written by Lovecraft, as well as memoirs, elegies, and homages written by his associates. Such texts served a hagiographic function, depicting Lovecraft as a (self-thwarting) genius and situating his work within—and as a natural product of—his own personality. Indeed, the heavy presence of biographical texts, frequently published alongside fiction written by Lovecraft and other Circle authors, increasingly cast the fiction itself as a form of Lovecraftiana. The 313 pages that make up Lovecraft's *The Shuttered Room*, for example, consist of only sixty-four pages of Lovecraft's fiction; the rest is taken up by working notes, memoirs, homages, and glossaries. As a result of this publishing program, by the end of the 1960s the Cthulhu Mythos not only appeared to be Lovecraft's own creation; it had also become fundamentally bound up with his personality and biography—a development further reinforced by Lovecraft's appearance as a character in a number of Mythos stories.

The only writer to whom Arkham House devoted similar publishing resources was Derleth himself, who by the end of the 1960s had published seventeen books through Arkham House. Although a number of these contained fiction and poetry that had nothing to do with Lovecraft or the Cthulhu Mythos, in most of these publications Derleth cast himself as Lovecraft's steward and authorial proxy. In part, these identities were logical corollaries of Derleth's possession of Lovecraft's manuscripts: after Barlow's death, there was simply no one else who had read more of Lovecraft's work or had greater familiarity with his biography. Of even greater significance, however, were Derleth's "posthumous collaborations" with Lovecraft, the first of which—*The Lurker at the Threshold*—was published in 1945. Two more coauthored volumes followed, and a number of coauthored short stories appeared in other Arkham House publications. Although based upon extremely short fragments (some no more than a sentence or two in length), the stories were marketed as unfinished tales that had been found among Lovecraft's papers and subsequently "completed" by Derleth.[136] Not only did crediting these stories (which Derleth had written almost entirely on his own) to Lovecraft reaffirm Derleth's qualifications as Lovecraft's authorial proxy, it also enabled Derleth to continue to develop the property without seeming to alienate it from Lovecraft's own personality or genius. Indeed, the posthumous collaborations—which, like Derleth's editorial contributions, tended to systematize and simplify the Mythos—represented Lovecraft's vision for the Mythos as identical to Derleth's: a complex pantheon of "bad" Gods long ago banished by "good" Gods but ceaselessly attempting to return to Earth by way, inevitably, of New England.

Thanks to both his posthumous collaborations with Lovecraft and his own single-authored Mythos fiction (which *Weird Tales* continued to publish into the 1950s), Derleth came to replace Lovecraft as the primary author of Mythos fiction by the middle of the twentieth century. In fact, excepting a few stories by Bloch, Derleth was the *only* producer of new Mythos fiction, a feat he achieved in part because of Arkham House's position in the United States as the industry's only serious publisher of weird/horror fiction in book form. After the pulp market began to dry up at the start of the 1950s, would-be Mythos writers simply had nowhere else to publish their work except Arkham House—a state of affairs that would remain unchanged until the paperback boom of the early 1970s. This publishing chokehold was reinforced by Arkham House's ostensible legal control of both Lovecraft's writing and the Mythos itself—which Derleth asserted in public venues, such as fanzines and magazines, and private correspondence with editors and authors.[137] Although, as discussed above, Arkham House's formal "rights" to the Mythos were at best extremely limited, the belief among fans and industrial actors that these rights, presumably authorized by Lovecraft himself, were genuine and capacious meant that, in practice, they were.

So effective were Derleth's claims of proprietary rights (sometimes backed up by threats of lawsuit) that only a single writer unaffiliated with Arkham House managed to publish Mythos fiction before the late 1960s: pulp writer C. Hall Thompson. After two of Thompson's Mythos stories appeared in *Weird Tales* in the mid-1940s, Derleth fired off letters explaining that "literary properties" such as Arkham, Miskatonic University, and the Book of Eibon were protected by copyright and that Thompson's use of them constituted "illegal borrowing."[138] Thompson's agent, Lurton Blassingame, responded immediately, promising that Thompson would not use the Mythos again.[139] That this dustup over Thompson's work appears to be the only time Derleth formally threatened legal action over another's use of Mythos assets demonstrates how quickly pulp editors and non-Circle writers came to understand and accept Derleth's control of the property. With the exception of Fred Chappell, whose *Dagon* (1968) made very limited use of Mythos assets, not a single other writer appears to have attempted to publish a piece of Mythos fiction while Derleth was alive without first securing his consent.

The portrait of Derleth that is suggested by my account may strike some readers as an unflattering one. Derleth, ignoring Lovecraft's own wishes, utilized his position as Lovecraft's publisher to assume for himself moral and legal authority over the Cthulhu Mythos, transforming what had been a communally produced property into a systematized—and heavily simplified—set of assets controlled by a single person, Derleth, who represented himself as both Lovecraft's moral steward and authorial heir. Such a portrait is not inaccurate; it is, however, incomplete, for Derleth's identification with Lovecraft ultimately cut both ways, positioning him not just as the property's "author" but also, as Lovecraft himself had been, mentor and friend to the property's young fans and would-be contributors. In fact, Derleth's management of the property eventually succeeded in reproducing the unique form of semantic/industrial equilibrium that had characterized the property while Lovecraft was living—with Derleth simultaneously exerting a centripetal or centralizing force in his role as "rightsholder" and authorial steward and a centrifugal or dispersing force in his role as mentor to a generation of new (male) weird fiction writers. To be sure, Derleth's style as mentor was different from Lovecraft's: he was harsher, more direct in his criticism, more geared toward commercial writing, and often (though not always) more serious in his approach to the Mythos. But like Lovecraft, he devoted significant time and care to the work of much younger writers and fans, many of whom began their careers with Mythos imitations. For some, Derleth also offered a kind of aid that Lovecraft had been unable to provide: a publishing contract.

Derleth encountered some of these young writers via fan mail or book orders placed through the mail. In the summer of 1964, for example, a teenage fan named Charles Swoope, introducing himself as a young man inspired by Derleth's work, wrote Derleth to see if the older man might provide him with feedback on a Mythos story he had written and also suggest a publishing venue.[140] To Swoope's surprise, Derleth replied with a warning that he controlled Lovecraft's work and that Swoope would need permission to employ Mythos assets. To Swoope's further surprise, however, Derleth's eventual response to Swoope's story (sent out to the young man less than a week after Swoope had placed the story in the post) proved to be a detailed letter containing praise and suggestions for revision and discounting the need for permission at all. In a later letter, Derleth also expressed interest in publishing a revised version of Swoope's story. Although Swoope appears to have stopped working on the story when he started college in the fall, he maintained correspondence with Derleth for at least a year, the subjects of which not only included Lovecraft and literature but also college classes and Swoope's nascent love life. The Swoope-Derleth letters are but one of many such exchanges, some of which are preserved in Derleth's papers at the Wisconsin Historical Society. In nearly all of them, Derleth asserts his "proprietary rights" over the Mythos assets only to waive them after reading and commenting upon the fiction, which he occasionally also offers to publish.[141]

I do not wish to overstate the importance of these exchanges: certainly they were less extensive and, to a degree, less intimate than Lovecraft's correspondence with similar young, would-be writers. Derleth provided less praise and, unlike Lovecraft, tended to emphasize the labor and financial precarity that typically characterized writing as a profession—thus effectively de-romanticizing it. Only a small portion of the amateur writers with whom Derleth corresponded thus eventually went on to publish fiction of any kind, let alone Mythos fiction. But the support Derleth provided proved instrumental for at least two of these young writers: Ramsey Campbell and Brian Lumley. Not only did both of these men eventually become extraordinarily successful authors of horror fiction, they also left a profound mark on the development of the Mythos, which in their hands—and with the encouragement and editorial input of Derleth—began to reacquire the playfulness and improvisatory qualities that had characterized it during Lovecraft's lifetime.

The nature of the editorial input Derleth provided Campbell and Lumley differed, reflecting significant differences in the kind of fiction each of the men was producing. To Campbell, whose first collection of Mythos stories was eventually published in 1964 as *The Inhabitant of the Lake & Less Welcome Tenants,* Derleth had surprisingly little to say about the somewhat idiosyncratic manner in which the young British fan had employed Mythos assets.[142] Despite Campbell's addition of new planets and new alien entities—and some of his stories' disregard for the systematized good-versus-evil narrative structures on which Derleth's own Mythos fiction relied—Derleth's only major revision request was that Campbell drop Lovecraft's fictionalized New England setting and move the stories to Britain. Derleth's request was made for the sake of providing the stories greater realism, but the request also had the effect of "freeing" the Mythos from the confines of its original setting and thereby broadening the kinds of histories, institutions, and peoples that Mythos stories could involve. Campbell's subsequent fiction for Arkham House made use of this expanded purview, both in Mythos stories such as "Cold Print" (first published in *Tales of the Cthulhu Mythos* [1969]) and in ostensibly non-Mythos fiction such as the stories in *Demons by Daylight* (acquired by Derleth but not published until after Derleth's death).

For Lumley, whose work at first appeared to constitute rather straightforward Lovecraft/Derleth pastiches, Derleth was harsher and more demanding in his comments. In addition to providing criticism and advice regarding tone, narrative structure, and basic plotting, Derleth frequently instructed Lumley on proper use of Mythos assets—particularly those that Derleth himself had invented, such as the Wind Walker and the five-pointed stars of the Great Old Ones.[143] Early in their correspondence, Derleth even encouraged Lumley to consult the two Lin Carter glossaries published in *The Shuttered Room* so that Lumley might better master the facts of the Mythos.[144] Such instruction seems not, however, to reflect any particular concern on Derleth's part that the Mythos be employed "correctly"; rather, it stems from Derleth's sense that Lumley in fact *wanted* to produce the kind of systematized, asset-heavy fiction suggested by the glossaries. Although Derleth thus advised him how to do so, he regularly encouraged Lumley to abandon this approach entirely, entreating Lumley, for example, in one of his first letters, to put the interests of storytelling above that of "the customary Cthulhu Mythos jargon."[145] Indeed, Derleth—who published Lumley's first Mythos fiction in *The Arkham Collector* and then in Lumley's own *The Caller of the Black*—frequently exhorted Lumley to follow Campbell's example by "leaning" less on Lovecraft and his version of the Mythos.[146]

As the examples of Swoope, Campbell, and Lumley suggest, in the 1960s Derleth—after two decades of vigilantly monopolizing the rights to Mythos fiction—began to use his presumed position as rightsholder to recreate, albeit in a more controlled form, the communal production conditions that had generated the Mythos during Lovecraft's lifetime. He did so in large part by encouraging new writers to bend, expand, and extend the Mythos or even to disregard it entirely. But he also encouraged more established writers, such as Colin Wilson and Lin Carter, to make free use of the Mythos, employing it as their own aesthetic projects dictated (for Carter, pastiche and extreme intertextuality; for Wilson, brooding existential horror). Although the resulting network of writers was at once weaker (owing to the lack of connections between Derleth's correspondents) and stronger (owing to Derleth's function as publisher) than that of the Lovecraft Circle, it resembled the Circle in the way it employed the Mythos less as a set of narrative assets and comportments than as a means of community, tutelage, and friendship. Indeed, Campbell has described his relationship with Derleth in much the same terms that Robert Bloch and other young members of the Lovecraft Circle described theirs with Lovecraft: "[N]ot only did I find him [Derleth] unfailingly helpful and patient and encouraging when I most needed this support, but in retrospect I'm doubly impressed that he could find anything worth encouraging among the second-hand Lovecraft I sent him."[147]

Conclusion

Derleth died in 1973, leaving Lovecraft's writing without a steward and the Cthulhu Mythos without a manager. Although Arkham House continued to function as the "official" proprietor of Lovecraft's work for licensing and reprint purposes, with Derleth no longer there to police the use of Mythos assets—and with new, higher-profile publishing opportunities emerging for horror-fiction writers—"unauthorized" use of the Mythos quickly became common. Some of the earliest of this work was produced by writers whom Derleth had mentored or encouraged, and who fans might thus see as having been granted license to continue producing Mythos work. But as more and more Mythos work came to be released by other publishers, and as writers, editors, and managers discovered that unauthorized use of Mythos assets would elicit neither comment nor threat from Arkham House, the Mythos gradually came to be seen as part of the public domain.

That Arkham House allowed this to happen was not an oversight but rather a deliberate change in policy conceived by Forrest Hartmann, the lawyer to Derleth's heirs, as part of a complex legal defense in a lawsuit brought by Donald Wandrei for control of the publisher. Hartmann, in a move very much resembling that made by L. Sprague de Camp against the Conan property's first book publisher (which we will explore in detail in chapter 5), sought to invalidate Wandrei's request for the copyrights to Lovecraft's fiction by presenting evidence that Arkham House owned no such rights, the U.S. copyrights having long ago expired.[148] The multiple judges' rulings for this case are mostly irrelevant to the history of the Mythos—and indeed fans, readers, writers, and even publishers knew nothing of the lawsuit's details until decades after it had been settled out of court. What does matter, however, is its effect on the property's development after Derleth's death. With Arkham House no longer asserting ownership of Lovecraft's stories or the Mythos, and with no other entity appearing to have the moral or legal authority to do so, the property became *in practice* a public good, and by the end of the century creative workers—not just prose writers but also comic book illustrators, toy designers, video game makers, and filmmakers—had come to employ Mythos assets, without permission, to create thousands of new entertainment products.

That there has been such a flourishing of Mythos-based content since the public domain status of Lovecraft's fiction was realized should not surprise, for that is exactly what the public domain is intended to enable. As work by legal scholars such Paul Heald, Christopher Buccafusco, and

Rebcca Giblin has suggested, public domain texts appear to stay in circulation longer and be more easily accessible than protected texts.[149] What is surprising, however, is the extent to which this new, public Mythos preserves the general shape in which Derleth had fashioned it: quasi-systematized, with H. P. Lovecraft at its center. The property's "fall" into the public domain has thus resulted in neither the Mythos's dissolution as an intertextual property nor its transformation into something radically different from what Lovecraft or Derleth had orchestrated. Rather, the property (if the word is still appropriate to use) remains both identifiable and coherent, with a relatively stable set of narrative assets and storytelling comportments and a commitment (albeit sometimes critical) to Lovecraft's authorial genius or personality. Although the post-Arkham House history of the "property" is well beyond the scope of this chapter, such a history, I suspect, would demonstrate that the Mythos's continued stability has been achieved not in spite but *because of* the radically expanded mode of communal production that now governs it. Whatever the case, the continued longevity of the "property" suggests the limited role copyright may actually play in ensuring intertextual coherence. Indeed, even for properties still protected by copyright, the absence of copyright protection for mere ideas means that other mechanisms for protecting narrative assets are, in many cases, of equal or greater importance. As this chapter has demonstrated, the principle of authorial genius served as one such mechanism of protection during the modern copyright era. So too were the consumption and production practices of fans and readers that the principal informed. As we will see in the next chapter, however, the outline of a much more powerful mechanism—trademark law—was beginning to take shape on the horizon, though it would take many decades for courts and property managers to recognize its application to narrative-based property.

Before moving on, however, it is worth asking whether it would be possible for a multiauthor, transmedia or multitext story world to emerge today, in the twenty-first century, along a route similar to that taken by the Cthulhu Mythos during the modern copyright era. The answer, for better or worse, is *probably not.* Although the Romantic figure of the author continues to loom large today in property management, the moral and property rights associated with it are now less hazy and ad hoc, more the product of formal contract and business strategy. In the comics industry, for example, the lawsuits of famous creators or their heirs, combined with a more competitive market for talent and a more vocal, activist fanbase, has led to the formal institutionalization of some kinds of moral right with respect to creators: textual credit given, at least by DC Comics, to original creators and a quasi-royalty (paid by both Marvel Comics and DC) to creators whose IP is adapted into other media.[150] And in all forms of media, amateurs and professionals, as well as fans and even casual consumers, have become more cognizant of the value of intellectual property rights. The kind of informal, improvised collaborations and repeated acts of disowning that characterized the development of the Cthulhu Mythos thus appears largely unthinkable today, even by well-meaning creators invested in some form of communal production.

That said, the horror genre itself has been irrevocably shaped by the Cthulhu Mythos and that property's idiosyncratic development. Although usually less freewheeling than during the modern copyright era, the welcomed lending and/or borrowing of certain kinds of narratological assets (names, places, monsters, Gods, books, etc.) has come to be a feature of late-twenty-first-century horror, as exemplified by such varied work as Thunderstorm Press's "Black Voltage Vs." series; PS Publishing's *Darker Companions*; Tim Seeley, Aaron Campbell, and Jim Terry's *West of Sundown*; Double Take Comics' comics universe; and Brian Keene and Christopher Golden's upcoming *The Drive-In: Multiplex.* What is more, the Cthulhu Mythos itself remains a narratological keystone for a tremendous range of horror fiction in all media, which regularly borrow from, alter, and expand upon the property's narratological assets in ways that require no rights-clearing and typically establish little to no new property rights on the revised (and revitalized) narrative Mythos assets. Examples include Caitlin Kiernan's *Houses under the Sea*; Matt Ruff's book and HBO television series *Lovecraft Country*; Chaoism's Call of Cthulhu roleplaying game; and From Software's *Bloodborne.* This is the legacy of Lovecraft as unified author figure, but it is also the legacy of Lovecraft's vision for the horror genre; for when horror is defined in terms of cosmicism—that is, as humans' encounters with phenomena that exceed our capacity for comprehension—then we are likewise dealing with narratological assets that by their very nature reject the specificity needed to secure them by copyright law. Cosmic horror's resistance to twenty-first-century norms of intellectual property development is thus not just a product of the communal form of production from which it originated but also of the thematic and storytelling aim of that production. Paradoxically, Lovecraft's fiction—so interested in questions of inheritance—has helped to give rise to a kind of narrative genre that resists controlling author-Gods, spreads rhizomatically, and continually invites writers, young and old, to make it their own.

CHAPTER 4

When Is a Copyright Not a Copyright?

Unfair Competition and Cartoon and Comics Characters in the Modern Copyright Era

> "A legal concept begins its career as smooth and as perfect as an egg. But if the concept has economic or social consequences and leads to controversy and contention between interest groups, litigation can batter and bruise it out of shape; or turn it into a rat's nest of complexity."
>
> —Lawrence Friedman, A History of American Law[1]

As the previous chapters have demonstrated, copyright, particularly as it has applied to literary, motion picture, and broadcasting works, has always been a complicated area of U.S. law, especially in the decades of the twentieth century that constitute what this book names the modern copyright era. But for all its complexity, the law was relatively coherent and consistent. Even in cases involving literary characters like Sam Spade, the governing legal logic was clear and comprehendible despite its application being something of an art form. Such was not the case, however, when it came to what entertainment professionals and the general public called "cartoon characters": characters that originated in comic strips, comic books, or animated films. From near the beginning of the twentieth century to today, courts have applied—sometimes implicitly, sometimes explicitly—a radically different conception of copyright law to lawsuits involving such characters and the texts they appeared in than they have done to those involving other kinds of characters and texts. Beginning in the late 1930s, well-positioned commentators routinely bewailed the split in the case law, with Kenneth Umbreit arguing, for example, in an influential 1939 piece for *The University of Pennsylvania Law Review*, that the reasoning contained in the court decisions involving cartoon characters was circular and difficult to square with the more general principles of copyright law.[2] For all their opaque reasoning, however, the decisions' practical significance, taken as a whole, was unmistakable. As Walter Derenberg, one of the founders of the Copyright Society of the U.S.A., observed bemusedly in a 1953 piece titled "Copyright No-Man's Land," "it is a strange fact that the originator of a cartoon or the person permitted to exploit it probably enjoys broader all-around legal protection than any other person in the law."[3]

Since the 1990s, it has become fashionable for legal scholars to cite the divergent case law as evidence of the need for a new *copyright in characters*, which would resolve the divergence and forfend the sometimes shaky legal reasoning that has accompanied cartoon cases by granting common law or (ideally) statutory protection to characters themselves and not just the texts in which they appear.[4] The decisions in the cartoon cases, which often seemed to have covertly granted such protection, are now thus regularly represented as "correct" or "fair" despite their idiosyncratic reasoning, and not as the aberrations earlier commentators saw them as.

This chapter parts ways with contemporary legal scholars by bracketing off the needs, real or imagined, of twenty-first-century media producers and instead adopting a perspective closer to that of early commentators like Umbreit and Derenberg, who wrestled with the question of why cartoon characters were repeatedly granted by judges what, at the time, seemed to be exorbitant protections. This chapter offers an answer, demonstrating, through the anlysis of three legal cases with precedential significance, how legal actors (both formal and informal) imported principles into copyright law that we would today recognize as more properly belonging to unfair competition or trademark law. This importation occurred in part because, with few exceptions, legal actors did not yet conceive of an action for unfair competition as a reliable means of protecting (or, to be more precise, *constituting*) literary and artistic property. Creators, business executives, lawyers, and judges thus regularly smuggled into copyright disputes principles that, from a later vantage point, appear not to belong there, in the process producing a confused and frequently confusing case law. That they did so was partly the result of what we might call a category error: legal actors took for granted that legal disputes involving the alleged "copying" of fictional characters were, because they dealt with copyrighted material, by definition copyright cases. For many judges, this category error was reinforced by a wary judicial conservatism: few courts were willing to risk potentially undermining the regulatory power of copyright law (or worse, being overturned on appeal) by introducing a new, judge-made form of IP with its own separate rights and responsibilities. This was not an unfounded worry, for as we will see the differing "rules" that governed the two kinds of intellectual property that then existed—copyrights and patents—were already in the early twentieth century beginning to create logical problems for courts adjudicating copyright suits. Copyright law was thus gradually stretched out of shape, at least for cartoon characters, as courts and legal actors applied it to enforce rights and protections that conflicted with both the letter of the copyright statute and the common law principles (such as that of the idea-expression dichotomy) that had developed to enforce it.

In demonstrating the law's confused approach to cartoon characters, I do not wish to suggest that there was something inevitable about its confusion. The common law did not passively reflect an inchoate entertainment industry's own preconceptions and priorities. Lawyers and judges had agency here. And yet this agency was often constrained by the basic logic of the U.S. legal system. This chapter's second goal is thus to illustrate how both the adversarial structure of the U.S. court system and the practical employment of stare decisis (i.e., precedent) tended to aggravate the IP problems posed by cartoon characters, resulting in a case law (and by extension lay knowledge) that was frequently unclear, contradictory, and confusing. Together these two features of U.S. law at times give tremendous weight to arbitrary and/or contingent aspects of formal disputes: the skill of counsel, the precedent that is deemed controlling, the language of an opinion, the temperament of a judge, even the personal conduct of a party to the suit. This is by no means a novel observation,[5] but it is one that has posed problems for legal historiography, and for this reason has been frequently ignored by historical accounts of IP law. This chapter, like the book's other chapters, aims to resolve—or perhaps sidestep—some of these problems, laying out a history in which arbitrariness and contingency have as much causal force as logic and necessity.

Unlike the previous chapters, each of which introduced one or more of the modern copyright regime's key legal principles, here the emphasis is on the *absence* of a legal principle: unfair competition/trademark law. In focusing on its absence, the chapter is not intended to suggest that unfair competition law, so important to narrative-based property management in the late twentieth and early twenty-first centuries, *should have been* part of the modern copyright regime's approach to narrative-based property. Its argument is rather that the absence of the principle was itself a kind of presence, a constitutive aspect of how the regime functioned as a system. The principle of unfair competition was thus not something that was merely missing, and thus easy to add in later; its absence was built into the fundamental framework of how modern copyright law worked.

This chapter consists of four sections. In the first, I briefly introduce the missing principle of unfair competition law by laying out its basic differences from copyright law. Following that, I devote one section each to three important legal cases, starting with the earliest and ending with the latest. The first of these cases, *Star Co. v. Press Publishing Co.*, is not a copyright case, nor does it seem, on a strict reading, to involve a dispute over narrative-based property.[6] I nevertheless begin with it for two reasons. First, the case provides an exceptionally clear picture of how cartoon characters were treated by creators, publishers, and courts at the beginning of the modern copyright era. As we will see, at this time the rights to a comic strip artist's continuing labor were often seen as more valuable than the characters the artist created. Second, the case has regularly been misrepresented in scholarship as one of the earliest instances of a lawsuit over the rights to a cartoon property, thus granting it a kind of lay precedential value that it does not appear to deserve. In its examination of the case, the chapter thus offers a helpful corrective to the early history of cartoon characters and intellectual property law.

The second and third cases discussed below directly concern copyright. *King Features Syndicate v. Fleischer*, concerning an allegedly illegal toy version of a cartoon horse, established the precedent by which cartoon characters would come to receive greater rights under copyright law than characters from other media.[7] My account of this case reconstructs the way case law was used (or perhaps misused) by the plaintiff in order to persuade the appellate court of the defendants' guilt. *Detective Comics v. Bruns Publications*, concerning an alleged copy of Superman, further cemented the precedent established in *King Features Syndicate v. Fleischer*.[8] It also reveals how the trial court judge's disposition determined the outcome of the case, not only as decided by that judge but even by circuit judges on appeal.

Before we proceed, however, two quick notes about the prose are in order. First, in keeping with the language of the decades about which I am writing here, I use the term *cartoon character* throughout the chapter to refer to any character created by a visual artist using pencil, ink, or paint. Such a character may thus have originated in an animated film (what is referred to today as a *cartoon*), but it could also have originated in a comic strip or comic book. Indeed, none of the cases described in this chapter involve cartoon characters in the twenty-first-century sense. For the purposes of clarity and precision, however, I also occasionally use the terms *comic-strip character* or *comic-book character*, even though such terms would most likely not have been employed as general categories before the 1940s.

Second, the particular details of the cases recounted here present difficulties for the consistent employment of stylistic rules governing titles of works. For early comic strips, series titles were often, as we will see, post hoc constructions: they were not reliably associated with individual installments of the strip in either a legal sense (i.e., copyright registration) or an aesthetic sense (i.e., printed somewhere on the strip). Individual published installments of the series traditionally referred to as The Yellow Kid or Hogan's Alley, for example, did not originally contain such titles. Until the 1920s (at which point such titles began appearing at the top of published strips), series titles were thus extratextual and extralegal constructions. Indeed, the series titles' reliance upon the names of specific narrative assets (usually characters) already points to the confusion that the law would have in conceptualizing disputes involving them: was the title signifying a text (and if so, which one?) or a character? In an effort to capture the conditions for such confusion in my prose, I do not italicize the names of series titles except when the works in questions were actually published under such titles; I merely capitalize them. I should also note that although I use the word "series" in its twenty-first-century sense, in the 1910s and 1920s the word was typically used to refer to what we today would call an individual instalment or strip. An early reader might thus have referred to the July 21, 1922, installment of Barney Google as a *series*. The earlier usage reflects the industrial and aesthetic understanding at the time, which viewed a comic strip as a "series" of drawings (what today we would call *panels*).

A related but ultimately different problem involves the correct treatment of newspaper titles. Confusingly, the title of a newspaper is sometimes also the title of the company that publishes the paper. At some points, the same proper noun might thus be italicized or not depending upon its meaning in a sentence. When I refer to a newspaper as such (i.e., a printed work), I italicize its name. When I refer to a newspaper as a business enterprise—as, for example, an employer—I do not italicize its name but merely capitalize it.

The (Missing) Principle of Unfair Competition/Trademark Law

A trademark is a visual mark that designates (at least under "traditional" legal thinking[9]) a good's "origin," that is, the source responsible for its production, thereby communicating information about the product to potential customers. These visual marks, which are placed upon a package, a label, an advertisement, or the good itself, can include logos, illustrations, or words, such as the name of a product or firm. When a mark is used to indicate the source of a *service*, as opposed to a good, it is sometimes called a service mark rather than a trademark. The legal principles and procedures underlying both kinds of mark, however, are generally the same (despite slightly different statutory histories), such that, when scholars speak of "trademark law" in the abstract, they are usually speaking of both.[10] Although something like a trademark was employed by merchants and guilds as early as the Middle Ages, trademark law in the modern sense did not emerge until the nineteenth century, at which time it developed in court (and was eventually codified by statute) as a means of preventing a specific kind of fraud committed by businesses.[11] As the U.S. Supreme Court explained in *Canal Co. v. Clark* (1872), "The first appropriator of a name or device pointing to his ownership, or which, by being associated with articles of trade, has acquired an understood reference to the originator, or manufacturer of the articles, is injured whenever another adopts the same name or device for similar articles, because such adoption is in effect representing falsely that the productions of the latter are those of the former."[12] Put more simply, the fraud consists of falsely representing one's products as the products of another. Because consumers are misled by such fraud, scholars have often located the legal basis for trademarks on a theory of consumer protection.[13] As in *Canal Co. v. Clark*, however, the plaintiff is almost exclusively a producer (i.e., business), acting to protect its own profits and/or market share—not a consumer.

Because trademark law functions to protect businesses—specifically the marks that represent them—rather than ideas or inventions, modern trademark law has often been considered a branch of what is called "unfair competition law." The law of unfair competition, not to be confused with antitrust law (which approaches competition from a broader public policy perspective), originated in a 1706 English case involving one man ruining the business of another through what the court found to be illegitimate means.[14] Although this case did not involve any sort of attempted misattribution, by the early twentieth century misattribution or what came to be called "passing off" was one of the two main kinds of infringement dealt with as unfair competition.[15] Such an infringement almost always concerned the appropriation or imitation by one business of another's trademark, such that a complaint of "passing off" under unfair competition law was invariably also a complaint of trademark infringement. Courts thus regularly treated the latter as a species of the former—as in *Hanover Star Milling Co. v. Metcalf* (1916), where Justice Mahlon Pitney observed succinctly that "the common law of trade-marks is but a part of the broader law of unfair competition."[16]

The link between trademark law and unfair competition is worth stressing because a trademark, though today commonly considered a species of intellectual property, is fundamentally different from a copyright or a patent. Unlike copyrights and patents, trademarks are not recognized by the U.S. Constitution; instead, they are a product of common law, codified by state and federal statutes, with some of the latter originally prompted by the treaty demands of international trade. A trademark is also not really—at least not during the modern copyright era—a property right, even in the temporally limited sense that a copyright or patent is, as trademarks are traditionally both provisional and inalienable. The owner of a trademark must continually employ the trademark to maintain its validity, and the owner cannot sell or transfer the mark (at least in theory) unless the sale or transfer includes the source (such as a factory) the mark has come to represent. What is more, the validity of the mark—that is, the right to exclude others from using or imitating it—is contingent upon the specific circumstances accompanying an infringement claim, circumstances that include public perception of the mark's meaning with regard to its source. For this reason, a trademark infringement claim does not require (and has never required) the mark in question to have been formally registered; nor does registration of a trademark establish an indisputable right (again, at least in theory) to restrict others from using the mark. As Justice Helen Nies explained in her decision for *In re DC Comics, Inc.* (1982), "Trademark rights can only be found to exist or not to exist at a particular point in time, and registration neither extends the period of one's right of exclusive use nor guarantees protection at any time in the future."[17] A trademark is thus a very different kind of intellectual property—if it is to be considered property at all—from a copyright.

This brief description of trademark law admittedly simplifies a branch of law that not only has a long and tortuous history but has also become in the twenty-first century especially complex, replete with its own abstruse (and controversial) principles, such as trademark incontestability and dilution, as well as jurisdiction-based differences.[18] During most of the period with which this book is concerned, however, trademark law was significantly underdeveloped, especially when it came to narrative-based property. Lawsuits involving such property rarely involved trademark claims, and when they did, they were straightforward and conservatively construed (dealing, for example, with a fictional work's title, advertising, or trade dress). Indeed, for most of the modern copyright era—and especially prior to the implementation of the Lanham Act in 1946, which sought to systematize what had become a confusing mix of state unfair-competition laws[19]—trademark law did not seem appropriate for the protection of stories, characters, and other fictional "assets," the "theft" of which was invariably pursued in federal court under copyright law. Indeed, for most narrative-based properties during the modern copyright era, including that of literature, film, and radio, copyright law seemed sufficient for preventing trespass and theft. Comic strips and comic books, however, posed unique problems to the application of copyright law, problems that stemmed from the two media's respective forms and from the rapid-paced, iterative mode that characterized their production and publication. Although the industry nevertheless relied upon copyright law to protect characters originating in these media, the problems led legal actors to reimagine and in part remake copyright law—at least as it applied to cartoons—along the lines of what we would today recognize as trademark and unfair competition law.

Star Co. v. Press Publishing Co.

Descriptions of intellectual property disputes feature so regularly in the histories of U.S. comic strips and comic books that they appear to be one of the primary means by which comics history has come to be narrated. Inevitably, the narrations take up a David-versus-Goliath perspective, with the historian's sympathy typically falling on the disenfranchised comics creator, in spite of—or perhaps because of—courts' tendencies to rule on behalf of his much better resourced employer. For early comic-strip disputes in particular, as Mark Winchester has observed in "Litigation and Early Comic Strips," the "prototypical conflict" is represented as involving a "rebellious cartoonist and a greedy newspaper in a bitter court battle."[20] As Winchester's essay goes on to demonstrate, however, such histories are historiographically problematic, relying upon multiple references to lawsuits but refraining, almost as a rule, from citing actual opinions or other evidence of legal action.[21] Winchester, although exhibiting a healthy skepticism toward such histories, nevertheless refrains from dismissing them as apocryphal; instead, in acts of speculative generosity, he tries to imagine the legal issues that such cases might have involved and to let such imagining guide him in search of material evidence.

To his credit, Winchester's method succeeds in dredging up sources (court opinions, advertisements, comic strips, etc.) that can be marshalled to fill in some of the comic strip's longstanding historical blank spots. The result is a revised history that, though still patchy and uncertain, feels considerably more reliable than what it has replaced. Unfortunately, it is also a history that suggests that Winchester's initial diagnosis of the historiographical problem was incomplete. While it is true that earlier accounts had failed to consult material sources, they had also fundamentally misconceived what the law is and how it functions. The law, in these accounts, had been imagined as a simple, historically stable system of formal rules, which courts applied straightforwardly to settle disputes of an individual (as opposed to social, public, or industrial) nature. Having mistaken the problem, Winchester's reconstructed history is doomed to repeat it: his acts of legal speculation employ this same conception of the law. Shored up by previously absent sources, the results seem sometimes plausible, as, for example, when Winchester describes the legal strictures that likely governed comics artist R. F. Outcault's work with The Yellow Kid for The New York Journal. But they often feel overly abstract and mechanistic, as though the formal law, at this early point in comic-strip history, were not only settled but could be counted on to reliably govern individual behavior. Occasionally, the article's taking for granted of legal truth even leads to outright mistakes, as when, for example, Winchester states that titles and names of characters could be copyrighted or when he incorrectly glosses *New York Herald Co. v. Star Co.*—which does not address the question of trademarking or copyrighting characters—as ruling that "the characters [of the Buster Brown strip] were not tangible enough to merit copyright or trademark."[22] The historiographical problem that needs solving, it would seem, is not just an absence of references; it is also a failure to conceive of the law as inchoate, in-process, or even (perhaps) outright confused.

Of the multiple disputes Winchester's piece examines, the battle for control of the Katzenjammer Kids strip receives the least attention. This is likely because the dispute is, in theory, the most easily verified. One need only read (as Winchester does) New York Supreme Court Judge Ingraham Scott's 1914 opinion for *Star Co. v. Press Pub. Co.* to learn what the case was about and discover how comic-strip history has gotten it wrong.[23] The case, which revolved around what we would today call a "noncompete clause" in an employment contract, has been from the late 1940s to the present day repeatedly described—even by the occasional legal scholar—as centering on artist Rudolph Dirks's rights to the comic strip characters he created.[24] Let us take, as a typical example of such description, the account of "The Lawsuit" provided by Jim Lowe's *The Katzenjammer Kids* fansite:

> The short version is this: After drawing a weekly Katzenjammer Kids page for 15 years or so, Rudolph Dirks wanted to take a break, something like Garry Trudeau and others have done in recent times. His boss at the Hearst newspaper syndicate didn't see it that way. Dirks left anyway and his duties were assigned to other artists.
>
> Dirks felt that he owned the rights to his characters and a lawsuit followed. The popular strip dropped out of the Sunday funnies for more than a year. Ultimately, the Katzenjammer Kids were continued for the Hearst papers by Harold H. Knerr, and the court awarded Dirks the right to continue drawing his characters, so long as they were not entitled "The Katzenjammer Kids." This, he proceeded to do for the rival Pulitzer newspapers.
>
> The end result was that two separate, but very similar strips ("The Original Katzenjammer Kids" and "The Captain and the Kids") ran in competing Sunday papers for more than a century.[25]

Other accounts are identical in substance, although some further characterize the lawsuit as "notorious," "legendary," or "well-publicized," with one additionally claiming that the "battle became a precedent for many cartoonists in trouble with their newspaper or syndicate."[26]

Some of the features of this history—the presenting of Dirks as the aggrieved party, the claim for the trial's importance—are easy to explain: they come from an essay written (or so it would seem) by Dirks himself.

In 1947, in celebration of the Katzenjammer Kids' fiftieth anniversary, United Features Syndicate (which had taken over the distribution of Dirks's strip from the New York World in 1931) issued a press release that included a biographical essay ostensibly authored by the comic strip's creator. In it, Dirks presents himself as an exhausted cartoonist who, after having been pressured into signing a contract with the New York Journal that he did not want, was hounded by the Journal's editor while traveling through Europe on vacation.[27] Although never stated outright, the essay strongly implies that Dirks left William Randolph Hearst's Journal for Joseph Pulitzer's World because the former had mistreated him. The resulting lawsuit, which Dirks frames as concerning his right to work for The World, "made front-page news," he claims, for a year.[28]

Ironically, given the article's framing of the lawsuit in terms of an author's right to his creations, the text of the article was not in fact written by Dirks at all but was lifted almost verbatim from a portion of early comic-strip historian Martin Sheridan's *Comics and Their Creators* (1942) (Dirks's edits were largely limited to changing the original third-person pronouns to first-person pronouns).[29] The essay, both as published by Dirks and by Sheridan (whose book was regularly reprinted up through the 1970s) seems to have established for subsequent fans and historians the basic terms of Dirks's dispute with Star Company's American Journal.[30] Jim Walsh's article on Dirks for a 1953 issue of *Hobbies—The Magazine for Collectors*, to give but one example, explicitly bases its account on the 1947 essay, which Walsh takes to have been authored by Dirks.[31]

Historians' reliance upon Dirks's/Sheridan's essay, however, cannot account for the eventual transformation of what was quite explicitly a case about the enforceability of an employment contract—as Dirks and Sheridan both characterized it—into a case about intellectual property rights to fictional characters. It is possible we are dealing here with the historian's version of a game of telephone. As information about Dirks was relayed through time and across sources, errors accidentally slipped in. More likely, however, latter day scholars and fans were struck by what appeared to them a historical puzzle: how was it that there were published, simultaneously for multiple decades, two competing comic strips featuring identical characters, near-identical situations, and extremely similar art styles? The received information about Dirks's lawsuit not only did not seem to account for it but also seemed hardly to acknowledge the situation as legally noteworthy. To most late-twentieth- and early-twenty-first-century observers, it would be inconceivable that this puzzling state of affairs did not involve some kind of dispute over IP rights. And so the late-twentieth- and early-twenty-first-century solution was projected by historians backwards: what had been a legal tussle over a noncompete clause was reimagined as a battle for the rights to Hans, Fritz, and the other characters that appeared in Dirks's comic strip.

If *Star Co. v. Press Publishing Co.* was not a dispute over the rights to narrative-based property, what was its legal significance? And how might its details help us understand how intellectual property law applied in practice to cartoon characters at the start of the modern copyright era? The facts of the dispute, accepted by both sides, are as follows. In 1897, Rudolph Dirks—then an aspiring and largely unknown comics artist—was hired by Rudolph Block, editor of the comics section of Hearst's *New York Journal*, to develop a comic strip modeled upon German artist Wilhelm Busch's popular illustrated story, *Max und Moritz: Eine Bubengeschichte in sieben Streichen*, which had been published in the United States as *Max and Maurice, a Juvenile History in Seven Tricks* since at least the 1870s. On December 12, 1897, The Journal published the first of Dirks's strips in its Sunday comics magazine section. The two-row, six-panel strip, sans captions or balloons, depicted three unidentified boys playing a prank on an older man in revenge for his having mean-spiritedly sprayed them with a garden hose. The strip, which has traditionally been referred to as The Katzenjammer Kids, quickly became a hit, and Dirks a national—and then international—celebrity, whose pay increased from $25 per single strip when he first started to $200 per strip in 1912.

By the end of 1911, however, Dirks had begun to tire of the steady demands of producing the high-profile weekly strip. With his current contract with The Journal set to expire the following October, Dirks informed Block of his desire to take a vacation the following year. A new contract was developed that would, in theory, enable him to do so without the newspaper having to pause the strip. For three years, beginning October 20, 1912, The Journal agreed to pay Dirks $250 per week in exchange for "a page series of 'Katzenjammers' or such other series as may be desired by the Star Company."[32] But it also agreed, in an unusual clause, to accept up to fifty-two strips the year prior to the start of the contract, for which it would pay $250 "for each and every series upon its receipt and approval."[33] Since Dirks would already during that year have been producing for The Journal (under the terms of his old contract) a weekly strip at a $200 pay rate, this special clause, in essence, would have allowed him to turn in and be paid in advance for strips due during the first year of the new contract.

The exact reason for the insertion of this clause was disputed in court. Dirks claimed that, desiring a trip abroad where he could "learn better how to paint," he had informed Block that he wanted to "be free from any regular work" after his present contract expired on October 19, 1912.[34] Both Block and Solomon Carvalho, president of the Star Company, assured him this "could be arranged," and, after several rounds of interviews, inserted the special clause so as to give Dirks the "privilege . . . of submitting drawings in advance."[35] Carvalho, however, denied at trial that he had ever "told Mr. Dirks that it could be arranged" nor that "it was with that understanding that the contract was drawn."[36] The clause, Block explained, was inserted to provide Dirks with the funds he needed to go to Europe: "Mr. Dirks stated to me that he would like to have a year in Europe, but that he could not afford this unless some way could be devised for securing him an income during said period."[37]

Whatever the reasoning behind the clause, Dirks found himself unable to avail himself of the opportunity it offered and, claiming that The Journal had "entirely departed from its contract with me," proceeded to resign by letter on January 1, 1913.[38] From that point on, Dirks ceased submitting drawings to or being paid by the Star Company, and by March 1913 his work stopped appearing in the company's papers.[39] In May, Dirks was approached by Pulitzer's Press Publishing Company, which offered to hire him to create strips for its paper, the *World*. After Dirks informed Block that he "had accepted a new position . . . and intended to begin drawing for the 'World' very soon," Star Company filed suit in New York State court against Dirks and the Press Publishing Company, alleging that Dirks had violated his contract—which required him, if "unwilling or incapacitated from furnishing to the Star Company the weekly series," to refrain from "furnish[ing] any drawings to any other newspaper or publication" until the contract's end date[40]—and that the Press Publishing Company had knowingly induced him to do so.[41] A request for a preliminary injunction to restrain Dirks from working for the Press Publishing Company was quickly heard and granted—and then affirmed on appeal (albeit with two judges dissenting) in a per curiam decision.[42] When the actual trial finally concluded on January 16, 1914, the court found for Star Company, granting it injunctive relief against Dirks until his contract expired in October 1915.[43] On appeal, however, the New York State Supreme Court came to Dirks's rescue, overturning the ruling and finding for the defendants on May 15, 1914.[44] Shortly thereafter, Dirks's cartoons featuring the Katzenjammer Kids began appearing in the Press Publishing Company's newspapers while Dirks's strip for Star Company was taken over by the relatively unknown artist Harold Knerr.

On the face of it, this was not a dispute over intellectual property. Neither the word *copyright* nor *trademark* appears even once in the bill of complaint or appellate court decisions (nor any of the other case files I was able to review). Rather, it was a dispute over the enforceability of what the law refers to as a *negative covenant*: a contractual provision in which a signee promises *not* to do something—in this case, Dirks's promise not to sell drawings to other newspapers. Although Dirks had, by signing the contract, ostensibly agreed to the covenant, his signature was not by itself dispositive. Under common law principles originating in *Lumley v. Wagner*, an English case decided in 1852, state courts determined the legality of such a covenant (i.e., whether or not they would enforce it) by evaluating its "reasonableness" in restraint of trade.[45] As Judge John W. Goff explained in his opinion granting Star Company a preliminary injunction, the mere existence of the covenant "is not controlling on the court, which will decide that question on the merits, irrespective of what the parties may agree to."[46]

To persuade the court, Star Company relied upon two arguments. The first, and most important, was that the services Dirks had contractually agreed to provide the newspaper were, as the contract itself stated, "special, unique and extraordinary."[47] This meant that his work as a comic-strip artist was so inimitable that there was no other artist Star Company could have hired to replace him. Some U.S. courts (including those in New York State) had at this time begun to require, as a condition for even considering granting this kind of injunction, that the labor in question must be, in some sense, irreplaceable.[48] If Dirks's labor were considered replaceable, Star Company might thus have had no case. The company's second argument was, essentially, that Dirks had acted in bad faith. His contract with Star Company had not only granted him a high rate of pay but had been specially developed to accommodate Dirks's desire to travel—and Dirks had found it satisfactory until the opportunity arose for him to receive even higher pay from one of Star Company's competitors. Dirks's claim that Star Company had not honored its side of the contract, the company contested, was merely a post hoc justification for breaking his contract.

The defense relied, although with some disagreement, on three arguments. For its part, Press Publishing Company denied that Dirks's labor was "special, unique, and extraordinary"—thus disputing the grounds on which an injunction might be considered. Dirks, however, disagreed, perhaps because he failed to understand the legal meaning of the phrase and took it as a judgment of his ability. Whatever his reason, he was nevertheless willing to point out in his answering affidavits some of the inconsistencies in Star Company's characterization of his labor as such. For example, noting that Block regularly attempted to direct Dirks's drawing and, in the year preceding the start of the contract, continually rejected his work as unsatisfactory, Dirks snidely observed, "under the directions that were given me, and that I was informed I must comply with, my drawings would not have been unique or special, but, on the contrary, very ordinary."[49]

Second, Dirks averred that, by placing unreasonable and unprecedented impediments in the way of his submitting work in advance, Star Company had itself acted in bad faith and thus failed to live up to its end of the contract. In legal terms, Dirks was thus arguing—as had by that time become a common strategy in cases involving contractual clauses of this kind—that the negative covenant was unenforceable because of "lack of mutuality." "Mutuality," as Harlan F. Stone explained in a 1916 essay for *Columbia Law Review*, "refers to the rule very generally applied in equity that specific performance of a contract will not be decreed unless the defendant has received or the court is in a position to give to the defendant all that he is entitled to receive under the contract in exchange for the performance of it on his part."[50] In other words, a court of equity—which is the court one petitions in order to force a party to perform or refrain from performing a specific action (as opposed to a court of law, which is the court where one seeks monetary damages)—will not order a defendant to perform part of a contract unless the plaintiff has performed or is capable of being ordered by a court to perform its part of the contract.[51]

Third, and perhaps most ingeniously, Dirks argued that he had never been an employee at all and the contract was not an employment contract. "The custom has been merely to pay me upon an accepted drawing," explained Dirks. "When they did not accept a drawing then I received no pay whatever. . . . [T]he 'American' has never for years past tendered any pay to me by way of salary, except as it has actually accepted drawings."[52] Although it is not clear, based upon the documents I have access to (which do not include the actual legal briefs submitted by counsel), how seriously Dirks and his lawyer meant this argument, the argument pointed to a profound problem with how comics creators were contracted, which would remain unsolved until the very end of the modern copyright era (and which would, as a consequence, give rise to multiple legal disputes up to the present day over creators' rights to comics IP): were comics creators employees selling their labor or independent contractors selling their art?[53]

Based upon the opinion Judge Goff wrote granting the plaintiff's motion for a preliminary injunction, Goff was unimpressed by the defendants' arguments. Although recognizing that the contract was poorly drafted in its "promiscuous and interchangeable use of the words 'employment,' 'services,' and 'purchase,'" he found that its intent to function as an employment contract had been clear to both parties at the time of signing.[54] Nor did he doubt that Dirks's services were unique and extraordinary, for it was not the creation of a comic strip that Star Company had contracted for but the creation of a comic strip by Dirks specifically, whom had long since "become identified" with The Journal and its Katzenjammer Kids series.[55] As for mutuality, the judge had little patience for the "exhaustive" review of the common law both sides offered, which he concluded was mainly "illustrative of the skill of the advocates in supporting their contentions by quotations from the same authorities."[56] There was in fact mutuality here, Goff concluded, and the negative covenant should be enforced.

On appeal, the New York supreme court judges, after some initial uncertainty (a divided court had affirmed the preliminary injunction[57]), denied that a permanent injunction was warranted. This was not because Judge Goff had been wrong on the question of mutuality, "a question upon which the court was not agreed on the former appeal, and is not agreed at present," but for a technical reason unrelated to the arguments put forth by either party.[58] In the original contract the clause requiring Dirks to refrain from working for a competitor in the case of his "incapacity or unwillingness to furnish the whole or part" of the comic strip was additionally modified by an addendum making it "optional," in such circumstances, to "the Star Company whether it shall purchase any of said series from Mr. Dirks on the terms and conditions aforesaid."[59] Star Company had likely intended this addendum to provide it protection from potential inconsistency or capriciousness on the part of Dirks, for the newspaper could have otherwise been put in the bad situation of finding itself obliged to buy sporadic drawings from Dirks when what it had wanted to buy from him was a three-year series. However reasonable its intent, the state supreme court concluded that the addendum, by its mere inclusion, rendered the negative covenant unenforceable, since the clause as a whole "imposes no fixed and definite obligation under Dirks to furnish drawings to plaintiff, or upon plaintiff to accept such drawings as Dirks might offer, and no obligation upon plaintiff's part to pay Dirks anything unless he shall furnish drawings which are accepted."[60] The result is a negative covenant "unsupported by any positive covenant" binding the plaintiff, a set of circumstances that under the basic rules of New York State contract law rendered that part of the contract unenforceable.[61] The decision does not seem to have prompted much comment by law reviews—nor was ever it much cited by future judges—although at least one commentator found the court's reasoning flawed.[62]

Given that the lawsuit had ultimately nothing to do with the Katzenjammer Kids as intellectual property, what are we to make of the peculiar state of affairs following the trial, which saw the Kids live on for decades in two different strips, drawn by two different artists and published by two competing newspapers? If a court did not grant each party some sort of right to the strip, why did the parties allow this? Why wasn't there, as comic strip historians have imagined there was, a copyright or trademark suit over the rights to the strip?

Perhaps the most important reason—and it is a reason that may be difficult for present-day comics fans to appreciate—is that, for the first few decades of the twentieth century, copying was rampant within the comic-strip/newspaper industry. The content of strips was routinely imitated—not just the characters and situations but even the general art style. Dirks's Katzenjammer Kids is a case in point. Until Dirks came to work for The World in 1914, the paper had been publishing Gene Carr's Step-Brothers for seven years. Clearly modeled upon the Katzenjammers, Carr's strip featured two mischievous boys who resembled in appearance Dirks's Hans and Fritz and who also, like them, spoke in a German accent. Nate Collier's The Kelly Kids, syndicated by World Color Printing from 1924 to 1939, similarly centered on the mischief-making of two boys, Tim and Tom, though this time of Irish not German descent. But the most flagrantly imitative of them all was Knerr's Der Feinheimer Twins, a straight up clone of Dirks's strip, which Keystone Syndicate had been distributing for years before Star Company hired Knerr to replace Dirks.

Why didn't comic strip creators and/or their publishers bring copyright suites to stop such copying? There are three reasons, the first and most simple being that up until the end of the 1930s publishers were sloppy with registering comic strips (and comic books) for copyright. In part their sloppiness was a result of the strict demands made by the modern copyright regime's heavily formalized system (described in chapter 1), which—for daily and weekly strips—was especially burdensome. Failure to copyright even one strip correctly could result in significant problems in pursuing a copyright suit down the line (as occurred, for example, in *National Comics Publications v. Fawcett Publications*).[63]

Second, and more in line with comic-strip creators' own thinking at the time, imitative strips—even grossly imitative strips such as Knerr's Der Feinhemier Twins—were not perceived as copyright violations until the end of the 1930s. Copyright law was understood to protect against someone reproducing the actual drawings of a strip (in the way one might reproduce the actual words of a prose story), but that is not what imitative strips did. They reproduced a type of character, a kind of situation, and/or an artistic style. Although an early-twentieth-century court might nevertheless have found such reproduction to be a violation of copyright law, the legal argument for doing so would not have been straightforward, and, as early cases involving the imitation of dramatic/literary characters and plots suggested, the verdict in such a case would almost always have been something of a crapshoot.[64]

But all this, at least during the twentieth century's first few decades, would have been of minimal importance because, in the final analysis, what mattered to a publisher was the comic strip creator, not the content of the strip. There was thus no reason to try to prevent or suppress imitations, for an imitation did not take from the publisher what was of primary value. Such logic is evidenced by the lawsuit over Dirks's comic strip, which was a breach of contract case alleging unfair competition rather than a copyright case. What Star Company was after by it was control over Dirks's authorial genius as a cartoonist, not the strips' IP "assets," which—at least in the court documents—were never presented by either side as having intrinsic value of their own.

So much for copyright; but what about trademark? Why didn't either party resort to a suit for trademark infringement? At the most basic level—and as explained in the chapter's previous section—trademark was not understood at this time, by industry professionals or legal experts, as having any bearing on the imitation of characters, narrative situations, or artistic styles. Those subjects fell under copyright law. All that a trademark suit could have addressed was the rights to a strip's title. But even there, which party, Star Company or Dirks, would have been found by a court to have a valid claim to the title was not clear. Because Block had come up with the title of the strip, because Dirks had been an employee of Star Company, and because the strip had become associated with Hearst's Journal, Star Company would seem to have had a valid claim to Katzenjammer Kids as a trademark. But perhaps Dirks—as he had argued in *Star Co. v. Press Publishing Co.*—had never been an employee at all but was rather an independent contractor. And perhaps the source to which the words "Katzenjammer Kids" pointed was not the newspaper after all but was rather Dirks, the artist and creator. Strong arguments could have been made for either party, which made the prospect of a lawsuit especially risky.

There was, however, an even bigger problem, one that I have tried to honor in my account of the case above by refraining from italicizing the words "The Katzenjammer Kids." For the fact was that up until right before the start of the trial, "The Katzenjammer Kids" had never been consistently used *as* a title. The custom was rather for Dirks or Block to give each day's strip its own specific title, which sometimes contained the words "Katzenjammer Kids" but more often did not. Here, for example, is a relatively random sample of titles appearing atop Dirks's strip from the first decade of the twentieth century:

- "Mrs. Katzenjammer Entertains Royalty." (March 2, 1902)
- "Der Captain and Uncle Heinie on Skis." (January 3, 1904)
- "Extracts from the Diary of Hans and Fritz." (January 24, 1904)
- "DER CAPTAIN BRINGS A HAPPY NEW YEAR PRESENT (And Takes It Back!)" (January 1, 1905)
- "IT WAS THE LAST DAY OF SCHOOL!" (June 6, 1905)
- "$2." (July 16, 1905)
- "They're Off! Hoora-a-a-ay!" (March 4, 1906)
- "Those Poor Innocent Rackety Rax Boys Are Just Piling Up Trouble for Themselves!" (April 12, 1908)
- "Hawaii? The Katzies Are on the Way!" (August 22, 1909)

Although I have not been able to review *every* strip from this period, the vast majority that I have examined do not contain the words "The Katzenjammer Kids" at all. Indeed, the title does not begin appearing regularly until Dirks quit the Journal in mid-1914, at which point it begins appearing atop every strip. A competent lawyer for the defense would have thus been able to make a strong argument that the Star Company's late attempt to claim the title (had such a claim ever been made) was itself a form of unfair competition.

In any case, I suspect that Star Company nevertheless sent notice to Dirks and Press Publishing Company warning them of a trademark or unfair competition suit if they made use of the phrase. And Dirks and Press Publishing did, at least, refrain from employing it as the title to Dirks's new strip, which they called The Captain and the Kids instead. But trusting that Dirks himself had some claim to it as well, they used it freely in advertising and marketing copy. Ads appearing after the supreme court's final decision printed it in large letters, often multiple times per ad, as a way of promoting Dirks's new strip. See, for example, figure 1. Books featuring the characters, such as The Saalfield Publishing Company's 1917 *Funny Larks of Hans und Fritz* proclaimed across the cover, "By R. Dirks, originator of the KATZENJAMMER KIDS" (capitalized in original). Dirks's early strips for Pulitzer even made use of the phrase in the comic's title line, as in that of his April 4, 1915, strip: "Boots! By Rudolph Dirks, *Originator of the Katzenjammer Kids*" (italics in original).

What does all this tell us about intellectual property protection for cartoon characters at the start of the modern copyright era? That, when dealing with the strips themselves (and excepting those strips that were adapted from other media, such as Tarzan), what mattered was the artist/creator, not the characters. And because the artists were what mattered, copyright was not an especially important tool in adjudicating conflicts. Contracts and unfair competition suits (though not trademark suits) were much more important. Indeed, we might even say that comic strip IP during this time was primarily regulated by "private law"—contracts and industry custom—rather than intellectual property law. For this reason, courts were rarely called upon to decide disputes over the rights to use characters in comic strips. As a result, courts were never forced to develop coherent principles regarding what a copyright in a comic strip actually protected: certainly the right to mechanically reproduce the strip, but what else beyond that? Courts and creators were thus left unprepared for the difficult cases revolving around the question of adaptation rights to cartoon characters (particularly with respect to toys and merchandise) that would soon follow.

King Features Syndicate v. Fleischer

Beginning in the first months of 1923, advertisements for an unusual looking toy horse began appearing in trade papers (see fig. 2). The horse closely resembled a fictional racehorse named Sparkplug, which had debuted in the July 17, 1922, offering of William DeBeck's enormously popular comic strip, Barney Google (see fig. 3). The toy even featured the comic-strip horse's nickname, Sparky, stitched across the blanket that covered most of its frame. Despite these similarities, the toy's manufacturer, Fleischer Toy Manufacturing Company, had neither received

Fig. 1. Advertisement from the *Pittsburgh Gazette Times*, June 15, 1914.

nor requested from the comic strip's copyright holder, King Features Syndicate, permission to produce the toy. The toy company had instead acquired rights to the design from a former dental hygienist named Blanche Burnett, who had, with the help of a Detroit patent attorney, acquired a valid patent for the toy's design in January 1923.[65] Upon being made aware of the ads in April of that same year, King Features' attorney, William DeFord, mailed a cease-and-desist letter to the toy manufacturing company, which—believing DeFord to be mistaken about King Features' rights—forwarded the letter to Burnett's lawyer, Rex Frye.[66] Frye's response, mailed near the end of April, succinctly summarized the legal question that would come to serve as the center of the resulting lawsuit:

> We note your claim that the manufacture and sale of the Horse Doll on which my client claims patent rights is an infringement of the copyright owned by the King feature Syndicate, Inc. which publishes the "Barney Google Cartoons." We are somewhat surprised at your view of the matter, and believe that the patent rights to the manufacture and sale of an article are entirely distinct from the copyright protection afforded under the Copyright Laws.[67]

DeFord disagreed, and on June 20, 1923, King Features filed suit in the Southern District of New York against Fleischer Manufacturing for copyright infringement.

Unlike *Star Co. v. Press Publishing Co.*, which both parties had assumed to revolve around questions of fact, neither King Features nor Fleischer Manufacturing had any illusions that contested facts were relevant to their case. Their dispute clearly hinged upon a question of law. Given (1) that the *Rules and Regulations* of the Copyright Office explicitly excluded toys and dolls from the purview of copyright and (2) that toys and dolls, as items of manufacture, were eligible under statute and common law for patent protection, could a copyright for a cartoon strip provide, by itself, a monopoly over the manufacturing of toys resembling aspects of that strip?[68] Or stated more simply: could copyright law be used to enjoin the manufacture of a toy? Because this was a legal question, the path to victory in court lay ultimately not in witnesses and evidence but rather in the ability of each lawyer to marshal precedent to persuade the court of his respective interpretation of the law. At the appellate level in particular, the victor would be the side whose lawyer wrote the more convincing legal brief.

Before we turn to those briefs, however, it is worth examining an alter-

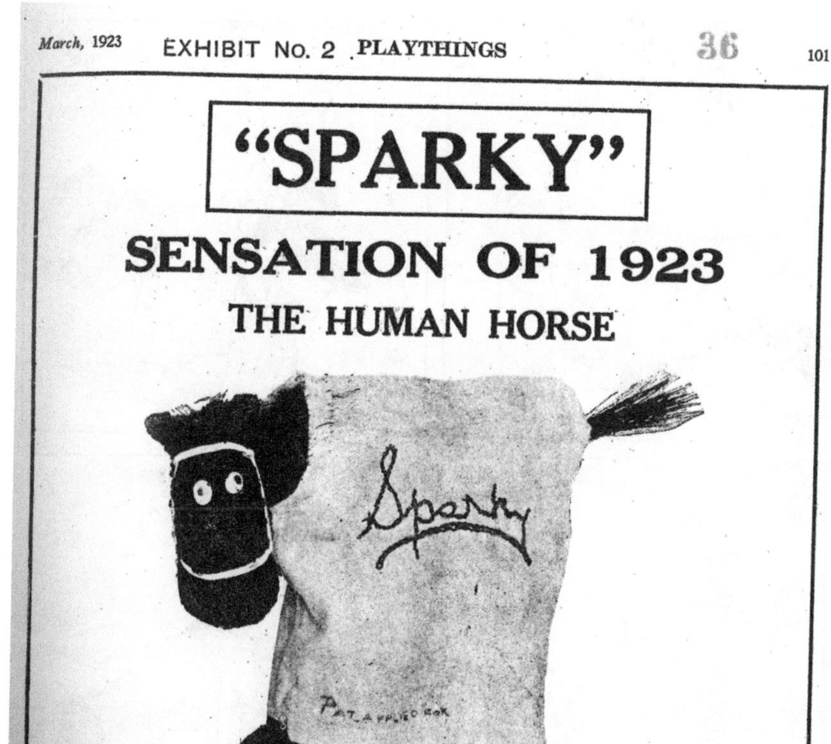

Fig. 2. Fleischer Toy Manufacturing Company, "Sparky" Advertisement, *Playthings*, March 1923.

Fig. 3. William DeBeck, Barney Google, King Features, July 21, 1922.

native strategy attempted by DeFord for King Features in the trial court. Essentially, DeFord argued via affidavits from Moses Koenigsberg, president of King Features, and Frank Klaproth, manager of the American Toy Department of George Borgfeldt & Co., that entertainment-industry custom was for toy manufacturers to license rights to comic strip characters from the strips' copyright holders. As Klaproth explained,

> It has become common practice for concerns engaged in our line of business to keep in touch with the popular interest in cartoons and illustrations in newspapers, books and periodicals and whenever such figures are found to command sufficient public interest to warrant it,

> we seek out the owners of the copyrights and, after securing a license, we convert the pictures into three-dimensional form.[69]

Although the toys were a different medium from the strips on which they were based, the former nevertheless constituted, in Klaproth's words, "ordinary" copies, requiring no "special genius" to make; "[w]hatever genius" they possess was that of their original comic strip creator.[70] Indeed, the Sparkplug toy's entire value—as two retailers and two (somewhat random) everyday consumers similarly attested for the plaintiff—was based upon the fact that it was a copy of DeBeck's cartoons.[71]

Although courts sometimes did (and still do) take industry custom into account when deciding copyright cases (see, for example, chapter 2), DeFord's argument suffered a number of problems that ultimately kept it from persuading the lower court judge—who denied the plaintiff's requests for an injunction. For one, neither Koenigsberg nor Klaproth were disinterested observers. Koenigsberg was employed by the plaintiff, and Klaproth's company had secured a license from the plaintiff right before the start of the trial to make its own Sparkplug toys. Klaproth was also unwilling, despite arguing that custom recognized copyrights in comic strips as securing the right to make toy versions of their characters, to deny the toys patent protection as well:

> In making the copies of these cartoons the fact that we are operating in a different medium . . . sometimes calls for a certain departure from the details of the original cartoon which we are copying. In designing these departures, the effort is, of course, to create as near as possible the effect of a perfect copy, but, nevertheless, there is in these departures an element of designing skill which is entitled to recognition and which we protect by applying for design patent.[72]

The custom argument thus seemed to hurt as much as it helped Fleischer's case. For if copyright protected the right to make toy versions of cartoon characters, then why was it also industry custom—as the affidavit of patent lawyer Charles Havell similarly averred—for such toys to be patented?[73]

From the perspective of a twenty-first-century legal observer, there appears yet one more problem with DeFord's strategy: the justifications the affiants offered in support of the industry's supposed custom supported a claim of unfair competition and/or trademark infringement, *not* copyright infringement. Indeed, the use of everyday consumers' observations that the toys struck them as "copies" of DeBeck's comic strip resembles less sophisticated versions of the kind of evidence routinely put forward in present-day trademark cases to establish a mark's secondary meaning. Additionally, all the theories put forth by the affiants (though clearly coached by DeFord to ensure that the language of their observations aligned with that of the copyright case law he would elsewhere emphasize) were rooted in the unfair-competition concept of *passing off*: the representation of one's goods or services as another's. James Averill, manager of retail store Madame Georgene, thus attested that "the buying public would not have looked for toy horse Sparky were it not for the mental picture of the horse which they, the public had after having seen the newspaper cartoon of 'Sparky' [*sic*]."[74] And yet so entrenched in the 1920s was the belief that disputes involving copyrighted characters were *copyright* disputes that it does not seem to have occurred to DeFord that King Features might file suit against Fleischer instead for unfair competition.

Ultimately, however, the problem that the trial judge John C. Knox had with this line of argument was that he believed it irrelevant. The numerous affidavits, provided by DeFord as part of his re-argument of the motion for a preliminary injunction, failed to convince Knox that his initial denial was wrong. In the memo accompanying that denial, Knox had stated that the protection King Features sought was not "within the contemplation of the copyright statutes," nor supported by case law.[75] His reasoning remained unchanged after re-argument, despite what he praised as "the unusually lucid and impressive reasons advanced" by the plaintiff.[76] Noting in a second memo that there "is little that I care to add to my previous memorandum," he not only denied once again the request for injunction but also granted the defendant's motion for a dismissal.[77] The logic he employed, rooted in that of *Baker v. Selden* and *Royal Sales Co. v. Gaynor*, insisted on the legal distinction between a copyright and a patent:

> A particular design may be copyrightable, and at the same time be capable of being made into an article of manufacture, which may be the subject matter of a design patent. The fact, I think, remains that if the protection secured be limited to copyright, it must exclude that which may be had only by virtue of the design patent law. Otherwise, the latter may, for many practical purposes, be all but nullified.[78]

Despite dismissing the case and thus, in effect, finding for the defense, Knox nevertheless believed Fleischer to be *morally* guilty. Having been persuaded that the toy manufacturer had acted unfairly, the judge refused to award the defendants legal costs:

> In my judgment defendants have capitalized an idea of the plaintiff's assignor and that no premium should be placed upon doing so. Defendants should be satisfied with obtaining what I believe I had to give them but which nevertheless from the standpoint of good conscience, I should have been glad to withhold.[79]

Under the norms of practical legal hermeneutics, this explanation, provided in a separate memo as to costs, was not meant to bear upon the underlying legal question of the case. On appeal, however, DeFord would treat the explanation as though it did, citing it as evidence that Knox's rulings were inconsistent and that Knox had, in fact, recognized Fleischer's guilt.[80]

Given the plaintiff's intention to appeal, however, the portion of Knox's ruling that mattered most to the two parties was his citation of case law. Because the case's underlying legal question did not appear to be original, Knox's ruling would stand or fall based upon whether or not it was in line with precedent. Central to the arguments of both DeFord for the plaintiff and Frye for the defendant in their respective appeals briefs were thus the two cases upon which Judge Knox had avowedly based his dismissal, *Baker v. Selden* and *Royal Sales Co. v. Gaynor.*[81] Before we examine the use to which counsel put these cases, it is thus worth my briefly summarizing them here.

Heard by the U.S. Supreme Court in 1879, *Baker v. Selden* revolved around a dispute over one author's copying of another's bookkeeping (i.e., accounting) system. The facts are as such: in 1859, 1860, and 1861, Charles Selden published and secured valid copyrights for various editions of a book, *Selden's Condensed Ledge, or Book-keeping Simplified,* which described an original system of bookkeeping. Subsequently, Mr. Baker published his own book, which—though not directly copying any of the actual pages of Selden's book—made use of the same system introduced by Selden. Alleging copyright infringement, Selden filed suit, with the circuit court for the Southern District of Ohio eventually ruling in his favor. On appeal, however, the Supreme Court disagreed, reasoning that since the system that Selden presented could not itself have been copyrighted (only, potentially, patented), Baker's employment of it in his own book could not be deemed a copyright violation. The explanation Judge Joseph Bradley provided in the opinion was clear and straightforward—at least at first. Halfway through the opinion, however, in what many lawyers would likely consider dicta, Bradley attempted to distinguish the aforesaid line of reasoning from that which would apply to situations in which "ornamental designs" or "pictorial illustrations" are copied.[82] Here, in language that already by the 1920s seemed to belong to another century, Bradley recast the fundamental logic of copyright law in almost metaphysical terms. Of designs and illustration, he explained, "it may be said, that their form is their essence, and their object, the production of pleasure in their contemplation. This is their final end." Inventions, such as methods of bookkeeping, by contrast "have their final end in application and use."[83] Therein, Bradley explains—in tortuous language that makes paraphrase challenging—lies the distinction between copyright and patent: published "descriptions," verbal or pictorial, that are ends-in-themselves may be copyrighted; descriptions whose object is "use," by contrast, "can only be secured, if at all, by letters-patent."[84] Dicta aside, however, the precedent the case established would have struck most early-twentieth-century lawyers as simple: the copyrighting of a text does not secure the right to prevent uses of that text that could have been secured by a patent.

The second cited case, *Royal Sales Co. v. Gaynor,* concerned a dispute over the rights to the design of a monogram composed of the letters *T A F T*. In 1908, the defendant, Gaynor, who was not incidentally a registered attorney in the U.S. Patent Office, assigned the copyright in a book of designs and sayings—which included the *T A F T* monogram—to the plaintiff, Royal Sales Company, which subsequently sold copies of the book with a badge featuring the monogram pinned to each one. Later that year, Gaynor proceeded to copyright another book, *Republican Platform Planks,* which he himself published and sold, attaching identical badges to the covers. Royal Sales Company filed suit for copyright infringement in New York district court and requested a preliminary injunction, to which Gaynor responded by filing a demurrer (a pleading challenging the legal sufficiency of a cause of action). Judge Henry Galbraith Ward understood from the facts that Gaynor had acted in "bad faith" by having "assured the complainant and its assignor that the copyright which he was selling did cover the making and selling of the monogram."[85] Nevertheless, he denied Royal Sales Company's request for preliminary injunction and effectively granted the demurrer:

> The copyright under consideration is for the book, and not for the monogram, and I think the monogram is not a subject within the copyright law. If it were, any one could get, by means of a copyright,

> what would be substantially a patent for a design for a longer term and upon payment of less fees than Rev. St. U.S. 4929–4933 . . . prescribes in the case of design patents. . . . It is as if one were to ask the court, in a suit brought upon a patent for a machine, to enjoin because of his assignor's bad faith in the publication of a book. The complainant's remedy, if any, must be sought in the courts of the state.[86]

The decision, unlike *Baker v. Selden,* is clear and legible throughout, but the logic is the same: a copyright for a book cannot be used to enforce rights provided under law by patent. Even in the case of misrepresentation or "bad faith," a federal copyright suit cannot be maintained; the proper remedy is a suit in state court alleging unfair competition.

Because the rule established by the two cases cited by Judge Knox appeared to be both straightforward and consistent with contemporary copyright and patent statutes, King Features' path to victory must have seemed, at the time, steep. To secure a reversal, DeFord would need to convince at least two of the three circuit judges hearing his case that Knox's reading of precedent had been erroneous. In theory, there were two means by which DeFord might do this: (1) he could cite additional case law that seemed to contradict *Baker v. Selden* and *Royal Sales Co. v. Gaynor* and/or (2) he could directly impugn Knox's interpretations of these two cases. DeFord ultimately pursued both strategies, although none of the additional case law cited in his appeals brief speaks directly to the legal question at the heart of his client's dispute with Fleischer. Case law is instead employed in what appears to have been an attempt to displace that question by establishing an unusually expansive definition of what constituted copying under both U.S. and English copyright law.[87] This definition, which was elaborated over multiple pages of the plaintiff's brief, seems to negate the idea-expression dichotomy by attributing copyright protection to almost anything an author produces: "The Copyright Act protects the intellectual product of the author, whether a concept of beauty or humor, and secures to him the full commercial value of that product and of any species of publication which he selects for its embodiment."[88] Under this very broad definition, Fleischer's horse would clearly constitute copyright infringement. Such a conclusion, however, only begged the question that it sought to displace: why did *Baker v. Selden* and *Royal Sales Co. v. Gaynor* seem to suggest otherwise? The more important part of DeFord's brief was thus its readings of those two cases, which were given considerably more attention than other cases cited within.

Let us start with DeFord's handling of *Royal Sales Co. v. Gaynor,* which ultimately had less of an impact on the court than his treatment of the other case. DeFord asserts that the circuit court's ruling here had become "bad law," out of sync with that of numerous other cases. Rather than explain how it was out of sync, however, DeFord relies entirely upon a long quotation from the appeals court's opinion in *Jeweler's Circular Pub. Co. v. Keystone Pub. Co.*, which stated that "the *Gaynor* case . . . may be difficult to reconcile" with four other cases.[89] DeFord did not himself discuss *Jeweler's*, which was an extraordinarily messy case dealing with a very narrow—and seemingly unrelated—question of law (can a compilation of trademarks be protected by copyright). Nor does the opinion, considered in full, provide the support he suggested it did. Not only was the section quoted clearly dicta (Judge Henry Wade Rogers had preceded his critique of *Gaynor* by noting that that case, even "if correctly decided," did not "touch this case"), the opinion gave rise to a vociferous dissent from Judge Charles Merrill Hough, who rejected not only the logic of the majority's ruling but also what he claimed was a misuse of case law.[90] DeFord ignored all of this, wisely substituting for actual analysis of the case and its ruling a single long quotation, which—stripped of its context—framed the opinion as having a definitive bearing on the trial court's ruling in his client's own case. In doing so, he also flatteringly misrepresented to the three appeals court judges hearing his case—who had been the same three judges to hear the *Jeweler's* case—their own prior ruling as more coherent and definitive than it had in fact been.

For *Baker v. Selden*, DeFord's strategy was more radical—and, potentially, riskier. Rather than reject the case as bad law, he argued that the rule it established was exactly the opposite of what Judge Knox had taken it to be. To pull off this sleight of hand, he relied once more upon dicta. Largely ignoring the case's actual ruling, DeFord's reading of the opinion drew heavily upon the unusual copyright metaphysics Judge Bradley had offered there. DeFord quoted a long section of this, which includes the lines I quoted while discussing the opinion above (with DeFord's emphasis):

> *Of course, these observations are not intended to apply to ornamental designs, or pictorial illustrations addressed to the taste. Of these it may be said that their form is their essence, and their object the production of pleasure in their contemplation. This is their final end. . . .*[91]

This meant, according to DeFord, that what copyright in a pictorial form protected was the form's final end: the unique "pleasure in contemplation" that it produced. Use of the form to produce a similar end would thus constitute a copyright violation. Application of the rule to the Sparkplug dispute was thus, according to DeFord, straightforward:

> The form of the horse (to use the language of the Court in *Baker v. Selden*), embodying the artist's concept of humor, was the essence of the cartoon, its end within the artist's purpose, and its object the production of amusement in contemplation. The Copyright Law was intended to give protection to the creator of that form, protection to its value in that form, to give amusement in contemplation.[92]

This was a bizarre argument, radically out of keeping with almost all legal actors' understandings of copyright law in the 1920s. And its assumption that toy versions of pictorial forms by definition trespass upon monopolies given those forms for "amusement in contemplation" seems easily assailable (aren't toys, after all, usually *played with*?). Nevertheless, DeFord went all in with the argument, weaving the language of *Baker v. Selden*'s dicta throughout the brief, which not only repeatedly frames the Sparkplug dispute in its terms but even recasts other case law in its language. Indeed, DeFord's brief is quite explicit about the implications of its reading of *Baker v. Selden*: "The practical effect of interpreting the Copyright Law (as the complainant-appellant claims it should be interpreted), would be, that the author of an original concept of humor, expressed in the form of a copyrighted cartoon, would obtain complete protection against its use by another, in any form, without his license."[93]

The defense, for its part, did its best to persuade the court of its own readings of *Baker v. Selden* and *Royal Sales Co. v. Gaynor*. And it offered up several other examples of cases involving patents for dolls. But in hindsight Frye appears to have been operating at a disadvantage, for the opinions he cited appeared so clearly and straightforwardly to set forth the rule that a copyright could not be used to protect things that are governed by patent, that there was little Frye could do except to provide quotes from them stating as much. In comparison to DeFord's brief, Frye's thus appears both less clever and less carefully argued. Frye also appears to have been less willing to critique the rulings of past judges. He thus refrains from attacking the plaintiff's importation of *Baker v. Selden*'s strange copyright metaphysics and even appears content, at times, to make use of the language of "concepts" and "ends."[94] Perhaps out of fear of angering Judges Rogers and Martin Thomas Manton, Frye also refrains from pushing back against DeFord's repudiation of *Royal Sales Co. v. Gaynor* except to suggest very delicately that DeFord had taken the two judges' criticism of that case in *Jeweler's* out of context.[95] I do not mean to suggest that Frye put forth a bad defense, but rather that the case law—especially when coupled with considerations of policy of the kind put forth by Judge Knox—appeared to support the defendant's position so strongly that a more aggressive, let alone clever, defense seemed unnecessary.

Unfortunately for Fleischer, however, the appeals court ultimately ruled unanimously for King Features, thus finding that the defendant's toy horse constituted an infringement of the plaintiff's copyright. In making this decision, the court may well have been prompted by the instinctive conviction—which Judge Knox had felt as well—that what the defendant had done was *unfair.* But in the manner in which they cast the decision, they were clearly influenced by DeFord. The expansive definition of copyright the opinion puts forth, rooted in the metaphysics of "concepts" and "ends," is adopted wholesale from DeFord's brief. Indeed, it is even reproduced at one point almost verbatim:

> The form of the horse, embodying the aspect of humor, was the essence of the cartoon; its end, within the artist's purpose, and its object, the production of amusement in contemplation. We think the copyright law was intended to give protection to the creation of that form, protection to its value in that form, to give amusement in contemplation.[96]

The result was a new precedent—establishing that copyright by itself protected the adaptation of cartoon characters into toys and other kinds of physical merchandise.[97] It was also a precedent whose reasoning was well outside the norms and language of contemporary copyright law and was, at times, even harder to parse than that of Judge Bradley's dicta in *Baker v. Selden.* For example, toward the end of the opinion in *King Features,* Judge Rogers wrote (again echoing DeFord's own language), "The protection accorded the owner of the copyright is of the intellectual product of the author. . . . The question is: To what is the artist or author entitled as his conception and what if such original conception has been appropriated? He is entitled to any lawful use of his property whereby he may get a profit out of it." On the face of it, as future commentators would note, the opinion thus seemed to be defying the idea-expression dichotomy by granting copyright protection to mere ideas.[98] Although the new rule it established regarding cartoon characters was easy enough to understand, the logic supporting such a rule was not. The rule also appeared to contradict the case law as it applied to fictional characters originating in prose fiction, theater, or live-action film. Why was a cartoon character granted greater protection than those from other media?

Despite the strangeness of its logic, *King Features Syndicate v. Fleischer* was seen by most contemporary commentators as the right decision.[99] That is because, despite the patent owner's claim to have come up with the design for the toy without ever having seen a Barney Google comic strip, one would be hard-pressed upon seeing the toy to believe that it was not a deliberate imitation of DeBeck's cartoon horse. What Burnett and Fleischer Manufacturing had done by producing it was thus *unfair.* But under the law as it then stood, their actions should not have been considered a copyright violation. "It is fairly clear that what is being protected in these cartoon by-product cases is neither an idea, a character, nor a design," copyright lawyer Kenneth Umbreit complained fifteen years later, "but a popularity value, a sort of psychological property."[100] From the vantage point of today, the property at issue appears very similar—even a kind of historical precursor to—a contemporary trademark. But in the 1920s and 1930s such a conception of trademark law was well outside the legal imaginations of judges and lawyers. Even Umbreit himself, more adventurous in his thinking than most legal practitioners, found it hard to square the ruling in *King Features Syndicate v. Fleischer* with trademark and unfair competition law as it was then understood: "We are dealing here with a type of property unknown to the older economics on which the law is based. It does not represent a 'practical' value based on the assumption that the 'trademark' is a warranty of quality; it represents a sentimental value based on the fact that the article bears the 'trade-mark.'"[101] Today, we recognize the new economics that supports such value, but to courts, lawyers, and creative talent during most of the modern copyright era these "economics" did not yet exist. In *King Features Syndicate v. Fleischer* we thus have an early instance of a dispute over such value, remade by a clever lawyer into a run-of-the-mill copyright case so that an early-twentieth-century court could understand it. His victory there would ultimately do much more than simply win his client an injunction: through the power of precedent, it smuggled recognition of this new form of value into copyright law as it would henceforth be practiced and understood, at least when it came to cartoon characters.

Detective Comics v. Bruns Publications

In the early spring of 1939, John M. Woolsey, a judge for the Southern District of New York, found himself assigned a "plagiarism" case involving two comic-book characters, one published by the plaintiff Detective Comics, the other by its competitor, Bruns Publications. In its answer to the complaint and in its briefs, the defense argued that the character it was alleged to have copied, a super-powered and flamboyantly dressed hero named Superman, was not itself an original creation and thus not "susceptible of monopolization under the copyright laws."[102] Woolsey, an "idiosyncratic" judge who prided himself in his literary sensibility (he had famously ruled in 1933 that James Joyce's *Ulysses* had literary merit), could not have been pleased.[103]

Five years earlier, in *Sheldon v. Metro-Goldwyn Pictures Corp.*, a suit that had attracted wide attention and was sometimes referred to as the "Lettie Lynton" case, Woolsey had been presented with a very similar defense to copyright infringement.[104] That case, which Woolsey subsequently described as "probably the most important copyright case that has been up for a long time," had been especially complex, involving five texts: a published description of a real-world trial, as well as a play, a novel, a film treatment, and a motion picture all based upon that trial.[105] After undertaking a painstaking analysis of the texts, "not only comparatively, but, as it were, genealogically," Woolsey had found himself persuaded by the defense's argument:[106]

> I find, therefore, that, whilst the defendants' writers had access to the Play and undoubtedly had it constantly before their minds when they were making the scenario for the Picture, they did not copy anything therein or take anything therefrom which was protected by copyright, and that, as a matter of law, therefore, they did not infringe the plaintiffs' copyright.[107]

On appeal, judges Learned Hand, Thomas Swan, and Harrie Chase disagreed. In a characteristically artful opinion, Hand—who like Woolsey took great stock in his own literary sensibility—found for the plaintiffs, thereby reversing Woolsey's decision. In what reads like a direct admonishment of Woolsey, Hand's opinion explicitly repudiates the reasoning on which Woolsey had decided the case:

> We are to remember that it makes no difference how far the play was anticipated by works in the public demesne which the plaintiffs did not use. The defendants appear not to recognize this, for they have filled the record with earlier instances of the same dramatic incidents and devises, as though, like a patent, a copyrighted work must be not only original, but new.[108]

No judge likes to be reversed, and this reversal must have especially smarted. Still angry and abashed three years later, Woolsey could only have been frustrated to find what appeared to be in *Detective Comics v. Bruns Publications* a nearly identical copyright case on his docket.

Speculating about a person's emotional state—let alone a judge's—is a risky business, usually dependent upon a host of psychological assumptions that are difficult to prove. In this case, however, the transcript to *Detective Comics v. Bruns Publications* can stand as confirming evidence. Throughout the trial, Woolsey was impatient, irascible, and aggressive. His instructions to the lawyers on the first day of testimony set the general tone for the proceedings:

> I understand in a general way what this is about. Now, you better make your record. There is no use having an elaborate opening or anything like that. Make your record by showing your contracts and show what you have got in the way of rights and then we will deal with that question.[109]

As the trial continued, Woolsey repeatedly rushed the testimony, complaining, for example, that "I do not want to waste much time on this" and asking "How long will this take?"[110] In another striking example, toward the end of testimony, facing the prospect of having to listen the next day to two additional witnesses for the plaintiff offered in rebuttal of witness testimony for the defense, he cautioned counsel to move quickly so that he could get on with his ruling: "You will have to argue this thing right away as soon as you get through and if I am satisfied about it maybe I will decide it right away. I can't tell; it depends on how it strikes me. You better be ready with everything."[111] On the day of that testimony, however, Woolsey had so little prepared that he was unable even to recall "the names of the people who were on the stand yesterday," despite the whole purpose of the new witnesses being to rebut the previous day's testimony.[112]

Because he was so impatient, Woolsey also continually interrupted the witness examinations, sometimes highjacking them for considerable lengths of time. His questions to the witnesses occasionally rephrased or (ostensibly) corrected the counsel's own questions.[113] At other times they constituted digressions that appeared to have little bearing on what either party thought important.[114] More often, however, his interruptions aimed to cut off examination entirely. In an antagonistic exchange with Samuel Fried, lawyer to the defendant distributors, Judge Woolsey—well aware of the frustration he had caused—justified his behavior as judicial philosophy:

MR. FRIED: If your Honor please, I have practiced law in these courts for more than twenty-five years and I believe I have some ideas of the conduct of a case.

THE COURT: Now I am trying this case, remember that. The trouble is lawyers think they try the cases and I don't believe in that, the judge tries the case.[115]

Anger at being reminded of his reversal in *Sheldon v. Metro-Goldwyn Pictures Corp.* notwithstanding, Woolsey's conduct can also be explained by the lesson he had taken from that reversal: for this kind of copyright case—one where access by the defendant to the plaintiff's work could not be denied—testimony, supplementary evidence, and even legal arguments were irrelevant. All that mattered was whether or not, upon sitting down and closely comparing the texts in question, a judge found the defendants' work to be a copy of the plaintiff's. Woolsey thus repeatedly insisted that everything else was a waste of time. "I want to get through with this," he complained to Asher Blum, counsel for Bruns Publications, early on in the testimony. "All I want do is look at the magazines."[116] And later, to Fried, "When you have a lot of these things to look at I just look at them and make up my mind."[117] And again, in a heated exchange with Blum on the method by which infringement is determined, "You can do it by looking at it. That is the way you do it. I am very used to these cases. All I have to do is look at the two things and determine it."[118]

So set was Woolsey on this method—and so determined not to commit the same mistake he had in *Sheldon v. Metro-Goldwyn Pictures Corp.*—that he continuously sought to squelch in court Blum's argument as to originality. This argument, in essence, posited that the concept of a superpowered individual who fought injustice on behalf of the weak while wearing a skintight costume was not original to Superman. As proof, Blum repeatedly attempted to offer up the example of *The Phantom,* a comic strip series featuring just such an individual that was first published two years *before* the debut of Superman. How Blum's argument at trial was supposed to have worked is unclear: the weakest version would have argued that Superman himself was unoriginal; a slightly stronger one, that Superman's creators had based him off the Phantom; and a stronger one still, that Brun's alleged copy, Wonder Man, had itself been based off of the Phantom. Whatever the form Blum meant the argument to take, Woolsey was not having it: he continually interrupted lines of question that got anywhere near it (usually triggering harried complaints by Blum) and resisted introducing into evidence examples from

The Phantom comic strip or other earlier works.[119] Indeed, in one astonishing interjection, he even seemed to confuse Blum with the defense lawyer (Nathan Burkan) in the Lettie Lynton case: "That case we had, and that I got reversed in, that I first decided in your favor involved just the same sort of question we have here."[120] Perhaps this was a slip of the tongue or perhaps Woolsey—who was prone during the trial to hasty ineloquence—had become jumbled in his expression. Whatever the explanation, the import was clear: Woolsey was not going to be tricked by Blum into falling for the same defense he had last time.[121]

Although Blum suffered most in Woolsey's courtroom, all four lawyers (Blum, Fried, and Raphael Koenig for the defense and Horace Manges for the plaintiff) struggled to perform competently in the face of the judge's behavior. Manges's stiffness and inflexibility with witnesses often made him seem as if he were working through a list of questions that could not change regardless of a witness's answers. He regularly led his own witnesses, and when he received answers that he did not like or expect on cross-examination, he often kept repeating the question, sometimes earning multiple rebukes from Woolsey for doing so.[122] His single-mindedness also led him to regularly ignore—or at least attempt to ignore—Woolsey's interruptions, sometimes resulting in almost comical confusion, at other times causing Woolsey to lose his temper.[123] In one instance, Manges, seemingly oblivious to Woolsey's sweeping rejection of Blum's originality argument, even reintroduced the argument during cross-examination by asking factual questions about the Phantom.[124]

Fried, who took a back seat to Koenig and Blum during the examination of witnesses, had much less to say to either witnesses or the judge. Nevertheless, he managed to commit errors that annoyed Woolsey, at one point direct examining instead of cross-examining a witness for the plaintiff and, at another, demonstrating a flagrantly faulty understanding of very basic copyright law principles.[125] For his part, Koenig, senior partner of the law firm handling Brun's defense, appears to have become so frustrated with Woolsey that he quickly handed the case off to Blum. The final straw may have been the explanation Woolsey gave for overruling one of Koenig's objections: "We are [in dealing with comics] in a zone of the grotesque. Don't be so serious about the thing." This seems to have been too much for Koenig, whose angry response stopped just short of contempt: "[m]aybe I can't impel myself into the grotesque, your Honor, from lack of experience in this type of imaginative litigation."[126]

No one, however, struggled as much as Blum. "Pitch-forked into this case" with little notice, he nevertheless gave it his full attention and appears to have been a smart lawyer with a decent knowledge of copyright case law.[127] But to no avail. Unable to build his argument around a question of law and unable to introduce into the record information to support such an argument upon appeal, he was forced to frame the dispute as a question of fact: specifically, the defendants' access to the plaintiff's work. Because Superman had appeared in print for many months before Wonder Man had, and because Superman had immediately become well-known in the comics and magazine industry, the only way access might be denied was by proving that Wonder Man had been created *before* Superman was published. Even with testimony claiming as much by Wonder Man's creators, however, this was a tough argument to prove, and at the end of the trial Blum's strategy for doing so had become so convoluted that he found himself arguing, absurdly, that Superman was a copy of Wonder Man! Indeed, as the trial neared its finish, Blum had become worn down by interruptions and denials to such an extent that he sometimes seemed confused as to what was even happening in court. In one instance, he even came close to badgering a witness by refusing to accept his answer about a prior pleading. The exchange that followed Woolsey's intervention is worth quoting in full:

> THE COURT: You asked him if he pleaded guilty in the Federal Court and he said he didn't plead guilty in the Federal Court. Are you certain he didn't?
>
> MR. BLUM: Yes. What happened is I didn't hear very well and Mr. Manges said "you are incorrect" and I thought he meant "he is incorrect"—just a case where my hearing should be a little better.
>
> THE COURT: All right, then I think you should apologize to the witness for talking to him in that way when he said definitely he had not been indicted in this court. . . .
>
> MR. BLUM: I would not have asked that question except that my hearing is getting worse. I am very sorry I asked that question.[128]

In its absurdity (and perhaps also pathos), the exchange demonstrates what a mess the trial had become by its end. With a defense unable to argue the underlying question of law and a judge convinced that everything but his own comparison of the texts was a waste of time, the trial devolved into farce. Indeed, Woolsey's opinion reads as though he ignored the proceedings almost entirely, relying instead solely upon a side-by-side comparison of excerpts from the texts. Astonishingly, the opinion does not even mention the defense's argument as to originality, nor does it cite any precedent other than *King Features v. Fleischer Syndicate* and *Fleischer Studios, Inc. v. Ralph A. Freundlich, Inc.* (another cartoon-character–toy case decided on identical grounds to the earlier case). Finding for the plaintiff, Woolsey ordered an injunction, the wording of which was in places vague and confusing:

> Said defendants . . . are perpetually enjoined and restrained from printing, publishing, offering for sale or selling or in any way distributing any cartoon or cartoons, or any periodical, book, magazine or other publication containing any cartoon or cartoons, portraying the figure of or embodiment of plaintiff's cartoon character "Superman" as set forth in plaintiff's said copyrighted works (Plaintiff's Exhibits 12 to 22 inclusive in evidence here) or any figure which is a copy or imitation thereof.[129]

Not only did the order seem to enjoin the illustration of any man (as the defense would complain on appeal) "dressed in gymnasium costume," it also distinguished, strangely, between the "figure of" Superman and the "embodiment" of Superman, granting equal protection to both. Whatever the distinction meant, it seemed to far overstep the protections traditionally offered fictional characters by copyright law, in part by jettisoning, for cartoon characters, the idea-expression dichotomy. Certainly, an artist could be barred, under standard copyright reasoning, from reproducing a published image (just as a writer could be barred from reproducing the words of a published novel); that is indeed what copyright, at its core, is designed to prevent. But what principle justifies granting a comic book publisher a monopoly on the production of any figure remotely resembling the one depicted in the comic books it published—even when the new figure is engaged in different actions, wearing different clothing, and situated within a different narrative? Woolsey's decision appears to grant protection to a generalized idea—that of the cartoon superhero.

Unfortunately, a mess of a trial can have implications far beyond that of the trial's outcome. Through path dependency, the appeal can become logically tainted: a product of the same disorder present at trial. In the case of *Detective Comics v. Bruns Publications,* the disorder was in part textually transmitted. The trial-court transcript of record bequeathed to the appeals court a morass of argument, in which basic questions of fact were unclear and underlying questions of law obscured. But the disorder was also transmitted by the lawyers themselves, who had been deprived at trial of the opportunity to develop strong or even coherent arguments. This is in part because the judge's handling of precedent was clumsy and distorting, thus forcing the defense in particular to wrestle with caricatures of case law. But it was also because the judge, by "trying the case" himself, prevented the adversarial process from doing its normal job (as we saw it do, for example, in chapter 2) of prompting counsel to revise strategies and finetune lines of argument. Both sides' appeals briefs thus ended up weaker than they would have likely been had the trial been better run. Manges's brief for the plaintiff, for example, devotes substantial attention to simply re-narrating the trial (even so far as quoting some of Woolsey's interruptions)—under the theory, I suspect, that the transcript would not have been by itself legible to the appeals court.[130] The defendant's brief, written by Koenig (back for the appeal) and Fried, devotes more attention to questions of law, but its arguments appear fueled by the conviction that they had been unfairly treated in court.[131] Lacking nuance, its discussions of case law are employed not to establish that their reading of the law is the better one but rather to prove that Judge Woolsey had been wrong and/or ignorant.

An especially committed appeals court might, on being handed such an appeal, work through these problems (or even, if deemed especially egregious, order a rehearing), but that does not appear to be what judges Learned Hand, Augustus Hand, and Harrie Chase did with *Detective Comics v. Bruns Publications.* Instead, Augustus Hand (Learned Hand's cousin), seemingly as confident in his own aesthetic sensibility as Woolsey had been in his, performed the same kind of simple, even simplistic, comparison that Woolsey did (i.e., "I just look at them and make up my mind"). In a short opinion, the bulk of which was spent listing instances of copying, the court affirmed Woolsey's finding of copyright infringement. The opinion cites only two past cases, and one of them, *Nichols v. Universal Pictures Co.*, is especially strange in this context.[132] In his 1930 opinion for that case, Judge Learned Hand had introduced what quickly became core copyright doctrine as to the protectability of fictional characters in the second circuit: "[T]he less developed the characters, the less they can be copyrighted; that is the penalty an author must bear for marking them too indistinctly."[133] In *Detective Comics v. Bruns Publications,* however, the case is cited to support a revision to the language of the district court's injunction that, in effect, gives the injunction—bizarrely—even wider breadth than the original:

> Since the complainant is not entitled to a monopoly of the mere character of a "Superman" who is a blessing to mankind (*Nichols v. Uni-*

> *versal Pictures Corp* . . .), we think the language of clause 4(c) of the decree somewhat too sweeping. It should be modified so as to read as follows: "(c) From printing, publishing, offering for sale or selling, or in any was distributing any cartoon or cartoons, or any periodical or book portraying any of the feats of strength or powers performed by 'Superman' or closely imitating his costume or appearance in any way whatever."[134]

On the face of it, the revision appears to defy the logic of both the precedent cited and the aim of the court itself, which claims here to be trying to make the injunction *less* sweeping. By barring Bruns from "portraying any of the feats of strength or powers performed by 'Superman,'" however, it went considerably further than Judge Woolsey's original order. Under the new language, Bruns was barred even from publishing an illustration of Hercules, Samson, or some other strong man in the public domain. Citing this and other problems with the injunction, Blum petitioned for a rehearing, but to no avail.[135] What had begun as a mess at trial concluded as a mess on appeal.

Up to this point, this chapter's presentation of *Detective Comics v. Bruns Publications* has employed the logic of path dependency to place the blame for the lawsuit's confusing results on Judge Woolsey. Starting with the depiction of a district court judge still smarting from being reversed on appeal, it sought to show how something as arbitrary as a judge's disposition can shape the ultimate outcome of a lawsuit. Although the influence of judges' dispositions has long been recognized by legal scholars (not to mention practicing lawyers), the judicial behavior scholarship often suggests that a judge's mood and/or ideological values determine a dispute's outcome in simple, almost mechanistic fashion, with re-election worries, for example, resulting in harsher sentencing or conservative values resulting in rulings against Establishment Clause claimants.[136] Woolsey's conduct in *Detective Comics v. Bruns Publications,* however, reveals a more complicated and holistic causal process, one where a primary cause, such as a judge's disposition, can matter but its impact still be mediated, over the course of a trial, by contingency. In other words, although possessing different degrees of power, each participant in the lawsuit remains relevant to the causal path, so that to leap descriptively from Woolsey's disposition to his ruling would misrepresent how the outcome was actually determined. What is more, attending, as actor-network theory would suggest we do, to the multiple actors involved in a lawsuit as it unfolds enables us to recognize how the arbitrary forces that bear on a dispute at trial can continue to exert influence on appeal.

We can thus better see how an appeal is not, as popular understanding would portray it, a "re-do" or "do over," but is rather, in many respects, a continuation of what came before.

There is, however, another, important explanation for the confusing results of *Detective Comics v. Bruns Publications*, and that is the absence of unfair competition and trademark law as recognized claims of action when it came to fictional characters during the modern copyright era. Today, assuming competent judges and lawyers, Bruns would be found guilty, if at all, of unfair competition or trademark infringement, not copyright infringement. This is because, in 2022, the feats and features Bruns imitated are simply too commonplace and generic to constitute illegal copying, even if—contra *Sheldon v. Metro-Goldwyn Pictures Corp.*—they were inspired by the drawings of Superman in Action Comics. This was arguably true in 1939 as well, but less obvious to judges and lawyers unversed in pulp fiction and popular culture. But it is not just a change in the visibility of superheroes that would result in a different ruling today; it is also a change in the realm of law under which the dispute would be fought. What Bruns appeared to have done had been sneaky and underhanded.[137] If it had not been, the witnesses for the defense would have had no reason to lie about it upon the stand—as the evidence, taken as a whole, suggests they did. Woolsey and the appeals court judges thus both reasonably concluded that the creators of Wonder Man had set out, with the example of Superman before them, to create an imitation that would benefit from Superman's popularity, potentially by diverting sales away from Detective Comics. To a judge more concerned with fair play than the economic function of competition in capitalism, the defense's actions might thus be deemed today "unfair." A judge might even rule that the published depictions of Wonder Man are so similar to Superman as to be likely to mislead consumers as to the comic's source, thus constituting trademark infringement. But federal judges in 1939 would not have conceived of such rulings—nor was it their charge to come up with them. Indeed, federal court would probably have been the wrong place to file such claims at that time, had a lawyer conceived of them.

In *Detective Comics v. Bruns Publications* we thus have a federal judge wanting to punish "unfair" behavior but only having copyright law available with which to do so. Just as the appeals court judges had been in the Sparkplug case fifteen years earlier, Woolsey was thus forced to bend copyright law out of shape in order to find for the plaintiffs. Indeed, Woolsey's own language in the opinion inadvertently registers the confusion between copyright law and unfair competition: "I find that . . .

there has been unfair use by the defendant of the plaintiff's copyrighted pictures and unfair paraphrase of the plaintiff's text accompanying its picture."[138] But the confusion is not just Woolsey's, for in the common law, examples are also precedent. *Detective Comics v. Bruns Publications'* confusion is thus also *King Features Syndicate v. Fleischer's*, which it cites; and subsequent cases involving similar kinds of "copying" will themselves inherit the same confusion. From this perspective, Woolsey appears less the primary cause for the lawsuit's messiness than a single node in a chain of effects that long preceded him and will long follow him.

Conclusion

For all its pretensions—or perhaps the better word is *aspirations*—to logic, the common law is a form of knowledge production subject to the limitations of human learning. As such, it is imperfect and at times incoherent and even irrational. Like other kinds of knowledge production, the common law develops in fits and starts, makes mistakes, and pursues hypotheses that take time to be proven correct or faulty. Unlike other forms of knowledge production, it also develops via an adversarial system designed for the primary purpose of achieving justice. For this reason, the immediate practical outcome of the work of jurisprudence is as important as—or sometimes of even greater importance than—the logic by which it is reached.

As the accounts above have demonstrated, such was the case with the common law's approach to copyright for cartoon characters and, more generally, the law of unfair competition as it applied to narrative-based properties during the modern copyright era. Not having yet discovered the utility of applying unfair competition law to fictional characters, judges introduced new rules in the effort to punish perceived wrongdoings, in the process rendering copyright law's treatment of characters incoherent and self-contradictory. In grafting reasoning that would eventually come to be identified with unfair competition and trademark law onto copyright law but limiting this reasoning's application to one specific kind of fictional character, judges inadvertently bent the law out of shape. The knowledge produced by decisions like *King Features Syndicate v. Fleischer* and *Detective Comics v. Bruns Publications* about what copyright protected and why can thus fairly be judged, with the benefit of decades of hindsight, as faulty.

Unlike other forms of knowledge production, however, the common law suffers a major weakness when it comes to correcting mistakes. Thanks to stare decisis, judges cannot (except in extraordinary circumstances) ignore or repudiate the rules and logic set forth in previous opinions. To the contrary, they must incorporate them into their own reasoning when deciding a case. Mistakes in jurisprudence in this manner tend to compound themselves over time. One wrong or suboptimal method of deciding a case can thus, through the power of precedent, have implications for countless others over multiple decades.

That said, precedent is not as binding as it might at first seem. Although forced to account for precedent, lawyers and judges can, through creative readings of past opinions, modify what the precedent is understood to mean. Such acts of reinterpretation can be difficult, especially when the precedent is old and regularly cited. But they can also occur without conscious effort at all, through lazy, obdurate, and/or prejudiced approaches to the law. While the tactic of reinterpretation can thus be used to correct past errors in the common law, it can just as often be used—as the above account of *King Features v. Fleischer Syndicate* and *Detective Comics v. Bruns Publications* both demonstrate—to reinforce them and introduce new ones. Indeed, the primary "error" introduced in these cases regarding cartoon characters has never been corrected and, for better or worse, persists today.

The broader historical circumstances that informed these decisions, however, have changed. Today, the applicability of unfair competition and trademark law to narrative-based properties is almost universally accepted. As a result, the "owners" of fictional characters are not forced to rely solely upon copyright law to maintain control over the use of their characters. At the same time, through the entertainment industry's adoption of multimedia, transmedia, and widescale cross-media adaptation, fictional characters of all kinds have developed in such a way that they, like early cartoon characters, lack a single textual origin. Indeed, in many so-called transmedia properties, the cartoon or comic book serves as a key component. The owners of fictional characters in any big media property can thus today not only rely upon the protections afforded by unfair competition and trademark law but, if necessary, can even make a reasonable claim in court to the extra protections still afforded to cartoon characters by copyright law.[139] Property-owners would no doubt call this a good thing, and perhaps it is—but it is hardly the product of the kind of coherent reasoning that we expect (perhaps unwisely) from the law.

CHAPTER 5

Conan, the Syndicate

Informal Contracting and the Making of Narrative-Based Property

> "For the meaning of the law in life and in the practice of lawyers is its meaning not to courts, but to laymen."
> —Karl Lewellyn, *The Bramblebush*[1]

In the book's three previous chapters, lawyers (and the sons of lawyers) have appeared as key figures in the histories of narrative-based properties. Sometimes, as in the lawsuits described in chapters 2 and 4, lawyers were driving forces in the fates of such properties; other times, as in the handling of Lovecraft's literary estate in chapter 3, their influence was more circumscribed. But in all three chapters, lawyers played significant roles in the stories of the properties' development. This chapter is different. Lawyers do not appear until near the chapter's end, and when they do, they function more as tools employed by the property's managers than as actors in their own right. Instead of lawyers, we have laypersons. The absence of lawyers, however, does not mean that the history of the property presented here is lacking in legal wrangling. To the contrary, the history's main actors evoke, employ, and even (like a lawyer might do) interrogate the law throughout. They write and challenge contracts, threaten lawsuits, undertake copyright searches, and invent novel legal strategies to save a property and secure a film deal. As the chapter demonstrates, legal action, formal and informal, can occur with little involvement by lawyers and legal knowledge can flourish among laypersons. The chapter's main protagonist, Lyon Sprague de Camp, is just such a layperson—although one possessing, from early in his career, greater legal bona fides than most.

In 1936, at the age of twenty-nine, a relatively inexperienced de Camp completed his first book, *Inventions and Their Management,* coauthored with a young MIT graduate named Alfred Berle. One of the first general-audience books on U.S. intellectual property law, *Inventions and Their Management* served both as a standalone resource for aspiring inventors and, after being split up into a series of booklets, as the main text for a correspondence course offered by the publisher's parent company, International Correspondence of Scranton. In detailed but accessible prose, the book introduces the legal and economic logics underpinning the concept of intellectual property, summarizes relevant legislation and case law, and provides step-by-step instructions on how to register patents and copyrights. Trained as engineers—and both of them only recently out of graduate school—neither de Camp nor Berle possessed any formal legal training nor practical experience in IP law.[2] Nevertheless, their book went through four editions between 1937 and 1959 and seems to have been held in fairly high esteem, not only by would-be inventors but also by lawyers, lawmakers, and judges.[3] No less an authority than the U.S. Supreme Court, for example, cited the second edition of Berle and de Camp's book twice in support of its opinion in the 1963 patent case *Sperry v. Florida.*[4]

For all its success, however, *Inventions and Their Management* had been something of an accident for de Camp. Although long passionate about engineering and its history, he had never had much interest in law and had only stumbled into writing the book through his employment at an organization called the Inventors Foundation. His first employer after de Camp received his master's degree (as de Camp recalled, "nobody else seemed willing to pay me anything at all"), the understaffed and low-paying Inventors Foundation had directed him, as it appears to have done most of its workers, to do a bit of everything. For de Camp, this included substitute teaching for the Foundation's classes, evaluating student inventions, and writing the *Inventions* book.[5] The job thus trained De Camp, interested or not, in the fundamental principles of patent law, and it taught him to consider what we would today call "opportunities for monetization" when evaluating whether potential intellectual property was worth the time and expense of registration.[6]

By 1938, however, de Camp had left behind the field of inventions altogether and—save for a short stint working for the U.S. Navy during World War II—devoted his labor entirely to popular writing.[7] Success came quickly in the genre of science fiction, and, through considerable hustling and a willingness to write in multiple genres, de Camp was eventually able to support his family on the proceeds of writing alone. When he first became involved with Robert E. Howard's Conan character in the 1950s, de Camp was thus a smart, seasoned, and hardworking professional writer, who was especially well-known among science-fiction fans for his foundational work in time-travel fiction. Thanks to his career as a writer, he was also an astute, albeit amateur, student of copyright law. Most writers, if they have any success, come to possess a general understanding of copyright law. But de Camp paid more attention to the law than most. Although he was surely influenced by his former work with patents, the reason for de Camp's interest was primarily practical, as is suggested by the revisions he contributed to the fourth edition of his *Inventions* textbook, published in 1959 under the slightly expanded title *Inventions, Patents, and Their Management.*[8] In addition to updates to the patent case law (presumably based on research conducted by Berle), de Camp added sections on copyright indivisibility and the legal protections available to fictional characters—hardly issues relevant to would-be inventors but of importance to writers of genre fiction like de Camp. Indeed, de Camp's account of indivisibility reads more like an impassioned complaint by an affected author than an objective account of the principle's origins and function.[9]

In the 1950s and for the subsequent decades he served as steward to the Conan property, de Camp was thus a layperson with respect to copyright law, but a layperson with an unusually keen understanding of the law's principles and their practical applications. Operating without the assistance of a lawyer, he employed this understanding to transform Howard's original pulp-fiction Conan stories into a business enterprise that closely resembled—and, as Carlos Scolari, Paolo Bertetti, and Matthew Freeman have suggested, prefigured—the kind of narrative-based properties that critics and industry workers call "franchises" or "transmedia" today.[10] Given de Camp's lack of formal legal training, as well as serious problems with what constituted Howard's literary estate, what de Camp achieved was no small accomplishment, especially under a copyright regime that seemed increasingly ill-suited to the needs of a rapidly evolving entertainment industry. Nor was his success without controversy. As we will see, the history of the property up through the late 1970s revolves around a series of contractual disputes among stakeholders that nearly came to destroy it. And yet, through improvisation, threats, creativity, and compromise, the property survived; and Conan and his world continue to this day to be licensed to a wide range of entertainment companies.

In addition to lacking much involvement by lawyers, the property discussed here is unlike those covered in previous chapters due to its reliance upon the kind of tight intertextuality usually identified (rightly or wrongly) with narrative-based properties today. Although the Conan property lacked such intertextuality during its first decades, by the 1950s de Camp, with some assistance, had begun to transform it into something much closer, narratologically, to a late-twentieth-century or twenty-first-century story world. The primary goal of this chapter is to show how such a transformation occurred, both textually and legally. In doing so, the chapter builds upon the Conan scholarship of Scolari, Bertetti, and Freeman, as well as Paul Sammon's excellent (though non-scholarly) *Conan: The Phenomenon.*[11] But it also diverges considerably from these earlier histories of the property by rooting its account in the property's evolving legal framework. This new approach was enabled—and indeed prompted by—consultation of the (as yet unsorted) Lynn Sprague and Catherine Crook de Camp Papers held at the Harry Ransom Center at the University of Texas Austin. Drawing heavily from these papers, which were supplemented by additional archival material (most of which was provided me informally by fans), the history of the Conan property offered in this chapter sheds new light on the property's textual and narratological innovations, which, it turns out, emerged not in the interest of developing a complex transmedia story world but rather as solutions to difficult legal and contractual problems.

In addition to presenting a revised history of the Conan property's development, this chapter also aims, like the chapters that preceded it, to illustrate and explain an important, taken-for-granted legal/industrial principle that governed the development of narrative-based intellectual property during the modern copyright era. In this chapter, that principle is what contract scholars call *informal contracting*: contracting that is tacit, ambiguous, and/or questionable as to whether a court would enforce it. Informal contracting is hardly unique to the modern copyright era but was both far more ubiquitous and accepted during that time than it is today. As the first section of this chapter explains, for most freelance creators working before the end of the 1970s, informal contracts were not an aberration but a regular (and often taken-for-granted) aspect of how the entertainment industry functioned. What is more, such contracts typically caused few problems. Although it might seem astonishing to a twenty-first-century reader, large portions of the entertainment industry did not seem to require the careful, formalized rendering of rights and responsibilities that the industry as a whole appears to require today. The example of Conan demonstrates why this was the case, but also shows how informal contracting could risk imperiling properties as the modern copyright era gave way to the period that followed.

In tracing the Conan property's development, the chapter also seeks to provide a detailed case study of how a series of disputes arising (in part) from informal contracting during the modern copyright era played out in practice. Contract disputes in the entertainment industry have long been a rich subject matter for media studies and legal scholars, many of whom have dedicated substantial energy to documenting and sometimes decrying the injustices caused by unfair contracts and to tracing the efforts—usually organized—taken by creators to secure more advantageous and regularized terms. Such scholarship includes recent work on the Writers Guild, Dramatists Guild, and Radio Writers Guild;[12] comic book creators' efforts to claim or establish legal rights to characters;[13] and lawsuits involving top-name Hollywood talent (sometimes over what is pejoratively known as "Hollywood accounting").[14] Most of this scholarship, however, focuses on disputes characterized by extreme differences in bargaining power, with, on the one side, creative employees or independent contractors (typically lacking in power except when represented collectively via a union or guild) and, on the other, management professionals or even entire corporations (better able to set contractual terms in their favor and possessing greater resources for legal battles). To be sure, scholarship exploring contractual disputes of this kind is vitally important. Not only does it help us better understand how industries employ and/or exploit creative workers, it can also help explain why labor, authorship, and publishing/exhibition practices have evolved differently across media industries.[15]

But the study of contracts can be valuable even when they lack extreme power differences and avoid giving rise to lawsuits. Indeed, a large part of (usually invisible) media-industry activity involves the negotiation and renegotiation of contracts, as well as dispute-resolution processes occurring outside of a court of law or even formalized guild framework. Although there has been media and communication scholarship that touches upon these aspects of contractual labor, most of it has taken a macroscopic approach, describing general norms and practices or kinds of negotiation.[16] This chapter takes a different approach, examining a long-running sequence of contractual conflicts and compromises, exacerbated and enabled by informal contracting, in which two parties with roughly identical power were continually engaged, sometimes as allies, sometimes as enemies. The result is a picture of contract negotiation and dispute that is at once much messier, more mundane, and even (perhaps) more irrational than typically offered elsewhere—but no less realistic or representative.

This chapter consists of five sections. The first provides a succinct description of the principle of informal contracting. The second describes the genesis of Robert E. Howard's Conan stories and their fate upon his death. The third traces the transformation of these stories, partially at the hands of fans-turned-professionals, into a narrative-based property organized around intertextuality. In the fourth section, I examine the legal and business strategies employed by L. Sprague de Camp and Glenn Lord, which resulted, paradoxically, in the stories' loss of copyright protection *and* the property's tremendous business success in the 1970s. The fifth and final section focuses on the Conan Syndicate, a novel and arguably ingenious contractual strategy for protecting the property that also, in the conflicts it prompted, nearly destroyed it.

Before we proceed, however, two brief caveats are warranted. First, although this chapter places special emphasis on the principle of informal contracting, the complicated history of the Conan property cannot be understood without reference to the principles discussed in previous chapters as well. Short duration of copyright, copyright formalities (including indivisibility), the idea-expression dichotomy, authorial genius—even the inchoate state of unfair competition law with respect to fictional works—all matter here to such an extent that they cannot be bracketed off without both significantly distorting the Conan property's history and misrepresenting how the disputes over rights to the property played out. Despite the emphasis on contracting, this chapter thus proceeds as a holistic, fine-grained legal history of a narrative-based property that is causally maximal: that is, emphasizing multiple forces at once. Maximal causality does not, of course, make for succinct or simple history, but I have nevertheless endeavored to provide a story here that is clear and even eloquent, despite its assumption that readers will be familiar with the principles discussed in previous chapters. I make no assumptions, however, that readers possess a similar familiarity with the Conan character or stories.

Finally, a brief word on the politics of Conan historiography. Since the start of the twenty-first century, de Camp has fared poorly at the hands of Conan fans, with the Robert E. Howard Foundation, Robert E. Howard scholars (both academic and amateur), the editors of the recent Del Rey editions of Howard's work, and large segments of the organized fan community having rather firmly rejected de Camp as a selfish, greedy adulterator of Howard's work and vision. That fans have not been kinder to him is in part a result of de Camp's patrician and judgmental approach to Howard in writing, as well as his decision to refrain from responding publicly to the ethical charges leveled at him in the 1980s and 1990s by Glenn Lord (who we will come to know as the Conan property's co-manager). My main goal with this chapter is to illuminate the process of narrative-based property development; the question of de Camp's ethical culpability (or, for that matter, Lord's) is irrelevant to me. That said, the history provided here has much to offer readers that are interested in that question, and I encourage them to borrow from it as they elaborate and refine what an ethics of narrative-based property development might mean.

The Principle of Informal Contracting

Although some sections of the entertainment industry, usually at the instigation of a guild or union, eventually came to adopt standard, formalized contracts for creative workers, such contracts were rare even up until the 1970s for the majority of freelance writers and artists.[17] For virtually all prose-fiction writers, essayists, comic book writers, and comic book artists, substantial numbers of screenwriters and journalists, and a minority of radio and teleplay writers, contracts varied so widely both between and within their respective fields that one cannot meaningfully speak of a "typical" contract for intellectual property production during the modern copyright era. What all these creators did have in common, however, was that—except when governed by a minimum basic agreement secured by a guild or union—the contracts under which their work was sold exhibited a high degree of informality and vagueness. In the newspaper and magazine industries, for example, freelance creators often sold rights to their work without any formal contract at all, relying instead upon verbal promises, examples of past performance (especially on the issue of payment rates), and the expectation of fair play. As Franklin Laskin pithily observed in a 1954 law review article, "The bargain in the magazine field is usually submission by the author followed by acceptance by the publisher. Rarely is there a preexisting contract to cover the rights of the parties."[18] In lieu of a contract, creators in most cases received a post-publication check, upon which was printed a legend indicating that by endorsing the check the payee surrendered a specified set of rights (or in some cases, all rights) to his or her work.[19] What a court would make of such a contract—often delivered and signed long after the story had already been published and copyrighted in the publisher's name—is an open question, not only because of the check's necessarily terse and ambiguous descriptions of terms, but also because courts sometimes held, under the principle of copyright indivisibility, that rights could not be divided in this fashion at all. That the contracts were legally problematic, even under the United States' especially liberal common law approach to contracts, was widely acknowledged by commentators on the industry. In the 1913 debut issue of *The Bulletin of the Authors' League of America*, for example, the League asked, "Is such a transaction legal? Can the author without prejudice alter this enforced 'contract' and cash the cheque?"[20] No answer was provided.

Although no industries so routinely forewent written contracts as the newspaper and magazine industries, in virtually every industry contracts for the work of many freelance creators shared an underlying vagueness, so that even when written and signed in advance, the parties were forced to rely upon understandings or agreements not formally detailed in the contracts themselves. Procedures relating to copyright formalities, for example, were often incompletely detailed or left out entirely, the result of which was that parties needed to rely upon best practices or unwritten agreements to ensure that copyrights were properly registered, assigned, and renewed. Given the stringent formalities associated with copyright during this time, such vagueness had the paradoxical effect of increasing the likelihood that statutory formalities might not be correctly observed while simultaneously providing courts the "wiggle room" to find that they had been (as the Second Circuit Court of Appeals did, for example, in *Dam v. Kirk La Shelle Co.*).[21] Similarly vague were contractual designations of what the purchase of a specified right or set of rights was actually conveying. Although contracts referred in seemingly straightforward language to such things as "serial rights," "dramatic rights," and "book rights," different parties—not to mention judges—often had different understandings of what such terms meant. Author Arthur Train, who before undertaking a career as a writer had practiced for many years as a lawyer, thus recounts his surprise at learning that S. S. McClure (publisher of *McClure's Magazine*)—to whom Train had sold "serial rights" in the story "C.Q."—had sold the British rights in the story to a magazine in London:

> What were "serial rights"? What had I intended to sell to McKenzie [at *McClure's*] and he to buy? Had there been the necessary "meeting of minds"? Certainly I hadn't intended to dispose of my newly-discovered British birthright. In fact, I hadn't known it existed! "Serial rights" might mean almost anything. There was no satisfactory adjudication in the books. To me "serial rights" meant the right to publish *once* serially—in a specified magazine—nothing else.[22]

Despite pressure from the Authors' League (for which Train came to serve as legal counsel) and the gradual adoption of more detailed contracts by the larger book publishers, such vagueness remained a common aspect of many contracts well into the 1970s.[23] Freelance artists and writers working for Marvel Comics, for example, were operating without formal contracts as late as 1980.[24]

Industry observers put forth many explanations for the lack of formal contracting in the early entertainment industry, the most common of which—and the one most frequently cited by guilds and unions—being that publishers and film studios used informality and vagueness to take advantage of authors.[25] Others suggested that authors' distinctive psychologies or their inherent lack of interest in business were to blame.[26] The more likely explanation, however, is that only in very rare cases was the value of clear formal contracts worth the costs to both parties of drafting, negotiating, and signing them. In part, this was because first publication rights (whether serial or book) were, for the overwhelming majority of original work, the only rights that mattered. For every *Tarzan of the Apes* (first serialized in *All-Story Magazine*) or *The Postman Always Rings Twice* (first published as a book by Alfred A. Knopf), there were a thousand other published stories that were never adapted or reprinted. What is more, even for those works that *were* republished (via serial reprints or books, in domestic or foreign markets) or adapted into other media, the price paid for the original first publication right typically dwarfed that paid for any other right, save, in the case of the most popular stories, that of motion picture rights.[27] Indeed, for the first half of the twentieth century, magazines functioned as the industrial base or "keystone" for the entire market ecosystem for fiction: not only did they serve as the primary forum for first publication, they also provided virtually every author with the bulk of his or her yearly earnings.[28] "Frankly, unless the young author wishes to become a script writer," explained Train, "he had better look to the magazines for his living and regard anything substantial in the way of book, film, or radio sales as 'riots, hurricanes, or Acts of God,' of which the tables of common sense actuaries do not take account and against which the insurance policies for happiness do not run."[29] Given the unlikelihood that the secondary rights to a story were of any value, most authors (who, like their publishers, always had the option of hiring a lawyer or negotiating when selling work) rarely paid them much mind.

Industrial actors had yet another reason, however, for relying upon informal contracts, and that is that the structure of the entertainment industry deprived either party to a deal of the incentive to cheat. Except in the early film and broadcast industries, where creators were usually paid employees and subject to very different working arrangements, the fact that creators were independent contractors meant that publishers relied upon a regular series of one-off contracts in order to acquire content. So long as demand for content was high—which it was for virtually the entire period with which we are concerned—friendly relationships between buyers and sellers were essential. A publisher who mistreated or took advantage of a writer, for instance, risked cutting off his or her business not only from that writer's future work but also—thanks to word of mouth and guild advisory reports—from the work of other writers.[30] This dynamic prevailed for both shoestring operations, such as the pulps, and highly capitalized ones, such as film studios and million-circulation magazines. Publishers of all kinds were thus incentivized to treat their creative-workers-cum-independent-suppliers fairly (at least, relatively speaking) and to resolve amicably any disputes that arose. This does not mean that authors were always happy with the deals they received. Countless writers charged editors, publishers, and producers with poor judgment and lack of business sense, while some—most famously, James Cain—impugned the fairness of publishers' demands for a share of subsidiary rights.[31] For the most part, however, independent creators got along well with the people who bought their work, and lawsuits were rare. The Authors' League thus regularly characterized the bad or cheating publisher as the exception, noting, for example, in the inaugural issue of its *Bulletin*, that "[t]he existing relations between author and publisher are in many cases—most cases, we believe—pleasant."[32]

For a twenty-first-century reader, especially one whose experience of contracts has primarily consisted of end-user licenses, credit card agreements, and housing contracts (leases, mortgages, etc.), the idea that formalized contracts often play a minimal role in managing exchange relationships might seem farfetched—or perhaps a quirk of the entertainment industry. Empirical work on contracting, however, has suggested that the "non-use" of contracts in business is relatively common—and for many of the same reasons I have suggested above. Such work began with Stewart Macaulay's groundbreaking 1963 essay, "Contractual Relations in Business: A Preliminary Study," which, drawing primarily on interviews, seemed to show that many businesses in the manufacturing industry, despite employing contracts, rarely used them in court (or even threatened to do so) in order to resolve disputes; what is more, many of the contracts these businesses used were vague or unspecified in one or more key areas, and a few were, as a matter of state law, unenforceable (a fact that the lawyers who drafted them seemed to recognize).[33] Subsequent studies reliably reproduced Macaulay's findings to such an extent that it is now widely accepted among legal scholars (or at least law and society scholars) that in most business contracting, "planning for the risk of nonperformance often is not too careful, and disputes are seldom resolved by litigation or even by applying the norms of contract law outside of litigation."[34] Scholarly adherents to what has come to be called "relational contract theory" explain this seemingly counterintuitive conclusion by arguing that, when dealing with potentially long-term business relationships, the relationship itself often takes priority over the discrete transaction. As Robert Gordon has influentially put it,

> parties treat their contracts more like marriages than like one-night stands. Obligations grow out of the commitment that they have made to one another, and the conventions that the trading community establishes for such commitments; they are not frozen at the initial moment of commitment, but change as circumstances change. . . . In bad times parties are expected to lend one another mutual support, rather than standing on their rights; each will treat the other's insistence on literal performance as willful obstructionism; if unexpected contingencies occur resulting in severe losses, the parties are to search for equitable ways of dividing the losses; and the sanction for egregiously bad behavior, is always, of course, refusal to deal again.[35]

The entertainment industry's approach to contracting in the modern copyright era, while admittedly less formal than its approach today, was thus well in keeping with approaches in other industries. Custom, the importance of reputation and good business relations, ethical norms such as the value of one's word, and the codependency of suppliers and buyers all worked to regulate exchange relationships as much as—or more than—formalized legal contracts did.

One might suppose that however well informal contracting worked for the typical entertainment industry deal, such contracting inevitably broke down when new technologies/media (such as film, sound film, radio, television, syndicated comic strips, and mass market paperbacks) appeared on the scene. To some extent this is true, since in such cases parties could not rely upon custom or shared understanding. For the most part, however, the contractual confusion caused by new technologies would likely not have been avoided by formal contracting either. Drafters of such contracts would have had to know in advance not only what new technologies might appear but also how these new technologies might impact already existing rights. Would, for instance, a silent film constitute a dramatic representation, a series of photographic illustrations, or something else entirely? And if silent films were a special kind of dramatic representation, how did this impact the value of dramatic rights in stories? That these kinds of questions are impossible to answer adequately in advance is suggested by their persistence into the twenty-first century, most notably with respect to "streaming" media rights, which—despite the existence of highly standardized, union-negotiated contracts—caused such rancorous disagreement between Hollywood writers and film/television studios in the early 2000s that the former struck for six months from 2007 to 2008 before securing what they felt was an adequate deal regarding them.[36]

When disputes over new technologies/media did arise, they occasionally ended up in court, as rightsholders put forth incompatible interpretations of how the new technologies were covered by preexisting contracts. Rather than resolve the confusion, however, the judicial system typically exacerbated it, as different courts issued incompatible rulings. Let us take, for example, the question of whether a silent film was or was not, under the law, a drama. In *Photo Drama Motion Picture Co. v. Social Uplift Film Corp.* (1914), a court in the Second Circuit ruled that a film was not.[37] Three years later, in *Hart v. Fox* (1917), a New York state court ruled that a film was.[38] The question in any event quickly ceased to matter, for as motion pictures became less novel, contracts became more specific regarding them, and courts began to treat film rights as an issue of contractual expectation rather than ontology, with the U.S. Supreme Court holding in *Manners v. Morosco* (1920) that the parties would have used the words "motion picture rights" if they had meant to convey them.[39] A similar sequence took place with respect to sound films and then television: initial confusion, which found its way into court where it was there replicated, followed by both more detailed contracts and new industry routines.[40]

Robert E. Howard's Conan

Hailed today by both adventure-fiction fans and American-literature scholars as one of America's greatest pulp fiction writers, Robert E. Howard was little recognized for his writing during his short life, ended by his own hand in 1936 at the age of thirty. An autodidact who never traveled far from his parents in rural central Texas, Howard published close to one hundred fifty stories in pulp and amateur magazines during his lifetime, many of them adventure tales set in semi-lawless geographical and political frontiers and featuring strong, self-sufficient male heroes. Although such motifs were hardly unique to Howard's fiction, Howard tended to employ them in distinctive fashion, grounding them in historical and geographical fact, and building out of them an almost mournful skepticism toward the values of civilization, ancient and modern. Widely if eccentrically read in the areas of ancient history, ethnology, and turn-of-the-century racial theory (including the spiritualist works of theosophists such as William Scott-Elliot), Howard treated the genre of pulp fiction as a means of both making a living telling stories and exploring the historical and existential ideas that most excited him. Whether or not these ideas were also what attracted pulp editors and readers, Howard, by the time of his death, had found considerable success with both *Weird Tales* and *Action Stories*, having developed for each of these magazines a popular series character: Conan the Cimmerian, a fierce barbarian adventurer, and Breckinridge Elkins, a larger-than-life Western mountain man. Today, Breckinridge Elkins—along with the entire genre of Western comedic adventure in which his stories were set—is largely forgotten. Conan, by contrast, has proven to be one of the most enduring pulp fiction characters of all time.

Conan debuted in the December 1932 issue of *Weird Tales* in a short story titled "The Phoenix on the Sword."[41] This first Conan story—a revision of an earlier, unsold tale about a barbarian king named Kull[42]—situates the barbarian as reluctant ruler of the kingdom of Aquilonia, where he is beset by disloyal subjects resentful of being ruled by a king of foreign blood. In the following month's issue of the magazine, Conan appeared in a second tale, "The Scarlet Citadel," where he was similarly portrayed as a brooding, melancholy ruler who misses his carefree days as an adventurer.[43] With his third appearance in the March 1933 issue, however, Conan underwent a change, becoming in "The Tower of the Elephant" a young thief whose thirst for adventure leads him to attempt the robbery of a powerful sorcerer.[44] Over the next three years, Conan appeared in twenty-five issues of *Weird Tales,* sometimes as a young man, sometimes a pirate, sometimes an experienced adventurer or military commander, and once more (in the multipart "The Hour of the Dragon"[45]) as the king of Aquilonia.

Like the stories that constituted other early-twentieth-century pulp franchises, the Conan tales employed a consistent set of storytelling comportments. Almost every story featured, for example, a damsel (usually scantily clad) whom Conan (also scantily clad) would at some point rescue. And there were usually gory battle sequences, evil sorcerers, magical treasure, and giant, often biologically impossible, monsters. Most of the stories also exhibited a complex theory of racial development, equal parts essentialist (with the story's different human races having different abilities and personality predispositions) and evolutionary (with a lack of interracial exchange, for example, put forth as a cause of racial stagnation and decay).

Beyond its reliance upon a small set of storytelling comportments, however, the Conan series was atypical of early pulp properties. Its most obvious difference was the fact that Conan's identity changed significantly from story to story across multiple variables, including age and appearance, profession, and even (to some degree) personality. The older King Conan, for example, exhibits a melancholia that bears little resemblance to the boisterous joie de vivre of Conan at his youngest, while only the pirate Conan of "Queen of the Black Coast" seems to be open to experiencing love.[46] To be sure, other franchise characters from this period sometimes also changed between stories, but they tended to do so linearly, aging as the stories proceeded, and with their underlying personalities remaining largely the same.

More unusual—and perhaps more difficult for twenty-first-century readers to appreciate—the Conan stories ranged widely across pulp genres. Today, the stories' fantastic preindustrial settings would situate them squarely within the "fantasy" or "swords and sorcery" genre. In the 1930s, however, no such genres existed, and Howard—an aspiring commercial writer whose primary exposure to fiction was the pulps—built each of his Conan stories upon the conventions of a popular contemporary pulp genre or subgenre. "Red Nails" and "The Pool of the Black One," for example, are lost race tales; "Beyond the Black River" a Western; "Jewels of Gwahlur" an African adventure (or "jungle") tale; "The Scarlet Citadel" an adventure tale in the vein of Walter Scott's historical romances; and "The God in the Bowl" (rejected by *Weird Tales*) a locked-room mystery.[47] To be sure, the stories do not slavishly adhere to genre conventions, and some—like "The God in the Bowl"—even cleverly subvert them. Relying on so many genres may even have served as a kind of insurance for Howard, as a Conan tale rejected by *Weird Tales* might without too great a difficulty be stripped of the Conan character, minimally revised, and then submitted to another pulp magazine. Such, for example, seems to have been Howard's practice with the "The Black Stranger," a Conan pirate story, which—after failing to find a home at *Weird Tales*—was rewritten as "Swords of the Red Brotherhood" (with Conan replaced by a pirate named Black Vulmea) and presumably sent out to other magazines, such as *Pirate Stories*.[48] Whatever Howard's reasoning was, the Conan stories' generic range was unprecedented for the time and also somewhat at odds with pulp publishing logic, as it deprived the stories of the kind of predictability that made series fiction so appealing to publishers in the first place.

In service to the variety of genres, the Conan stories also made use of a wide range of settings, including deserts, snowy mountains, "Western" frontier towns, "medieval" cities, pirate ships, and Oriental palaces. None of these were out of keeping with contemporary adventure fiction, although such fiction was typically set in real-world places, such as Africa, Afghanistan, and the Himalayas. The settings in Howard's Conan stories by contrast were made up—or at least partially made up, as they deliberately echoed real geographic regions and nations, past and present. Aquilonia, for example, is modeled upon ancient Rome, Stygia upon Egypt, Vendhya upon India, and Afghulistan upon Afghanistan. The Conan stories' made-up races had similar real-world inspirations, with the Picts modeled first upon the British Picts and then indigenous North Americans, the Kushites sub-Saharan Africans, and the Shemites ancient Semites. Today, for reasons that will be discussed later in this chapter, scholars and fans typically view these quasi-imaginary places and peoples as comprising a unified, imaginary world, sometimes called Hyboria. At the time the stories were first published, however, the existence of this world was only minimally evident. Although multiple stories contained descriptive allusions to the same places and peoples, each story tended to be geographically self-contained, with specific places rarely employed as settings more than once across the series. What is more, because these places so clearly echoed real-world locations, the stories made no demands upon readers to keep track of—or even recognize the existence of—a shared story world. Indeed, there was little benefit to be had by doing so: like most other early narrative-based properties—but unlike those of the twenty-first century—the stories lacked the requisite intertextuality.

Given the importance of intertextuality to the development of the Conan property after Howard's death, its absence from Howard's original stories is striking. With the exception of the names of places and races—and of Conan himself, notwithstanding the changes his identity undergoes—the stories contain nothing that would be called an "asset" today: no recurring characters, objects, or events. Like most fiction from this era, they also exhibit no textual memory across stories. Unlike the static virtual beginnings that typified other memory-less series, however, the beginnings of Howard's Conan stories were unstable, with both Conan himself and the genre in which he is situated changing with each iteration. The stories thus broke from the approach to iterative storytelling as it was typically practiced elsewhere while preserving the textual amnesia that Umberto Eco has identified as a hallmark of this form of narrative.[49] As we will see, readers of *Weird Tales* sometimes tried rearranging and synthesizing Howard's iterations to produce for themselves plausible biographies of Conan, thereby supplying the stories with a fan-made intertextuality. But with the exception of Conan's changing age and the different locations of the stories (which one might use to try to "map" his travels), the stories offered scant textual support for this kind of reading.

Before we turn to what became of the property after Howard's suicide, it is worth asking why his Conan series appears so different from other early series fiction. Although relatively unusual, series fiction that progressed temporally from story to story was not unheard of in the 1930s; indeed, Howard was familiar with both Burroughs's Tarzan and his John Carter/Barsoom series—and may even have modeled Conan upon Burroughs's protagonists. Howard could have thus—in theory—written stories that were explicitly intertextual, with Conan aging as the series progressed. Unlike Burroughs's heroes, however, Howard's Conan was relatively unknown (the stories were not distributed in general-audience magazines nor was there much prospect of them being made into Hollywood films), and his primary venue was the short story, not the novel. These factors made it risky to deploy intertextuality in the way

Burroughs did, not only because Howard could not have relied upon new or sporadic *Weird Tales* readers to know Conan's backstory, but also because *Weird Tales*' editor, Farnsworth Wright, sometimes rejected Howard's stories outright. Had the stories been sequential, these rejections would have seriously complicated and slowed down Howard's production of them. And yet Howard also forwent the more common model of the static, endlessly repeating, virtual beginning—a model that was well-suited for the pulps and was associated with some of their most popular and longest-lasting series (such as that of Seabury Quinn's occult detective Jules de Grandin in *Weird Tales*).

One possible explanation is that Howard wrote unreflectively, paying little attention to how the stories fit together until after he had finished writing them. Howard himself sometimes suggested as much. In an oft-quoted letter to Clark Ashton Smith, for example, he describes the stories as almost writing themselves: "the man Conan seemed suddenly to grow up in my mind without much labor on my part and immediately a stream of stories flowed off my pen—or rather off my typewriter—almost without effort on my part. I did not seem to be creating, but rather relating events that had occurred. Episode crow[d]ed on episode so fast that I could scarcely keep up with them."[50] There are reasons, however, to doubt this account. We know, for instance, that the first Conan story involved quite a bit of labor, as Howard had produced it by heavily revising a non-Conan story that had been rejected by *Weird Tales*. And he regularly rewrote and revised tales, often swapping characters, in order to sell them. Nevertheless, it is true that Howard as a writer devoted much less attention to the long-term financial viability of his creations than did most of the more successful pulp writers. The sequence of the Conan stories was quite clearly not the subject of rational planning. This was partially an issue of values. Despite writing for the pulps, Howard endeavored to produce what he understood to be high-quality literary fiction. He thus utilized his stories to experiment with (rather than slavishly reproduce) generic conventions and to explore the ideas that most interested him: ancient history, ethnology, civilization versus barbarism, and so on. This explains the generic range of his fiction as well as his practice of cycling through different fictional characters rather than developing them into long-running series.

There is, however, another possible explanation for the uniqueness of Howard's Conan series. Today, many fans and scholars attribute to the Conan stories a kind of backdoor or covert intertextuality. In this reading, Howard's Conan stories only *appear* to be disconnected; when read properly, they demonstrate both a stable narrative arc or "career" for the series's main character and a painstakingly constructed, multitext story world. From this perspective, the Conan stories not only demonstrate a textual memory; they in fact prefigure the detailed, multitext epics of late-twentieth-century fantasy fiction, with "Hyboria" functioning as a kind of proto-Middle Earth. Interpreted in this fashion, the series's differences from other early franchises are primarily the result of Howard's approach being ahead of its time, a kind of storytelling mutation that would one day prove adaptive but was tragically ill-suited for the publishing environment of the 1930s. The evidence usually put forth for this interpretation is, however, not the stories themselves (subjected, as one might expect, to careful close reading) but rather a remarkable paratext titled "The Hyborian Age," which did not see print during Howard's lifetime but would come to play an important role in the development of the Conan property after Howard's death.

The "Hyborian Age" is a peculiar essay, described by Howard in a 1936 parenthetical addendum as fictional background material. "When I began writing the Conan stories a few years ago," he explains, "I prepared this 'history' of his age and the peoples of that age, in order to lend him and his sagas a greater aspect of realness."[51] In providing such a history, "The Hyborian Age" might be thought to resemble an IP bible of the kind utilized today—but the resemblance is slight, as the presumed setting of the Conan stories occupies only a sliver of the history the essay lays out: a mere six of the essay's sixty-five paragraphs. Conan himself receives no mention at all, while a hero named Arus—who comes to power *after* the period in which Conan's stories seem to be set—serves as the essay's primary historical figure. Indeed, assessed purely by its content, "The Hyborian Age" appears more a kind of imaginative ethnology than a platform for telling stories. In its careful tracing of the descent and dispersion of Picts and Shemites across tens of thousands of years as a result of geological change, the essay reads more like the early segments of H. G. Well's *The Outline of History* (a book Howard knew well) than it does any traditionally conceived literary setting.[52] Even from the standpoint of production history, there is reason to doubt Howard's claim that the essay functioned in any significant way as background material. As Patrice Louinet has argued, Howard's conception of Conan's world developed gradually over time, and "The Hyborian Age," begun after his third Conan story, underwent continual revision and expansion as Howard produced additional stories.[53]

Whatever the reasons for the Conan series's distinctive structure,

Howard's commitment to it was short-lived. By mid-1935, after only three years of work on the character, Howard abandoned him, focusing instead on the popular and equally short-lived Western mountain man, Breckinridge Elkins.[54] Though there is no evidence that Howard planned to someday return to Conan, the opportunity would in any case never arise: in June 1936 Howard shot and killed himself. Having left no will, the rights to his literary work passed to his widowed father, Isaac. These rights, along with what little physical property Isaac possessed, passed upon his death in November 1944 to a friend, Dr. Pere Kuykendall, who held them until his own death in May of 1959. They then passed to Kuykendall's wife, Alla Ray Kuykendall, and his daughter, Alla Ray Morris, with whom they remained until the mid-1990s.[55]

Although this descent of rights is supported by legal documents and has gone uncontested in a number of court proceedings, the exact substance of these rights has at times—and particularly in the years immediately following Howard's death—been uncertain. There was no doubt that the rights included common law copyrights in Howard's letters, unpublished poetry, and unpublished fiction, though most of this material was for all intents and purposes lost until the 1950s.[56] As for the presumably more valuable published stories, at times key stakeholders doubted whether the heirs had any rights to them at all. Such was the state of pulp publishing in the early 1930s that authors regularly parted with many of the rights to their material when selling to periodicals. As noted in the previous section, the terms of ownership were also rarely secured by clear, formal contracts, but often instead via either tacit understanding or a simple check from the publisher, such as the one Howard's father received from Farnsworth Wright, editor of *Weird Tales,* shortly after his son's death. "I note on the back of this check," Isaac complained to his son's agent, Otis A. Kline, "that [upon signature] this Popular Fiction Publishing Co. claims First American Magazine and Radio Rights to Manuscripts. I did not know and cannot tell under what terms Robert carried on with Farnsworth."[57] Indeed, there was no way Howard's father could have known, for his son kept no records of his sales—and neither did his agent.

Although the fact that Howard did not keep records may strike us today as inexplicable, such behavior (or lack thereof) was not unusual at the time (for another example, see chapter 3). To some extent, writers did not keep detailed records because rudimentary copying technology made it difficult and expensive for them to do so: unless carbon paper, which was costly, was used at the time a document was first generated, copies had to be handmade—a laborious and error-prone process. Moreover, because the vast majority of material produced for the periodical market was perceived to have little or no value beyond its first publication, careful recordation of secondary rights seemed rarely warranted in the first place. Though ultimately wrong with respect to Howard's work, this perception was not unfounded, at least through the 1940s, as there were very few markets for reprints of most pulp fiction. Indeed, Kline was unable to sell any Howard reprints, even in foreign markets, and—as he explained to Howard's father in 1941—the typical rate for reprints was so low that it hardly justified trying.[58] Though a few authors—usually writing for the better pulps such as *Argosy*—were able to further exploit their stories through book, radio, or film deals, these were rare exceptions; for the vast majority of pulp fiction, the demand was simply too small to support their development in other media. Given the time and costs associated with formal legal contracts, the careful management of rights in magazine fiction (excepting the work of already famous writers) was thus not worth the bother.

Howard's father was nevertheless appalled by such a cavalier approach to his son's fiction, though it was an approach that Howard and his agent seemed to share. Isaac, desperate to secure the rights for the Conan stories, which he shrewdly imagined "would make a fine book," spent almost five years after Robert's death attempting through letters to get an accounting from *Weird Tales*—or to force Kline to get such an accounting—as to what rights the magazine publisher possessed.[59] Farnsworth Wright, editor of *Weird Tales*, though occasionally in correspondence with Isaac, seems never to have provided him with such an accounting—at least in part, I would guess, because the publisher itself did not know. Whatever the reason, after Kline informed Isaac in a 1941 letter that *Weird Tales* had most likely bought almost all of Howard's rights and that these rights were not anyway worth the cost of a suit to secure them, Isaac appears to have abandoned his efforts.[60] To Isaac and to Kline, the rights to Howard's stories were thereafter presumed to belong to the registered owner of the stories' copyrights, Popular Fiction Publishing Co.

As accurate as the preceding account of the rights is, however, it is likely to be unsatisfactory to many Howard fans and scholars, whom—as a group—have spilt much ink questioning who, in the days immediately following Howard's death, *really* owned the rights to these stories. Was it Isaac or was it *Weird Tales* (i.e., Popular Fiction Publishing Co.)? Although discussions around this question typically revolve around the registered copyright themselves, which—in keeping with both the strictures of indivisibility and the interests of efficiency—were undeniably held by the publisher, the presumption that Robert Howard had reserved at least some of the rights to some of the stories via informal contracting seems warranted. That said, what Robert may or may not have done—or, for that matter, what *Weird Tales* may or may not have done—is ultimately irrelevant, for in practice, in the absence of a court ruling on the matter, the "real" owner was whomever relevant stakeholders held to be the owner. In the case of Conan, for at least the first decade after Howard's death, relevant stakeholders were simply not sure. Isaac, for example, seems to have held the owner to be *Weird Tales,* while the writer and publisher August Derleth assumed—at least until Isaac informed him otherwise—that the owner was Isaac.[61] Further complicating the issue was the fact that stakeholders sometimes ascribed to Isaac a kind of second-order or "moral" right to Howard's stories, which superseded the formal legal right. Derleth, for example, indicated that he preferred his payment for anthology rights to one of Robert's stories be made to Robert's father, "regardless of the fact of ownership."[62] As stakeholders became accustomed to making this exception, the exception gradually ceased to be seen as an exception at all. By the time Dr. Kuykendall had inherited Isaac's estate (and Oscar Friend replaced Kline in managing Howard's literary rights), would-be licensors treated Kuykendall—who, never having known Robert and having no familial or genetic relationship to him, should have possessed no "moral" rights—as the legal holder of most of Howard's previously published work.

The Production of Intertextuality: From Fans to L. Sprague de Camp

In the decade following Howard's death, the Conan stories disappeared entirely from print. Memories of the property, however, persisted among important members of the nascent science-fiction/fantasy fan community, especially Donald Wollheim, future Ace Books editor and DAW Books founder. In 1936, the twenty-two-year-old fan published parts of Howard's "The Hyborian Age" in his short-lived fanzine, *The Phantagraph.* Two years later, LANY Cooperative Publications, an amateur publishing venture consisting of Wollheim and four other fans, published the complete essay in chapbook form.[63] To this chapbook, two other Howard fans—Peter Schuyler Miller and John D. Clark—contributed a bio-bibliographic account of Howard's hero titled "A Probable Outline of Conan's Career." Originally written between 1935 and 1936 and sent upon completion to Howard as a piece of fan mail, the outline (which Howard returned after making a few changes) reorders the stories according to what its authors perceived in the series as an implicit narrative chronology, beginning with Conan as a young thief in "The Tower of the Elephant" and ending when Conan "is about 45" in "The Hour of the Dragon."[64] As we will see, "A Probable Outline" would come to play an important role in the development of the Conan property. At the time it was published, however, very few saw it, and outside of a tiny community of early Howard devotees, Conan was either forgotten or unknown until the publication of *Skull-Face and Others* by Arkham House almost a decade later.

As described in chapter 3, Arkham House had originally been formed for the purpose of commemorating via a series of books the author H. P. Lovecraft, who had died in 1937—and who had been, incidentally, a friend and regular correspondent with Howard. The publishing house's remit soon expanded, however, to include other authors of weird or "macabre" fiction, with the intent, according to co-owner August Derleth, of "corner[ing] the market" in this genre.[65] Accordingly, Derleth assembled *Skull-Face*, a collection, eventually published in 1946, containing twenty-one of Howard's *Weird Tales* stories (six featuring Conan), as a representative sample of Howard's contribution to the genre. Acquiring the rights to these stories, however, proved frustrating to Derleth. Howard's father, whom Derleth at first assumed possessed at least some of these rights, insisted that he did not have them and, wary of getting into legal trouble, demanded that Arkham House secure formal releases from the owner of *Weird Tales* before he signed any licensing agreement or accepted payment.[66] Based on existing correspondence between Derleth and *Weird Tales*, Derleth seems ultimately not to have done this, the likely explanation being that after Isaac died in late 1944, Derleth no longer felt any moral or legal compulsion to do so. In any case, *Skull-Face* proved moderately successful for Arkham House, even receiving a (mixed) review in a 1946 issue of *The New York Times Book Review*;[67] nevertheless, the book probably did little to generate sustained interest in Conan, focusing as it did less on Conan himself than on Howard and the genre of weird fiction.

In 1948 and 1949, Wollheim, having broken into the publishing industry earlier in the decade and now editor at Avon Books, published in Avon's digest-size reprint magazine, *Avon Fantasy Reader*, two of the *Weird Tales* Conan stories Derleth had left out of *Skull-Face*.[68] Part of a general effort by the former fanzine author to bring attention to Howard and other *Weird Tales* authors he had loved in his youth, these stories were third and fourth in a series of seven Howard tales (six of which were reprints) printed in the magazine before it was cancelled in 1952. As with Derleth's *Skull-Face*, the *Avon* publications present the Conan stories not as a self-sufficient property but rather as merely one piece of both Howard and the weird tale's larger literary legacy. Outside of this limited context, Conan appeared to have neither audience nor monetary value.

With the publication of the first Conan hardcover by Gnome Press in 1950, however, Conan began to develop a life of his own. Founded in 1948 and run by Martin Greenberg, Gnome Press was a small publisher remembered today both for its important science fiction publications and its chronic undercapitalization.[69] Although no records of the initial negotiations for the Conan stories exist, Greenberg, not especially familiar with Howard's work and typically uninterested in fantasy or weird fiction, was likely assisted in licensing the rights by longtime Howard fan and former fanzine publisher John Clark, whom Greenberg employed to serve as initial editor of the series. Having acquired exclusive publishing rights to all seventeen *Weird Tales* Conan stories from the Kuykendalls through their agent, Oscar Friend, Greenberg worked with Clark to arrange the stories into a five-book series beginning with the novel-length story of King Conan, "The Hour of the Dragon"—renamed *Conan the Conqueror* so as to better spotlight its hero.[70] For the remainder of the books, Clark drew upon his fifteen-year-old "A Probable Outline of Conan's Career" to group the stories together according to Conan's imagined age. *The Coming of Conan*, for example, featured stories starring a young Conan, while *The Sword of Conan* focused on a mid-career Conan. Unfortunately, Gnome Press's publishing program obscured Clarke's careful sequencing: the books were published without regard to their underlying chronology and lacked titles or series number that might indicate to a retailer or consumer their places in that chronology.

Both Wollheim's publishing efforts and Clark's editorship highlight two important issues for the history of the Conan property and that of narrative-based properties in general. The first is the vital role fans frequently serve in developing and maintaining these properties. As Conan's early publishing history demonstrates, Howard's literary revival (admittedly, in the 1950s, still an inchoate one) was not the inevitable outcome of abstract cultural forces or of the intrinsic quality of Howard's writing but was rather the result of a few self-avowed fans and erstwhile amateurs (from the Latin *amatores*, i.e., "lovers"), who acted to promote

Howard's work in professional production contexts. It is not quite right to call this "fan labor," as Kristina Busse, Suzanne Scott, and other fan studies scholars have employed the term, since Wollheim and Clark had, by this point, become professional participants in the industry.[71] But there is no doubt that the methods of reading, writing, and collaborating that they had learned as young fans significantly informed their interests and practices as professionals. A similar kind of fan-informed labor would become common later in the century as fans took jobs with entertainment companies such as Marvel Comics working on the properties they loved;[72] but in the cases of Wollheim and Clark—like that of Derleth before them—we have a fan who, having acquired power or influence within the publishing industry, utilized it to advocate for a property that had been otherwise forgotten or deemed worthless.[73] This is not to suggest that organized fan communities in the early twentieth-century had significant market-shaping power (of the kind sometimes attributed by scholars to twenty-first-century fandoms[74]), for in the examples of Wollheim and Clark we are not dealing with organized fandom at all, but rather with individual fans who used positions of power within the publishing industry to bring Howard's work back into print. That said, what constitutes the professional publishing industry—and what differentiates a fan from a professional—has never been clear-cut and was especially not in the case of early genre work, such as fantasy and science fiction. Clark's work with Conan is a case in point, as his "A Probable Outline of Conan's Career," though produced while he was a young, self-professed fan and originally published in an amateur chapbook, not only came to serve as a credential justifying his editorship of the Conan series at a for-profit publishing house but also repeatedly functioned for subsequent editors as a publishing blueprint for the entire Conan property.

The second issue raised by Wollheim and Clark's involvement is the important role publishers and editors play in transforming individual works of fiction into fully-fledged narrative-based properties. For the Gnome Press series, Clark took a collection of stories whose relation to each other was, at best, quasi-iterative and transformed them into a single chronological saga. He did this by reordering the stories, making slight alterations to names and verb tenses, and writing what de Camp calls "bridging paragraphs" that served to connect the stories via extremely condensed accounts of Conan's activities during the gaps between Howard's tales.[75] In giving the character of Conan a coherent history that exceeded what was provided in Howard's prose, Clark thus began the transformation of the Conan stories from mere instances of *Howardiana*, of virtually no general interest, into a full-fledge narrative-based property whose primary assets were not just the texts that Howard had written but also its characters, its world, and its intertextual story and chronology.

Although Clark's original editorial vision governed the Gnome Press series until its final volume in 1957, beginning in 1952 Clark's stewardship of the property was gradually transferred to L. Sprague de Camp, who in November 1951 had discovered three previously unpublished Conan stories at the apartment of the Kuykendall's agent, Oscar Friend. Describing the find in his biography, de Camp explains that Friend "lent me the three Conan manuscripts to see if, with editing, I could fit them into the Conan Saga that Greenberg was publishing and make it possible to sell them for magazine publication."[76] To do this, de Camp undertook a rapid self-education in all things Conan, a process that included not only careful readings of all the Conan tales but epistolary consultation with Peter Schuyler Miller, Clark's original coauthor on "A Probable Outline of Conan's Career" and an old friend of de Camp's.[77] None of this work was paid for, nor did any kind of formal contract exist between Friend and de Camp. Instead, the work proceeded on trust: that de Camp, functioning as both editor and surrogate agent, would, if successful in publishing the stories, share the proceeds fairly with the Kuykendalls.

By the beginning of 1952, de Camp had developed enough familiarity with the stories to join Clark, whom de Sprague knew well and counted a friend, as an unofficial and unpaid editor of the Gnome Press series, and in late January the two worked with Greenberg to plan out the remaining books in the series.[78] The revised plan included spots for de Camp's three unpublished Conan stories, which he subsequently edited "with a heavy hand" so as both to better integrate them into Clark's chronology and to correct the narrative problems that had led to their original rejections by *Weird Tales* in the 1930s.[79] Appearing also in Del Rey's *Fantasy Fiction* and *Space Science Fiction* magazines between 1952 and 1953 (in issues edited by Wollheim), the stories were promoted as "hitherto unpublished" Conan stories "by Robert E. Howard (edited by L. Sprague de Camp)"—and treated legally by stakeholders as coauthored works.[80] These coauthored stories—as well as the introductions de Camp provided for the third and fourth Gnome Press volumes—gradually established de Camp as the property's foremost authority and primary steward.

Up to this point in the property's history, Conan and his world had not yet transcended their association with their original creator. Though newly chronologized—albeit somewhat opaquely—via the first half of the Gnome Press series, the stories remained semantically wedded to their original author. Like the works of Howard's friend and peer H. P. Lovecraft, the Conan stories had become materially, editorially, and legally constructed as the personal legacy of a singular authorial genius. So much did this Howardian construction of the property dominate the involved stakeholders' approach to it that after the supply of unpublished Conan stories had been exhausted, de Camp turned to *non-Conan* Howard stories as a means of further extending the series. Beginning in 1953, de Camp thus "Conan-ized" four of Howard's unsold adventure tales by replacing their original protagonists with Conan, altering place names, substituting magic for guns and explosives, and making alterations to the plots so as to fit them into Conan's official Gnome Press biography. In doing so, de Camp, ironically, employed the same practice but in reverse that Howard had used when trying to salvage rejected Conan stories.

In maintaining—even extending—Howard's legacy in this fashion, however, de Camp was coming to function as an extra-authorial supplement to the Conan property: "a ghost of a ghost," as de Camp would later put it.[81] As posthumous ghost writer for Howard, de Camp was, we might even say, the entrepreneurial ghost in the Conan literary machine, for it was primarily his own economic self-interest—and not what for Wollheim and Clark had been a fanatical attachment to Howard the author—that both kept de Camp involved with the property and kept the property developing and expanding. Such involvement even included rewriting a novel-length work of fan-fiction that Greenberg had received, unsolicited, in 1956 from a Swedish Air Force officer named Björn Nyberg.[82] Though de Camp always spoke kindly of Nyberg's book, which Nyberg had written "just for fun" and as a means "to practice his English," the published version—titled *The Return of Conan*—is a substantial dip in quality for the series, and one suspects there was little pleasure to be had for de Camp in rewriting it beyond that of a paycheck and a claim to future royalties.[83]

Given de Camp's primarily *economic* interest in the Conan property—and his subsequent financial claims upon it—fans and scholars have often accused him of illegitimately commandeering the property from its rightful owners, the Kuykendalls.[84] Before we turn to the Conan boom of the 1960s and 70s, it is thus worth querying de Camp's legal relationship to the property during the Gnome Press era. The seventeen *Weird Tales* Conan stories, which make up the bulk of the Gnome Press series, were recognized at this time as belonging to Isaac Howard's heirs, the Kuykendalls. A detailed accounting of the exact rights the Kuykendalls possessed had still never been made, and the copyrights, having never been formally transferred, were still registered to the Popular Fiction Publishing Co. For the purposes of magazine and book publishing, however, none of this mattered: in every instance after Isaac's death, interested parties licensed the rights from the Kuykendalls. This included Gnome Press, which had acquired exclusive book rights to the *Weird Tales* Conan stories from the Kuykendalls through their agent, Oscar Friend. Although this practice represents an institutionalization of the *moral* approach to the rights that stakeholders had followed when Howard first died, it was no doubt reinforced by *Weird Tales*' diminishment in importance in the 1940s and eventual disappearance as a business entity in 1954.[85]

That leaves the seven posthumously published Howard stories and Nyberg's *The Return of Conan*, all heavily edited and/or coauthored by de Camp under the encouragement (never formalized by contract) of the Kuykendall's agent. De Camp registered the posthumously published stories for copyright in both his name and that of the Kuykendalls. For Nyberg's novel the registration was made in his name and Nyberg's. For these texts, de Camp was thus part-owner—both in practice and under the formal letter of the law.

Rusty Burke, president of the Robert E. Howard Foundation at the time I am writing this, has objected in print that de Camp's work on these stories was "essentially 'work for hire'—work he was hired to do by Dr. Kuykendall through Oscar Friend."[86] U.S. work-for-hire law, like intellectual property law itself, underwent constant development throughout the twentieth century, with courts and statutes treating it very differently in the 1980s than they had in the 1930s or 1950s. As Peter Jaszi and Martha Woodmansee have argued, although the Copyright Act of 1909 included (in Section 62) a provision recognizing that employers were to be treated as authors in cases of "work . . . made for hire," it was not till many decades later that the law began to "shift toward" the "eventual position" that "employers were entitled to claim copyright" in the works their employees created under the employers' supervision and expense.[87] Indeed, the Copyright Act of 1909 neglected to provide a definition for "work made for hire," perhaps because—as Borge Varmer reported in a 1958 study of the doctrine produced for Congress—the legislature (at least judged by records of its proceedings) did not think the issue of much importance at the time.[88] In any case, by the 1950s, case law had developed establishing a right of employers to the works authored by their employees; little case law had emerged, however, involving the rights to work produced by independent contractors, such as de Camp, and the general thrust of the common law seemed to differentiate contractors from employees. As Varmer explained,

> In broad terms, the acts of an employee as such are imputed to his employer, but those of an independent contractor are not imputed to the person for whom he performs a special commission. Underlying this distinction is the premise that an employer generally gives more direction and exercises more control over the work of his employee than does a commissioner with respect to an independent contractor.[89]

The lack of cases suggests that there were few intractable disputes concerning the ownership of contracted work at the time, perhaps because customary and/or contractual practices worked sufficiently in the absence of formalized law. Such practices might also explain why, even as late as the 1950s, work-for-hire doctrine was still being left out of copyright manuals and how-to guides aimed at laymen.[90]

What Rusty Burke seems to be arguing about de Camp is thus not that his labor on behalf of the Conan property was "work for hire" as a publisher or rightsholder would have understood it in the 1950s, but rather as a publisher or rightsholder would have understood it at the end of the twentieth century, at which point labor contracts regularly stipulated that work by independent contractors was "work for hire" and as such belonged exclusively to the employer.[91] On that point, Burke is probably right: today, no competent rightsholder (or its agent) would contract with an independent laborer to develop a preexisting property without being careful to contractually maintain ownership over whatever that laborer produced. From this anachronistic perspective, de Camp might be seen to have "grafted himself onto the Conan stories . . . before anyone was the wiser," as Howard fan Vernon Clark argued in a 1989 piece for the Robert E. Howard Amateur Press Association.[92]

Given the particularly inchoate state of the Conan property in the 1950s, however, the parallel drawn between de Camp and today's typical contractor is misleading. Unlike such workers today, usually hired for specific projects under formal contracts and given property bibles and/or editorial supervision to guide their work, de Camp's involvement with the Conan property was undertaken on his own initiative, for no pay, and from very early on he remained almost entirely self-managing. The unpublished Conan stories, though in the possession of Friend, were only discovered after de Camp sought to look for them, and his work on them—which included both revising them and managing and elaborating Conan's transtextual biography—was produced, in contemporary lingo, "on spec," with no guarantee of payment unless the stories sold.[93] That the stories did sell was also in large part thanks to de Camp himself, who interfaced directly with the magazine publishers (many of whom knew him well), marketed the property in fan publications such as *AMRA*, and provided unpaid editorial assistance to Greenberg and Clark on the Gnome Press series.[94] Even more unusual for contemporary contractors, de Camp also took formal legal action (which I will examine in greater detail in the following section) at his own expense in the 1960s in order to recover the publishing rights from Greenberg so that he might license them—for both his own and the Kuykendalls' benefit—to a larger publishing house for greater profit. If we are to imagine, counterfactually, that Friend *had* acted like a modern rightsholder (for the Kuykendalls themselves appear to have paid virtually no attention to the Conan property) by insisting upon a work-for-hire designation with respect to de Camp, secured by formal contract, the likely outcome would have *not* been the separation of de Camp from any rights in the stories on which he worked (which is what Burke seems to imagine) but rather de Camp's refusal to have worked on them—and the larger property—at all. Whatever the case, there is yet an even more compelling reason not to consider the de Camp-authored Conan stories "work for hire," and that is that no legal stakeholder ever considered them such. Although, as we will see shortly, Glenn Lord, the official manager of the Howard "literary estate" starting in 1965, regularly disputed de Camp's moral right to the texts, he never sought to challenge de Camp's legal right.

From Gnome Press to the Public Domain

In early 1963, the Kuykendalls' literary agent, Oscar Friend, passed away, leaving his agency (and the formal responsibility for managing the Conan stories) in the hands of his daughter, Kittie West. A year later, in preparation for shutting the agency down, West began seeking out new homes for her father's clients. For the Kuykendalls, West identified de Camp as the most obvious replacement, as he had been informally managing the Conan property for the past decade. De Camp, however, rejected the offer, in part because the peculiar ownership structure of the Conan property created what he would later call a "conflict of interest," but also because de Camp seems to have judged the financial return from serving as agent to be simply not worth his time.[95] Acting on de Camp's advice, West thus eventually offered the position to Glenn Lord, a thirty-three-year-old Texan and devoted Howard fan with no experience as an agent and little familiarity with the professional publishing industry. Lord accepted, and on April 1, 1965, he was officially made the Kuykendalls' sole representative in matters relating to what was still being called "The Robert E. Howard Estate."[96]

De Camp had become acquainted with Lord during the mid-1950s, when Lord had sought his assistance in putting together *Always Come Evening*, a book of Howard's poetry that Lord eventually paid to have published through Arkham House in 1957.[97] By the early 1960s, thanks in part to Lord's success at tracking down some of the scattered remnants of Howard's "unpublished" literary output, Lord had begun to develop a reputation among fantasy publishers and Howard fans as the foremost expert—after de Camp—of all things Howard-related.[98] Beginning in 1961, Lord gradually published these once-lost writings—along with letters, tributes, bibliographic information, and reviews—in a sleek fanzine titled *The Howard Collector*, which ran until 1973, and which many identify today as the beginning of serious, scholarly minded Howard fandom.[99]

That de Camp recommended Lord in place of himself to serve as the estate's agent provides some indication of how well the two men got on together in the early 1960s. Indeed, their correspondence during this period is remarkably polite, friendly, and even intimate given the enmity that would come to characterize their later relationship. Ironically, their first collaboration on estate-related business—in early 1964, a year before Lord had officially become the Kuykendalls' agent—concerned the very issue that would eventually turn them into enemies: the copyrights for Howard's Conan stories.

As explained in chapter 1, under the Copyright Act of 1909, U.S. copyright law divided the period of a copyrighted text's protection into two separate twenty-eight-year spans. To claim the second twenty-eight years, the correct stakeholder (or his or her legal representative) had to file a formal renewal through the Copyright Office in the last year of the work's initial period of protection. By doing so, the stakeholder simultaneously renewed the copyright and became the registered owner of it—regardless of whether or not he or she had owned it at the time the renewal was filed. As designated by statute, which had been designed to enable authors to reclaim the copyrights to their works after the first period of protection had expired, the stakeholder who filed the renewal had to be the original author.[100] If the author were no longer living, the right of renewal passed to his or her spouse, then children, then next of kin, and then finally—in the absence of any surviving family—the legal representative of the estate. According to the letter of the statue (which the common law's own construal of the renewal process tended to support for most of the modern copyright era), a person who was not a member of one of these classes could not file a renewal, even if that person were the legal owner of the copyright at the end of the first period of protection.

In 1964, twenty-eight years after the publication date of the last *Weird Tales* Conan stories, the majority of the Conan corpus was either entering its second period of copyright, with the Kuykendalls having become the rightsholders, or entering the public domain—depending upon whether or not copyright renewals had been formally submitted to the Copyright Office by the correct stakeholders. Although literary agents usually assisted their clients in managing copyrights, renewals sometimes fell through the cracks, especially in cases (like that of the Kuykendalls) where the clients remained almost wholly uninvolved with the management of their property.[101] Given the ill-health of Oscar Friend throughout the early 1960s and his death in 1963[102] (precisely the years in which the renewals would have needed to be submitted), de Camp suspected that the estate had in fact not taken action to renew the copyrights—an oversight that would have radically altered the profit potential of the Conan property. Concerned, de Camp consulted Lord, whose work acquiring and publishing *Howardiana*, de Camp believed, may have given him direct knowledge of how the copyrights were being managed.[103] As of 1964, however, Lord had only published work in *The Howard Collector* that was in the public domain (often because it had not been registered when originally published in amateur publications). He thus knew no more than de Camp but believed, especially after consultation with the more experienced August Derleth, that de Camp's suspicions were justified.[104] In January of 1965, de Camp reported to Lord that he had taken matters into his own hands and undertaken formal copyright searches of a handful of Conan stories. "Not one," he informed Lord, "has been renewed."[105]

The lack of renewal would quickly become the most important factor in the development of the Conan property, but before we examine its effects, it is worth asking why neither de Camp nor Lord tried to intervene in 1964 to protect the two Conan stories still eligible for renewal ("The Hour of the Dragon" and "Red Nails"). Though both men were aware by April that renewals were soon due, neither seemed to have informed the Kuykendalls or Kittie West (who was still operating as the Kuykendalls' representative at that time) that action was needed. Indeed, de Camp appears to have waited till *after* the renewal period had ended to inform West of the copyright issue.[106] From a moral perspective, both men might be seen as having willfully neglected to protect the "Howard estate."

From an industrial or economic perspective, however, the better question might be why de Camp or Lord *should* have intervened to protect the property. Neither man would have benefitted financially from doing so and both would have incurred costs (in time, postage, telephone charges, and photocopying) for trying. What is more, both had significant incentives *not* to protect the remaining stories. For Lord, whose zine depended upon public domain material, the more Howard material that was out of copyright, the more material there was available for him to publish freely. To some extent, the same is also true for de Camp, who sometimes reprinted Howard stories in anthologies he edited. But de Camp had yet another reason—this one curiously in alignment with the economic interests of the Kuykendalls—for wishing to see as many of the stories as possible enter the public domain: doing so would invalidate Gnome Press's exclusive rights to the material.

As early as 1961, de Camp, like many other established science-fiction writers, had become fed up with Martin Greenberg's management of Gnome Press. Although its publications sold reasonably well for a publisher of its size, Gnome Press's lack of capital reserves meant that production costs for new books were regularly met (or so authors alleged) by misappropriating the royalties owed to authors for already published books. Greenberg's failure to pay what was owed and his supposedly manipulative handling of authors who complained (in one instance, according to Isaac Asimov, he even succeeded in getting Asimov to lend *Greenberg* money) instilled in de Camp a vitriolic hatred.[107] In a 1962 letter to Asimov, for example, de Camp characterized Greenberg as an opportunistic thief who should only be dealt with by catching him "by the balls and twist[ing]."[108] By balls-twisting, de Camp, who by this time had successfully sued Greenberg for money owed on his nonfiction book *Lost Continents*, seems to have meant legal action for contract violation.[109] But as royalties for the Conan books failed to appear, de Camp thought up an additional legal strategy.

Recognizing the potential value of the new paperback (or "reprint") market of the 1960s, de Camp approached Larry Shaw at Lancer Books in the summer of 1964 to see if Lancer would be interested in publishing the newly codified Conan saga as an eight-book paperback series.[110] Lancer agreed, on the condition that de Camp could secure the book publishing rights to the stories—rights that were unfortunately in the hands of Greenberg for as long as the Gnome Press Conan books were kept in print. Greenberg, de Camp knew, would never agree to release these rights (at least not without a financially crippling royalty commitment from Lancer). Rather than attempt to negotiate, de Camp thus set out, with the support of Kittie West, to invalidate these rights, a process made possible in large part thanks to the failure of the Kuykendalls to renew the Conan copyrights.[111] If the copyrights for the *Weird Tales* Conan stories were in the public domain, de Camp reasoned, then Greenberg's exclusive license to the book rights was no longer valid. Concerned about a potential lawsuit from Greenberg, Lancer asked that de Camp get a court to ratify this reasoning, which he did by filing suit against Gnome Press in mid-1965 on behalf of himself, Nyberg, and the Kuykendalls.[112] By May of the following year, the judge presiding over the case issued a declaratory judgment on behalf of the plaintiffs: the *Weird Tales* Conan stories were found to be in the public domain and thus free to be used without Greenberg's consent.[113]

This left under Greenberg's control the book/reprint rights to the stories coauthored by de Camp, all of which were still near the beginning of their first period of copyright protection. De Camp, with Lord now assisting as agent for the estate, proceeded with his suit against Greenberg to regain control of them, arguing that Greenberg had failed to fulfill their contract with respect to royalties and the provision requiring that the books be kept in print.[114] As both of these were issues of fact, they would necessitate an actual trial, which could potentially take months or even longer and might not result in the verdict de Camp wanted. The claim that the final two books were out of print was particularly difficult to prove, as the books technically remained in print, according to custom if not the actual letter of the contract (which was silent on this issue), so long as Gnome Press was able to fill bona fide orders for them, even if it did not market them or ensure their availability with retailers. Slyly, de Camp attempted to hasten the exhaustion of Gnome Press's inventory (which by 1966 reportedly consisted of only unbound sheets) by placing his own advertisements for the books in magazines such as *Fantasy & Science Fiction*.[115]

In the meantime, however, Lancer was now willing to begin publishing the Conan series, with the proviso that de Camp leave out of it all of the stories still under dispute with Greenberg. Since de Camp was committed to what had become among fans a firmly established chronological ordering of the stories in terms of Conan's "career," this meant that the Lancer books could only consist of whatever legally unencumbered stories happened also to be chronologically sequential. Only three paperback-length sets of stories (one of these being the long story "The Hour of the Dragon," now published as a standalone novella by the same name) unambiguously met these criteria. Wanting to strike while the sci-fi/fantasy paperback market was still hot, Lancer and de Camp quickly prepared these sets of stories for print as *Conan the Adventurer*, *Conan the Warrior*, and *Conan the Conqueror*. Because the volumes would not together constitute an uninterrupted series, de Camp framed them editorially in much the same way the Gnome Press books had been—that is, without reference outside of the introductions to where the books fit into the larger saga. The covers instead touted the books' places in the *publishing* order: "Volume One of the Complete Conan," for example, despite that volume coming somewhere near the middle in terms of narrative order.[116] To help get around the lack of material legally available to him, de Camp (still working without pay or a formal contract) also began work completing an assortment of Conan fragments Lord had discovered in San Francisco in 1965, the first of which was published in *Conan the Adventurer* as "Drums of Tombalku." Unfortunately, these fragments were not a perfect solution for de Camp, as not only did many of them require extensive work to complete, each of them could fit intertextually only within very specific gaps in the preexisting saga. They thus, in some cases, even added to the difficulty of planning out publishable volumes. Some other solution was urgently needed, and just as the first Lancer book was preparing to ship, de Camp hit upon it. He, working with a young author named Lin Carter, would write their own Conan stories.

By the 1970s, these non-Howard Conan stories—usually referred to as *pastiches*—would come to be framed by fan discourse as the ultimate cause of the breakdown between Lord and de Camp, with Lord cast as the defender of a "purist" Howardian Conan and de Camp as the money-hungry "vulture" fattening himself on Howard's literary legacy.[117] In 1966, however, de Camp's idea for creating pastiches was neither controversial nor even particularly novel: one seventh of the official Conan saga, as represented by the Gnome Press series, already consisted of a pastiche (Nyberg and de Camp's *The Return of Conan*). Lord thus readily assented to de Camp's idea for more Conan stories, even offering suggestions—as he had done with the unfinished Conan tales he'd given de

Camp—as to how they might fit into the larger saga.[118] Both men understood that the pastiches would, as de Camp put it in a letter to Robert Heinlein, enable them "to get around Greenberg's claims" and earn all of the involved parties money.[119] Accordingly, de Camp and Carter got to work producing short pastiches set at the beginning of Conan's career. These allowed de Camp to break up the first chronological volume of the Lancer series—which, as originally planned, required rights to some of the legally contested stories—into two books, the first of which could then be published without waiting for the outcome of the lawsuit.[120] By mid-1967, Carter and de Camp had also begun work on an "old-[man-] Conan novel," which Lord also approved, set in narrative time after the events of Nyberg's book.[121]

Although neither Lord nor de Camp could have predicted it in 1966, the pastiches ultimately proved unnecessary for the survival of the Lancer Conan series. Before any of the newly planned volumes had even been finished, Greenberg agreed to settle the lawsuit out of court. In May of 1968, in exchange for a release from all liabilities and $500 (paid out-of-pocket by de Camp), Greenberg relinquished his claims to the coauthored Conan stories, leaving Lancer free to publish the "original" Gnome-Press Conan saga in its entirety.[122] With the pastiches already under contract, however—and with the already-published volumes selling in record numbers—Lancer agreed to expand the series beyond the eight books initially planned. By the time the series had officially "ended" in 1977 (by which time Ace had acquired the publishing contract from a bankrupt Lancer), additional pastiches and coauthored pieces had brought it up to twelve books, ordered chronologically (with volume numbers now clearly signaling the order) from Conan's earliest adventures as a young man to his final quest as an aging king.

As the 1960s came to a close, the Conan property had thus evolved a great deal from its original form as a series of disconnected pulp stories written by Robert E. Howard. Thanks to the work of fans, editors, pasticheurs, and—most of all—de Camp, as well as the vagaries of copyright renewal and publishing contracts, the property now boasted discrete, separable assets, including fully developed characters, some with rich, detailed histories; a story world that was both intricate and coherent; visual material such as maps and character art (in the form of Frank Frazetta's highly esteemed cover art for the Lancer books); a highly developed narrative through-line; and an approach to storytelling that was so recognizable that it almost constituted a genre in its own right ("sword and sorcery"). The property had also become relatively, though not yet completely, detached semantically from its original creator, thus allowing for the development of narrative- and asset-based marketing and development strategies to replace the original creator-based strategy that Derleth, Wollheim, and Clark had first employed. Although strict adherence to the chronology of Conan's "career" risked eventually impeding the generation of new content, for the time being there was ample room for what twenty-first-century transmedia scholars such as Carlos Scolari, Paolo Bertetti, and Colin Harvey have called "narrative expansion": the elaboration of an existing story through the addition of new, related texts.[123] Indeed, de Camp and Carter, following a strategy first employed by Burroughs in his Barsoom and Tarzan series, even created a son for Conan, named Conn, who—if need be—could be used by the writers to extend the series past Conan's old age (and eventual death) without abandoning its established continuity.[124] Perhaps the best proof, however, of the Conan property's transformation into a viable long-term narrative-based property, was that by the end of the 1960s, producers of other media forms, including comic books and film, had begun expressing interest in it.

From a formal legal perspective, however, the Conan property was in even worse shape than it had been at Howard's death. De Camp's method for invalidating the Gnome Press contract had likewise invalidated the primary legal protection on which narrative-based property depends. As ruled by a trial court, at least one-third of the stories that made up the property now belonged to the public. That the stories suffered this fate was in part an accident, the freak result of a confluence of unrelated events: had the Kuykendalls paid attention to their property, had their agent(s) ensured that the copyrights were properly renewed, had a potentially lucrative business opportunity never arrived with Lancer Books, or had Gnome Press adhered to its publishing contract or (failing that) freely relinquished its rights to the Conan stories, de Camp (with West and Lord's support) would never have sought to invalidate the stories' copyrights. But this freak result was also, in a sense, *primed* by the property's disorganized and informal system of production, which relied almost entirely upon fans, agents with little to no skin in the game, small-press publishers, and freelance writers/editors working without a contract. In the absence of a formalized business enterprise with a delineated hierarchy and a clear incentive/remuneration structure, stakeholders such as Lord and de Camp naturally sought to maximize their own individual returns, even when this risked undermining the value and legal standing of the property itself. The invalidated copyrights are the most obvious example, but equally problematic were the remaining copyrights, which were held by various combinations of four different parties: the Kuykendalls, de Camp, Carter, and Nyberg. With so many parties possessing distinct and separable rights in the Conan "property," and with no structure in place capable of coordinating their interests, the property risked becoming a legal minefield. Were Conan little capable of generating a profit, the diffused rights posed little problem; with bigger companies outside of the book-publishing world, such as Marvel Comics, Dino De Laurentiis's production company, and (eventually) Mattel, showing interest, however, the diffused rights soon became a recipe for disaster.

The Short, Troubled Life of the Conan Syndicate

Before 1966, de Camp and Lord had viewed the Kuykendalls' failure to renew the Conan copyrights as a lucky break—the trump card in their long-running dispute with Martin Greenberg. Indeed, until Greenberg had finally relinquished his claims to Conan, both men had viewed the court's formal invalidation of the copyrights as a mostly positive outcome for the property, as it allowed the Lancer publishing deal to proceed (almost) as planned. That neither man understood the tremendous problems the public domain stories posed can partly be blamed on the lack of long-term profit potential they attributed to the property. Conan's recent small-scale success, after all, might have been a fluke. Best to make as much money off the property as they could *now* without worrying about tomorrow.

But as de Camp's early book on intellectual property law demonstrates, the men's lack of concern also stemmed from their underestimation of what copyright protection likely provided. Since the 1954 *Warner Bros. v. Columbia Broadcasting System* decision (if not earlier), de Camp had understood separable narrative assets, such as characters and places, to be unprotectable under U.S. copyright law. Toward the end of a section titled "What May Be Copyrighted" in the 1959 edition of *Inventions, Patents, and Their Management,* de Camp introduces the subject of such protection with the blunt statement, "It is not possible to copyright fictitious or fanciful characters or settings, used in . . . stories or cartoons, so as to keep others from imitating them."[125] He elaborates, using Burroughs's Tarzan as an example:

> [I]t would not violate the copyright on any of these works, or any other rights of the owner of the Burroughs copyrights, if another writer brought into his own story a character named Tarzan, like Burroughs' hero even unto the leopard-skin loincloth, so long as there was no chance of a reader's mistaking the later work for a genuine Tarzan story by Burroughs. . . .
>
> Suppose, however, that a later author writes a story called *Tarzan the Egregious*, in which his muscular hero swings from branch to branch and discovers lost races in the African jungle just as Burroughs' character did, and the plagiarist moreover signs his work with the pseudonym "Edward Rich Burrows." The Burroughs copyright would still not be violated, so long as the story itself was original and not a copy or a paraphrase. But the Burroughs interests would have a promising case of unfair competition against the later writer. They could sue him for injunction and damages for falsely passing off his book as part of the authentic Burroughs canon.[126]

So confident was de Camp that fictional characters could not be protected by copyright that he regularly advised fans by letter that they did not need his permission to publish a Conan or "Hyborian Age" story, since, as he told one teenage letter-writer, "there is no copyright on fictional persons and places."[127] That de Camp believed this to be true explains why he did not fear that the loss of copyright on most of Howard's Conan stories might usher in a wave of new competing Conan stories. Were other people interested in publishing their own Conan tales, de Camp figured, copyright would not stop them.

Whether de Camp was right or wrong about copyright is ultimately impossible to say; he was certainly not alone in his belief (as we saw in chapter 2, no less than the U.S. Court of Appeals for the Ninth Circuit appeared to have reasoned similarly), although the certainty with which he appeared to hold it is surprising given how ambiguous the law on this issue had become—and arguably had always been. From a practical perspective, however, the validity of his view is ultimately beside the point: once the Conan stories were ruled in court to belong to the public, anyone *could* legally publish a new Conan story without de Camp or Lord's permission, regardless of whether they could have done so had the stories remained copyrighted. By formally invalidating the copyrights of Howard's original stories, Lord and de Camp had thus imperiled their control not only of the Conan property's textual past but its textual future as well. Although Lancer was, for the time being, willing to pay de Camp for the public domain stories in order to gain access to the stories still protected by copyright, there was no guarantee that Lancer would always be so willing—especially since nothing prevented Lancer's competitors from publishing the public domain stories *without* paying for them. In fact, another company or enterprising author could now even legally develop its own Conan saga, building off the original *Weird Tales* stories exactly as de Camp had done. In the short term, however, the worst effect of the court's ruling was that it had rendered the legal plank necessary for selling subsidiary rights extremely wobbly. Just as any author could now publish his own Conan story without permission, so too could a comic-book or film company—in theory at least—develop its own Conan texts without permission.

To de Camp's credit, he recognized these problems quickly and, as soon as the Greenberg case had ended, advocated a two-pronged strategy for dealing with them. The first and simplest part of this strategy required the four stakeholders (de Camp, Lord [representing the Kuykendalls], Nyberg, and Carter) to keep secret the fact that the *Weird Tales* stories had entered the public domain.[128] To this end, de Camp began responding to permission requests using a careful double-speak. In reply to a 1969 request to use Conan in a comic strip, for example, de Camp explained to the requestor that granting this permission might "jeopardize our chances of making a comic-book deal." "I am therefore," he continued, "most regretfully, unable to extend any permission in this matter, to do anything with Conan beyond what you would already have a legal right to do so."[129] This strategy was not tenable long-term, as de Camp could not legally prevent people from using the Conan character without his permission; nor did it solve the problem of subsidiary rights, as any big client (such as a Hollywood studio) would require a document establishing the descent of rights before concluding a deal. Indeed, as early as 1969, lawyers representing a potential film producer were already requesting such a document.[130] As we will see, however, the strategy was successful at misleading less-sophisticated licensees, such as Marvel Comics. Hiding the stories' lack of copyright protection would also buy the stakeholders time to implement the second, and more difficult, part of de Camp's strategy: pooling together the copyrights they still had into a single unified package.

How such a unified package would solve the public domain problem was not immediately obvious to any of the property's stakeholders, including de Camp, who initially advocated for it as a solution to a different problem faced by the Conan property: its plethora of legally autonomous rightsholders. Although by 1968 the Lancer book series had been sufficiently successful to begin attracting interest from Hollywood, de Camp rightly feared that such interest would evaporate were a buyer required to negotiate separately with four different rightsholders.[131] In the unlikely event that a buyer remained interested, more problems awaited. A single holdout among the four rightsholders could scuttle a deal. Knowing that, a buyer might "try to play one of us off against the other," de Camp explained to Lord, ultimately leaving the four "with little if any profit and probably a lot of hard feeling."[132] As a solution, de Camp proposed that the men form a "united front"—what he would eventually call "the Conan syndicate"—by agreeing in advance to treat their separate rights as a single saleable package, with proceeds being divvied up according to a predetermined formula.[133]

De Camp proposed that this formula be applied both to the sale of rights for "the *whole* corpus or saga of Conan stories, past and future" and for the sale of individual stories or smaller groups of stories from the saga.[134] For sales of the entire saga, de Camp saw the predetermined formula as absolutely essential: "The choice is between making [such] an agreement and having no such sale at all."[135] The benefit of applying the same formula to sales of individual stories, however, was less obvious, as it would have required the official copyright holders of the material sold to share proceeds with members of the Syndicate who did not officially possess rights in that material. For example, were a buyer to purchase a license for only *The Return of Conan* (copyrighted in de Camp and Nyberg's names), Lord (acting as proxy for the Kuykendalls) and Carter would still receive a share of the proceeds. De Camp argued that the alternative—what he described as "every man's selling for himself whatever he has the right to sell"—would, despite its ostensible fairness, ultimately be to the group's collective disadvantage.[136] Such an "individualistic plan," reasoned de Camp, "would make for hard feelings on the part of those who did not make the sale and might scare off a buyer for the whole series if he saw some of the stories being exploited by a rival firm."[137]

Although de Camp appears not to have consciously understood this at the time he proposed the contract, the Syndicate plan had yet another benefit, in that it might allow the stakeholders to invoke the law of unfair competition to help protect the Conan property. As described in chapter 4, unfair competition was a branch of law that had originated in a 1706 English case in which one person had ruined the business of another through what the court found to be illegitimate means. By the twentieth century, it had come to focus primarily on what was known as "passing off." As legal scholar Zechariah Chafee, Jr. explained in a 1940 piece for the *Harvard Law Review*, in a passing off case, "the defendant is diverting business from the plaintiff to himself by a particular kind of falsehood. The device [used to effect the diversion] tells potential customers that the goods come from the plaintiff, whereas in fact they come from the defendant."[138] Passing off thus involves some form of misattribution on the part of a seller, typically by using a distinct mark (or *trademark*) that had become associated in the mind of the public with some other seller or business enterprise. Such marks had received federal protection since the beginning of the twentieth century, but—as discussed in the previous chapter—lawyers, judges, and entertainment professionals rarely applied trademark law to fictional characters themselves during the modern copyright era. They did, however, recognize its applicability to other aspects of the publishing enterprise: the *names* of texts, series, authors, and even characters, as well as any distinctive advertising or trade dress associated with a text or series. Indeed, de Camp's reference to unfair competition in *Inventions, Patents, and Their Management* (quoted above) suggests that he understood, in at least a general sense (some of the details are arguably wrong), how it might be used to protect aspects of a narrative-based property.

How would the Syndicate have enabled the rightsholders to invoke unfair competition law to protect the Conan property? Were de Camp able to have established in the late 1960s that the name *Conan* had acquired what courts called "secondary meaning"—association in the eyes of the public with the specific business enterprise run by the Conan Syndicate—de Camp would have had a legal path to preventing the use of the name by any new businesses seeking to exploit the character.[139] Enterprising publishers would have been still free to publish the public domain stories; de Camp was powerless to ask a court to stop that. But anyone publishing a *new* Conan story or saga would have been, in theory, vulnerable to allegations of "passing off" or "unjust enrichment" unless prior permission had been granted them by the Syndicate. In effect, unfair competition law, which Justice Learned Hand called in a 1925 decision the most "plastic" law in the United States, could have been employed by the Conan stakeholders to try and minimize the damage caused by the loss of copyrights on the *Weird Tales* stories.[140] Whether or not a court would have found for the Syndicate had such a case gone to trial is an open question, but the mere threat of such a lawsuit would be enough to dissuade most would-be competitors from making use of the character. The one catch, of course, was that for such a strategy to have worked, there had *to be* a Syndicate. Were the four rightsholders to function as separate business entities, selling rights individually and even in competition with each other, the name *Conan* could have no single secondary meaning, and thus could not be trademarked.

That de Camp did not understand right away all of the advantages his proposed Conan Syndicate would provide is in part because the doctrine of unfair competition had by the late 1960s not yet become a regular tool in the management of fictional characters and properties. Much greater emphasis, both in trade publications and in court, was put on copyright. That de Camp's proposal enabled the establishment of trademark protection should not, however, be seen as an accident or stroke of luck. The fictional-property market de Camp found himself in encouraged a specific form of business setup so as to maximize both the revenue potential of Conan as a property and the returns accruing to the four rightsholders. That this setup likewise facilitated what would eventually become a powerful and, within the media industries, ubiquitous means of protecting characters via trademark law indicates clear congruence between developing legal practices in the United States, the business structures of new fictional-property enterprises, and the formal law itself. The three fields of practice, we might say, were becoming, as the modern copyright era drew to a close, homologous. What we should not lose sight of, however, is that this new homology was itself the product of the kind of seemingly arbitrary or accidental actions instituted by individuals like de Camp, who in improvising new kinds of responses within a set of given legal or financial contexts was simultaneously altering these very contexts so as to better enable these new kinds of responses. Through a process resembling what Anthony Giddens famously called "structuration," de Camp's proposed Syndicate was thus not just reactive but also generative.[141] For all its seeming idiosyncrasy, it was part of the same process of industrial change that led eventually to the wide-scale employment of unfair competition/trademark law to protect fictional properties.

In the short term, however, de Camp's proposal suffered one serious flaw: Glenn Lord would not agree to it—at least not in the terms de Camp originally proposed. In part, Lord's resistance was financially motivated. Under the original Lancer contract between de Camp and Lord, de Camp paid the Kuykendalls a flat rate of two cents per word for previously unpublished Howard Conan material, one cent per word for previously *published* Howard Conan material, and nothing at all for stories in the public domain.[142] The Kuykendalls would also receive no royalties for book sales. Though these rates seem miniscule today, they were standard for the early 1960s, and Lord agreed to them without debate when the contract was signed in September of 1966. The more important compensation was in licensing and foreign sales, for which the Kuykendalls were awarded one-half of all proceeds derived from Howard material still under copyright.[143] Foreign sales promised to be particularly remunerative for the Kuykendalls, since the *Weird Tales* Howard stories would still be under copyright in Britain for many more decades. By 1968, however, the relatively small amount of money so far paid to the Kuykendalls had come to be seen by Lord as unreasonable, since by that time the Conan series was fast becoming one of the first fantasy paperback blockbusters in the United States.[144] Lord thus refused to agree to de Camp's proposed Syndicate unless de Camp agreed to revise the Lancer contract's terms so as to increase the Kuykendalls' compensation for use of the Howard material.

Underlying Lord's financial objection, however, was, for de Camp, a much harder to accommodate moral objection. Although no member of the Kuykendall family had ever interacted with Robert E. Howard, and although no family member had ever shown much interest in the Conan property, Lord considered the Kuykendalls the rightful beneficiaries of Howard's work. Indeed, Lord rarely referred to them in business correspondence as the Kuykendalls; he called them, rather, "the Howard Estate." As the legal heirs of Howard's fiction, Lord argued, the Kuykendalls were morally and legally closest to the property's originating source; they, through their legal proxy (Lord himself), should thus have primary control of the property and benefit financially from this control. For Lord, the descent of rights via inheritance—however uncertain or arbitrary (recall that Howard's fiction was not mentioned in either his or his father's wills)—had a greater claim to legitimacy than did the operations of copyright law. Lord thus rejected de Camp's proposal regarding subsidiary rights, complaining in a 1968 letter that it was unfair for original *Weird Tales* Conan stories to be valued at less than the rate of the newer stories. Noting that the estate had received "not one cent" for these stories from the Lancer deal, Lord insisted that he was no longer willing "to 'donate' these stories" to de Camp or another: "I may not be able to prevent their confiscation by anyone who is determined to use them without payment, but I will not cooperate in any such deal."[145] As Lord's language in this letter suggests, his demand for greater remuneration is ultimately founded in a refusal to accept—or perhaps a failure to fully understand—what the court's judgment regarding the Conan copyrights had actually effected. From the perspective of U.S. copyright law, the lawsuit, though instrumental in turning Conan into a profitable book series, had shifted legal control of the property to de Camp by invalidating most of the estate's solely held copyrights. The court's judgment had in effect taken the estate's portion of the property and removed the legal sanctions necessary for it to exist as property at all. But Lord persisted in treating the public domain stories as property belonging to the estate, albeit property significantly devalued. His objection to de Camp's proposal frames use of the public domain stories in terms of *confiscation* and *donation*, actions that can only meaningfully be performed on property. The increase in compensation he demanded of de Camp would thus, he proposed, be best effected by treating the public domain stories as though they were still under copyright—and belonging to the estate—when determining the estate's share of proceeds from a sale of rights in the Conan saga as a whole.

In arguing on behalf of greater control for the Kuykendalls, Lord was, to be sure, doing so out of self-interest; his income as agent depended upon the amount he brought in from licensing Howard's stories. Lord was, however, also motivated by what appeared to be a genuine devotion to Robert E. Howard, and this devotion partly explains the legitimacy Lord granted the idea of the "Howard Estate." Once Lord became agent for the estate, he seemed to see himself—much as fans would later see him—as working not on behalf of the Kuykendalls at all but rather on behalf of Howard himself and his legacy. From this perspective, de Camp was not a partner but was rather what Lord would later call a "vulture," constantly picking at the literary remains of Howard, which had been left exposed by the imperfect workings of U.S. copyright law.[146] Although open, under the right terms, to de Camp's proposal that the stakeholders form a united front for the sale of the Conan saga *as a whole*, Lord thus objected to any deal that would require him to share profits for individual sales of any of Howard's original stories—even those stories that legally belonged to the public. As de Camp tried in vain to explain to Lord, this position would hurt the Estate, as Lord could exert no legal control over the public domain stories: "As you doubtless realize, since the material in public domain is nobody's exclusive property, any one of the authors, in the absence of an agreement to the contrary, would have an equal right to 'sell' this material and keep whatever he could get in this manner."[147] Lord, however, was adamant. For him to join the Syndicate, its purview must be limited to sales of the saga as a whole. The Howard Conan stories rightfully belonged only to the Howard Estate.

In order to gain Lord's participation in the Syndicate, de Camp eventually gave in to all of Lord's requests. For the public domain stories used in the Lancer series, de Camp agreed to pay a per-word rate.[148] He also agreed to a fifty-fifty split of proceeds earned from the publication of any new, previously unpublished, book-length Howard material.[149] In determining the division of proceeds for sale of subsidiary rights in the entire Conan saga—which de Camp calculated by determining the amount of words each stakeholder had contributed to the saga's total word count—de Camp counted the public domain stories as though they belonged to the estate, though he discounted their value by two-thirds.[150] As for the Syndicate's scope, only sales of subsidiary rights for the entire Conan saga would be covered. The sale of rights in individual stories would remain uncoordinated and require no profit sharing among stakeholders.[151] All four of the stakeholders—Lord (acting on behalf of the Kuykendalls), de Camp, Carter, and Nyberg—agreed to these terms as set out in a relatively simple contract drafted by de Camp himself (with no assistance from a lawyer) and dated June 8, 1968.[152]

Viewed retrospectively, the contractual creation of the Conan Syndicate was a major success, even a triumph. Just as de Camp had intended, the "united front" effectively dissuaded potential competitors from publishing the public domain stories or creating new Conan material. It helped the group recover the publishing rights to the stories after a bankrupt Lancer attempted to sell them to another publisher. And, once legally incorporated as Conan Properties, Inc. (with substantial assistance by lawyer Arthur Lieberman), the Syndicate enabled the sale of subsidiary rights in a manner that brought its members large financial returns, including the sale of film rights to Hollywood producer Edward Pressman in 1978. Even more importantly, however, the Syndicate managed to keep the four stakeholders working in concert (albeit often at loggerheads) long enough to build up what was in practice a unified business, represented by Conan and protectable from the late twentieth century through today under trademark law. Without the Syndicate, none of the major licensing deals—including the 1982 Milius-Schwarzenegger film, Funcom's *Age of Conan* MMORPG (launched in 2008), toy deals with Mattel and McFarlane Toys, the Dark Horse comics series of the early 2000s, and the Marvel Comics series of the 2010s—would have been possible.

For all its long-term success, however, during most of the 1970s the Syndicate was barely functional and in near-constant danger of collapse. De Camp's failure to get Lord to "unite" on the sale of rights in single stories not only left the group only partially unified, it even incentivized the four men to compete among themselves in the sale of individual story rights. Just as de Camp had feared, this "every-man-for-himself" approach led to inefficiency, bungled deals, and an extraordinary (among Howard fans even *legendary*) degree of enmity between Lord, on the one hand, and de Camp and Carter on the other. Indeed, an entire book could be written tracing the fights and reconciliations the members of the Syndicate underwent during its ten-year existence (to say nothing of those that developed after Conan Properties, Inc. was established). For my purposes, however, there are two specific "episodes" in the Syndicate's history that are worth briefly examining for the light they shed on the complex workings of contract enforcement and intellectual property law in practice. The first of these involves a rights deal made by Lord with Marvel Comics in 1970.

In September 1968, Roy Thomas, a writer and editor at Marvel, wrote to Lord with news of Marvel's plans to launch a sword-and-sorcery comic book series, and expressed his hope that the publisher might license Conan for it, at the rate of $150 to $200 per issue. Lord was inclined to accept the offer, despite its vagueness, but mindful of the Syndicate agreement (signed just three months earlier), he dutifully submitted the offer to de Camp, Carter, and Nyberg.[153] Carter was the first to respond, noting that the offer was far too little, that the Syndicate should also request a share of "subsidiary stuff" (such as posters and T-shirts Marvel might make), and that Lord should retain an agent, specifically, Henry Morrison (who was handling Conan's film and television sales), to negotiate the deal for them.[154] Lord agreed at first to hold off making a deal himself, but over the next month he increasingly challenged the Syndicate's contractual authority to restrain him, at one point even retaining his own agent and deliberately withholding the agent's identity and terms from the other Syndicate members.[155] When de Camp finally gave in, consenting to the sale with the proviso that the proceeds be split among the Syndicate members in accordance with the group's 1968 contract, Lord was livid. In an angry letter, he rejected that de Camp, Carter, or Nyberg "would come in on this" under the terms of their agreement. Because Howard had created Conan and his world, Lord argued, Lord had the right to sell the rights to this world—and that sale of these rights did not constitute sale of the series as a whole. "You, Carter, and Nyberg have freely used the character and milieu created by Howard without any restraint, earning quite handsomely thereby," he concluded; "consequently, any sale of the character by the Howard interests should by all means be equally as free of restraint."[156]

Underlying the conflict were two distinct issues, one moral and one contractual, with Lord recognizing only the first and de Camp proceeding primarily in terms of the latter. Lord's continued insistence that Conan belonged to the "Howard estate," irrespective of the various stories' copyright statuses, was founded upon a moral argument that the creator of a property (or the creator's heirs) has a natural and thus never completely alienable right to profit from his creation. De Camp, by contrast, saw the language of their agreement—and its implication for the property as a whole—as the crux of the matter. "As for the pending question of the sale of comic-book rights," he replied to Lord, "since this depends upon differing interpretations of the phrase 'subsidiary rights in and to all the Conan stories as a group,' my reply will require careful thought."[157] Although the question hinged upon the ambiguous language of an informal contract, it also reflected a more profound uncertainty with respect to intellectual property law itself: when dealing with a coherent, intertextual, narrative-based property, on what exactly were the legal rights to a "character" and fictional "milieu" founded? In the first works to feature that character, in the "Conan stories as a group," or—as de Camp himself had believed—nowhere at all? Given the lack of copyright protection for the original stories, de Camp reasoned, the answer had implications far beyond that of Lord's deal with Marvel, for if the character and milieu could be sold separately by each member of the Syndicate without regard for the legal status of the existing stories, the Syndicate would dissolve, no film deal would be possible, and the lack of copyright for the original stories would quickly become known.[158]

In the short term, Lord won the dispute, completing the deal with Marvel Comics before de Camp had time to consult a lawyer and keeping the profits for the heirs. Just as de Camp and Carter had warned, however, the deal quickly revealed itself to be a bad one for Lord, who had substantially underpriced the license and failed to reserve or take a cut in subsidiary rights to the comics. Conan fast became one of Marvel's top-selling titles, expanding to a second series in 1974; and Marvel took advantage of the subsidiary rights Lord had granted it, releasing a variety of Conan merchandise without oversight by Lord or the Syndicate, thus effectively preventing the Syndicate's sale of merchandise rights to other parties. So great was the publisher's need for content—and so popular were the adaptations of the existing stories among comic book readers—that Marvel also ended up using not just the "character" and "milieu" but the entire Conan saga, including Carter, de Camp, and Nyberg's stories (for which Marvel had to negotiate separately). De Camp was thus proven right in the end, and once Conan Properties, Inc. was formed, the distinction between "character" and "stories as a group" was erased and the deal with Marvel renegotiated so as to better favor the former Syndicate members.

That the group did not come together sooner to renegotiate with Marvel was in large part a consequence of the second episode I wish to examine here, which revolves around the complexity of copyright formalities, specifically those relating to the renewal process and its potential intersection with the principle of copyright indivisibility. Sometime between 1974 and 1975, Lord, working with an agent named Kirby McCauley, discovered that Blanchard Press (or its predecessor, Steinerberg Press), owner of many of Popular Fiction Publishing Co.'s assets, had filed copyright renewals for seven of the *Weird Tales* issues in which Howard's Conan stories had first appeared. Did this mean that the stories *were not* in the public domain? Hoping that this was the case, Lord submitted the question to Blum, Moscovitz, Friedman & Kaplan, a law firm specializing in intellectual property. In October 1975, Alex Friedman responded with a twelve-page review of the "problem," organized around a single question of law: does a copyright renewal registration for a composite work such as a magazine "preserve" the copyrights for the works contained therein? Although admitting that his answer made a number of assumptions regarding the facts of the case, Friedman was surprisingly definitive in his conclusion: "we do not believe that a Court would hold . . . that the works have fallen into the public domain."[159] Despite citations from *Nimmer on Copyright* and a large number of court opinions, his reasoning is primarily based on the relatively simple recognition that "courts, in recent years, have demonstrated a great reluctance to permit copyrighted works to fall into the public domain where there was evidence of an intention to maintain a valid copyright."

One is tempted to imagine Lord's response as incensed, even apoplectic, given that the structure of the Syndicate had been built upon the assumption that most of the original Howard stories were *not* protected by copyright. And there is no doubt that he saw the law firm's report as further evidence that de Camp had cheated him. His communication with de Camp about this issue (handled mostly by McCauley), however, remained composed, with expressions of moral outrage excised in favor of demands for an increased share of the publishing profits and veiled threats of legal action.[160] De Camp responded cautiously, refusing to take Friedman's report (forwarded to him by McCauley) as definitive. That he did not do so is almost certainly because he recognized that the facts of the case were more complicated than what Lord had represented to Friedman. Most simply, that the estate *intended* to maintain a valid copyright was uncertain at best, given that de Camp had—with the written authorization of the estate and the support of Lord—earlier asked a court of law to declare them *invalid*. What is more, the murkiness of the original assignment of rights between Howard and Popular Fiction Publishing Co. evoked all of the problems and uncertainties of copyright indivisibility—a subject that the law firm (somewhat surprisingly) had failed to take up, but which de Camp well understood, however imperfectly. Had Howard only sold *Weird Tales* first serial rights to the stories, for example, all bets were off regarding the validity of the renewal.

Ultimately, the legal answer as to whether the renewals were valid is irrelevant—and, never having been tried in a court of law, indeterminable. Of importance to us, rather, is what the episode reveals about how "professional" legal advice is used by the nonlegal experts who solicit and receive it when fighting over the meaning and validity of an ambiguous contract. In practice, such advice functions not as a definitive statement of the law but as a tool whose meaning and use value are heavily determined by the goals, beliefs, and lay knowledge of those who solicit and/or receive it. In their communication of the renewal question to Friedman's firm, for example, Lord and McCauley subtly misrepresented the facts at issue, resulting in a conclusion of questionable applicability to their dispute with de Camp but useful as a negotiating tactic. Indeed, Lord and McCauley appeared less interested in how the law works (or was purported to work) than in the fact that Friedman's firm had concluded that it works in their favor. As McCauley noted in a threatening letter to de Camp, "I've not myself read the source material, nor I think has Glenn, since we are placing confidence in their research as copyright specialists and their ability to defend the renewals if ever there should be a legal challenge."[161]

To de Camp, however, Friedman's report was merely the opening in a series of contractual—and even intellectual—salvos. Drawing on his own experience as both a litigant and a published expositor of intellectual property law, de Camp undertook his own research, reviewing some of the works cited in Friedman's report (de Camp's papers, for example, contain copies of *Nimmer on Copyright*), undertaking formal renewal searches via the U.S. Copyright Office, and eventually consulting a law firm of his own—to which he presented a more comprehensive account of the facts.[162] Knowledgeable of both the messiness of the property's history and of Lord's limited financial resources, he also seemed to have wagered that—whatever the law was on this matter—Lord was unlikely to risk a lawsuit. More importantly, de Camp recognized that Lord and the other Syndicate members' interests in protecting the property were ultimately the same and that, were the group to reunite, Friedman's conclusion stood to benefit them all. By the time Conan Properties, Inc. was formed, de Camp and Lord had thus become aligned in their response to the report and the arguments it contained. No longer a crux in their battle with each other, the report provided the "legal" evidence the men needed in order to make a good faith representation to Pressman in 1978 that the Conan franchise was legally protected and owned by a single legal entity. As this surprisingly happy conclusion suggests, for scholars of narrative-based property, the most important question to be asked when dealing with professional legal "advice" is probably not whether such advice is correct—nor even whether it is followed—but rather how it is understood and employed by those who receive it.

Conclusion

As the above sections have demonstrated, the contracts employed by those involved with the Conan property were, for much of the property's early history, often tacit, ambiguous, and of questionable legality in court—qualities that characterize what this chapter, following decades of legal and economic scholarship, has called *informal contracts.* Such contracts were used, at the property's beginning, by Howard and *Weird Tales* to exchange some or all of the publication rights to the original Conan stories. They were used after Howard's death to create and manage relationships between the rightsholders and those, such as Friend, West, de Camp, and Lord, who acted as their agents. Informal contracts were further used to sell publishing and other subsidiary rights. They were also used, starting with de Camp's involvement with the property, to prompt and manage the production of new Conan material or—in the case of Nyberg—to retroactively authorize such production. And they were used, finally, in the form of the Syndicate agreement(s) to try to salvage the property as a long-term business concern.

The degree of informality varied across these contracts. Many of them were so informal as to lack written terms altogether; instead, they were made orally or through one or two sentences contained within a personal letter or stamped on the back of a check. All were ambiguous in some respect, though some more than others. The contracting and subcontracting of "agents," for example, relied heavily upon tacit understandings of what an agent was supposed to do (and not do). And some of the contracts were almost certainly more enforceable in a court than others—though importantly the only one to be brought to court (the publishing contract with Gnome Press) was more formal than most. Even that contract, however, had been missing specifications regarding a vital detail: the responsibility of the rightsholders to renew the copyrights.

Today, in the twenty-first century, none of the contracting involved with a narrative-based property would be conducted as the Conan contracts were. Today's contracts would be drafted by lawyers, with details clearly spelled out and all contingencies—or at least all that are imaginable—accounted for. For example, while working on this book, I was approached by a production company interested in producing a television episode about a real-life event in which I had been involved several years earlier. Would I, they inquired, be willing to grant them rights to my story? The resulting (unratified) contract was more than ten typed pages of terms, conditions, and waivers in language that was at once highly specific and carefully broad—and very difficult for a nonlawyer (even one, such as myself, who studies IP law) to understand. In one clause, common to entertainment contracts today, the production company claimed the right to use my likeness in "any and all media, now known or hereafter devised" "throughout the universe, in perpetuity."[163] Such clauses, representing efforts to ensure that the rights acquired will persist in any possible future, would have been unimaginable to anyone involved with the Conan property during its early decades. Indeed, such clauses would have been unimaginable to almost anyone working in the entertainment industry during the modern copyright era.

Galactic overreach notwithstanding, the abandonment of informal contracting practices by today's entertainment industry might be counted as a positive development in the history of narrative-based property management. Informal contracting, after all, appears to have nearly destroyed the Conan property on multiple occasions. In an era of more formal contracts, where the responsibilities and punitive consequences of failing to adhere to them are clearly and carefully articulated, such destruction may appear less likely. What is more, with relationships between parties to a contract now specified in clear, written detail—with contingencies accounted for—we might expect relationships between parties to be less likely to devolve into enmity or dispute.

Or would we? As the high-profile lawsuits filed in recent years by Scarlett Johansson against the Walt Disney Company (regarding the film

Black Widow), Frank Darabont and CAA against AMC Networks (regarding the television show *The Walking Dead*), and Emily Deschanel and David Boreanaz against Fox (regarding the television show *Bones*) suggest, the ubiquity of formal contracting seems not to have decreased the need for lawsuits over contractual violations—nor does it appear to have done much to improve relationships among contractees in the entertainment industry. Indeed, for all the damage that informal contracting seems to have wrought on the Conan property, we might nevertheless read that property's history as an argument in *favor* of informal contracting. As this chapter has demonstrated, the success and survival of the Conan property depended upon a degree of improvisation, responsiveness, and creativity that formalized contracts would almost certainly have squelched. In today's era of formal contracting, it is impossible, for example, to imagine someone like de Camp undertaking the kind of work he did to fashion and refashion the Conan property without contractual guarantees of (considerable) pay, royalties, and expenses. And it is equally impossible to imagine any rightsholder—especially those, like the Kuykendalls, who held rights that appeared to have little profit potential and who possessed little capital to devote to their exploitation—agreeing to such guarantees. The likely outcome today of circumstances similar to that in which the Conan stakeholders found themselves many decades ago would thus not be more secure development of the property but the absence of any property development at all. Perhaps for this reason, informal contracts, though rare today, are not extinct, especially those involving high-level creative talent in Hollywood. As legal scholar Jonathan Barnett has argued, so-called soft contracts continue to play an important role (despite occasionally giving rise to major lawsuits) in managing the "reputational issues," "high specification and enforcement costs," and "outcome uncertainty" associated with the business of Hollywood.[164]

Of course, that the Conan property's fate would be different if it originated today is not merely because the principle of informal contracting has been supplanted. So too have nearly all of the legal principles that informed the development of the Conan property, as well as those properties discussed in previous chapters. In place of short copyright duration, copyrights now last a relatively long time: the life of the author plus seventy years or, for the case of works made for hire, one hundred twenty years from creation or (if shorter) ninety-five years from publication. Copyright formalities are almost nonexistent, and indivisibility has been dead for so long that many young lawyers have never heard of it. While authorial genius continues to be recognized by fans and sometimes—when dealing with works made for hire before 1978—by entertainment companies, it has ceased to mean much in a court of law, nor does it seem especially relevant to the development and/or textual semantics of recently produced properties, which are frequently presented as the creations not of individuals but of corporations, such as Warner Bros. or Marvel Comics (a marketing tactic that Jerome Christensen has suggested has its origins in the branding practices of classical Hollywood).[165] As for the idea-expression dichotomy, its development after 1978 is unfortunately beyond the scope of this book, and its fate arguably still undetermined. What can be safely said, however, is that its relevance to the management of narrative-based property has decreased as trademark law and unfair competition have come to serve as the primary tools for protecting fictional characters and other kinds of narrative assets. Whereas cartoon characters, which courts protected through the application of unfair competition principles to copyright law, had once represented an *exception* to the protections afforded fictional characters by the law, today they are the paradigmatic example of the protections the law provides.

What remains true today, however, is that the history of any narrative-based property's development is almost never straightforward, nor is it unshaped by disputes of a broadly legal kind, even if such disputes end up resolved outside of a courtroom. Likewise, the authoring/management of narrative-based property remains today, as it was then, ultimately about (to borrow Derek Johnson and Johnathan Gray's language) "control, power, and the management of meaning and people as much as it is about creativity and innovation."[166] The story of any narrative-based property's development is thus always, for better or worse, multicausal, shaped by personality, morality, and financial opportunity; by accident, contingency, and irrationality; and by a range of legal, creative, and managerial actions—some formal, some informal, some effective, some ineffective, and some (perhaps more than we might wish to recognize) the product of simple dumb luck.

Coda

What Comes After? Toward a Periodization of U.S. Intellectual Property Law

With the implementation of the Copyright Act of 1976 in 1978, the modern copyright era came to an end. Its ending was not, in all regards, instantaneous. As Jessica Litman has demonstrated, judges sometimes resisted abandoning case law that the new statute appeared to abrogate—in part, she suggests, because both the statute itself and its documented legislative history were unusually complicated and often "unclear."[1] In addition, works that were already under copyright before 1978 remained, in some important respects, still governed by provisions of the 1909 Act and the case law supplementing it. "If, as of 1978, it [the old Act] will be dead," warned Melville Nimmer on the eve of the new act's implementation, "it will nonetheless in many ways rule us from the grave."[2] For most legal actors, however—including judges—the old act quickly became irrelevant. Replacing it, as Barbara Ringer, register of copyrights from 1973 to 1980, noted, was a statute so "profound" in its revisions to the law, that it might represent "a shift in the direction of the very philosophy of copyright itself."[3]

Previous chapters have relayed the fate of the legal principles most important to narrative-based property during the modern copyright era. The duration of copyright protection was extended from what was, even in 1909, a short fifty-six years (split into two twenty-eight-year terms) to today a term equal to the life of the author plus seventy years (or, for works made for hire, ninety-five years from publication or one hundred years from creation, whichever is shorter). Copyright formalities, including indivisibility, were ended, making copyright effectively automatic. Formal contracts became the rule across all industries, in part due to the new statute's revision to the work-for-hire doctrine, though also thanks to the growing involvements of agents, managers, and lawyers in the entertainment industry. Although codified by the Act of 1976, the idea-expression dichotomy has seen its importance wane in resolving copyright disputes—as has the principle of authorial genius, which no longer appears to play the key role in judicial opinions that it once did. As for what chapter 4 referred to as the "missing principle" of trademark and unfair competition law, it is today no longer missing—quite the contrary.

But what, taken together, do the above changes mean for intellectual property as a whole? And what new legal principles became important after 1978? If, as Ringer, suggested, we are dealing with a new "philosophy of copyright itself," what is this philosophy? How might we label and thus periodize it? Previous chapters have tried to avoid these questions, largely for methodological reasons. The approach to legal historiography taken by this book—one that privileges the micro, the archive, the idiosyncratic, and the contingent—does not lend itself well to quick, generalized transhistorical comparisons. The post-1978 period is, to be blunt, outside this book's scope, and to bring it fairly within would require the kind of careful tracing of principles and properties that formed the substance of the previous five chapters. What comes after the modern copyright era is thus, for better or worse, a question for another book.

That said, it may be useful to speculate here, by way of conclusion, what such a book would look like. In what follows, I thus offer up brief descriptions of what strike me as the three most important post-1978 legal principles governing narrative-based property after the end of the modern copyright era. Although these descriptions lack the scope and detail of those presented in previous chapters for the most important *modern-copyright-era* principles, they provide together an immediate sense of how radically intellectual property law has changed since the passage of the 1976 Act. They also point, albeit provisionally, to how one might approach periodizing post-1978 intellectual property law in the United States—at least with respect to narrative-based property.

Transformative Use

Traditionally viewed as supporting the interests of free expression (guaranteed under the First Amendment) and various goals of public policy, the doctrine of fair use permits non-rightsholders to make use of copyrighted material—under special conditions—without permission from its rightsholders. Legal scholars usually trace the origins of the doctrine to eighteenth-century common law, and the principle can be found at work in judicial opinions throughout the modern copyright era, albeit in ways that suggest its meaning was still unstable during this time.[4] As Saul Cohen noted in a 1953 piece for *Copyright Law Symposium*, "there is some disagreement as to whether fair use is an infringement of copyright which is privileged or whether fair use simply does not infringe the copyright."[5] In the latter case, one was arguably dealing not with a special kind of judicially authorized use at all but merely use that was, under the letter of copyright law, non-infringing.

Whatever its meaning during this earlier era, the doctrine as we recognize it today is a product of the Copyright Act of 1976, which both codified and formalized the common law by mandating a four-factor test for fair use.[6] In determining fair use, judges were henceforth required to consider (1) "the purpose and character of the use," (2) "the nature of the copyrighted work," (3) "the amount and substantiality of the portion" of the work used, and (4) "the effect of the use upon the potential market for or value of the copyrighted work."[7] Despite this formalization, however, judges continued to struggled with "fair use" decisions after 1978, resulting in a case law that was, for at least the next fifteen years, at best, inconsistent, and at worst—to adopt the language of Second Circuit Judge Pierre Leval—chaotically confused.[8]

To try and resolve this confusion, Judge Leval introduced in a 1990 *Harvard Law Review* article a new legal principle, which he termed *transformative use* and which he argued should serve in fair-use determinations as the crux of first-factor consideration. "The question of justification," he explained, "turns primarily on whether and to what extent, the challenged use is *transformative*. The use must be productive and must employ the quoted matter in a different manner or for a different purpose from the original."[9] Four years after the article's publication, the U.S. Supreme Court, in *Campbell v. Acuff-Rose Music, Inc.*, adopted Leval's new principle as the law of the land, defining *transformative* as "altering the original with new expression, meaning or message" and instructing readers that "[t]he more transformative the work, the less will be the significance of other factors . . . that may weigh against a finding of fair use."[10]

Since *Campbell v. Acuff-Rose*, the number of fair use cases revolving around transformative use has exploded, with more than 90 percent of fair use decisions in 2019 relying upon it.[11] The principle has not, however, brought the clarity Judge Leval had intended and, has for over two decades now, been the subject of intense criticism by lawyers, creators, and a growing number of judges. "[C]ourts have disagreed," observes legal scholar Brian Sites, "both in practice and in definition, about what qualifies as transformative."[12] The result has been a "muddled" doctrine[13] that, as it has grown in employment by defense lawyers, has subjected the entertainment industry to increasing amounts of uncertainty. This uncertainty has been especially worrisome to managers of narrative-based property, since, as Jiarui Liu has demonstrated, courts appear more likely to find transformative use when dealing with literary and audiovisual works than with other kinds of work, such as music and software[14]—and since a finding of transformative use almost always leads to a finding of fair use.[15] The principle of transformative use also risks undermining the statutory right to prepare derivative works granted copyright owners by the 1976 Act.[16] "Transformation is the hallmark of a derivative work too," cautioned Diane Zimmerman a few years after *Campbell v. Acuff-Rose*, "and copyright owners are ordinarily allowed to decide by whom, whether and when such works can be produced."[17] Indeed, managers of narrative-based property depend upon a monopoly over such transformation in order to create adaptations and story worlds and to license and merchandise their characters. If transformation has indeed become the privileged mode of fair use, such a monopoly is, at best, provisional, and the legal grounds on which these managers' businesses depend has been rendered unstable. Worse still, the identification of transformation with fair use means that a key right guaranteed by the Act of 1976 has, at the hands of judges (albeit perhaps with good intentions), been undermined. For these and other reasons, the future of transformative use is uncertain. Whatever its future, however, its current role in U.S. copyright law represents a radical change from that of the modern copyright regime.

Trademark Law

Trademark law, as described in previous chapters, was originally an outgrowth of unfair competition law, designed to protect businesses (and secondarily consumers) from unfair injury due to misrepresentation of the origin of a good. Such misrepresentation was most often effected through the misappropriation of a name or mark associated with the good's producer—i.e., a trademark. During the modern copyright era, trademark law was in its infancy, at least as it applied to narrative-based property, and thus had relatively little impact on the development of fictional characters and their story worlds. Even after the passage of the Lanham Act in 1946, which supplemented state laws with a federal trademark system, narrative-based property managers continued to rely primarily upon copyright law to protect against competing or derivative uses that involved what we would today identify as misappropriation of a trademark. As chapter 4 argued, the efforts by lawyers and judges to employ copyright law in this manner sometimes bent that law out of shape, resulting, for example, in a separate case law for cartoon characters from that for other kinds of fictional characters.

By the end of the twentieth century, however, trademark law had grown to be an important and ubiquitous tool in the management of narrative-based property—and it has only grown in importance since. Today, fictional characters and other kinds of narrative assets are not only copyrighted but also routinely trademarked, such that many are now protected under two very different fields of intellectual property law. Whereas superheroes originating in comic books, to give but one example, were trademarked, when at all, in tiny numbers in the years constituting the modern copyright era, trademark applications by Marvel and DC skyrocketed after 1977, with DC alone applying for more than 150 in 1979, more than 325 in 1991, and more than 150 in 2016.[18] During the modern copyright era, by comparison, DC filed an average of fewer than four a year, and in most years filed zero.[19] Whereas none of the legal disputes over properties considered in previous chapters of this book involved trademark claims, similar disputes (for example, over the right of an author to continue employing a character he created or a toymaker to sell a toy that resembled a cartoon character belonging to someone else) would thus invariably involve them today.

In large part, the growing importance of trademark law to narrative-based property reflects a shift in legal understanding, spurred by new legislation, in what a trademark represents. No longer merely signaling the provenance of a good, a trademark is now widely understood as accruing an inherent value of its own: a kind of repository for meaning and/or generalized good will. As Mark Lemley worried in a 1999 piece for the *Yale Law Journal*,

> Commentators and even courts increasingly talk about trademarks as property rights; as things valuable in and of themselves, rather than for

> the product goodwill they embody. Courts protect trademark owners against uses that would not have been infringements even a few years ago and protect as trademarks things that would not have received such protection in the past. And they are well on their way to divorcing trademarks entirely from the goods they are supposed to represent.[20]

New doctrines such as trademark dilution, first introduced by states such as Massachusetts, then made federal law by the Federal Trademark Dilution Act of 1995 (strengthened in important respects by the Trademark Dilution Revision Act of 2006), institutionalized these changes.[21] Today, even noncompetitors can thus be barred—or held liable for damages—for the misuse or imitation of a well-known trademark.

Trademark law has become so powerful that today it arguably even rivals copyright law as a means of protecting narrative-based property. Copyrights can—and, for all works, eventually will—expire. Trademark protection, by contrast, is unending (at least, if managed correctly). A property owner can thus, at least in theory, continue via trademark law to monopolize the use of fictional characters and story worlds even after the copyrights in the underlying texts have expired. Although few twentieth-century texts featuring characters still popular today have yet entered the public domain, many soon will, including the first cartoons to feature Mickey Mouse. For those few that have already—including John Carter of Mars and Conan the Barbarian—the former copyright owners have in many cases been able to continue to charge licensing fees for the use of the properties. Legal scholars have been warning of a coming crisis for more than a decade, and there appears to be little clear case law to help guide judges in these kinds of disputes.[22] In conducting research for this book, the entertainment lawyers I consulted suggested to me different solutions, with one predicting that trademark law would eventually be sanctioned for the barring of derivative merchandise or services but not aesthetic content (i.e., texts), once the original text had entered the public domain. Whatever the answer, trademark clearly functions today—and will likely continue to function in the future—as a powerful new tool, unimagined by earlier property managers, for the protection of narrative-based property.

Safe Harbor Provision

The term "Safe Harbor provision" refers to exemptions from liability for copyright infringement granted by the Online Copyright Infringement

Liability Limitation Act to online service providers for content that is posted to or distributed through their systems by users. Also referred to as Section 512, the provision was passed in 1998 as part of the Digital Millennium Copyright Act, where it was intended to strike a balance between the needs of new technology services and the rights of copyright holders.[23] In exchange for implementing systems for reporting and "expeditiously" taking down infringing content, service providers were given protection from suits alleging direct infringement.[24] Such systems, in turn, were imagined to benefit copyright holders by enabling them to get infringing content removed without needing to file expensive and time-consuming lawsuits.

In the years since the Safe Harbor provision was enacted, it has proven to be both more controversial and, in important respects, less effective than its drafters had hoped. Among legal scholars, the primary criticism has been the "chilling effect" the notice-and-takedown systems have had on users, who—though granted the right to file counternotice—are usually poorly positioned to challenge the take-down requests of large entertainment companies.[25] Although empirical data on notices and take downs are rare, what studies exist strongly suggest that a significant portion of requests are problematic or "fundamentally flawed," resulting in the regular takedown of non-infringing content.[26] At the same time, rightsholders have often found it difficult to employ the system to respond to wide-scale infringement, in part because individual notices must be sent for each individual file or link. No sooner is one infringing file taken down, then a new copy is posted back up, sometimes by the same user, a problem commonly referred to as "whack-a-mole."[27] As a result, especially when sites that hosted user-generated content such as YouTube were in their infancy (and thus positioned *against* the professional entertainment industries), unlicensed copyrighted material has often been easy to find online—even on legal non-pirate sites located in the United States. Such material includes digital copies of films, comic books, and television shows, as well as unauthorized derivative works.

Despite—or because of—its failures, the Safe Harbor provision's influence on the management of narrative-based property has been monumental. Not only did Section 512 give rise to powerful technology companies like Alphabet, Meta, and TikTok—which have often served an outsized role in managing and distributing consumer attention—it also fundamentally remade most, if not all, of the entertainment industries. It did this in part by destroying legacy business models and forcing companies to reimagine their product offerings so as to better compete with "free" pirated content. But it also, in enabling an explosion of fan-produced content, including fan art, fan wikis, and fan fiction, forced property managers to interact with their audiences in a more strategic manner than had been desired—or even possible—during the modern copyright era. To be sure, in emphazing such change, I may appear to be pointing as much to the impact of the consumer Internet (itself a post-1978 technology) as I am a new, post-1978 legal principle. In reality, however, the consumer Internet as we know it is in many ways a *product* of the Safe Harbor provision. Without Section 512—or some other provision in its place—a very different Internet would almost certainly have developed, and with it a different set of forces impacting narrative-based property managers.

From Post-modern Copyright to Copyright in the Digital Era

As the above descriptions should suggest, periodizing the intellectual property era that comes after 1978—at least with respect to narrative-based property—is not as easy as periodizing the era that comes before. Part of the challenge is the number of significant statutes that have been passed over the last five decades, each of which has in important respects altered the workings of intellectual property law. Whereas between 1909 and 1978, few major statutes of relevance to narrative-based property were passed and implemented, in the years since 1978 numerous important statutes have passed, as well as key international treaties. Radical new principles have also been introduced by judges, while key questions concerning important legal doctrines remain unanswered. Due to the growth of trademark law, any post-1978 periodization must also wrestle with the timelines of two different bodies of law, each of which, taken separately, would appear to suggest incompatible periodization schemes.

The plethora of important post-1978 laws is, however, not the only factor making periodization difficult. Just as challenging are the rapid and multiple changes in how narrative-based property has been produced, distributed, and consumed. The appearance of video games as an important product category, for example, might conveniently be located right at the tail end of the modern copyright era (the Atari 2600 was released in September 1977). But that date is rather far off from the beginning of the consumer Internet (which we might date around the launch of America Online in 1991) and that itself some distance from the start of what media scholars and journalists call the "streaming era" (which, if identified with the launch of Netflix's streaming site, is 2007; if identified with broadcasters' and cable companies' own shift to streaming, closer to 2020). And what to make of the very recent rise of artificial intelligence? Is that a continuation of the same era that gave us file sharing and the search engine or is it the start of something new?

Existing legal scholarship, unfortunately, does not provide much help. For a few decades after the passage of the Copyright Act of 1976, legal scholars spoke (albeit sometimes disparagingly) of a *postmodern* or *post-modern copyright.*[28] Some were no doubt inspired to do so by the rise of postmodern theory in the humanities and cultural criticism. But even when more concretely tied to the task of periodization, it is not always clear what the markers of a postmodern copyright era might be. Pamela Samuelson, for example, suggested in 2003 that "post-modern copyright" (which she framed as a problematic expansion of rights to rightsholders) is marked, first, by the "great success of U.S. copyright industries" and, second, by "information technology," such as new "global digital networks."[29] This last factor, however, has also inspired legal scholars to adopt an alternate mode of periodization, which places the Internet as the primary driver of legal change. Numerous law review articles since the start of the twenty-first century thus speak of a "digital era," "network era," or "Internet era," with respect to intellectual property law.[30] Although few of these articles are interested in defining in detail the markers of this era, including its start date, they suggest that in the post-1978 period—in a way that was less true for the modern copyright era (despite the introduction of new technologies such as sound film, radio, and television)—it is technological change that has driven legal change.

Given the above complications, I suspect the best way of periodizing is to demarcate, at least with respect to narrative-based property, two different periods of intellectual property law between 1978 and 2023. The first I would tentatively label *the post-modern copyright era,* with the hyphen indicating that the word *post-modern* is meant to signify merely what comes after the *modern* and not the kind of special theoretical construct elaborated in works like Frederic Jameson's *Postmodernism, or, The Cultural Logic of Late Capitalism.*[31] This would extend from 1978 to 1998, with the Copyright Act of 1976 and the Digital Millennium Copyright Act of 1998 serving as endpoints. It would be marked by the continued importance of copyright law, as laid out in the 1976 Act and interpreted/embellished by subsequent case law. And it would be marked, aesthetically, by the growth of what I called in chapter 2 sequential and rhizomatic modes of storytelling as alternatives to (but not replacements for) iterative storytelling.

The second period I would label *the trademark era,* which I would date from the passage of the first Federal Trademark Dilution Act in 1995 to the present. It would be marked by the new role of trademark law as both a complement—and, increasingly, a replacement—for copyright law. Aesthetically, it would see the biblical mode of storytelling take prominence via the employment of reboots, loosely related spin-offs, transmedia adaptations, and the increasing circulation of trademarked characters outside the context of any recognizable narrative whatsoever (as in, for example, Marvel's Luke Cage or Ubisoft's Assassin's Creed characters appearing in shaving advertisements/product packaging[32]). It would also see the proliferation of numerous versions of the same characters (as in superhero multiverses), thus shifting the concept of character, both narratively and legally, away from both the essence of the "story being told" and "the chessman in the game of telling the story" (to return to Judge Stephens's language in *Warner Bros. v. Columbia Broadcasting System*) toward something else entirely: a sort of generalized symbol or brand.

This is, of course, a rough, provisional periodization of post-1978 intellectual property law—and only as it applies to narrative-based property. A very different periodization would be needed if one were to focus, for example, on the genre of music or the business of online advertising. But even in its roughness, it helpfully points to the significance of the changes in intellectual property that have taken place since the passage of the Copyright Act of 1976. In doing so, it also underscores how different from today—and how comparatively stable—the modern copyright era was. Between 1909 and 1978, a single system governed how narrative-based property was managed legally in the United States. The system was not without its contradictions and its confusions, and it was in practice (as all legal systems are) subject to accident and contingency, but it worked—or worked well enough—for almost seven decades. Whatever its faults (and there were certainly many), we will unlikely be able to say the same about what comes or has already come after.

Notes

Abbreviations

ADP August Derleth Papers (Wisconsin Historical Society. Madison, Wisconsin)
DCB Transcript of Record, *Detective Comics v. Bruns Publications* (No. 16907)
KFF Transcript of Record, *King Features v. Fleischer*
NAKC National Archives at Kansas City (Kansas City, Missouri)
PLSDC The Papers of L. Sprague de Camp and Catherine Crook de Camp (The Harry Ransom Center, The University of Texas at Austin)
RDP Rudolph Dirks Papers, 1860–1971 (Archives of American Art, Smithsonian Institution. Washington, DC)
SCPP Transcript of Appeal to New York Supreme Court, *Star Co. v. Press Pub. Co.*
WBA Warner Bros. Archives (University of Southern California. Los Angeles, California)

Introduction

1. E.g., Derek Johnson, *Media Franchising: Creative License and Collaboration in the Culture Industries* (New York: NYU Press, 2013); Carlos Scolari et al., *Transmedia Archaeology: Storytelling in the Borderlines of Science Fiction, Comics and Pulp Magazines* (New York: Palgrave, 2014); Kyle Meikle, *Adaptations in the Franchise Era, 2001–16* (New York: Bloomsbury, 2019); Tim Molloy, "Blacklight Does Transmedia: The Future of Storytelling—and End of Lame Movie Tie-Ins," *The Wrap*, April 22, 2011, https://www.thewrap.com/transmedia-death-lame-movie-tie-ins-26718

2. E.g., Henry Jenkins, *Convergence Culture* (New York: New York University Press, 2006); James Fleury et al., eds., *The Franchise Era* (Edinburgh: Edinburgh University Press, 2019); Peter Caranicas, "Bibles Hold Tentpole Revivals: Biz Moves Backstory to Forefront," *Variety*, July 12, 2009, 5; Steven Zeitchik, "Can Corporate Hollywood Make Peace with Voice-Minded Directors?" *Los Angeles Times*, June 21, 2017, https://

www.latimes.com/entertainment/movies/la-et-mn-star-wars-lord-miller-20170621-story.html; Ben Fritz, *The Big Picture* (New York: Houghton Mifflin Harcourt, 2018).

3. Wanda Orlikowski, "Sociomaterial Practices: Exploring Technology at Work," *Organization Studies* 28.9 (2007): 1435–48; Paul Leonardi, *Car Crashes without Cars* (Cambridge: MIT Press, 2012).

4. Bruno Latour, *An Inquiry into Modes of Existence: An Anthropology of the Moderns*, trans. Catherine Porter (Cambridge: Harvard University Press, 2013).

5. See Catherine Fisk, *Working Knowledge: Employee Innovation and the Rise of Corporate Intellectual Property, 1800–1930* (Chapel Hill: University of North Carolina Press, 2009); Alain Pottage, *Figures of Invention: A History of Modern Patent Law* (Oxford: Oxford University Press, 2010); and Robert Merges, *American Patent Law: A Business and Economic History* (New York: Cambridge University Press, 2022).

6. See Lionel Sobel, "The Law of Ideas, Revisited," *UCLA Entertainment Law Review* 1.1 (1994): 9–94; Robert Denicola, "The New Law of Ideas," *Harvard Journal of Law & Technology* 28.1 (2014): 195–236; and Kurt Sanders, *Intellectual Property and the Law of Ideas* (London: Routledge, 2021).

7. For discussions of the history of U.S. trademark law that are not limited to its application to narrative-based property, see Frank Schechter, *The Historical Foundations of the Law Relating to Trade-marks* (Clark: Lawbook Exchange, 2012 [originally published in 1925]); Daniel McClure, "Trademarks and Unfair Competition: A Critical History of Legal Thought," *Trademark Reporter* 69 (1979): 305–56; Keith Stolte, "A Response to Jerome Gilson's Call for an Overhaul of the Lanham Act," *Trademark Reporter* 94 (2004): 1335–59; and Mark Bartholomew, "Advertising and the Transformation of Trademark Law," *New Mexico Law Review* 38 (2008): 1–48.

8. Jessica Litman, "Copyright, Compromise and Legislative History," *Cornell Law Review* 72 (1987): 858.

9. Litman, 858.

10. Barbara Ringer, "First Thoughts on the Copyright Act of 1976," *New York Law School Law Review* 22 (1976): 479.

11. Melville Nimmer, "The Old Copyright Act as a Part of the New Act," *New York Law School Law Review* 22 (1976): 471–76.

12. See David Bordwell, Janet Staiger, and Kristin Thompson, *The Classical Hollywood Cinema* (New York: Columbia University Press, 1985); Jerome Christensen, *America's Corporate Art: The Studio Authorship of Hollywood Motion Pictures* (Stanford: Stanford University Press, 2012); Gary Edgerton, *The Columbia History of American Television* (New York: Columbia University Press, 2007); Richard Fine, *James M. Cain and the American Authors' Authority* (Austin: University of Texas Press, 1992); Jean-Paul Gabilliet, *Of Comics and Men: A Cultural History of American Comic Books*, trans. Bart Beaty and Nick Nguyen (Jackson: University of Mississippi Press, 2010); Ian Hamilton, *Writers in Hollywood: 1915–1951* (New York: Carroll & Graf, 1991); Michele Hilmes, *Radio Voices: American Broadcasting 1922–1952* (Minneapolis: University of Minnesota Press, 1997); Shawna Kidman, *Comic Books Incorporated: How the Business of Comics Became the Business of Hollywood* (Oakland: University of California Press, 2019); Thomas Schatz, *The Genius of the System: Hollywood Filmmaking in the Studio Era* (New York: Henry Holt and Company, 1986); David Sumner, *The Magazine Century: American Magazines Since 1900* (New York: Peter Lang, 2010).

13. Pamela Samuelson, "Copyright and Freedom of Expression in Historical Perspective," *Journal of Intellectual Property Law* 10 (2003): 319–44.

14. Brad Sherman and Lionel Bently, *The Making of Intellectual Property Law: The British Experience, 1760–1911* (New York: Cambridge University Press, 1999), 3, 2–3.

15. E.g., Wenqi Liu, "Reform of China's Copyright Legislation," *Journal of the Copyright Society of the U.S.A.* 59 (2011): 843–63.

16. Ronald Gard and Elizabeth Townsend Gard, "The Present (User-Generated Crisis) Is the Past (1909 Copyright Act): An Essay Theorizing the 'Traditional Contours of Copyright' Language," *Cardozo Arts & Entertainment Law Journal* 28 (2011): 455, 459.

17. Gard and Gard, 460.

18. Gard and Gard, 460.

19. See, for example, Peter Baldwin, *The Copyright Wars: Three Centuries of Trans-Atlantic Battle* (Princeton: Princeton University Press, 2014); Martin Buinicki, *Negotiating Copyright: Authorship and the Discourse of Literary Property Rights in Nineteenth-Century America* (New York: Routledge, 2006); Peter Decherney, *Hollywood's Copyright Wars* (New York: Columbia University Press, 2012); Siva Vaidhyanathan, *Copyrights and Copywrongs: The Rise of Intellectual Property and How It Threatens Creativity* (New York: New York University Press, 2001).

20. Dorothy Howell, *Intellectual Properties and the Protection of Fictional Characters: Copyright, Trademark, or Unfair Competition?* (New York: Quorum Books, 1990).

21. See Bruno Latour, *Reassembling the Social: An Introduction to Actor-Network Theory* (New York: Oxford University Press, 2005); John Law, *After Method: Mess in Social Science Research* (New York: Routledge, 2004); John Law and John Hassard, *Actor Network Theory and After* (Oxford: Blackwell Publishers/The Sociological Review, 1999); Mike Michael, *Actor-Network Theory: Trials, Trails and Translations* (London: Sage, 2017).

22. Latour, *Reassembling*, 75–78; Bruno Latour, *We Have Never Been Modern*, trans. Catherine Porter (Cambridge: Harvard University Press, 1993).

23. Clifford Geertz, "Thick Description: Toward an Interpretive Theory of Culture," in *The Cultural Geography Reader* (New York: Routledge, 2008); Joseph Ponterotto, "Brief Note on the Origins, Evolution, and Meaning of the Qualitative Research Concept 'Thick Description,'" *Qualitative Reporter* 11.3 (2006): 538–49.

24. Latour, *Reassembling*, 165.

25. Latour, *Reassembling*, 25.

26. The few book-length works in media studies include Mike Ananny, *Networked Press Freedom* (Cambridge, MA: MIT Press, 2018); Joshua Braun, *This Program Is Brought to You By . . . : Distributing Television News Online* (New Haven: Yale, 2015); and Marijke de Valck, *Film Festivals: From European Geopolitics to Global Cinephilia* (Amsterdam: Amsterdam University Press, 2007); Emma Hemmingway, *Into the Newsroom: Exploring the Digital Production of Regional Television News* (London: Routledge, 2007); Anita Lam, *Making Crime Television* (London: Routledge, 2013); Helen Thornham, *Ethnographies of the Videogame* (London: Routledge, 2016). In sociolegal studies and law and society, ANT has occasionally been used to study techno-legal issues and lay experiences of the legal process. E.g., Emilie Cloatre, "Trips and Pharmaceutical Patents in Djibouti: An ANT Analysis of Socio-Legal Objects," *Social & Legal Studies* 17.2 (2008): 263–81; Dave Cowan and Helen Carr, "Actor-Network Theory, Implementation, and the Private Landlord," *Journal of Law and Society* 35 (2008): 149–66; Andrea Quinlan, "Visions of Public Safety, Justice, and Healing: The Making of the Rape Kit Backlog in the United States," *Social & Legal Studies* 29.2 (2019): 225–45; Tarleton Gillespie, *Wired Shut: Copyright and the Shape of Digital Culture* (London: MIT Press,

2007); Irene van Oorschot, *The Law Multiple: Judgment and Knowledge in Practice* (Cambridge: Cambridge University Press, 2021). It has also been used by Bruno Latour himself to write an unusual ethnography of the Conseil d'État. Bruno Latour, *The Making of Law: An Ethnography of the Conseil d'État*, trans. Marina Brilman and Alain Pottage (Cambridge: Polity, 2010).

27. The exception has been several theoretical provocations—sometimes under the label of "ANTi-history"—most of which have been limited to the field or organizational studies. See Gabrielle Durepos and Albert Mills, "Actor-Network Theory, ANTi-History and Critical Organizational Historiography," *Organization* 19.6 (2012): 703–21; Kim Myrick et al., "History-making and the Academy of Management: An ANTi-History Perspective," *Management & Organizational History* 8.4 (2013): 345–70; and Bert De Munck, "Re-assembling Actor-Network Theory and Urban History," *Urban History* 44.1 (2017): 111–22.

Chapter 1

1. E.g., Paul Saint-Amour, *The Copywrights: Intellectual Property and the Literary Imagination* (Ithaca: Cornell University Press, 2003), 4–5.

2. Act of September 19, 1962, Pub. L. No. 87-668, 87th Cong., 2d Sess., 76 Stat. 555; Act of August 28, 1965, Pub. L. No. 89-142, 89th Cong., 1st Sess., 79 Stat. 581; Act of November 16, 1967, Pub. L. No. 90-141, 90th Cong., 1st Sess., 81 Stat. 464; Act of July 23, 1968, Pub. L. No. 90-416, 90th Cong., 2d Sess., 82 Stat. 397; Act of December 16, 1969, Pub. L. No. 91-147, 91st Cong., 1st Sess., 83 Stat. 360; Act of December 17, 1970, Pub. L. No. 91-555, 91st Cong. 2d Sess., 84 Stat. 1441; Act of November 24, 1971, Pub. L. No. 92-170, 92d Cong., 1st Sess., 85 Stat. 490; Act of October 25, 1972, Pub. L. No. 92-566, 92d Cong., 2d Sess., 86 Stat. 1181; Act of December 31, 1974, Pub. L. No. 93-573, 93d Cong., 2d Sess., 88 Stat. 1873.

3. Augustine Birrell, *Seven Lectures on the Law and History of Copyright in Books* (New York: Cassell and Co., 1899), 36–38.

4. Thorvald Solberg, *Report on Copyright Legislation, by the Register of Copyrights* (Washington, DC: Government Printing Office, 1904), 18–20. Note that at the time both of these surveys were conducted, the period of protection offered in the United States was one period of twenty-eight years (extended from fourteen years in 1831), followed by a second period of fourteen years. Stat. 436 (1831). The second period was extended to twenty-eight years in 1909. 35 Stat. 1075, Title 17 U.S.C., section 23.

5. Solberg, *Report on Copyright Legislation*, 20.

6. See Abe Goldman, "The History of U.S.A. Copyright Law Revision, 1901–1954" (Washington, DC: United States Government Printing Office, 1955).

7. See Stephen Ladas, *The International Protection of Literary and Artistic Property*, vol. 2 (New York: Macmillan, 1938), 879–1119; Herman Finklestein, "The Copyright Law—A Reappraisal," *University of Pennsylvania Law Review* 104.8 (1956): 1045–49. By the time Finklestein conducted his research, only the United States and the Philippines provided terms of protection not measured by way of the author's life—with the majority of nations providing terms set at or above the Berne minimum.

8. Barbara Ringer, *Study No. 31: Renewal of Copyright*, in *Copyright Law Revision Studies Prepared for the Subcommittee on Patents, Trademarks, and Copyrights of the Committee on the Judiciary Studies 29–31* (Washington, DC: Government Printing Office, 1961), 222.

9. Such was the fate, for example, of a number of early Sherlock Holmes stories

in the United States. Mattias Boström, *From Holmes to Sherlock,* trans. Michael Gallagher (New York: Mysterious Press, 2017), 254–55.

10. In practice, courts often allowed authors to sign away the renewal right (which under the Copyright Act of 1976 would be refashioned as a reclamation or reversion right) in advance, thereby undermining one of the purposes for the renewal right in the first place. Perversely, however, such assignments did not reliably secure the second copyright to the assignee either, since courts universally held that an a priori assignment of the renewal right constituted an *expectancy* (a pledge to do something) instead of a transfer of rights. As a result, the assignment would be negated if the author died before its completion, with the rights passing to the author's spouse or children (or, if none existed, the estate's executor or next of kin). See Samuel Spring, *Risks and Rights in Publishing, Radio, Television, Motion Pictures, Advertising, and the Theater* (New York: W. W. Norton, 1952), 94–95.

11. 90 Stat. 2541, Section 304.

12. 112 Stat. 2827.

13. Jane Ginsburg, "The US Experience with Formalities: A Love/Hate Relationship," in *Global Copyright: Three Hundred Years Since the Statute of Anne, from 1709 to Cyberspace,* eds. Lionel Bently, Uma Suthersanen, and Paul Torremans (Chelthenham, UK: Edward Elgar, 2010), 437.

14. Solberg, *Report on Copyright Legislation,* 20–21.

15. During the nineteenth century, registration and deposit were temporally separable actions: registration of title was required prior to publication while deposit could not occur until after publication. The Copyright Act of 1909 did away with the pre-registration of title; formal registration would henceforth occur only at the time of deposit. For complex reasons, courts nevertheless continued to speak of registration and deposit as two separate requirements. In practice, however, the two were separate parts of the same single act (under the Act of 1909 it was technically impossible to deposit a work without simultaneously registering it). In this chapter, I thus treat them as a single act.

16. International Copyright Act of 1891, 51 Cong. Ch. 565, 26 Stat. 1106, Section 4956.

17. An Act to Amend and Consolidate the Acts Respecting Copyright, Pub. L. 60-349, 35 Stat. 1075, Section 12.

18. *Washingtonian Publishing Co. v. Pearson* 360 U.S. 30 (1939).

19. 360 U.S. 30, 42.

20. The study is described in Benjamin Kaplan, *Study No. 17: The Registration of Copyright,* in *Copyright Law Revision Studies Prepared for the Subcommittee on Patents, Trademarks, and Copyrights of the Committee on the Judiciary Studies 17–19* (Washington, DC: Government Printing Office, 1960), 34.

21. Robert Wedgeworth and Barbara Ringer, "The Library of Congress Advisory Committee on Copyright Registration and Deposit—Letter and Report of the Co-Chairs," *Columbia-VLA Journal of Law and the Arts* 17 (1993): 290.

22. For example, Alf K. Berle and L. Sprague de Camp, *Inventions and Their Management,* corrected and revised printing (Scranton, PA: International Textbook Press, 1940), 550–52; Margaret Nicholson, *A Manual of Copyright Practice: For Writers, Publishers, and Agents,* 2nd ed. (New York: Oxford University Press, 1956), 16–18; Kaplan, *Study No. 17,* 34.

23. The Copyright Act of 1976 requires deposit of two copies of most kinds of work to the Library of Congress within three months of publication, under penalty of

fine but not invalidation of the copyright or denial of the right to register (17 U.S.C. § 407). Although empirical data regarding the levying of fines is unavailable, fines appear to be very rarely, if ever, levied, except in the extraordinary cases where the Register has made a formal demand for copies that has gone unfilled in a timely fashion. ACCORD's extensive 1992 report thus excludes fines from its list of incentives to deposit (Wedgewood and Ringer, 1993). As for registration, under present law there are two considerable penalties to delaying registration until after an infringement has occurred: (1) the late registrant forgoes rights to statutory damages and attorney fees (17 U.S.C. § 412) and (2) the court will not accord the validity of the copyright prima facie weight (17 U.S.C. § 410 (c)).

24. Harry Henn, "Magazine Rights: A Division of Indivisible Copyright," *Cornell Law Review* 40.3 (1955): 417.

25. Until the 1950s there was a third implication, which is outside the scope of this book but worth noting here: assignments were treated for tax purposes as capital gains; licenses were treated as income. See Lorna Margolis, "Supplement 1: Divisibility in Relation to Income Tax," in Abraham Kaminstein, *Study No. 11: Divisibility of Copyright*, in *Copyright Law Revision Studies Prepared for the Subcommittee on Patents, Trademarks, and Copyrights of the Committee on the Judiciary Studies 11–13* (Washington, DC: Government Printing Office, 1960), 39–56.

26. Kaminstein, *Study No. 11*, 1.

27. Morris Cohn, "Old Licenses and New Uses: Motion Picture and Television Rights," *Law and Contemporary Problems* 19.2 (1954): 186.

28. *Dam v. Kirk La Shelle Co.*, 175 F. 902 (2nd Cir. 1910).

29. Franklin Laskin, "All Rights Unreserved—The Author's Lost Property in Publishing and Entertainment," *Copyright Law Symposium* 7 (1954): 97.

30. Arthur Train, *My Day in Court* (New York: Charles Scribner's Sons, 1939), 311.

31. Kaminstein, *Study No. 11*, 4.

32. There are too many to list here, but as examples see: HR 11258, 68th Cong., 2d sess. (1925); S. 342, 73d Cong., 1st Sess. (1933).

33. Robert Burton, "Business Practices in the Copyright Field," in 7 *Copyright Problems Analyzed* (n.p.: Commerce Clearing House, 1952), 88.

34. For a review of the principle as applied by courts, see Kaminstein, *Study No. 11*; Elliot Groffman, "Divisibility of Copyright: Its Application and Effect," *Santa Clara Law Review* 171 (1979): 171–94.

35. The risk that an alleged act of infringement would become the subject of multiple suits was solved by § 501 (b).

36. Christopher Sprigman, "Reform(aliz)ing Copyright," *Stanford Law Review* 57.2 (2004): 488.

37. Berne Convention, Art. 5.2.

38. Lisa Parks, "Infrastructure," in *Keywords for Media Studies*, ed. Laurie Ouellette and Jonathan Gray (New York: New York University Press, 2017), 106–7.

Chapter 2

1. E.g., Patrick Goldstein, "It's a Super Deal," *Los Angeles Times*, September 1, 2009, https://www.latimes.com/archives/la-xpm-2009-sep-01-et-bigpicture1-story.html; Martin Peers, "Disney Marvels at Superhero Potential," *Wall Street Journal*, September 1, 2009, C10.

2. *Warner Bros.Pictures v. Columbia Broadcasting System*, 216 F. 2d 945 (9th Cir. 1954).

3. E.g., Kristen Knudsen, "Tomorrow Never Dies: The Protection of James Bond and Other Fictional Characters under the Federal Trademark Dilution Act," *Vanderbilt Journal of Entertainment Law & Practice* 2 (2000): 13–28; Gregory Schienke, "The Spawn of Learned Hand—A Reexamination of Copyright Protection and Fictional Characters: How Distinctly Delineated Must the Story Be Told?" *Marquette Intellectual Property Law Review* 9.1 (2005): 63–90; Kathryn Foley, "Protecting Fictional Characters: Defining the Elusive Trademark-Copyright Divide," *Connecticut Law Review* 41 (2009): 921–61; Geoffrey Scott and Karen Maul, "Kryptonite, Duff Beer and the Protection of Fictional Characters and Products in the Global Community," *Monash University Law Review* 38.1 (2012): 228–82; Tze Ping Lim, "Beyond Copyright: Applying a Radical Idea-Expression Dichotomy to the Ownership of Fictional Characters," *Vanderbilt Journal of Entertainment and Technology Law* 21 (2018): 95–144; Nicole O'Hara, "The Arc and Art of Protecting Fictional Characters," *Legal Intelligence*, April 2, 2018, https://perma.cc/YH49-VLAX

4. E.g., Lydia Lern and Joseph Miller, *Intellectual Property Law: Cases & Materials*, 7th ed. (Oregon City: Sempahore Press, 2021); Craig Joyce et al., *Copyright Law*, 10th ed. (Durham: Carolina Academic Press, 2016); Deborah Bouchoux, *Intellectual Property: The Law of Trademarks, Copyrights, Patents, and Trade Secrets*, 5th ed. (Boston: Cengage Learning, 2016).

5. E.g., Roger Schechter and John Thomas, *Intellectual Property: The Law of Copyrights, Patents and Trademarks* (St. Paul: West Group, 2003), 41; James Boyle and Jennifer Jenkins, *Intellectual Property: Law & The Information Society—Cases and Materials*, 4th ed. (n.p.: n.p., 2018), 407–8; Jeanne Fromer and Christopher Sprigman, *Copyright Law: Cases and Materials v. 1.0*, (n.p.: n.p., 2019), 299–301; Ralph Brown and Robert Denicola, *Copyright: Unfair Competition, and Related Topics Bearing on the Protection of Works of Authorship*, 10th ed. (New York: Thomson Reuters, 2009), 252–53. For an important exception see Melville Nimmer et al., *Cases and Materials on Copyright and Other Aspects of Entertainment Litigation including Unfair Competition, Defamation, Privacy*, 7th ed. (Newark: Lexis Nexis, 2006), 89–93.

6. E.g., Zarh Said, "Fixing Copyright in Characters: Literary Perspectives on a Legal Problem," *Cardozo Law Review* 35 (2013): 769–829; Missy Brenner, "Shadow of the Bat[mobile]: Character Copyright after *DC Comics v. Towle*," *Santa Clara Law Review* 57 (2017): 481–517.

7. E. Fulton Brylawski, "Protection of Characters—Sam Spade Revisited," *Bulletin of the Copyright Society of the USA* 22 (1974): 87.

8. Foley, "Protecting Fictional Characters," 929–30.

9. *Gaiman v. McFarlane*, 360 F.3d 644 (7th Cir. 2004), 660. The Ninth Circuit, more charitably, has set aside what is arguably the most important part of the decision by declaring it *dicta* (a kind of judicial aside or non sequitur, which does not bind future judges and so does not make law). *Olson v. National Broadcasting Company* 855 F.2d 1446 (9th Cir. 1988), 1451–52.

10. Although their access to information is much more limited—and they are present only (sometimes) in trial court—juries are tasked with producing a similar kind knowledge to enable them to render a verdict.

11. *Stowe v. Thomas*, 23. F. Cas. 201 (C.C.E.D. Pa. 1853), 206–7.

12. See, for example, *White Smith Music Publishing Co. v. Apollo Company*, 209 U.S. 1 (1908).

13. *Kalem Company v. Harper Brothers*, 222 U.S. 55 (1911), 63.

14. *Nichols v. Universal Pictures Co.*, 45 F.2d 119 (2nd Cir. 1930), 121.

15. Compare Hand's metaphor to that of Judge Charles Merrill Hough in *Dymow v. Bolton* (heard by Hough, Hand, and Martin Thomas Manton), four years earlier: "The incomplete skeleton the two plays have in common, but it is with real difficulty that the flesh and blood, the incidental, yet essential, adornment and trimming, of the plays can be cut away to show similarity between a few bones." *Dymow v. Bolton* 11. F.2d 690 (2nd Cir. 1926), 692. Hough's metaphor, with its construal of flesh and blood as "incidental . . . adornment and trimming," lies somewhere between the old and the new: the body as one part independent idea (the bones) and another part arbitrary clothing (the flesh).

16. E.g., John Ogilvie, "Defining Computer Program Parts under Learned Hand's Abstractions Test in Software Copyright Infringement Cases," *Michigan Law Review* 91 (1992): 526–70; Carl Mazurek, "Through the Looking Glass: Photography and the Idea/Expression Dichotomy," *NYU Journal of Intellectual Property and Entertainment Law* 6 (2016): 278–309.

17. *Peter Pan Fabrics, Inc. v. Martin Weiner Corp.*, 274 F.2d 487 (2nd Cir. 1960), 489.

18. 17 USC § 106 (2) (1978).

19. 17 USC § 101 (1978).

20. 17 USC § 1(B) (1909).

21. Edwin Hutchins, *Cognition in the Wild* (London: The MIT Press, 1995).

22. Umberto Eco, "The Myth of Superman," *Diacritics* 2.1 (1972): 14–22, 19.

23. Louis Frohlich and Charles Schwartz, *The Law of Motion Pictures Including the Law of the Theatre* (New York: Baker, Voorhis and Company, 1918), 53–54.

24. *Curwood v. Affiliated Distributors*, 283 F. 219, 222–223 (S.D.N.Y. 1922).

25. M. A. Mills, "The Protection of Titles," *The Bulletin of the Authors' League of America*. 1.4 (August 1913): 3–5.

26. *Atlas Mfg. Co. v. Street and Smith*, 204 Fed. 398 (C.C.A. 1913); *New York Herald Co. v. Star Co.*, 146 F. 204 (S.D.N.Y. 1906), *aff'd mem.*, 146 F. 1023 (2nd Cir. 1906); *Outcault v. New York Herald*, 146 F. 205 (S.D.N.Y. 1906).

27. Alf K. Berle and L. Sprague de Camp, *Inventions, Patents, and Their Management* (New York: D. Van Nostrand Company, 1959), 485.

28. William Mooney, *Dashiell Hammett and the Movies* (New Brunswick: Rutgers University Press, 2014), 2.

29. E.g., Karen Huston Karydes, *Hard-Boiled Anxiety: The Freudian Desires of Dashiell Hammett, Raymond Chandler, Ross MacDonald, and Their Detectives* (Salisbury: Secant, 2016); Ken Fuller, *Hardboiled Activist: The Work and Politics of Dashiell Hammett* (n.p.: Praxis Press, 2017).

30. "Dashiell Hammett Tour," *Trip Advisor*, accessed August 24, 2021, https://www.tripadvisor.com/Attraction_Review-g60713-d559451-Reviews-Dashiell_Hammett_Tour-San_Francisco_California.html

31. Don Herron, *The Dashiell Hammett Tour: Thirtieth Anniversary Guidebook* (San Francisco: Vince Emery Productions, 2010); Ed Sams, *Dashiell Hammett's San Francisco*, (n.p.: CreateSpace, 2014).

32. Oxford English Dictionary (website), accessed August 5, 2022, https://www.oed.com

33. Israel Kirzner, *Perception, Opportunity, and Profit: Studies in the Theory of Entrepreneurship* (Chicago: University of Chicago Press, 1979); Israel Kirzner, *Discovery and the Capitalist Process* (Chicago: University of Chicago Press, 1985).

34. Although theoretically possible for an author to exploit the capital without selling or licensing rights to it (for example, by self-publishing a book using his or her own printing press), this is, in reality, extremely rare and might, in any case, be better framed from an economics perspective in terms of the author licensing rights to his or her own publishing and printing businesses.

35. E.g., Sally Cline, *Dashiell Hammett: Man of Mystery* (New York: Arcade Publishing, 2014), 44; John Scaggs, *Crime Fiction* (New York: Routledge, 2005), 28, 58–59.

36. The contract is reproduced in Richard Layman, *Discovering the Maltese Falcon and Sam Spade*, rev. ed. (San Francisco: Vince Emery Productions, 2005), 159–64.

37. Dashiell Hammett, "From the Memoirs of a Private Detective," in *Crime Stories and Other Writings* (New York: Library Classics of the United States, 2001), 906.

38. Qtd. in William Nolan, *Hammett: A Life at the Edge* (New York: St. Martin's Press, 1983), 46–47.

39. Reproduced in Layman, *Discovering*, 86

40. E.g., James Moynahan, "Dashiell Hammett Confesses!" King Features Syndicate insert, 1934: reproduced in Layman, *Discovering the Maltese Falcon and Sam Spade*, 60; Elizabeth Sanderson, "Ex-Detective Hammett," in *The Bookman* (January–February 1933), reproduced in Layman, *Discovering*, 68–70; "Thou art the Man!" *Ellery Queen's Mystery Magazine* 10.44 (July 1947): 4–5; Nathan Ward, *The Lost Detective: Becoming Dashiell Hammett* (New York: Bloomsbury, 2015), xxi, 135; Cline, *Dashiell Hammett*, xix; Nolan, *Hammett*, 40, 46.

41. Dashiell Hammett, *The Maltese Falcon*, in *Dashiell Hammett: Complete Novels* (New York: Library Classics of the United States, 1999), 391.

42. Dashiell Hammett, *Selected Letters of Dashiell Hammett: 1921–1960* (Washington, DC: Counterpoint, 2001), 129, note 3. See also Richard Layman, *Shadow Man: The Life of Dashiell Hammett* (New York: Harcourt Brace Jovanovich, 1981), 166.

43. Hammett, *Selected Letters*, 133.

44. Hammett, *Selected Letters*, 518, 533.

45. These include a *Silver Theater* adaptation in 1942, a *Phillip Morris Playhouse* adaptation in 1942, a *Screen Guild Theater* adaptation in 1943, a *Lux Radio Theater* version in 1943, an *Academy Award Theater* adaptation in 1946—all on the CBS network. Radio Listings, *Lincoln Sunday Journal and Star*, February 1, 1942, D8, reproduced at https://www.newspapers.com/image/?clipping_id=2108785&fcfToken=eyJhbGciOiJIUzI1NiIsInR5cCI6IkpXVCJ9.eyJmcmVlLXZpZXctaWQiOjYzNTk5NDAwLCJpYXQiOjE1Nzc5ODc3MTQsImV4cCI6MTU3ODA3NDExNH0.rg2wTIEKUe0c3FN_hBcWA21vubSigvYY-R1A9nUFnsI; "WHP Radio Programs," *Harrisburg Telegraph*, August 8, 1942, n.p., reproduced at https://www.newspapers.com/image/?clipping_id=3043646&fcfToken=eyJhbGciOiJIUzI1NiIsInR5cCI6IkpXVCJ9.eyJmcmVlLXZpZXctaWQiOjQzMTU5NzE1LCJpYXQiOjE1Nzc5ODc4MjksImV4cCI6MTU3ODA3NDIyOX0.h_uKOtgjsxnl_2CaJzwZiUP720tCw2Xk4FK-9JmXMY4; for third show check: Vincent Terrace, *Radio Programs 1924–1984*, 1999; "Lux Radio Theater 382: The Maltese Falcon," *Old Time Radio Downloads*, https://www.oldtimeradiodownloads.com/drama/lux/lux-radio-theater-43-02-08-382-the-maltese-falcon; Layman, *Discovering*, 327.

46. WBA, Box 12600A, Folder: Dashiell Hammett v. Warner Bros. Pictures Inc. Folder 1.

47. 84 F. Supp. 28 (S.D.N.Y. 1949), 29.

48. WBA, Box 12600A, Folder: Dashiell Hammett v. Warner Bros. Pictures Inc. Folder 1.

49. *Hammett v. Warner Bros. Pictures*, 84 F. Supp. 28; affirmed, 176 F.2d 145 (1949).

50. 84 F. Supp. 28, 29.

51. 84 F. Supp 28.

52. 176 F.2d 145.

53. Morris Ebenstein to Gordon Files, March 7, 1950, WBA, Box 12560B, Folder: Dashiell Hammett v. Warner Bros. Pictures Inc.

54. Gordon Files to Morris Ebenstein, March 9, 1950, WBA, Box 12560B, Folder: Dashiell Hammett v. Warner Bros. Pictures Inc.

55. Amended Complaint for Copyright Infringements and Unfair Competition, Exhibit A in *Hammett v. Warner Bros. Pictures*, WBA, Box 12600A, Folder: Dashiell Hammett v. Warner Bros. Pictures Inc.

56. For more on the place of custom in formal law, see Michael Reisman, "The Cult of Custom in the Late 20th Century," *California Western International Law Journal* 17.1 (1987): 133–45; David Bederman, *Custom as a Source of Law* (New York: Cambridge University Press, 2010); Timothy Meyer, "Codifying Custom," *University of Pennsylvania Law Review* 160 (2012): 995–1069.

57. Louis Frohlich and Charles Schwartz, *Law of Motion Pictures Including the Law of the Theatre* (New York: Baker, Voorhis and Company, 1918); WBA, Box 12600A, Folder: *Hammett v. Warner Bros.* Drafts of Reply Brief; WBA, Box 12600A, Folder: *Hammett vs Warner Bros.* (Drafts and Notes).

58. Appellant's Opening Brief, *Warner Bros. Pictures v. Columbia Broadcasting System* (1954), WBA Box 19599A, Folder: Warner Bros. v. C.B.S.

59. E.g., George Files to Morris Ebenstein, September 28, 1950, WBA, Box 12560B, Accordion File: Dashiell Hammett v. Warner Bros. Pictures Inc.

60. Joseph Karp to George Files, December 27, 1950, WBA, Box 12527A, Folder: W.B.P., Inc. and *Knopf v. Columbia Broadcasting, et al.* (Misc. Letters & Correspondence) 1(2).

61. George Files to Joseph Karp, November 27, 1950, WBA, Box 12527A, Folder: W.B.P., Inc. and *Knopf v. Columbia Broadcasting, et al.* (Misc. Letters & Correspondence) 1(2).

62. WBA, Box 12599-B, unlabeled manilla envelope (no folder).

63. WBA, Box 12599-B, unlabeled manilla envelope (no folder).

64. John T. Winterich to Morris Ebenstein, February 4, 1955, WBA Box 12559-B, unlabeled manilla envelope (no folder).

65. Plaintiff's Brief in Support of Motion for Summary Judgment, *Hammett v. Warner Bros. Pictures*, 10, WBA, Box 12558A, Folder: *Hammett v. Warner Bros.* / Plaintiff's Main Brief.

66. Deposition of Dashiell Hammett, *Hammett v. Warner Bros. Pictures*, WBA, Box 12600A, Folder: Dashiell Hammett v. Warner Bros. Pictures Inc.

67. "A Man Called Spade," *American Magazine*, July 1932: 32–36; "Too Many Have Lived," *American Magazine*, October 19, 1932: 46–49; "They Can Only Hang You Once," *Collier's*, November 19, 1932: 22–24; *The Adventures of Sam Spade and Other Stories by Dashiell Hammett* (New York: Lawrence E. Spivak, 1944).

68. Plaintiff's Brief in Support of Motion for Summary Judgment, *Hammett v. Warner Bros. Pictures*, 10, WBA, Box 12558A, Folder: *Hammett v. Warner Bros.* / Plaintiff's Main Brief.

69. Plaintiff's Brief in Support of Motion for Summary Judgment, 10.

70. Testimony of Samuel Dashiell Hammett, *Warner Bros. Pictures v. Columbia Broadcasting System*, USC of Appeals for the Ninth Circuit, Transcript of Record, Volume 1, 214, WBA Box 12559A, Folder: Warner Bros. v. CBS.

71. Testimony of Samuel Dashiell Hammett, 217–18.

72. 102 F. Supp. 141, 145.

73. Contract between Jack Warner and Dashiell Hammett, January 23, 1931, Exhibit 6, *Dashiell Hammett v. Warner Bros. Pictures*, WBA, Box 12600A, Folder: Dashiell Hammett vs. Warner Bros. Pictures Inc. Folder 1; Deposition of Dashiell Hammett, *Hammett v. Warner Bros. Pictures*, WBA, Box 12600A, Folder: Dashiell Hammett v. Warner Bros. Pictures Inc.; Testimony of Samuel Dashiell Hammett, *Warner Bros. Pictures v. Columbia Broadcasting System*, USC of Appeals for the Ninth Circuit, Transcript of Record, Volume 1, 214, WBA, Box 12559A, Folder *Warner Bros. v. C.B.S.*, 195–205; Dashiell Hammett, *On the Make* (corrected copy), WBA, Box 12599A, Folder: Warner Bros. v. C.B.S. / On the Make.

74. Letter from Darryl Zanuck to Daniel Leonardson, April 28, 1931: Exhibit 7, WBA, Box 12600A, Folder: Dashiell Hammett v. Warner Bros. Pictures, Inc.

75. Deposition of Dashiell Hammett, *Hammett v. Warner Bros. Pictures*, WBA, Box 12600A, Folder: Dashiell Hammett v. Warner Bros. Pictures Inc.

76. Affidavit of Edward Muhl, November 18, 1948 and Affidavit of Helen Maloney, November 16, 1948, *Hammett v. Warner Bros. Pictures*, WBA, Box 12599A, Folder: Dashiell Hammett v. Warner Bros. Pictures, Folder 2.

77. Dashiell Hammett, *On the Make* (corrected copy), WBA, Box 12599A, Folder: Warner Bros. v. C.B.S. / On the Make.

78. Brief of Appellee, *Hammett v. Warner Bros. Pictures*, US Court of Appeals, 36, WBA, Box 12558A, Folder: Hammett v. Warner Bros.

79. Letter from Gordon Files to Joseph D. Karp, August 27, 1951, WBA, Box 12527A, Folder W.B.P. Inc. and *Knopf v. Columbia Broadcasting, et al.* (Misc. Letters & Correspondence) 1.

80. Appellant's Opening Brief, *Warner Bros. Pictures v. Columbia Broadcasting System*, Court of Appeals, 17–35, WBA Box 12559A, Folder: Warner Bros. v. C.B.S.

81. Appellant's Opening Brief, 17.

82. Appellant's Opening Brief, 36, underlining in original.

83. Unsigned letter to Gordon Files, February 17, 1949, WBA, Box 12600A, Folder: Hammett v. WB, File #4—Drafts and Notes.

84. Unsigned letter to Gordon Files.

85. Testimony of Howard Cady, *Warner Bros. Pictures v. Columbia Broadcasting System*, Transcript of Record, Volume 1, 238–47, WBA, Box 12559A, Folder: Warner Bros. v. C.B.S.

86. Brief of Appellee, *Hammett v. Warner Bros. Pictures*, 42, WBA, Box 12588A, Folder: Hammett v. Warner Bros.

87. Brief of Appellee Dashiell Hammett, *Warner Bros. Pictures v. Columbia Broadcasting System*, 23, WBA, Box 12559A, Folder: Warner Bros. v. C.B.S.

88. Brief of Appellees CBS, etc., *Warner Bros. Pictures v. Columbia Broadcasting System*, 27, WBA, Box 12559A, Folder: Warner Bros. v. C.B.S.; Brief of Appellee Dashiell Hammett, *Warner Bros. Pictures v. Columbia Broadcasting System*, 11, WBA, Box 12559A, Folder: Warner Bros. v. C.B.S.

89. Appellant's Opening Brief, *Warner Bros. Pictures v. Columbia Broadcasting System*, Court of Appeals, 36, WBA, Box 12559A, Folder: Warner Bros. v. C.B.S.

90. Appellant's Opening Brief, 35.

91. Letter from George Files to Morris Ebenstein, January 1949, WBA, Box 12560B, Accordion file: Dashiell Hammett v. Warner Bros. Pictures Inc.

92. Letter from Sidney Schrieber representing the Motion Picture Association

to "members of the Copyright Committee," December 7, 1954, WBA, Box 12558A, Folder: Warner v. C.B.S.—Sam Spade OPINION.

93. Raymond Nickerson, "Confirmation Bias: A Ubiquitous Phenomenon in Many Guises," *Review of General Psychology* 2.2 (1998): 175–220, 175.

94. Letter from Morris Ebenstein to George Files, February 8, 1950, WBA, Box12558A, Folder: Hammett v. Warner Bros. (Drafts and Notes).

95. See, for example, "Dictated by M. Ebenstein, December 23, 1954—Sam Spade Case," WBA, Box12558A, Folder: Hammett v. Warner Bros. (Drafts and Notes).

96. Walter Powell and Paul DiMaggio, "Introduction," in Walter Powell and Paul DiMaggio, eds., *The New Institutionalism in Organizational Analysis* (Chicago: University of Chicago Press, 1991), 11.

97. 216 F.2d 945, 948.

98. 216 F.2d 945, 948.

99. 216 F.2d 945, 950.

100. 216 F.2d 945, 950.

101. 216 F.2d 945, 950.

102. 216 F.2d 945, 950.

103. In the following chapter, I explore additional causes and consequences of this logic, which I call *the principle of authorial genius.*

104. 216 F.2d 945, 950.

105. 216 F.2d 945, 950.

106. Jenkins, *Convergence Culture.*

Chapter 3

1. H. P. Lovecraft and E. Hoffman Price, "Through the Gates of the Silver Key," in *Lovecraft: Collected Fiction*, vol. 3, Variorum Edition, ed. S. T. Joshi (New York: Hippocampus Press, 2017), 282.

2. Lovecraft and Price, 323.

3. See Raymond Sarraute, "Current Theory on the Moral Right of Authors and Artists under French Law," *American Journal of Comparative Law* 16.4 (1968): 465–86; Cyril Rigamonti, "Deconstructing Moral Rights," *Harvard International Law Journal* 47.2 (2006): 353–412; Peter Decherney, "Auterism on Trial: Moral Rights and Films on Television," *Wisconsin Law Review* (2011): 273–330; also, Berne Convention for the Protection of Literary and Artistic Works, July 24, 1971, 25 U.S.T. 1341, 828 U.N.T.S. 221, art. 6*bis*.

4. Suzanne Scott, "Who's Steering the Mothership? The Role of the Fanboy Auteur in Transmedia Storytelling," in *The Participatory Cultures Handbook*, ed. Aaron Delwiche and Jennifer Jacobs Henderson (London: Taylor and Francis, 2012).

5. Melanie Kohnen, "'The Power of Geek': Fandom as Gendered Commodity at Comic-Con," *Creative Industries Journal* 7.1 (2014): 76.

6. Anastasia Salter and Mel Stanfill, *A Portrait of the Auteur as Fanboy: The Construction of Authorship in Transmedia Franchises* (Jackson: University Press of Mississippi, 2020), xiv.

7. E.g., Stewart Macaulay, "Non-Contractual Relations in Business: A Preliminary Study," *American Sociological Review* 28.1 (1963): 55–67; Olav Sorenson and David Waguespack, "Social Structure and Exchange: Self-confirming Dynamics in Hollywood," *Administrative Science Quarterly* 51.4 (2006): 560–89; Richard McAdams and Eric Rasmusen, "Norms and the Law," in *Handbook of Law and Economics*, vol. 2, ed.

A. Mitchell Polinsky and Steven Shavell (Amsterdam: Elsevier, 2007); John Thornton Caldwell, *Production Culture: Industrial Reflexivity and Critical Practice in Film and Television* (London: Duke University Press, 2008); Stephen Zafiarau, "Reputation Work in Selling Film and Television: Life in the Hollywood Talent Industry," *Qualitative Sociology* 31 (2008): 99–127; Miranda Banks et al., *Production Studies, The Sequel!: Cultural Studies of Global Media Industries* (New York: Routledge, 2015).

8. E.g., S. T. Joshi, ed., *H. P. Lovecraft: Four Decades of Criticism* (Athens: Ohio University Press, 1980); David Simmons, ed., *New Critical Essays on H. P. Lovecraft* (New York: Palgrave Macmillan, 2013); S. T. Joshi, *Lovecraft and a World in Transition: Collected Essays on H.P. Lovecraft* (New York: Hippocampus Press, 2014); Carl Sederholm and Jeffrey Andrew Weinstock, *The Age of Lovecraft* (London: University of Minnesota Press, 2016).

9. E.g., George Wetzel, *The Lovecraft Scholar* (Darien: Hobgoblin Press, 1983); Chris J. Karr, "The Black Seas of Copyright: Arkham House Publishers and the H.P. Lovecraft Copyrights," Chris J. Karr (website), n.d., https://www.aetherial.net/lovecraft/arkham.html

10. Debora Threedy, "Legal Archaeology: Excavating Cases, Reconstructing Context," *Tulsa Law Review* (2006): 1197–1238.

11. Peter Jaszi, "Toward a Theory of Copyright: The Metamorphoses of 'Authorship,'" *Duke Law Journal* (1991): 455–502; Martha Woodmansee, "The Genius and the Copyright: Economic and Legal Conditions of the Emergence of the 'Author,'" *Eighteenth-Century Studies* 17.4 (1984): 425–48; Martha Woodmansee and Peter Jaszi, eds., *The Construction of Authorship: Textual Appropriation in Law and Literature* (Durham: Duke University Press, 1994).

12. Peter Jaszi and Martha Woodmansee, "Copyright in Transition," in *A History of the Book in America*, vol. 4, eds. Carl Kaestle and Janice Radway (Chapel Hill: University of North Carolina Press, 2009), 90.

13. See, for example, Michael Gamer, *Romanticism and the Gothic: Genre, Reception, and Canon Formation* (New York: Cambridge University Press, 2000); Anne Jamison, "Copyright and Collaboration: Wordsworth, Coleridge, and the Debate over Literary Property," *Romanticism* 17.2 (2011): 209–21; Peter Jaszi, "On the Author Effect: Contemporary Copyright and Collective Creativity," *Cardozo Arts and Entertainment Law Journal* 10 (1991–1992): 293–320; Rosemary Coombe, *The Cultural Life of Intellectual Properties: Authorship, Appropriation, and the Law* (Durham: Duke University Press, 1998); Lior Zemer, "'We-Intention' and the Limits of Copyright," *Cardozo Arts & Entertainment Law Journal* 24.1 (2006): 99–120.

14. Kathy Bowrey, *Copyright, Creativity, Big Media and Culture Value: Incorporating the Author* (New York: Routledge, 2022), 24–25.

15. Lee Marshall, *Bootlegging: Romanticism and Copyright in the Music Industry* (London: Sage, 2005), 4.

16. In legal and literary scholarship, cultural genealogy typically replaces formal definition. For an exception, see Andrew Bennett, *The Author* (London: Routledge, 2005), 55–71.

17. *Fox Film Corp. v. Doyal*, 286 U.S. 123 (1932), 127 quoting from *Kendall v. Winsor*, 62 U.S. 322, (1858), 328.

18. *Burrows-Giles Lithographic Company v. Sarony*, 111 U.S. 53 (1884), 58.

19. *Bleistein v. Donaldson Lithographic Company*, 188 U.S. 239 (1903), 250.

20. On the historical significance of *Burrow-Giles v. Sarony*, see Christine Haight Farley, "The Lingering Effects of Copyright's Response to the Invention of Photogra-

phy," *University of Pittsburgh Law Review* 65 (2004): 385–456. For a similar account of *Bleistein v. Donaldson*, see Baton Beebe, "*Bleistein*, The Problem of Aesthetic Progress, and the Making of American Copyright Law," *Columbia Law Review* 117(2017): 330.

21. E.g., Martha Woodmansee, "On the Author Effect: Recovering Collectivity," *Cardozo Arts & Entertainment Law Journal* 10 (1991–1992): 279–92, 288–92; Keith Aoki, "Foreword: Innovation and the Information Environment: Interrogating the Entrepreneurs," *Oregon Law Review* 75 (1996): 1–18; Lisa Ede and Andrea A. Lunsford, "Collaboration and Concepts of Authorship," *PMLA* 116.2 (2001): 354–69; Susan Scafidi, "Intellectual Property and Cultural Products," *Boston University Law Review* 81 (2001): 793–842. James Boyle offers a slightly different but equally influential critique of the law's dependence upon the principle of authorial genius in James Boyle, "A Theory of Law and Information: Copyright, Spleens, Blackmail, and Insider Trading," *California Law Review* 80.6 (1992): 1413–1540.

22. Jaszi, "On the Author Effect," 302.

23. Justin Hughes, "The Personality Interest of Artists and Inventors in Intellectual Property," *Cardozo Arts and Entertainment Law Journal* 16 (1998): 81–181, 92. See also, Jane Ginsburg, "The Author's Place in the Future of Copyright," *Willamette Law Review* 45 (2008–2009): 381–94.

24. In the music industry—which is beyond the scope of this book—the situation is more complicated. See, for example, Marshall, *Bootlegging*; Phillip McIntyre, "Copyright and Creativity: Changing Paradigms and the Implications for Intellectual Property and the Music Industry," *Media International Australia* 123.1 (2007): 82–94; Olufunmilayo Arewa, "Making Music: Copyright Law and Creative Processes," in *A Companion to Media Authorship*, eds. Jonathan Gray and Derek Johnson (Malden, MA: Wiley-Blackwell, 2013); Kylie Pappalardo and Patricia Aufderheide, "Romantic Remixers: Hidden Tropes of Romantic Authorship in Creators' Attitudes about Reuse," *Cultural Science Journal* 12.1 (2020): 1–12.

25. The identification of Doyle with Sherlock has been extensively explored by scholars. See, for example, Boström, *From Holmes to Sherlock*.

26. Jerry Siegel (writer) and Joe Shuster (artist), *Superman* 1, National Publications, May 1939, n.p. Reproduced in Jerry Siegel (writer), and Joe Shuster, Jack Burnley, and Wayne Boring (artists), *The Golden Age Superman Omnibus*, vol. 1 (Burbank, CA: DC Comics, 2013).

27. Siegel and Shuster, n.p.

28. See Ian Gordon, *Superman: The Persistence of an American Icon* (New Brunswick: Rutgers University Press), 93–115.

29. See Hamilton, *Writers in Hollywood*.

30. See Fine, *James M. Cain*, 43–44.

31. On Hammett, see chapter 2. On Fitzgerald, see Alan Margolies, "Fitzgerald and Hollywood," in *The Cambridge Companion to F. Schott Fitzgerald*, ed. Ruth Prigozy (New York: Cambridge University Press, 2002). On Faulkner, see Stefan Solomon, *William Faulkner in Hollywood: Screenwriting for the Studios* (Athens: University of Georgia Press, 2017).

32. Michael Stropper, "The Transition to Flexible Specialisation in the US Film Industry: External Economies, the Division of Labour, and the Crossing of Industrial Divides," *Cultural Journal of Economics* 13 (1989): 273–305; Asu Aksoy and Kevin Robins, "Hollywood for the 21st Century: Global Competition for Critical Mass in Image Markets," *Cambridge Journal of Economics* 16 (1992): 1–22. For an account of the breakdown of the Fordist system that pays special attention to the economic and

artistic demands of film authors, see Jeff Menne, *Post-Fordist Cinema: Hollywood Auteurs and the Corporate Counterculture* (New York: Columbia University Press, 2019).

33. E.g., *Fairbanks v. Winik* 201 N.Y.S. 487 (1923); *Rogers v. Republic Prod., Inc.*, 213 F.2d 662 (9th Cir. 1954).

34. Decherney, "Auteurism on Trial," 273.

35. E.g., Thomas Whiteside, *The Blockbuster Complex: Conglomerates, Show Business, and Book Publishing* (Middletown: Wesleyan University Press, 1981), 1; John Thompson, *Books in the Digital Age: The Transformation of Academic and Higher Education Publishing in Britain and the United States* (Malden, MA: Polity, 2005), 219; Joseph Marrisa, "Enter the Middleman: Legitimisation of Literary Agents in the British Victorian Publishing Industry, 1875–1900," *Business History* 62.6 (2020): 944. See also, John Thompson, *Merchants of Culture: The Publishing Business in the Twenty-First Century* (Malden, MA: Polity, 2010), 103–45.

36. This divergence in approaches to the rights of authors can be seen in the differing positions taken by Warner Bros. and Knopf in their "joint" suite against Dashiell Hammett, as described in the previous chapter.

37. As indicated by the August Derleth Papers, held by the Wisconsin Historical Society, publishers repeatedly refused to publish Derleth's Solar Pons detective stories—which were modeled upon the original Sherlock Holmes stories—for fear of angering Adrian Conan Doyle (Arthur's son), despite the fact (which the publishers recognized) that some of the original stories to feature Sherlock Holmes were not protected by copyright in the United States. See, for example, the letters contained in Box 20, Folder 7, ADP.

38. *Esquire, Inc. v. Varga Enterprises, Inc.*, 81 F. Supp. 306 (N.D. Ill. 1948), 308.

39. These numbers are based upon the 2017 variorum edition of Lovecraft's collected fiction, excluding those listed in the appendix, but including the story ghost written for Houdini, *Imprisoned with the Pharaohs*, which has been left out of the variorum edition.

40. H. P. Lovecraft, *Selected Letters*, vol. 3, eds. August Derleth and Donald Wandrei (Sauk City: Arkham House, 1971), 29; H. P. Lovecraft, *Selected Letters*, vol. 2, eds. August Derleth and Donald Wandrei (Sauk City: Arkham House, 1958), 232–233. According to Lovecraft's first biographer, of the $17.50 Lovecraft originally proposed, only $15.50 was ultimately paid. L. Sprague De Camp, *Lovecraft: A Biography* (New York: Doubleday, 1975), 294–95.

41. De Camp, *Lovecraft*, 112.

42. On the subject of Lovecraft's letter writing, see Joshi, *Lovecraft and a World in Transition*, 440–52.

43. De Camp, *Lovecraft*, 444.

44. S. T. Joshi, *I Am Providence: The Life and Times of H. P. Lovecraft*, vol. 2 (New York: Hippocampus Press, 2013), 1004–5.

45. For examples of other post-Derleth definitions (most emphasizing some or all of the features delineated above), see Lin Carter, *Lovecraft: A Look Behind the Cthulhu Mythos* (San Bernardino: The Borgo Press, n.d.); James Egan, "Dark Apocalyptic: Lovecraft's Cthulhu Mythos as a Parody of Traditional Christianity," *Extrapolation* 23.4 (1982): 362–76; Massimo Berruti, "H. P. Lovecraft and the Anatomy of the Nothingness: The Cthulhu Mythos," *Semiotica* 150 (2004): 363–418; Mark Lowell, "Lovecraft's Cthulhu Mythos," *The Explicator* 63.1 (2004): 47–50; S. T. Joshi, *The Rise and Fall of the Cthulhu Mythos* (Poplar Bluff: Mythos Books, 2008); T. Allan Bilstad, *The Lovecraft Necronomicon Primer: A Guide to the Cthulhu Mythos* (Woodbury: Llewellyn,

2009); John Haefele, *A Look Behind the Derleth Mythos: Origins of the Cthulhu Mythos* (n.p.: Cimmerian Press, 2014).

46. Joshi, *Rise and Fall*, 19; Chris Murray and Kevin Corstorphine, "Co(s)mic Horror," in *New Essays on H. P. Lovecraft*, ed. David Simmons (New York: Palgrave, 2013); Carl Sederholm, "H.P. Lovecraft, Heavy Metal, and Cosmicism," *Rock Music Studies* 3.3 (2016): 266–80; Rebecca Janicker, "Conveying Cosmicism: Visual Interpretations of Lovecraft," in *The Medial Afterlives of H. P. Lovecraft: Comic, TV, Film, Podcast, Games*, eds. Tim Lanzendörfer and Max José Dreysse Passos de Carvalho (New York: Palgrave, 2023).

47. Carter, *Lovecraft*, 59.

48. Robert Bloch, *Once Around the Bloch* (New York: Tor, 1993), 65.

49. H. P. Lovecraft, *Letters to Robert Bloch and Others*, eds. David Schultz and S. T. Joshi (New York: Hippocampus Press, 2015), 19–22.

50. E.g., John Tibbets, *The Gothic Imagination: Conversations on Fantasy, Horror, and Science Fiction in the Media* (New York: Palgrave, 2011), 9–54; Jack Koblas, *The Lovecraft Circle and Others as I Remember Them* (Eugenia: Battered Silicon Dispatch Box, 2012).

51. Lovecraft, *Letters to Bloch*, 53–57.

52. See, for example, Lovecraft, *Lovecraft: Letters to Bloch*, 44–45.

53. H. P. Lovecraft, *O Fortunate Floridian: H. P. Lovecraft's Letters to R. H. Barlow*, eds. S. T. Joshi and David Schultz (Tampa: University of Tampa Press, 2016), 73.

54. Bloch, *Once Around the Bloch*, 67.

55. Robert Bloch, *The Robert Bloch Companion: Collected Interviews—1969–1989*, ed. Randall Larson (Mercer Island: Starmont House, 1989), 31.

56. Lovecraft, *Letters to Bloch*, 96.

57. Lovecraft, 151.

58. Lovecraft, 53–54.

59. Lovecraft, 53–54.

60. Lovecraft, 108.

61. Lovecraft, 118.

62. Robert Bloch, "The Shambler from the Stars," in *Mysteries of the Worm*, ed. Robert M. Price (Hayward: Chaoism, 1991), 17.

63. Bloch, 18.

64. Bloch, 18.

65. Lovecraft, *Letters to Bloch*, 142.

66. B. M. Reynolds, untitled letter, *Weird Tales* 26.5 (November 1935): 652.

67. Bloch, *Once Around the Bloch*, 79.

68. H. P. Lovecraft, "The Haunter in the Dark," in *Lovecraft: Collected Fiction*, vol. 3, Variorum Edition, ed. S. T. Joshi (New York: Hippocampus Press, 2017), 477.

69. Maurice Lévy, *Lovecraft: A Study in the Fantastic*, trans. S. T. Joshi (Detroit: Wayne State University Press, 1988), 110.

70. Carter, *Lovecraft*, 97.

71. de Camp, *Lovecraft*, 405.

72. Lovecraft, *Letters to Bloch*, 139.

73. Lovecraft introduced Long to J. C. Henneberger, original owner of *Weird Tales*, in 1924, and at this meeting encouraged Henneberger to consider two of Long's short stories for publication in his magazines. Both were eventually published, with "The Desert Lich" appearing in the November 1924 issue of *Weird Tales*, the first *Weird Tales* issue edited by Farnsworth Wright. See Frank Belknap Long, *Howard Phillips Lovecraft: Dreamer on the Night Side* (Sauk City: Arkham House, 1975), 122.

74. For complex genealogical reasons having more to do with how Lovecraft scholarship developed than how Lovecraft himself worked, Lovecraft scholarship has tended to refer to Lovecraft's ghostwriting as "revision work" rather than "ghostwriting." Although "ghostwriting" has the disadvantage of sometimes suggesting that Lovecraft did greater substantial work on a story than he actually did, I nevertheless prefer it to "revision work," as it more clearly signals the economic and authorial aspects of Lovecraft's professional work on other's stories and thus better enables us to differentiate it from the writing and revising he did freely for friends and loved ones.

75. Such a view, for example, seems to be an underlying assumption in Lévy, *Lovecraft*; George Wetzel, "The Cthulhu Mythos: A Study," in *H. P. Lovecraft: Four Decades of Criticism*, ed. S. T. Joshi (Athens: Ohio University Press, 1980); Simon MacCulloch, "Lovecraft Waits Dreaming," in *Dissecting Cthulhu: Essays on the Cthulhu Mythos*, ed. S. T. Joshi (Lakeland: Miskatonic River Press, 2011). It also appears to serve as an unstated foundation of arguments that cast the Mythos stories written by others (including members of the Lovecraft Circle) as categorically different from and/or inferior to Lovecraft's own. See, for example, Dirk Mosig, "H. P. Lovecraft: Myth-Maker," in *Dissecting Cthulhu*, 111.

76. Joshi, *World in Transition*, 34. See also Joshi, *World in Transition*, 343–46.

77. Robert M. Price, "Lovecraft's 'Artificial Mythology,'" in *An Epicure in the Terrible: A Centennial Anthology of Essays in Honor of H. P. Lovecraft*, eds. David Schultz and S. T. Joshi (London: Associated University Presses, 1991), 253. See also Robert M. Price, "The Revision Mythos," in *H. P. Lovecraft and the Cthulhu Mythos* (San Benardino: Borgo Press, 1990).

78. Robert E. Howard and H. P. Lovecraft, *A Means to Freedom: The Letters of H. P. Lovecraft and Robert E. Howard*, vol. 1, eds. S. T. Joshi, David E. Schultz, and Rusty Burke (New York: Hippocampus Press, 2009), 40.

79. Howard and Lovecraft, 40.

80. On narrative expansion, see Scolari et al., *Transmedia Archaeology*, 9–10; Gregory Steirer, "Narrative Worlds: A Provisional Definition," *Cultural Production*, October 2, 2011, http://culturalproductionblog.com/?=480

81. Incidentally, the book's publication history appears also to have been shaped by Bishop's gender, as August Derleth (owner of Arkham House) required Bishop to contribute most of the cost of production for her book. Such a requirement does not appear to have been standard Arkham House publishing practice and did not apply to any of the male Mythos writers Arkham House published. See ADP, Box 5, Folder 4 [letters from August Derleth to Zelia Bishop, 1954].

82. Although different in important ways—not least of which is the lack of a nominal central author figure—twenty-first-century co-creation of the kind represented by fan fiction, user-generated video, mods, and social media platforms (as well as older forms of collectively produced work, such as quilts) raises the same legal issue concerning communal productions. Courts, in general, have struggled to recognize communally produced work in the absence of existing contractual frameworks designating ownership and rights. See, for example, Leanne Stendell, "Fanfic and Fan Fact: How Current Copyright Law Ignores the Reality of Copyright Owner and Consumer Interests in Fan Fiction," *Southern Methodist University Law Review* 58 (2005): 1551–82; Ann Bartow, "Fair Use and the Fairer Sex: Gender, Feminism, and Copyright Law," *American University Journal of Gender Social Policy and Law* 14 (2006): 551–84; and Tracy Harwood and Tony Garry, "Co-creation and Ambiguous Ownership within

Virtual Communities: The Case of the Machinima Community," *Journal of Consumer Behavior* 13.2 (2014): 148–56.

83. Farnsworth Wright to August Derleth, July 13, 1931, ADP, Box 60, Folder 1.

84. Upon hearing from Derleth of the rejection, Lovecraft responded with outrage:

> I *like* to have others use my Azathoths & Nyarlathoteps—& in return I use Klarkash-Ton's [Clark Ashton Smith's] Tsathoggua, your monk Clithanus, & [Robert E.] Howard's Bran. Indeed, I shall tell Wright of my attitude when next I write him. . . . The fellow seems to have absolutely no *flexibility* or sense of proportion in his judgments—everything is measured literally & pedantically. And his "idolatry" of one whose stuff he repeatedly rejects is surely a damn peculiar species. (August Derleth and H. P. Lovecraft, *Essential Solitude: The Letters of H. P. Lovecraft and August Derleth*, vol. 1, eds. David Schultz and S. T. Joshi [New York: Hippocampus Press, 2013], 353)

Though Wright subsequently accepted other Mythos stories from Derleth, he never accepted the story that prompted his initial objection, and it was not until after Lovecraft's death that the story was published (as "The Evil Ones") in another publisher's magazine.

85. H. P. Lovecraft, *Last Will and Testament of H.P. Lovecraft*, August 12, 1912. Scanned copy available at "Will of H.P. Lovecraft, August 12, 1912," Wikisource, https://en.wikisource.org/wiki/Will_of_H.P._Lovecraft,_August_12,_1912

For the sake of completeness, it is also worth noting that Lovecraft was married at the time of his death, having failed to sign or file the divorce papers that would have formally ended his marriage with Sonia Greene. How this might have affected the execution of his will remains a purely hypothetical question, however, as neither Sonia (who had remarried in 1936) nor anyone initially involved with Lovecraft's estate were aware of these serious omissions until many years later (although Donald Wandrei appears to have suspected them), and at no point did Sonia appear to have considered filing a claim for control of the estate. See Joshi, *I Am Providence*, vol. 2, 726–27; also Donald Wandrei to August Derleth, March 29, 1937, ADP, Box 54, Folder 2.

86. Robert Barlow, "The Wind That Is in the Grass: A Memoir of H. P. Lovecraft in Florida," in Lovecraft, *O Fortunate* Floridian, xxxii–xxxiii.

87. H. P. Lovecraft, "Instructions in Case of Decease," in Lovecraft, *Collected Essays*, vol. 5, ed. S. T. Joshi (New York: Hippocampus Press, 2006).

88. Lovecraft, 237–28.

89. For a recent journalistic account of their relationship, see Paul La Farge, "The Complicated Friendship of H.P. Lovecraft and Robert Barlow, One of His Biggest Fans," *The New Yorker*, March 9, 2017, https://www.newyorker.com/books/page-turner/the-complicated-friendship-of-h-p-lovecraft-and-robert-barlow-one-of-his-biggest-fans

90. For an overview of the young Barlow's publishing undertakings, see S. T. Joshi and David E. Schultz, "Introduction," in Lovecraft, *O Fortunate Floridian*, x–xiii.

91. For example, Joshi and Schultz, "Introduction"; George Wetzel, "Lovecraft's Literary Executor," in *Collected Essays on H.P. Lovecraft and Others* (Cabin John: Wildside Press, 2015), Kindle version; George Wetzel, "Copyright Problems of the Lovecraft Literary Estate," in *Collected Essays on H.P. Lovecraft and Others* (Cabin John: Wildside Press, 2015), Kindle version.

92. The contract's terms are discussed in Wetzel, "Lovecraft's Literary Executor."

93. Wetzel, "Lovecraft's Literary Executor."

94. E.g., Wetzel, "Lovecraft's Literary Executor"; Chris J. Karr, "The Black Seas of Copyright."

95. Annie Gamwell to August Derleth, originally undated, ADP, Box 20, Folder 1.

96. Wetzel, "Lovecraft's Literary Executor."

97. Albert Baker to Robert Barlow, October 19, 1938, reproduced in Wetzel, "Lovecraft's Literary Executor."

98. Donald Wandrei to August Derleth, March 23, 1937, ADP, Box 54, Folder 2.

99. Although Derleth served as the pair's primary point of contact with Gamwell, Wandrei assumed responsibility for their interactions with Baker, in part because he better understood how the management of literary rights worked. In October 1938, he instructed Baker to threaten Barlow with legal action and offered to pay Baker's legal fee. Donald Wandrei to August Derleth, October 3, 1938, and October 9, 1938, ADP, Box 54, Folder 3.

100. See Donald Wandrei to August Derleth, January 3, 1938, ADP, Box 54, Folder 3; Howard Wandrei to August Derleth, March 1937, ADP, Box 55, Folder 7; August Derleth to Glenn Lord, 1965, ADP, Box 137, Folder 7.

101. Peter Ruber, "Introduction: The Un-Demonizing of August Derleth," in *Arkham's Maters of Horror: A 60th Anniversary Anthology Retrospective of the First 30 Years of Arkham House*, ed. Peter Ruber (n.p.: Arkham House, 2000), 31.

102. Howard Wandrei to August Derleth, March 25, 1937, ADP, Box 55, Folder 7.

103. Howard Wandrei to August Derleth, April 1937, ADP, Box 55, Folder 7.

104. Howard Wandrei to August Derleth, April 1937, ADP, Box 55, Folder 7.

105. Farsnworth Wright to August Derleth, March 22, 1937, ADP, Box 60, Folder 3.

106. See, for example, Farnsworth Wright to August Derleth, April 12, 1937, ADP, Box 60, Folder 3; Farnsworth Wright to August Derleth, July 28, 1937, ADP, Box 60, Folder 3; Dorothy McIlwraith to August Derleth, May 9, 1941, ADP, Box 60, Folder 4.

107. See, for example, Donald Wandrei to August Derleth, March 23, 1937, ADP, Box 54, Folder 2; Donald Wandrei to August Derleth, January 16, 1938, ADP, Box 54, Folder 3.

108. See, for example, Donald Wandrei to August Derleth, March 25, 1937, ADP, Box 54, Folder 2.

109. Donald Wandrei to August Derleth, August 8, 1937, ADP, Box 54, Folder 3; Donald Wandrei to August Derleth, January 3, 1939, ADP, Box 54, Folder 3; Donald Wandrei to August Derleth, January 30, 1939, ADP, Box 54, Folder 3; Donald Wandrei to August Derleth, August 30, 1939, ADP, Box 54, Folder 3.

110. Joshi, *I Am Providence*, vol. 2, 1014.

111. Farnsworth Wright to August Derleth, March 22, 1937, ADP Box 60, Folder 3.

112. See, for example, Lovecraft's December 22, 1929, and February 19, 1932, letters to Derleth, in Derleth and Lovecraft, *Essential Solitude*, 238; August Derleth and H. P. Lovecraft, *Essential Solitude: The Letters of H. P. Lovecraft and August Derleth*, vol. 2, eds. David Schultz and S. T. Joshi (New York: Hippocampus Press, 2013), 454–55.

113. Howard Wandrei to August Derleth, March 1937, ADP, Box 55, Folder 7; Howard Wandrei to August Derleth, April 1937, ADP, Box 55, Folder 7.

114. Donald Wandrei to August Derleth, January 7, 1939, ADP, Box 54, Folder 3.

115. Donald Wandrei to August Derleth, August 30, 1939, ADP, Box 54, Folder 3.

116. Donald Wandrei to August Derleth, January 3, 1939, ADP, Box 54, Folder 3.

117. Donald Wandrei, Brief, *In the Manner of the Estate of August Derleth,* Sauk County, Wisconsin, County Court, Probate Branch, July 19, 1974, 2.

118. Annie Gamwell, Last Will and Testament of Annie Gamwell, January 10, 1940, reproduced at https://en.wikisource.org/wiki/Will_of_Annie_Gamwell,_January_10,_1940. A lawyer named Ralph Greenlaw served as executor after Lewis. Wetzel, "Copyright Problems."

119. Donald Wandrei to August Derleth, March 11, 1941, ADP, Box 54, Folder 3.

120. Wandrei to Derleth, March 11, 1941.

121. Donald Wandrei to August Derleth, March 13, 1941, ADP, Box 54, Folder 3. See also Dorothy McIlwraith to August Derleth, May 9, 1941, ADP, Box 60, Folder 4.

122. Wetzel, "Copyright Problems."

123. E.g., S. T. Joshi, "Forward," in *New Critical Essays on H. P. Lovecraft,* ed. David Simmons (New York: Palgrave Macmillan, 2013), xiv; Ben Indick, "The Sage of Sauk City," *Science Fiction Studies* 22.1 (1995): 134–35; "What Is Your Opinion of August Derleth?" *R/Lovecraft,* Reddit, 2010, https://www.reddit.com/r/Lovecraft/comments/gvmej/what_is_your_opinion_of_august_derleth/

124. Derleth first produced the quotation in two magazine articles published in 1937: August Derleth, "H. P. Lovecraft, Outsider," *River* 1.3 (June 1937): 88–89; August Derleth, "A Master of the Macabre," *Reading and Collecting* 1.9 (Aug. 1937): 9–10. It subsequently appeared in multiple Arkham House publications, including the following: Derleth and Wandrei, "Howard Phillips Lovecraft: Outsider," in H. P. Lovecraft, *The Outsider and Others* (Sauk City: Arkham House, 1939), xi; Francis Laney, "The Cthulhu Mythology: A Glossary," in H. P. Lovecraft, *Beyond the Wall of Sleep* (Sauk City: Arkham House, 1943); Lin Carter, "H. P. Lovecraft: The Gods," in H. P. Lovecraft and Divers Hands, *The Shuttered Room,* ed. August Derleth (Sauk City: Arkham House, 1959), 250–67; August Derleth, "A Note on the Cthulhu Mythos," in *Trail of Cthulhu* (Sauk City: Arkham House, 1962); August Derleth, "H. P. Lovecraft and His Work," in H. P. Lovecraft, *The Dunwich Horror and Others* (Sauk City: Arkham House, 1963); August Derleth, "The Cthulhu Mythos," in H. P. Lovecraft and Others, *Tales of the Cthulhu Mythos,* ed. August Derleth (Sauk City: Arkham House, 1969).

125. For more information on "The Black Magic Quote," see S. T. Joshi, *The Rise, Fall, and Rise of the Cthulhu Mythos* (New York: Hippocampus Press, 2015), 273–74; David Schultz, "The Origin of Lovecraft's 'Black Magic' Quote," in *Dissecting Cthulhu: Essays on the Cthulhu Mythos,* ed. S. T. Joshi (Lakeland: Miskatonic River Press, 2011); Haefele, *A Look Behind,* 304–21; William Fulwiler, "Three Quotations and a Fabrication," *Crypt of Cthulhu* 46 (1987): 13–14.

126. Derleth, "H. P. Lovecraft and His Work," xiii.

127. Qtd. In Haefele, *A Look Behind,* 137.

128. Laney, "The Cthulhu Mythos."

129. Section IV of Fritz Lieber, Jr., "A Literary Copernicus," in H. P. Lovecraft, *The Shuttered Room* (Sauk City: Arkham House, 1959).

130. Lin Carter, "H. P. Lovecraft: The Books," in H. P. Lovecraft and Divers Hands, *The Shuttered Room,* ed. August Derleth (Sauk City: Arkham House, 1959); Carter, "H. P. Lovecraft: The Gods"; Tom Cockroft, "Addendum: Some Observations on the Carter Glossary," in H. P. Lovecraft and Divers Hands, *The Shuttered Room,* ed. August Derleth (Sauk City: Arkham House, 1959). See also, Carter, *Lovecraft.*

131. August Derleth and Donald Wandrei, "By Way of Introduction," in H. P. Lovecraft, *Beyond the Wall of Sleep* (Sauk City: Arkham House, 1943).

132. Derleth, "H. P. Lovecraft and His Work," xiv.

133. Derleth, "Note on the Cthulhu Mythos," 247.

134. August Derleth, *Something Near* (Sauk City: Arkham House, 1945), front dust-jacket flap.

135. Frank Long, *Rim of the Unknown* (Sauk City: Arkham House, 1972), back dust-jacket flap.

136. H. P. Lovecraft and August Derleth, *The Lurker at the Threshold* (Sauk City: Arkham House, 1945), dust-jacket front flap; H. P. Lovecraft and August Derleth, *The Survivor and Others* (Sauk City: Arkham House, 1957), dust-jacket front flap.

137. See, for example, August Derleth, "Myths about Lovecraft," *The Lovecraft Collector* no. 2 [May 1949], 4, facsimile edition (Cranston: The Two Front Rooms, 2017). As early as 1937, Derleth was also suggesting that "permission" was required to use Mythos assets. See Derleth, "H. P. Lovecraft, Outsider."

138. August Derleth to Lurton Blassingame, May 3, 1947, ADP, Box 5, Folder 6.

139. Lurton Blassingame to August Derleth, May 5, 1947, ADP, Box 5, Folder 6.

140. The correspondence can be found in ADP, Box 51, Folder 2.

141. For another example, see Derleth's exchange with Frank Thayer Jr. (whose "Family Tree" Derleth published in *Travellers by Night*), ADP, Folder 51, Box 4.

142. Ramsey Campbell and August Derleth, *Letters to Arkham: The Letters of Ramsey Campbell and August Derleth, 1961–1971*, ed. S. T. Joshi (Hornsea: PS Publishing, 2014).

143. For example, August Derleth to Brian Lumley, October 26, 1967, ADP, Box 137, Folder 39.

144. Derleth to Lumley, October 26, 1967. Derleth regrets that he does not still possess proof pages of Carter's glossaries or he would send them to Lumley himself.

145. August Derleth to Brian Lumley, September 21, 1967, ADP Box 137, Folder 39.

146. For example, August Derleth to Brian Lumley, May 28, 1970, ADP, Box 137, Folder 39.

147. Ramsey Campbell, "Chasing the Unknown," in *Cold Print* (London: Headline Feature, 1993), 11.

148. The lawsuit was settled in 1986 without a judge ever ruling on the question of the copyrights to Lovecraft's stories. For a summary of the dispute—albeit one relatively uninterested in the legal questions the dispute raised—see D. H. Olson, "Of Donald Wandrei, August Derleth, and H. P. Lovecraft," in Donald Wandrei, *Don't Dream: The Collected Horror and Fantasy Fiction of Donald Wandrei* (Minneapolis: Fedogan & Bremer, 1997). Special thanks to Chris Karr, for providing me scans of the relevant court files.

149. Paul Heald and Christopher Buccafusco, "Do Bad Things Happen When Works Fall into the Public Domain," *Berkeley Technology Law Journal* 28.1 (2013): 1–43; Paul Heald, "How Copyright Keeps Works Disappeared," *Journal of Empirical Legal Studies* 11.4 (2014): 829–66; Rebecca Giblin, "A New Copyright Bargain? Reclaiming Lost Culture and Getting Authors Paid," *Columbia Journal of Law and Arts* (2018): 369–411; Jacob Flynn et al., "What Happens When Books Enter the Public Domain? Testing Copyright's Underuse Hypothesis across Australia, New Zealand, the United States and Canada," *University of New South Wales Law Journal* 42.4 (2019): 1215–53.

150. Ian Gordon, "Comics, Creators, and Copyright: On the Ownership of Serial Narratives by Multiple Authors," in *A Companion to Media Authorship*, eds. by Jonathan Gray and Derek Johnson (New York: Wiley, 2013); Alisa Perren and Gregory Steirer, *The American Comic Book Industry and Hollywood* (London: Bloomsbury, 2021), 47–74.

Chapter 4

1. Lawrence Friedman, *A History of American Law* (New York: Simon and Schuster, 1974), 152.

2. Kenneth Umbreit, "A Consideration of Copyright," *University of Pennsylvania Law Review* 87 (1939): 932–53. See also, as examples, "The Protection Afforded Literary and Cartoon Characters through Trademark, Unfair Competition, and Copyright," *Harvard Law Review* 68.2 (1954): 349–63; Leon Kellman, "Legal Protection of Fictional Characters," *Brooklyn Law Review* 25 (1958): 3–19.

3. Walter Derenberg, "Copyright No-Man's Land: Fringe Rights in Literary and Artistic Property, Part 1," *Journal of the Patent Office Society* 35.9 (1953): 627–57, 637.

4. E.g., David Feldman, "Finding a Home for Fictional Characters: A Proposal for Change in Copyright Protection," *California Law Review* 78 (1990): 687–720; Mark Bartholomew, "Protecting the Performers: Setting a New Standard for Character Copyrightability," *Santa Clara Law Review* 41 (2001): 341–78; Kathryn Foley, "Protecting Fictional Characters," *Connecticut Law Review* 41 (2009): 925–26.

5. E.g., Roscoe Pound, "Theory of Judicial Decision III. A Theory of Judicial Decision for Today," *Harvard Law Review* 36.8 (1923): 940–59; Karl Llewellyn, *The Common Law Tradition: Deciding Appeals* (Boston: Little, Brown and Co., 1960); Bruce Harris, "Final Appellate Courts Overruling Their Own 'Wrong' Precedents: The Ongoing Search for Principle," *Law Quarterly Review* 118 (2002): 408–27; Scott Moss, "Bad Briefs, Bad Law, Bad Markets: Documenting the Poor Quality of Plaintiffs' Briefs, Its Impact on the Law, and the Market Failure It Reflects," *Emory Law Journal* 63 (2013): 58–125; Erik Christiansen, "Misbehaving," *Litigation* 46.2 (2020): 51–56; Terry Maroney, "(What We Talk About When We Talk About) Judicial Temperament," *Boston College Law Review* 61 (2020): 2085–2153.

6. *Star Co. v. Press Pub. Co.*, 162 App. Div. 486 (N.Y. 1914).

7. *King Features v. Fleischer*, 299 F. 533 (2d Cir. 1924).

8. *Detective Comics v. Bruns*, 28 F. Supp. 399 (S.D.N.Y. 1939), *rev'd*, 111 F.2d 432 (2d Cir. 1940).

9. See Mark McKenna, "The Normative Foundations of Trademark Law," *Notre Dame Law Review* 82.5 (2007): 1839–1916.

10. E.g., Daphne Robert *The New Trade-Mark Manual: A Handbook on Protection of Trade-Marks in Interstate Commerce* (Washington, DC: The Bureau of National Affairs, 1947); Doris Estelle Long, "Rebooting Trademarks for the Twenty-first Century," *University of Louisiana Law Review* 495 (2011): 517–54.

11. Schechter, *Historical Foundations of the Law Relating to Trade-marks* (Clark, NJ: Lawbook Exchange, 2012).

12. *Canal Co. v. Clark*, 80 U.S. 311 (1872), 323.

13. E.g., Irene Calboli, "Overlapping Copyright and Trademark Protection: A Call for Concern and Action," *Illinois Law Review Slip Opinions* (2014): 27; "What Trademark Covers," *Digital Media Law Project*, September 10, 2022, https://www.dmlp.org/legal-guide/what-trademark-covers

14. Schechter, *Historical Foundations.*

15. The other kind of infringement is misappropriation or "reaping where one hasn't sown," which is usually held to have originated in the United States in *International News Service v. Associated Press*, 248 U.S. 215 (1918).

16. *Hanover Star Milling Co. v. Metcalf*, 240 U.S., 403 (1916), 413. The primary distinction between trademark and unfair competition infringements concerned registration under the Federal Trademark Act of 1905 (the first federal trademark act

was passed in 1870 but was declared unconstitutional in 1879; a revised act passed in 1881 but applied only to international law). Suits involving registered marks were heard in federal court; suits involving other kinds of unfair competition were heard in state courts.

17. *In re DC Comics, Inc.*, 689 F.2d 1042 (C.C.P.A. 1982), 1052. Since implementation of the Lanham Act in 1946, there have been significant legal benefits to registration, including the potential to achieve "incontestability," which some have argued have rendered trademarks closer in some respects to traditional notions of property. See Kenneth Port, "The Illegitimacy of Trademark Incontestability," *Indiana Law Review* 23 (1993): 519–87; Rebecca Tushnet, "Fixing Incontestability: The Next Frontier," *Boston University Journal of Science and Technology Law* 23 (2017): 434–55.

18. See Wendy Gordon, "Introduction: Ralph Sharp Brown, Intellectual Property, and the Public Interest," *Yale Law Journal* 108 (1999): 1611–17; Mark Lemley, "The Modern Lanham Act and the Death of Common Sense," *Yale Law Journal* (1999): 1687–1715; McKenna, "Normative Foundations"; Joe Cole, "Trademark Terms under the Lanham Act and State Law," *Journal of Contemporary Legal Issues* 19 (2010): 70–77; Sondra Levine, "The Origins of the Lanham Act," *Journal of Contemporary Legal Issues* 19 (2010): 22–27; Kenneth Port, "The Expansion Trajectory: Trademark Jurisprudence in the Modern Age," *Journal of the Patent and Trademark Office Society* 92.4 (2010): 474–97.

19. See James Kobak Jr., "Totem and Taboo: Growth of a Common Law of Unfair Competition in New York with Some Notes on the Effect of the Lanham Act of 1946," *New York Law Forum* 17 (1972): 941–82.

20. Mark Winchester, "Litigation and Early Comic Strips: The Lawsuits of Outcault, Dirks and Fisher," *Inks*, May 1995, 17.

21. Winchester, 17.

22. Winchester, 15, 21. In *New York Herald Co. v. Star Co.*, 146 F. 204, 204 the court states explicitly that, "This is a suit solely to restrain infringement of a trade-mark; no question as to copyright or as to unfair competition is presented. The trade-mark which complainant claims to own is the words 'Buster Brown' as a title or heading for a comic section of a newspaper. No claim is made as to any particular style of illustration, only to these words used in this connection."

23. 162 App. Div. 486.

24. These include, in addition to those cited in subsequent notes, E. Fulton Brylawski, "Protection of Characters—Sam Spade Revisited," *Bulletin of the Copyright Society of the USA* 22 (1974): 80; Ron Goulart, *The Funnies: 100 Years of American Comic Strips* (New York: Adams Pub., 1995), 53, 210; M. Booker, *Comics Through Time: A History of Icons, Idols, and Ideas*, vol. 1 (Santa Barbara: ABL-CLIO, 1914), 109; Don Markstein, "The Katzenjammer Kids," *Toonopedia*, n.d., http://www.toonopedia.com/katzen.htm, accessed July 15, 2022; "Harold H. Knerr, A Cartoonist, 66," *New York Times*, July 9, 1949, 13.

25. Jim Lowe, *The Katzenjammer Kids*, June 25, 1998, http://www.dumboozle.com/katzies/katzdex.html

26. "Rudolph Dirks," *Wikipedia*, https://en.wikipedia.org/wiki/Rudolph_Dirks, accessed July 18, 2022; "Rudolph Dirks," *Lambiek Comiclopedia*, June 21, 2021, https://www.lambiek.net/artists/d/dirks_r.htm; Jud Hurd, "Rudolph Dirks," *Cartoonist Profiles*, September 1974, 42. Cartoon historian Donald Crafton also calls the decision "precedent-setting" in Donald Crafton, *Before Mickey: The Animated Film 1898–1928* (Chicago: University of Chicago Press, 2015), 182.

27. A substantial portion of this essay is reproduced in Jim Walsh, "Classics of the Comics: *The Katzenjammers,*" *Hobbies—The Magazine for Collectors,* April 1953, 146–51, 163.

28. Walsh, 149.

29. Martin Sheridan, *Comics and Their Creators: Life Stories of American Cartoonists* (N.p.: Hale, Cushman & Flint, 1942), 57–63.

30. In addition to new editions of his book, Sheridan published a barely edited version of his section of Dirks for *The Quill* in 1958. Martin Sheridan, "The Kids that Never Grew Up," *The Quill,* October 1958, 11–12, 18.

31. Walsh, "Classics of the Comics."

32. SCPP, RDP, 15.

33. SCPP, RDP, 15.

34. SCPP, RDP, 33.

35. SCPP, RDP, 27.

36. SCPP, RDP, 38.

37. SCPP, RDP, 45–46.

38. SCPP, RDP, 33.

39. SCPP, RDP, 23.

40. SCPP, RDP, 16.

41. SCPP, RDP, 21; SCPP, RDP, 10–13.

42. SCPP, RDP, 63–67; *Star Co. v. Press Publishing Co.*, 143 N.Y.S. 1144 (1913)

43. 162 A.D. 486, 488.

44. 162 A.D. 486.

45. *Lumley v. Wagner,* 42 Eng. Rep. 687 (1852). See David Tannenbaum, "Enforcement of Personal Service Contracts in the Entertainment Industry," *California Law Review* 42 (1954): 18–27; Harlan Blake, "Employee Agreements Not to Compete," *Harvard Law Review* 73.4 (1960): 625–91.

46. SCPP, RDP, 64.

47. SCPP, RDP, 11.

48. Tannenbaum, "Enforcement," 21. See *Clark Paper 7 Mfg. Co. v. Stenacher,* 236 N.Y. 312 (1923).

49. SCPP, RDP, 34.

50. Harlan Stone, "The 'Mutuality' Rule in New York," *Columbia Law Review* 16.6 (1916): 443.

51. See also J. B. Amers, "Mutuality in Specific Performance," *Columbia Law Review* 3.1 (1903): 1–12.

52. SCPP, RDP, 35–36.

53. For more on this issue, see Alisa Perren and Gregory Steirer, *The American Comic Book Industry and Hollywood* (London: Bloomsbury, 2021), 47–49.

54. SCPP, RDP, 63.

55. SCPP, RDP, 65.

56. SCPP, RDP, 64–65.

57. *Star Co. v. Press Publishing Co.*, 143 N.Y.S. 1144.

58. 162 A.D. 486, 487.

59. SCPP, RDP, 16.

60. 162 A.D. 486, 491

61. 162 A.D. 486, 491–92. The specific rule being violated is the requirement that a contractual agreement must involve from both parties what is called "consideration," i.e., something offered in exchange.

62. Stone, "The 'Mutuality' Rule," 460–61.

63. *National Comics Publications v. Fawcett Publications,* 93 F. Supp. 349 (S.D.N.Y. 1950), *rev'd* 191 F.2d 594 (2d Cir., 1951), petition for injunction denied 198 F.2d 927 (2d Cir., 1952).

64. E.g., *Nichols v. Universal Pictures Co.* 34 F.2d 145; *Fendler v. Morosco* 253 N.Y. 281 (1930); *Rush v. Oursler* 39 F.2d 468 (2d Cir., 1930).

65. Transcript of Record, *King Features Syndicate v. Fleischer,* NAKC, 41–46.

66. Transcript of Record, 26–27.

67. Transcript of Record, 27–28.

68. *Rules and Regulations for the Registration of Claims to Copyright* (Copyright Office Bulletin No. 15) (Washington, DC: U.S.G.P.O, 1913), par 12 (g); *Manual of Classification of Subjects of Invention of the United States Patent Office* (Washington, DC: U.S.G.P.O., 1912), No. 46.

69. KFF, NAKC, 74.

70. KFF, NAKC, 76.

71. KFF, NAKC, 76, 82–83, 84–85, 86–88, 89–90.

72. KFF, NAKC, 77.

73. KFF, NAKC, 91–111.

74. KFF, NAKC, 85.

75. KFF, NAKC, 58–59.

76. KFF, NAKC, 117.

77. KFF, NAKC, 117.

78. KFF, NAKC, 117.

79. KFF, NAKC, 121.

80. KFF, NAKC, 6.

81. *Baker v. Selden,* 101 U.S. 99 (1880); *Royal Sales Co. v. Gaynor,* 164 F. 207 (2d Cir. 1908).

82. 101 U.S. 99, 103.

83. 101 U.S. 99, 103–4.

84. 101 U.S. 99, 104.

85. *Royal Sales Co. v. Gaynor,* 164 F. 207 (1908), 208.

86. 164 F. 207.

87. KFF, NAKC, 12–23.

88. KFF, NAKC, 22.

89. KFF, NAKC, 30–31; *Jeweler's Circular Pub. Co. v. Keystone Pub. Co.,* 281 Fed. 83 (2d Cir. 1922), 86.

90. 281 Fed. 83, 86.

91. KFF, NAKC, 26; *Baker v. Selden,* 101. U.S. 99, 103–4.

92. KFF, NAKC, 27.

93. KFF, NAKC, 34.

94. E.g., KFF, NAKC, 25–26.

95. KFF, NAKC, 35.

96. KFF, NAKC, 299 F. 533, 537.

97. The precedent would be reinforced by *Fleischer Studios, Inc. v. Ralph A. Freundlich, Inc.,* 73 F. 2d 276 (2d Cir. 1934), which held that a doll resembling the cartoon character Betty Boop constituted a copyright infringement.

98. For example, Edward Samuels, "The Idea-Expression Dichotomy in Copyright Law," *Tennessee Law Review* 56 (1989): 321–463, 339.

99. E.g., "Recent Cases," *University of Pennsylvania Law Review* 73.1 (1924): 96–113, 103–4.

100. Umbreit, "Consideration of Copyright," 939.

101. Umbreit, 940.
102. DCC, NAKC, 14.
103. Gary Rosen, *Adventures of a Jazz Age Lawyer: Nathan Burkan and the Making of American Popular Culture* (Berkeley: University of California Press, 2020), 269.
104. E.g., "'Lettie Lynton' Movie Ruled a Plagiarism," *New York Times*, January 18, 1936, 19.
105. DCC, NAKC, 143.
106. *Sheldon v. Metro-Goldwyn Pictures Corp.*, 7 F. Supp. 837 (S.D.N.Y. 1934), 842.
107. 7 F. Supp. 837, 844.
108. *Sheldon v. Metro-Goldwyn Pictures Corp.* 81 F. 2d 49 (2d Cir. 1936), 53.
109. DCC, NAKC, 24.
110. DCC, NAKC, 82, 84.
111. DCC, NAKC, 122.
112. DCC, NAKC, 126.
113. E.g., DCC, NAKC, 34.
114. E.g., DCC, NAKC, 100.
115. DCC, NAKC, 148, capitalization mine.
116. DCC, NAKC, 62.
117. DCC, NAKC, 64.
118. DCC, NAKC, 82.
119. E.g., DCC, NAKC, 54–55, 86–87, 109.
120. DCC, NAKC, 57.
121. As an intellectual property lawyer operating in New York, Blum must have encountered Woolsey in previous cases. Besides *Sheldon v. Metro-Goldwyn Pictures Corp.*, however, there appears to have been no IP case heard by Woolsey that involved anything remotely resembling the questions underlying this case and on which Woolsey was reversed.
122. E.g., DCC, NAKC, 92, 94, 96.
123. E.g., DCC, NAKC, 118–19, 121.
124. DCC, NAKC, 96.
125. DCC, NAKC, 74, 76.
126. DCC, NAKC, 37–38.
127. DCC, NAKC, 125
128. DCC, NAKC, 147.
129. DCC, NAKC, 180.
130. Brief of Plaintiff-Appellee, *Detective Comics v. Bruns Publications* (No. 16907), NAKC.
131. Brief for Defendants-Appellants, *Detective Comics v. Bruns Publications* (No. 16907), NAKC.
132. *Nichols v. Universal Pictures Co.*, 45 F.2d; 119 The other is *Shelden v. Metro-Goldwyn Pictures Corp.*, 81 F. 2d 49.
133. 45 F.2d 119, 121.
134. *Detective Comics v. Bruns Publications*, 111 F.2d 432, 434.
135. Petition for Rehearing, *Detective Comics v. Bruns Publications* (No. 16907), NAKC.
136. Sanford Gordon and Gregory Huber, "Accountability and Coercion: Is Justice Blind When It Runs for Office?," *American Journal of Political Science* 48 (2004): 247–63; Gregory Sisk and Michael Heise, "Ideology All the Way Down: An Empirical Study of Establishment Clause Decisions in the Federal Courts," *Michigan Law Review* 110 (2012): 1201–63.

137. In addition to copying Superman, Bruns appeared to have used its industry position to gain access to private sales information regard Action Comics.

138. *Detective Comics v. Bruns Publications*, 28 F. Supp. 399, 400.

139. Calboli, "Overlapping Copyright and Trademark."

Chapter 5

1. Karl Lewellyn, *The Bramblebush: On Our Law and Its Study* (Dobbs Ferry, NY: Oceana Publications, 1960).

2. According to de Camp, Berle did most of the research while de Camp himself did most of the writing. L. Sprague de Camp, *Time and Chance: An Autobiography* (Hampton Falls, NH: Donald Grant, 1996), 127.

3. A. K. Berle and L. S. de Camp, *Inventions and Their Management*, 1st ed. (Scranton, PA: International Textbook Company, 1937); Alf K. Berle and L. Sprague de Camp, *Inventions and Their Management*, 2nd ed. (Scranton, PA: International Textbook Company, 1947); Alf K. Berle and L. Sprague de Camp, *Inventions and Their Management*, 3rd ed. (Scranton, PA: International Textbook Company, 1951); Berle and de Camp, *Inventions, Patents, and Their Management.*

4. *Sperry v. Florida*, 373 U.S. 379 (1963), 390. Curiously, a U.S. District Court also cited the book in a 1974 case about school segregation. *Hart v. Community School Bd of Brooklyn.* 383 F. Supp. 699, 763.

5. De Camp, *Time and Chance*, 123, 125–27.

6. E.g., "After making a properly dated and witnessed drawing and description, I looked into the market. I found that, while the device might be patentable, its potential market was much too small to make the investment of more time and money worth while." De Camp, 125.

7. De Camp, 141–42.

8. Berle and de Camp, *Inventions, Patents, and Their Management.*

9. Berle and de Camp, 494–97.

10. Carlos Scolari, Paolo Bertteti, and Matthew Freeman, *Transmedia Archaeology: Storytelling in the Borderlines of Science Fiction, Comics and Pulp Magazines* (New York: Palgrave, 2014), 15–38.

11. Scolari et al.; Paul Sammon, *Conan: The Phenomenon* (Milwaukie: Dark Horse, 2013).

12. E.g., Michele Hilmes, "Never Ending Story: Authorship, Seriality, and the Radio Writers Guild," in *A Companion to Media Authorship*, eds. Jonathan Gray and Derek Johnson, 181–99 (Malden, MA: Wiley-Blackwell, 2013); Miranda Banks, *The Writers: A History of American Screenwriters and Their Guild* (New Brunswick: Rutgers, 2015); Catherine Fisk, *Writing for Hire: Unions, Hollywood, and Madison Avenue* (London: Harvard University Press, 2016); Thomas Walsh, *Playwrights and Power: The Making of the Dramatists Guild* (Hanover: Smith & Kraus, 2016); Matthew Bodie, "Lessons from the Dramatists Guild for the Platform Economy," *University of Chicago Legal Forum* (2017): 17–34.

13. E.g., Meredith Annan House, "*Marvel v. Kirby*: A Clash of Comic Book Titans in the Work Made for Hire Arena," *Berkeley Technology Law Journal* (2015): 933–64; Ian Gordon, "Comics, Creators, and Copyright: On the Ownership of Serial Narratives by Multiple Authors," in *A Companion to Media Authorship*, edited by Jonathan Gray and Derek Johnson (New York: Wiley, 2013); Marc Greenberg, *Comic Art, Creativity and the Law*, 2nd ed. (Northamption: Edward Elgar, 2022), 233–44.

14. E.g., Peter Decherney, "Auteurism on Trial: Moral Rights and Films on Tele-

vision," *Wisconsin Law Review* (2011): 273–330; Neal Robin, "Hit Losers: The Good (Faith) Fight for Net-Profits Payments from Blockbuster Hollywood Productions," *Case Western Reserve Journal of Law, Technology, & The Internet* (2012–2013): 445–82; Eric Strum, "Hollywood Accounting: Profit Participation and the Use of Mediation as a Mode of Resolving These Disputes," *Cardozo Journal of Conflict Resolution* (2016–2017): 457–87; Agata Frymus, "Jetta Goudal Versus the Studio System: Star Labour in 1920s Hollywood," *Historical Journal of Film, Radio, and Television* 39.1 (2019): 36–53; John Broderick, "*Warner Bros. v. Nelson*: A Prelude to the De Havilland Law," *Loyola of Los Angeles Entertainment Law Review* (2021): 111–49.

15. For example, Alisa Perren and myself have shown how the mainstream comics industry, because it lacked the kind of guilds and minimum basic agreements that arose to standardize creative labor contracts in the television industry, evolved in such a way that a creator-owned publishing model became a major component of the industry—a quite different evolutionary outcome than of television, despite the two industries both dealing heavily in a similar product: serialized, collectively produced, narrative entertainment. Alisa Perren and Gregory Steirer, *The American Comic Book Industry and Hollywood* (London: Bloomsbury, 2021), 47–74.

16. Examples of media studies scholarship that discusses routine contract negotiation and renegotiation (though usually involving power differences) include Tom Kemper, *Hidden Talent: The Emergence of Hollywood Agents* (Berkeley: University of California Press, 2009); John Thompson, *Merchants of Culture: The Publishing Business in the Twenty-First Century* (Malden, MA: Polity, 2010); Violaine Roussel, *Representing Talent: Hollywood Agents and the Making of Movies* (Chicago: University of Chicago Press, 2017); Ken Basin, *The Business of Television* (New York: Routledge, 2018); Jeffrey Ulin, *The Business of Media Distribution: Monetizing Film, TV, and Video Content in an Online World*, 3rd ed. (New York: Routledge, 2019); Kate Fortmueller, *Below the Stars* (Austin: University of Texas Press, 2021); and Perren and Steirer, *American Comic Book Industry*.

17. On the important role of guilds with respect to the historical development of formal contracting practices in the media industries, see Banks, *Writers*; Fisk, *Writing for Hire*; Walsh, *Playwrights and Power*. For an account of the historical development of formalized contracts for high-level talent in Hollywood, see Emily Carman and Philip Drake, "Doing the Deal: Talent Contracts in Hollywood," in *Hollywood and the Law*, eds. Paul McDonald et al. (London: BFI, 2015). For a discussion of the economic logic of the long-term contracting of stars in early Hollywood, see Darlene Chisholm, "Asset Specificity and Long-Term Contracts: The Case of the Motion-Picture Industry," *Eastern Economic Journal* 19.2 (1993): 143–55.

18. Franklin Laskin, "All Rights Unreserved—The Author's Lost Property in Publishing and Entertainment," *Copyright Law Symposium* 7 (1954): 96.

19. Alfred Wasserstrom, "Magazine, Newspaper and Syndication Problems," in *1953 Copyright Problems Analyzed*, ed. Theodore Kupferman (Chicago: Commerce Clearing House, 1953), 165.

20. "Needs of Such an Organization," *The Bulletin of the Authors' League of America* 1 (April 1913): 7. On the subject of nineteenth- and twentieth-century contract law in the United States, see Lawrence Friedman, *Contract Law in America: A Social and Economic Case Study* (Madison: University of Wisconsin Press, 1965).

21. 175 F. 902.

22. Arthur Train, *My Day in Court* (New York: Charles Scribner's Sons, 1939), 308.

23. Within the book publishing industry, contracts—even when detailed—tended to vary in form and language by publisher. Although the Author's League provided

a model for a standard contract, no major publisher made use of it. Edward Colton, "Contracts in the Entertainment and Literary Fields," in *1953 Copyright Problems Analyzed*, ed. Theodore Kupferman (Chicago: Commerce Clearing House, 1953), 140.

24. Gary Groth, "Pushing Marvel into the '80's: An Interview with Jim Shooter," *Comics Journal* 60 (1980): 55–86, 77.

25. E.g., *The Bulletin of the Authors' League of America* 1.7 (November 1913): 15.

26. E.g., Harry Ransom, *The First Copyright Statute: An Essay on an Act for the Encouragement of Learning* (Austin: University of Texas Press, 1956), 11.

27. For discussions of average rates, see Train, *My Day in Court*, 429–35; Theodore Peterson, *Magazines in the Twentieth Century* (Urbana: University of Illinois Press, 1964), 122–27.

28. Marco Iansiti and Roy Levien, *The Keystone Advantage* (Boston: Harvard Business School Press, 2004), 82–83.

29. Train, *My Day in Court*, 433.

30. The Authors' League, for example, collected reports of unfair or abusive publishers and routinely provided this information to members who requested it.

31. Such claims more commonly took the form of a percentage of revenue generated than outright ownership of the rights. For Cain's critique, see James Cain, "An American Authors' Authority," *Screen Writer*, July 1946, 1–18, 2–3.

32. Untitled article, *The Bulletin of the Authors' League of America* 1.1 (April 1913), 2.

33. Stewart Macaulay, "Non-contractual Relations in Business: A Preliminary Study," *American Sociological Review* 28.1 (1963): 55–67.

34. Stewart Macaulay, "Elegant Models, Empirical Pictures, and the Complexities of Contract," *Law & Society Review* 11.3 (1977): 507–28, 509.

35. Robert Gordon, "Macaulay, MacNeil, and the Discovery of Solidarity and Power in Contract Law," *Wisconsin Law Review* (1985): 565–80, 569

36. Peter Sanders et al., "Hollywood Is Going Off Script as Writers Gamble for Digital Pie," *Wall Street Journal*, November 6, 2007, B8; Michael Cieply, "Both Sides in Writers' Strike See New-Media Future at Stake," *New York Times*, December 1, 2007, C1, C4; Jonathan Handel, *Hollywood on Strike! An Industry at War in the Internet Age* (Los Angeles: Hollywood Analytics, 2011). See also Miranda Banks, "The Picket Line Online: Creative Labor, Digital Activism, and the 2007–2008 Writers Guild of America Strike," *Popular Communication* 8 (2010): 20–33.

37. *Photo Drama Motion Picture Co. v. Social Uplift Film Corp.*, 213 Fed. 374 (S.D.N.Y. 1914), *aff'd* 220 F. 448 (2d Cir., 1915).

38. *Hart v. Fox*, 166 N.Y. Supp. 793 (1917).

39. *Manners v. Morosco*, 252 U.S. 317 (1920).

40. On sound film, for example, see *Cinema Corporation of America v. De Mille*, 149 Misc. 358 (N.Y. 1933); on television, see Cohn, "Old Licenses and New Uses: Motion Picture and Television Rights," *Law and Contemporary Problems* 19.2 (1954): 190–93.

41. Robert E. Howard, "Phoenix on the Sword," *Weird Tales*, December 1932, 769–84.

42. Robert E. Howard, "By This Axe I Rule!" in *Kull: Exile of Atlantis* (New York: Del Rey/Ballantine Books, 2006).

43. Robert E. Howard, "The Scarlet Citadel," *Weird Tales*, January 1933, 51–77.

44. Robert E. Howard, "The Tower of the Elephant," *Weird Tales*, March 1933, 306–22.

45. Robert E. Howard, "Hour of the Dragon" was serialized in *Weird Tales*, Decem-

ber 1935, 658–84, *Weird Tales,* January 1936, 72–105, *Weird Tales,* February 1936, 72–105, *Weird Tales,* March 1936, 323–44, and *Weird Tales,* April 1936, 450–71.

46. Robert E. Howard, "Queen of the Black Coast," *Weird Tales,* May 1934, 530–49.

47. Robert E. Howard, "Red Nails" was serialized in *Weird Tales,* July 1936, 16–35, *Weird Tales,* August/September 1936, 205–21, and *Weird Tales,* October 1936, 334–53; Robert E. Howard, "Pool of the Black One," *Weird Tales,* October 1933, 447–66; Robert E. Howard, "Beyond the Black River" was serialized in *Weird Tales,* May 1935, 591–608, and *Weird Tales,* June 1935, 734–54; Robert E. Howard, "Jewels of Gwahlur," *Weird Tales,* March 1935, 299–327; Robert E. Howard, "The God in the Bowl," in *The Coming of Conan* (New York: Del Rey/Ballantine Books, 2005).

48. Robert E. Howard, "The Black Stranger," in *The Conquering Sword of Conan* (New York: Del Rey/Ballantine Books, 2005). For information on the story's history, see Patrice Louinet, "Hyborian Genesis, Part III," in *The Conquering Sword of Conan* (New York: Del Rey/Ballantine Books, 2005), 377–78.

49. Umberto Eco, "The Myth of Superman," *Diacritics* 2.1 (1972): 19.

50. Robert E. Howard, *The Collected Letters of Robert E. Howard,* vol. 2, eds. Rob Roehm and John Bullard (n.p.: Robert E. Howard Foundation Press, 2007), 150–51.

51. Robert E. Howard, *The Hyborian Age,* facsimile edition (Tallahassee: Skelos Press, 2015), 1.

52. The essay's lack of resemblance to postwar "world-building" or "world-mapping" documents has occasionally earned it harsh criticism from contemporary commentators. See, for example, E. Hoffmann Price, introduction, in *The Last Celt: A Biobibliography of Robert E. Howard, the Creator of Conan,* ed. Glenn, Lord (New York: Berkley Publishing Corporation, 1976), 15; Darrell Schweitzer, *Conan's World and Robert E. Howard* (San Bernardino: The Borgo Press, 1978), 52–53.

53. Patrice Louinet, "Hyborian Genesis," in *The Coming of Conan the Cimmerian,* by Robert E. Howard (New York: Random House, 2002), 429–52.

54. Mark Finn, *Blood and Thunder: The Life and Art of Robert E. Howard* (Austin: MonkeyBrain Books, 2006), 173–75.

55. Neither Isaac nor Pere Kuykendall's wills explicitly mention the rights to Howard's writing.

56. On the dispersion and rediscovery of Howard's unpublished work, see Rob Roehm, "The Legend of the Trunk," *REH: Two-Gun Raconteur,* January 14–April 17, 2014, http://www.rehtwogunraconteur.com/the-legend-of-the-trunk-part-1/

57. Isaac Howard, *The Collected Letters of Doctor Isaac M. Howard* (n.p.: Robert E. Howard Foundation Press, 2011), 79.

58. Howard, 181–82.

59. Howard, 154.

60. Howard, 174–85.

61. Howard, 193–96; August Derleth to Dorothy McIlwraith, February 3, 1944, ADP, Box 60, Folder 4; Dorothy McIlwraith to August Derleth, February 8, 1944, ADP, Box 60, Folder 4.

62. Isaac Howard, *The Collected Letters,* 194–95.

63. Jeffrey Shanks, "Introduction to the 2015 Fascimile Edition: Constructing an Age Undreamed Of," in *The Hyborian Age,* facsimile edition, by Robert E. Howard (Tallahassee: Skelos Press, 2015), vii–viii.

64. Peter Schuyler Miller and John D. Clark, "A Probable Outline of Conan's Career," in *The Hyborian Age,* facsimile edition, by Robert E. Howard (Tallahassee: Skelos Press, 2015), 17.

65. August Derleth, *Thirty Years of Arkham House: 1939–1969* (Sauk City, WI: Arkham House, 1970), 6.

66. Isaac Howard, *The Collected Letters,* 210, 215; Otis Kline to August Derleth, November 13, 1944, ADP, Box 28l, Folder 7.

67. H. R. Hays, "Superman on a Psychotic Bender," *New York Times Book Review,* September 29, 1946, 35.

68. For an account of Wollheim's transition from fan to professional, see Damon Knight, *The Futurians* (New York: John Day), 1977.

69. Jack Chalker and Mark Owings, eds., *The Science-Fantasy Publishers: A Critical and Bibliographic History,* 3rd ed. (Westminster, MD: Mirage Press, 1991), 192–96.

70. L. Sprague de Camp, "History of the Lord-De Camp Dispute," March 19, 1972, PLSDC. At the time I consulted these papers at The Harry Ransom Center, they had not yet been formally organized by the archive. Boxes were overstuffed with material; papers were often overflowing the folders they were in or in some cases not in any folder at all; duplicates were also scattered throughout the folders; and papers were sometimes arbitrarily organized. I thus do not cite the box or folder numbers for papers from this collection.

71. Kristina Busse, "Fan Labor and Feminism: Capitalizing on the Fannish Labor of Love," *Cinema Journal* 54.3 (2015): 110–15; Suzanne Scott, "'Cosplay is Serious Business': Gendering Material Fan Labor on *Heroes of Cosplay,*" *Cinema Journal* 54.3 (2015): 146–54.

72. See Perren and Steirer, *The American Comic Book,* 47–74.

73. For more on these three fans-turned-professionals, see Harry Warner, *All Our Yesterdays: An Informal History of Science Fiction Fandom in the Forties* (Chicago: Advent, 1969), 15, 79–80, 225; Knight, *Futurians*: 87–90, 132–33, 180–82, 245–46; Chalker and Owings, eds., *The Science-Fantasy Publishers,* 14–19, 335–36.

74. Henry Jenkins, "Fandom, Negotiation, and Participatory Culture," in *A Companion to Media Fandom and Fan Studies,* ed. Paul Booth (Oxford: Wiley Blackwell, 2018); Angela Ndalianis, "Female Fans, Female Creators, and Female Superheroes: The Semiotics of Changing Gender Dynamics," in *The Routledge Companion to Gender and Sexuality in Comic Book Studies,* ed. Frederick Luis Aldama (New York: Routledge, 2020); James Rampant, "The Manga Polysystem: What Fans Want, Fans Get," in *Manga: An Anthology of Global and Cultural Perspectives,* ed. Toni Johnson-Woods (London: Continuum, 2010).

75. De Camp, *Time and Chance,* 217.

76. De Camp, 230.

77. See, for example, L. Sprague de Camp to Peter Schuyler Miller, December 3, 1951, PLSDC; Peter Schuyler Miller to L. Sprague de Camp, December 16, 1951, PLSDC.

78. De Camp understates his involvement in the series in his biography: de Camp, *Time and Chance,* 229–32. Cf. L. Sprague de Camp to Isaac Asimov, February 6, 1952, PLSDC; L. Sprague de Camp to Peter Schuyler Miller, February 7, 1952, PLSDC.

79. De Camp, *Time and Chance,* 230.

80. Robert E. Howard, "The Frost-Giant's Daughter," ed. L. Sprague de Camp, *Fantasy Fiction,* August 1953, 78.

81. L. Sprague de Camp, "Conan's Ghost," in *The Spell of Conan,* ed. L. Sprague de Camp (New York: Ace, 1980), 42.

82. L. Sprague de Camp to Al Getcher, September 26, 1956, PLSDC.

83. Björn Nyberg, qtd. in James Sieger to L. Sprague de Camp, June 9, 1960, PLSDC; de Camp, *Time and Chance,* 231–32.

84. See especially Rusty Burke, "De Camp vs. Howard: Rewriting Conan," in *The Fantastic Worlds of Robert E. Howard*, second printing, ed. James van Hise (Yucca Valley, CA: James van Hise, 2001). [Originally published in *REHUPA* #104 (July 1990)].

85. The magazine ceased publication in 1954. The rights to it (the details of which were, as one might imagine, nebulous) were eventually purchased by Leo Marguiles, who relaunched it in the 1970s. Philip Sherman, *Leo Marguiles: Giant of the Pulps* (n.p.: Altus Press, 2017), 209–12.

86. Burke, "De Camp vs. Howard," 52.

87. Peter Jaszi and Martha Woodmansee, "Copyright in Transition," in *A History of the Book in America*, vol. 4, edited By Carl Kaestle and Janice Radway (Chapel Hill: University of North Carolina Press, 2009), 92–93.

88. Borge Varmer, "Study No. 13: Works Made for Hire and On Commission," in *Copyright Law Revision: Studies Prepared for the Subcommittee on Patents, Trademarks, and Copyrights*, 86th Congress, 2d session (Washington: U.S.G.P.O., 1960), 128.

89. Varmer, "Study No. 13," 142.

90. See, for example, Margaret Nicholson, *A Manual of American Copyright Practice* (London: Oxford University Press, 1945).

91. For work produced by independent contractors to be considered "work for hire," the Copyright Act of 1976 required that written agreement between the contractor and the employer expressly designate it as such. 17 U.S.C. §101 (1976). For more information on the evolution of work-for-hire doctrine as it pertains to writers, see Anne Marie Hill, "Work for Hire Definition in the Copyright Act of 1976," *Cornell Law Review* 74.3 (1989): 559–86.

92. Vernon Clark, "Dreams from Youharneth-Lahai," *REHUPA* 95 (January 1989): 42–47.

93. L. Sprague de Camp to Isaac Asimov, December 21, 1951, PLSDC.

94. See, for example, Lester del Rey to L. Sprague de Camp, June 23, 1952, PLSDC; L. Sprague de Camp to Edward Ferman, July 15, 1966, PLSDC.

95. De Camp, *Time and Chance*, 305; Glenn Lord to L. Sprague de Camp, March 19, 1965, PLSDC.

96. Untitled contract signed by P. M. Kuykendall, April 1, 1965, PLSDC.

97. Glenn Lord to L. Sprague de Camp, September 26, 1956, PLSDC; Kenneth Turan, "The Barbarian in Babylon: Conan's Greatest Challenge," *Savage Sword of Conan* no. 48, January 1980, 55–66 [originally published in *New West* magazine, August 27, 1979].

98. Many of these "unpublished" texts had, in fact, been published, albeit in amateur publications lacking professional, mass-market distribution.

99. Rusty Burke, "Glenn Lord: The Father of Howard Fandom," in *Anniversary: A Tribute to Glenn Lord and the Howard Collector*, ed. Dennis McHaney (Texas: Dennis McHaney, 2011); Sammon, *Conan the Phenomenon.*

100. 17 U. S. C. §23 (repealed 1976). By the 1960s, the renewal section had moved to §24 (the text remained unchanged).

101. Glenn Lord to L. Sprague de Camp, January 21, 1965, PLSDC.

102. De Camp, *Time and Chance*, 302.

103. L. Sprague de Camp to Glenn Lord, April 16, 1964, PLSDC.

104. Glenn Lord to L. Sprague de Camp, April 20, 1964, PLSDC. See also L. Sprague de Camp to Glenn Lord, October 11, 1964, PLSDC, and Glenn Lord to L. Sprague de Camp, October 23, 1964, PLSDC.

105. L. Sprague de Camp to Glenn Lord, January 1965, PLSDC.

106. L. Sprague de Camp to Glenn Lord, January 1965, PLSDC; L. Sprague de Camp to Kittie West, January 31, 1965, PLSDC.

107. Isaac Asimov to L. Sprague de Camp, January 29, 1961, PLSDC.

108. L. Sprague de Camp to Isaac Asimov, February 1, 1962, PLSDC.

109. L. Sprague de Camp to George Scithers, June 7, 1961, PLSDC; L. Sprague de Camp to Peter Schuyler Miller, November 28, 1964, PLSDC.

110. Though there are no records of de Camp's initial negotiations with Shaw, de Camp alludes to the deal in correspondence from August 1964 with both Lord and Schuyler Miller. See L. Sprague de Camp to Glenn Lord, August 22, 1964, PLSDC; L. Sprague de Camp to Peter Schuyler Miller, August 12, 1964, PLSDC. He discusses the number of volumes in L. Sprague de Camp to Edward Ferman, July 23, 1966, PLSDC.

111. L. Sprague de Camp to Lin Carter, January 27, 1965, PLSDC.

112. L. Sprague de Camp to Alan Nourse, May 3, 1965, PLSDC; L. Sprague de Camp to Frizt Leiber, October 30 1965, PLSDC.

113. L. Sprague de Camp to Glenn Lord, May 18, 1966, PLSDC; L. Sprague de Camp to Isaac Asimov, May 28, 1966, PLSDC; unsent letter from L. Sprague de Camp to Damon Knight, dated August 15, 1966, PLSDC. De Camp worked very closely with an attorney, Sydney Schwartz, in the suit, which de Camp oversaw and for which he served as liaison for the defendants.

114. L. Sprague de Camp to Lin Carter, January 27, 1965, PLSDC; L. Sprague de Camp to Isaac Asimov, August 4, 1966, PLSDC; unsent letter from de Camp to Damon Knight, dated August 15, 1966. Lord notifies de Camp of the specifics of the provision regarding print status in Lord to de Camp, May 3, 1965.

115. L. Sprague de Camp to Isaac Asimov, May 28, 1966, PLSDC; L. Sprage de Camp to Edward Ferman, September 6, 1967.

116. Robert E. Howard and L. Sprague de Camp, *Conan the Adventurer* (New York: Lancer Books, 1966).

117. Byron Roark, "Vultures over Cross Plains," *REH: Lone Star Fictioneer* 1.3 (Fall 1975): 40–45. Lord himself would later borrow Burke's language when characterizing de Camp: see Glenn Lord, "A Vulture Comes Up Snake Eyes," *The Cimmerian* 3.2 (February 2006): 24–26. For other examples, see Burke "De Camp vs. Howard"; James van Hise, untitled editorial, *Swords & Fantasy* no. 5 (January 2006): n.p.; Don Herron, acknowledgements, in *The Barbaric Triumph: A Critical Anthology on the Writings of Robert E. Howard,* ed. Don Herron (n.p.: Wildside Press: 2004), ix-x. For representations of the feud, see Turan, "The Barbarian in Babylon," 60–62; and Sammond, *Conan the Phenomenon,* 41–42.

118. L. Sprague de Camp to Glenn Lord, October 15, 1966, PLSDC; L. Sprague de Camp to Glenn Lord, October 26, 1966, PLSDC; L. Sprague de Camp to Glenn Lord, October 28, 1966, PLSDC; L. Sprague de Camp to Glenn Lord, November 7, 1966, PLSDC; Glenn Lord to L. Sprague de Camp, September 22, 1965, PLSDC; L. Sprague de Camp to Glenn Lord September 26, 1965, PLSDC; Glenn Lord to L. Sprague de Camp September 27, 1965, PLSDC; Glenn Lord to L. Sprague de Camp, May 29, 1966, PLSDC.

119. L. Sprague de Camp to Robert Heinlein, July 10, 1967, PLSDC.

120. L. Sprague de Camp to George Scithers, May 10, 1967, PLSDC; L. Sprague de Camp to Isaac Asimov, July 7, 1967, PLSDC.

121. L. Sprague de Camp to George Scithers, May 10, 1967, PLSDC; Glenn Lord to Larry Shaw, May 12, 1967, PLSDC.

122. L. Sprague de Camp to Isaac Asimov, May 16, 1968, PLSDC; L. Sprague de Camp to Lin Carter, Glenn Lord, and Björn Nyberg, June 8, 1968, PLSDC.

123. E.g., Scolari et al., *Transmedia Archaeology*, 3–4; Paolo Bertetti, "Transmedia Archaeology: Narrative Expansions Across Media before the Age of Convergence," in *The Routledge Companion to Transmedia Studies*, edited by Matthew Freeman and Renira Rampoazzo Gambarato (New York: Routledge, 2018); Colin Harvey, *Fantastic Transmedia: Narrative, Play and Memory across Science Fiction and Fantasy Storyworlds* (New York: Palgrave Macmillan, 2015). See also Gregory Steirer, "Narrative Worlds: A Provisional Definition," *Cultural Production*, October 2, 2011, http://culturalproductionblog.com/?p=480

124. L. Sprague de Camp and Lin Carter, *Conan of the Isles* (New York: Lancer Books, 1968).

125. Berle and de Camp, *Inventions, Patents, and Their Management*, 485.

126. Berle and de Camp, 486.

127. L. Sprague de Camp to Donald Schank, February 14, 1967, PLSDC; see also L. Sprague de Camp to Roy Capella, April 3, 1969, PLSDC.

128. L. Sprague de Camp to Lin Carter, Glenn Lord, and Björn Nyberg, June 8, 1968, PLSDC [this letter also functioned as a signed contract between the parties].

129. L. Sprague de Camp to Mark Ammerman, November 24, 1969, PLSDC; see also L. Sprague de Camp to Arthur Cooper, May 4, 1968, PLSDC.

130. L. Sprague de Camp to Glenn Lord, October 16, 1969, PLSDC.

131. L. Sprague de Camp to Glenn Lord, May 18, 1968, PLSDC.

132. L. Sprague de Camp to Glenn Lord, May 18, 1968, PLSDC.

133. L. Sprague de Camp to Glenn Lord, November 7, 1966, PLSDC; L. Sprague de Camp to Glenn Lord, Lin Carter, and Björn Nyberg, June 8, 1968, PLSDC; L. Sprague de Camp to Richard Gauger, January 13, 1970, PLSDC.

134. L. Sprague de Camp to Glenn Lord, May 18, 1968, PLSDC.

135. L. Sprague de Camp to Glenn Lord, May 18, 1968, PLSDC.

136. L. Sprague de Camp to Glenn Lord, May 18, 1968, PLSDC.

137. L. Sprague de Camp to Glenn Lord, May 18, 1968, PLSDC.

138. Zecheriah Chaffee Jr., "Unfair Competition," *Harvard Law Review* 53.8 (1940): 1301.

139. See, for example, *Time, Inc. v. Life Television.*, 123 F. Supp. 470 (1954); also, "The Protection Afforded Literary and Cartoon Characters," 352.

140. *Ely-Norris Safe Co. v. Mosler Safe Co.*, 7 F.2d 603, 604 (C.C.A. 2d, 1925).

141. Anthony Giddens, *The Constitution of Society: Outline of the Theory of Structuration* (Berkeley: University of California Press, 1986).

142. L. Sprague de Camp to Glenn Lord, September 14, 1966, PLSDC.

143. L. Sprague de Camp to Glenn Lord, September 14, 1966, PLSDC.

144. Glenn Lord to L. Sprague de Camp, May 13, 1966, PLSDC.

145. Glenn Lord to L. Sprague de Camp, May 13, 1968, PLSDC.

146. Lord, "Vulture Comes Up Snake Eyes."

147. L. Sprague de Camp to Glenn Lord, May 18, 1968, PLSDC.

148. L. Sprague de Camp to Glenn Lord, May 18, 1968, PLSDC.

149. L. Sprague de Camp to Glenn Lord, May 18, 1968, PLSDC.

150. L. Sprague de Camp to Lin Carter, Glenn Lord, and Björn Nyberg, June 8, 1968, PLSDC [this letter also functions as a contract].

151. L. Sprague de Camp to Lin Carter, Glenn Lord, and Björn Nyberg, June 8, 1968, PLSDC.

152. L. Sprague de Camp to Lin Carter, Glenn Lord, and Björn Nyberg, June 8, 1968, PLSDC.

153. L. Sprague de Camp to Lin Carter, Glenn Lord, and Björn Nyberg, September 8, 1969, PLSDC.

154. Lin Carter to Glenn Lord, September 9, 1969, PLSDC.

155. Glenn Lord to L. Sprague de Camp, October 10, 1969, PLSDC.

156. Glenn Lord to L. Sprague de Camp, November 3, 1969, PLSDC.

157. L. Sprague de Camp to Glenn Lord, November 12, 1969, PLSDC.

158. Surprisingly, none of the Syndicate members recognized the legal danger in selling rights to stories that had entered the public domain.

159. Kirby McCauley to L. Sprague de Camp, January 13, 1976, PLSDC.

160. Kirby McCauley to L. Sprague de Camp, January 13, 1976, PLSDC; Glenn Lord to L. Sprague de Camp, December 17, 1975, PLSDC.

161. Kirby McCauley to L. Sprague de Camp, January 13, 1976, PLSDC.

162. Henry Paul and Henry Paul Jr. to L. Sprague de Camp, January 27, 1976, PLSDC.

163. Dionne Searcey and James Hagerty, "Lawyerese Goes Galactic as Contracts Try to Master the Universe," *Wall Street Journal*, October 29, 2009, https://www.wsj.com/articles/SB125658217507308619

164. Jonathan Barnett, "Hollywood Deals: Soft Contracts for Hard Markets," *Duke Law Journal* 4.64 (2015): 607, 608. See also Gary McLaughlin, "Oral Contracts in the Entertainment Industry," *Virginia Sports & Entertainment Law Journal* (2000): 101–34.

165. Jerome Christensen, *America's Corporate Art: The Studio Authorship of Hollywood Motion Pictures* (Stanford: University of California Press, 2012). In U.S. television, Catherine Johnson has suggested that a similar kind of corporate author-function took shape in the 1980s with the "emergence of niche [cable] channels that were deliberately constructed with a distinct authorial voice and individual brand identity." Catherine Johnson, "The Authorial Function of the Television Channel: Augmentation and Identity," in *A Companion to Media Authorship*, eds. Johnathan Gray and Derek Johnson (Malden, MA: Wiley and Sons, 2013), 281.

166. Jonathan Gray and Derek Johnson, "Introduction: The Problem of Media Authorship," in *A Companion to Media Authorship*, eds. Johnathan Gray and Derek Johnson (Malden, MA: Wiley and Sons, 2013), 4.

Coda

1. Jessica Litman, "Copyright, Compromise, and Legislative History," *Cornell Law Review* 72.5 (1987): 860.

2. Melville Nimmer, "The Old Copyright Act as a Part of the New Act," *New York Law School Law Review* 22 (1976): 471.

3. Barbara Ringer, "First Thoughts on the Copyright Act of 1976," *New York Law School Law Review* 22 (1976): 479.

4. See, for example, *Shipman v. R.K.O. Radio Pictures*, 100 F.2d 533 (2d Cir. 1938), 537, where fair use is defined as "copying the theme or ideas rather than their expression."

5. Saul Cohen, "Fair Use in the Law of Copyright," *Copyright Law Symposium* 6 (1953): 48.

6. 17 U.S.C. § 107 (1976).

7. 17 U.S.C. § 107.

8. Pierre Leval, "Nimmer Lecture: Fair Use Rescued," *UCLA Law Review* 44.5 (1997): 1450.

9. Pierre Leval, "Toward a Fair Use Standard," *Harvard Law Review* 103 (1990): 1111.

10. *Campbell v. Acuff-Rose Music, Inc.*, 510 U.S. 569 (1994), 579.

11. Jiarui Liu, "An Empirical Study of Transformative Use in Copyright Law," *Stanford Technology Law Review* 22 (2019): 163–241; Clark Asay et al., "Is Transformative Use Eating the World?" *Boston College Law Review* 61 (2020): 905–70.

12. Brian Sites, "Fair Use and the New Transformative," *Columbia Journal of Law & Arts* 39 (2016): 518.

13. Matthew Bunker and Clay Calvert, "The Jurisprudence of Transformation: Intellectual Incoherence and Doctrinal Murkiness Twenty Years After *Campbell v. Acuff-Rose Music*," *Duke Law & Technology Review* 12.1 (2014): 125.

14. Liu, "An Empirical Study," 166.

15. Liu, 167.

16. 17 U.S.C. § 106 (1976).

17. Diane Zimmerman, "The More Things Change the Less They Seem 'Transformed': Some Reflections on Fair Use," *Journal of the Copyright Society of the U.S.A.* 46 (1998): 251–69, 261.

18. Mitchell Adams, "The Secret Commercial Identity of Superheroes: Protecting the Superhero Symbol," in *The Superhero Symbol: Media, Culture, and Politics*, ed. Liam Burke et al. (New Brunswick, NJ: Rutgers University Press, 2019), 93.

19. Adams, "Secret Commercial Identity of Superheroes," 93.

20. Mark Lemley, "The Modern Lanham Act and the Death of Common Sense," *Yale Law Journal* (1999): 1687–88.

21. Pub. L. 104–98, 109 Stat. 985 (1996); Pub. L. 109–312, 120 Stat. 1730.

22. E.g., Kathryn Foley, "Protecting Fictional Characters: Defining the Elusive Trademark-Copyright Divide," *Connecticut Law Review* 41 (2009): 921–61; Irene Calboli, "Overlapping Copyright and Trademark Protection: A Call for Concern and Action," *Illinois Law Review Slip Opinions* (2014): 25–34.

23. 17 U.S.C. § 512 (1998).

24. 17 U.S.C. § 512(c)(1)(C); 17 U.S.C. § 512(d)(3).

25. E.g., Jennifer Urban and Laura Quilter, "Efficient Process or Chilling Effects—Takedown Notices under Section 512 of the Digital Millennium Copyright Act," *Santa Clara High Technology Law Journal* 22.4 (2006): 621–93; Emily Asp, "Section 512 of the Digital Millennium Copyright Act: User Experience and User Frustration," *Iowa Law Review* 103 (2018): 751–83; Joel Matteson, "Unfair Misuse: How Section 512 of the DMCA Allows Abuse of the Copyright Fair Use Doctrine and How to Fix It," *Santa Clara High Technology Law Journal* 35.2 (2018): 1–22.

26. Urban and Quilter, "Efficient Process"; Jennifer Urban, Joe Karaganis, and Briana Schofield, *Notice and Takedown in Everyday Practice*, version 2 (Berkeley: BerkeleyLaw, 2017), https://files.osf.io/v1/resources/59m86/providers/osfstorage/578939e6594d9001f1859ef7?action=download&direct&version=2

27. Register of Copyrights, *Section 512 of Title 17* (Washington, DC: United States Copyright Office, 2020), https://www.copyright.gov/policy/section512/section-512-full-report.pdf, 1.

28. E.g., Margaret Chon, "Postmodern 'Progress': Reconsidering the Copyright and Patent Power," *DePaul Law Review* 43 (1993): 97–146; Elton Fukumoto, "The Author Effect After the 'Death of the Author': Copyright in a Postmodern Age," *Washington Law Review* 72.3 (1997): 903–34; Peter Jaszi, "Is There Such a Thing as Postmodern Copyright?" *Tulane Journal of Technology and Intellectual Property* 12 (2009): 105–21.

29. Pamela Samuelson, "Copyright and Freedom of Expression in Historical Perspective," *Journal of Intellectual Property Law* 10.2 (2003): 326, 327.

30. E.g., Martin Kretschmer, "Digital Copyright: The End of an Era," *European Intellectual Property Review* 25.8 (2003): 333–41; Lulin Gao, "Intellectual Property Rights in the Internet Era: The New Frontier," *John Marshall Review of Intellectual Property Law* 5 (2006): 589–95. See also Jerry Jie Hua, *Toward a More Balanced Approach: Rethinking and Readjusting Copyright Systems in the Digital Network Era* (Berlin: Springer, 2014).

31. Frederic Jameson, *Postmodernism, or, The Cultural Logic of Late Capitalism* (Durham: Duke University Press, 1992).

32. Gina Acosta, "Magic Shave Enlists Luke Cage in Fight for Close Shave," *Drug Store News*, May 25, 2016, https://drugstorenews.com/beauty/magic-shave-enlists-luke-cage-fight-close-shave; Brian Ashcraft, "*Assassin's Creed Unity* DLC Bundled with . . . Shaving Gel," *Kotaku*, November 5, 2014, https://kotaku.com/assassins-creed-unity-dlc-bundled-with-shaving-gel-1654876969

Bibliography

Works Cited

Acosta, Gina. "Magic Shave Enlists Luke Cage in Fight for Close Shave." *Dug Store News,* May 25, 2016, https://drugstorenews.com/beauty/magic-shave-enlists-luke-cage-fight-close-shave

Adams, Mitchell. "The Secret Commercial Identity of Superheroes: Protecting the Superhero Symbol." In *The Superhero Symbol: Media, Culture, and Politics,* edited by Liam Burke, Ian Gordon, and Angela Ndalianis, 89–104. New Brunswick, NJ: Rutgers University Press, 2019.

Aksoy, Asu, and Kevin Robins. "Hollywood for the 21st Century: Global Competition for Critical Mass in Image Markets." *Cambridge Journal of Economics* 16 (1992): 1–22.

Amers, J. B. "Mutuality in Specific Performance." *Columbia Law Review* 3.1 (1903): 1–12.

Ananny, Mike. *Networked Press Freedom: Creating Infrastructures for a Public Right to Hear.* Cambridge, MA: MIT Press, 2018.

Aoki, Keith. "Foreword: Innovation and the Information Environment: Interrogating the Entrepreneurs." *Oregon Law Review* 75 (1996): 1–18.

Arewa, Olufunmilayo. "Making Music: Copyright Law and Creative Processes." In *A Companion to Media Authorship,* edited by Jonathan Gray and Derek Johnson, 69–87. Malden, MA: Wiley-Blackwell, 2013.

Asay, Clark, Arielle Sloan, and Dean Sobczak. "Is Transformative Use Eating the World?" *Boston College Law Review* 61 (2020): 905–70.

Ashcraft, Brian. "*Assassin's Creed Unity* DLC Bundled with . . . Shaving Gel." *Kotaku,* November 5, 2014, https://kotaku.com/assassins-creed-unity-dlc-bundled-with-shaving-gel-1654876969

Asp, Emily. "Section 512 of the Digital Millennium Copyright Act: User Experience and User Frustration." *Iowa Law Review* 103 (2018): 751–83.

Baldwin, Peter. *The Copyright Wars: Three Centuries of Trans-Atlantic Battle.* Princeton: Princeton University Press, 2014.

Banks, Miranda. "The Picket Line Online: Creative Labor, Digital Activism, and the 2007–2008 Writers Guild of America Strike." *Popular Communication* 8 (2010): 20–33.

Banks, Miranda. *The Writers: A History of American Screenwriters and Their Guild.* New Brunswick: Rutgers, 2015.

Banks, Miranda, Bridget Conor, and Vicki Mayer. *Production Studies, The Sequel! Cultural Studies of Global Media Industries.* New York: Routledge, 2015.

Barlow, Robert. "The Wind That Is in the Grass: A Memoir of H. P. Lovecraft in Florida." In H. P. Lovecraft, *O Fortunate Floridian: H. P. Lovecraft's Letters to R. H. Barlow,* edited by S. T. Joshi and David Schultz, xxix–xxxvi. Tampa: University of Tampa Press, 2016.

Barnett, Jonathan. "Hollywood Deals: Soft Contracts for Hard Markets." *Duke Law Journal* 4.64 (2015): 605–69.

Bartholomew, Mark. "Advertising and the Transformation of Trademark Law." *New Mexico Law Review* 38 (2008): 1–48.

Bartholomew, Mark. "Protecting the Performers: Setting a New Standard for Character Copyrightability." *Santa Clara Law Review* 41 (2001): 341–78.

Bartow, Ann. "Fair Use and the Fairer Sex: Gender, Feminism, and Copyright Law." *American University Journal of Gender Social Policy and Law* 14 (2006): 551–84.

Basin, Ken. *The Business of Television.* New York: Routledge, 2018.

Bederman, David. *Custom as a Source of Law.* New York: Cambridge University Press, 2010.

Beebe, Baton. "*Bleistein,* The Problem of Aesthetic Progress, and the Making of American Copyright Law." *Columbia Law Review* 117 (2017): 319–97.

Bennett, Andrew. *The Author.* London: Routledge, 2005.

Berle, Alf K., and L. Sprague de Camp. *Inventions and Their Management,* 1st ed. Scranton, PA: International Textbook Company, 1937.

Berle, Alf K., and L. Sprague de Camp. *Inventions and Their Management,* corrected and revised printing. Scranton, PA: International Textbook Press, 1940.

Berle, Alf K., and L. Sprague de Camp. *Inventions and Their Management,* 2nd ed. Scranton, PA: International Textbook Company, 1947.

Berle, Alf K., and L. Sprague de Camp. *Inventions and Their Management,* 3rd ed. Scranton, PA: International Textbook Company, 1951.

Berle, Alf K., and L. Sprague de Camp. *Inventions, Patents, and Their Management.* New York: D. Van Nostrand Company, 1959.

Berruti, Massimo. "H. P. Lovecraft and the Anatomy of the Nothingness: The Cthulhu Mythos." *Semiotica* 150 (2004): 363–418.

Bertetti, Paolo. "Transmedia Archaeology: Narrative Expansions Across Media before the Age of Convergence." In *The Routledge Companion to Transmedia Studies,* edited by Matthew Freeman and Renira Rampoazzo Gambarato, 263–71. New York: Routledge, 2018.

Bilstad, T. Allan. *The Lovecraft Necronomicon Primer: A Guide to the Cthulhu Mythos.* Woodbury, MN: Llewellyn, 2009.

Birrell, Augustine. *Seven Lectures on the Law and History of Copyright in Books.* New York: Cassell and Co., 1899.

Blake, Harlan. "Employee Agreements Not to Compete." *Harvard Law Review* 73.4 (1960): 625–91.

Bloch, Robert. *Once Around the Bloch.* New York: Tor, 1993.

Bloch, Robert. *The Robert Bloch Companion: Collected Interviews—1969–1989.* Edited by Randall Larson. Mercer Island, WA: Starmont House, 1989.

Bloch, Robert. “The Shambler from the Stars.” In *Mysteries of the Worm*, edited by Robert M. Price, 16–23. Hayward, CA: Chaoism, 1991.

Bodie, Matthew. “Lessons from the Dramatists Guild for the Platform Economy.” *University of Chicago Legal Forum* (2017): 17–34.

Booker, M. *Comics Through Time: A History of Icons, Idols, and Ideas*, vol. 1. Santa Barbara: ABC-CLIO, 1914.

Bordwell, David, Janet Staiger, and Kristin Thompson. *The Classical Hollywood Cinema: Film Style & Mode of Production to 1960*. New York: Columbia University Press, 1985.

Boström, Mattias. *From Holmes to Sherlock*. Translated by Michael Gallagher. New York: Mysterious Press, 2017.

Bouchoux, Deborah. *Intellectual Property: The Law of Trademarks, Copyrights, Patents, and Trade Secrets*, 5th ed. Boston: Cengage Learning, 2016.

Bowrey, Kathy. *Copyright, Creativity, Big Media and Culture Value: Incorporating the Author*. New York: Routledge, 2022.

Boyle, James. “A Theory of Law and Information: Copyright, Spleens, Blackmail, and Insider Trading.” *California Law Review* 80.6 (1992): 1413–1540.

Boyle, James, and Jennifer Jenkins. *Intellectual Property: Law & The Information Society—Cases and Materials*, 4th ed. N.p.: n.p., 2018.

Braun, Joshua. *This Program Is Brought to You By . . . : Distributing Television News Online*. New Haven: Yale University Press, 2015.

Brenner, Missy. “Shadow of the Bat[mobile]: Character Copyright after *DC Comics v. Towle*.” *Santa Clara Law Review* 57 (2017): 481–517.

Broderick, John. “*Warner Bros. v. Nelson*: A Prelude to the De Havilland Law.” *Loyola of Los Angeles Entertainment Law Review* (2021): 111–49.

Brown, Ralph, and Robert Denicola. *Copyright: Unfair Competition, and Related Topics Bearing on the Protection of Works of Authorship*, 10th ed. New York: Thomson Reuters, 2009.

Brylawski, E. Fulton. “Protection of Characters—Sam Spade Revisited.” *Bulletin of the Copyright Society of the USA* 22 (1974): 77–103.

Buinicki, Martin. *Negotiating Copyright: Authorship and the Discourse of Literary Property Rights in Nineteenth-Century America*. New York: Routledge, 2006.

The Bulletin of the Authors' League of America 1.7 (November 1913).

Bunker, Matthew, and Clay Calvert. “The Jurisprudence of Transformation: Intellectual Incoherence and Doctrinal Murkiness Twenty Years After *Campbell v. Acuff-Rose Music*.” *Duke Law & Technology Review* 12.1 (2014): 93–128.

Burke, Rusty. “De Camp vs. Howard: Rewriting Conan.” In *The Fantastic Worlds of Robert E. Howard*, second printing, edited by James van Hise, 41–53. Yucca Valley, CA: James van Hise, 2001.

Burke, Rusty. “Glenn Lord: The Father of Howard Fandom.” In *Anniversary: A Tribute to Glenn Lord and the Howard Collector*, edited by Dennis McHaney, 31–40. N.p.: Dennis McHaney, 2011.

Burton, Robert. “Business Practices in the Copyright Field.” In *7 Copyright Problems Analyzed*, 87–117. N.p.: Commerce Clearing House, 1952.

Busse, Kristina. “Fan Labor and Feminism: Capitalizing on the Fannish Labor of Love.” *Cinema Journal* 54.3 (2015): 110–15.

Cain, James. “An American Authors' Authority.” *The Screen Writer*, July 1946, 1–18.

Calboli, Irene. “Overlapping Copyright and Trademark Protection: A Call for Concern and Action.” *Illinois Law Review Slip Opinions* (2014): 25–34.

Caldwell, John Thornton. *Production Culture: Industrial Reflexivity and Critical Practice in Film and Television*. Durham: Duke University Press, 2008.

Campbell, Ramsey. "Chasing the Unknown." In *Cold Print*, 9–19. London: Headline Feature, 1993.

Campbell, Ramsey, and August Derleth. *Letters to Arkham: The Letters of Ramsey Campbell and August Derleth, 1961–1971*. Edited by S. T. Joshi. Hornsea, UK: PS Publishing, 2014.

Caranicas, Peter. "Bibles Hold Tentpole Revivals: Biz Moves Backstory to Forefront." *Variety*, July 12, 2009, 5.

Carman, Emily, and Philip Drake. "Doing the Deal: Talent Contracts in Hollywood." In *Hollywood and the Law*, edited by Paul McDonald, Eric Hoyt, and Emily Carman, 209–34. London: BFI, 2015.

Carter, Lin. "H. P. Lovecraft: The Books." In H. P. Lovecraft and Divers Hands, *The Shuttered Room*, edited by August Derleth, 212–49. Sauk City, WI: Arkham House, 1959.

Carter, Lin. "H. P. Lovecraft: The Gods." In H. P. Lovecraft and Divers Hands, *The Shuttered Room*, edited by August Derleth, 250–67. Sauk City, WI: Arkham House, 1959.

Carter, Lin. *Lovecraft: A Look Behind the Cthulhu Mythos*. San Bernardino, CA: The Borgo Press, n.d.

Chaffee, Zecheriah, Jr. "Unfair Competition." *Harvard Law Review* 53.8 (1940): 1289–1321.

Chalker, Jack, and Mark Owings, eds. *The Science-Fantasy Publishers: A Critical and Bibliographic History*, 3rd ed. Westminster, MD: Mirage Press, 1991.

Chisholm, Darlene. "Asset Specificity and Long-Term Contracts: The Case of the Motion-Picture Industry." *Eastern Economic Journal* 19.2 (1993): 143–55.

Chon, Margaret. "Postmodern 'Progress': Reconsidering the Copyright and Patent Power." *DePaul Law Review* 43 (1993): 97–146.

Christensen, Jerome. *America's Corporate Art: The Studio Authorship of Hollywood Motion Pictures*. Stanford: University of California Press, 2012.

Christiansen, Erik. "Misbehaving." *Litigation* 46.2 (2020): 51–56.

Cieply, Michael. "Both Sides in Writers' Strike See New-Media Future at Stake." *New York Times*, December 1, 2007, C1, C4.

Clark, Vernon. "Dreams from Youharneth-Lahai." *REHUPA* 95 (January 1989): 42–47.

Cline, Sally. *Dashiell Hammett: Man of Mystery*. New York: Arcade Publishing, 2014.

Cloatre, Emilie. "Trips and Pharmaceutical Patents in Djibouti: An ANT Analysis of Socio-Legal Objects." *Social & Legal Studies* 17.2 (2008): 263–81.

Cockroft, Tom. "Addendum: Some Observations on the Carter Glossary." In H. P. Lovecraft and Divers Hands, *The Shuttered Room*, edited by August Derleth, 268–77. Sauk City, WI: Arkham House, 1959.

Cohen, Saul. "Fair Use in the Law of Copyright." *Copyright Law Symposium* 6 (1953): 43–73.

Cohn, Morris. "Old Licenses and New Uses: Motion Picture and Television Rights." *Law and Contemporary Problems* 19.2 (1954): 184–202.

Cole, Joe. "Trademark Terms under the Lanham Act and State Law." *Journal of Contemporary Legal Issues* 19 (2010): 70–77.

Colton, Edward. "Contracts in the Entertainment and Literary Fields." In *1953 Copyright Problems Analyzed*, edited by Theodore Kupferman, 139–58. Chicago: Commerce Clearing House, 1953.

Coombe, Rosemary. *The Cultural Life of Intellectual Properties: Authorship, Appropriation, and the Law*. Durham: Duke University Press, 1998.

Cowan, Dave, and Helen Carr. "Actor-Network Theory, Implementation, and the Private Landlord." *Journal of Law and Society* 35 (2008): 149–66.

Crafton, Donald. *Before Mickey: The Animated Film 1898–1928.* Chicago: University of Chicago Press, 2015.

"Dashiell Hammett Tour." *Trip Advisor.* Accessed August 24, 2021. https://www.tripadvisor.com/Attraction_Review-g60713-d559451-Reviews-Dashiell_Hammett_Tour-San_Francisco_California.html

de Camp, L. Sprague. "Conan's Ghost." In *The Spell of Conan,* edited by L. Sprague de Camp, 38–43. New York: Ace, 1980.

de Camp, L. Sprague. *Lovecraft: A Biography.* New York: Doubleday, 1975.

de Camp, L. Sprague. *Time and Chance: An Autobiography.* Hampton Falls, NH: Donald Grant, 1996.

de Camp, L. Sprague, and Lin Carter. *Conan of the Isles.* New York: Lancer Books, 1968.

Decherney, Peter. "Auteurism on Trial: Moral Rights and Films on Television." *Wisconsin Law Review* (2011): 273–330.

Decherney, Peter. *Hollywood's Copyright Wars.* New York: Columbia University Press, 2012.

De Munck, Bert. "Re-assembling Actor-Network Theory and Urban History." *Urban History* 44.1 (2017): 111–22.

Denicola, Robert. "The New Law of Ideas." *Harvard Journal of Law & Technology* 28.1 (2014): 195–236.

Derenberg, Walter. "Copyright No-Man's Land: Fringe Rights in Literary and Artistic Property, Part 1." *Journal of the Patent Office Society* 35.9 (1953): 627–57.

Derleth, August. "The Cthulhu Mythos." In H. P. Lovecraft and Others, *Tales of the Cthulhu Mythos,* edited by August Derleth, vii–xii. Sauk City, WI: Arkham House, 1969.

Derleth, August. "H. P. Lovecraft and His Work." In H. P. Lovecraft, *The Dunwich Horror and Others,* ix–xx. Sauk City, WI: Arkham House, 1963.

Derleth, August. "H. P. Lovecraft, Outsider." *River* 1.3 (June 1937): 88–89.

Derleth, August. "A Master of the Macabre." *Reading and Collecting* 1.9 (August 1937): 9–10.

Derleth, August. "Myths about Lovecraft." *The Lovecraft Collector* no. 2 [May 1949], facsimile edition, 1, 3–4. Cranston, RI: The Two Front Rooms, 2017.

Derleth, August. "A Note on the Cthulhu Mythos." In *The Trail of Cthulhu,* 245–48. Sauk City, WI: Arkham House, 1962.

Derleth, August. *Something Near.* Sauk City, WI: Arkham House, 1945.

Derleth, August. *Thirty Years of Arkham House: 1939–1969.* Sauk City, WI: Arkham House, 1970.

Derleth, August, and H. P. Lovecraft. *Essential Solitude: The Letters of H. P. Lovecraft and August Derleth,* vol. 1. Edited by David Schultz and S. T. Joshi. New York: Hippocampus Press, 2013.

Derleth, August, and H. P. Lovecraft. *Essential Solitude: The Letters of H. P. Lovecraft and August Derleth,* vol. 2. Edited by David Schultz and S. T. Joshi. New York: Hippocampus Press, 2013.

Derleth, August, and Donald Wandrei. "By Way of Introduction." In H. P. Lovecraft, *Beyond the Wall of Sleep,* ix–x. Sauk City, WI: Arkham House, 1943.

Derleth, August, and Donald Wandrei. "Howard Phillips Lovecraft: Outsider." In H. P. Lovecraft, *The Outsider and Others,* xi–xiv. Sauk City, WI: Arkham House, 1939.

de Valck, Marijke. *Film Festivals: From European Geopolitics to Global Cinephilia.* Amsterdam: Amsterdam University Press, 2007.

Durepos, Gabrielle, and Albert Mills. "Actor-Network Theory, ANTi-History and Critical Organizational Historiography." *Organization* 19.6 (2012): 703–21.

Eco, Umberto. "The Myth of Superman." *Diacritics* 2.1 (1972): 14–22.

Ede, Lisa, and Andrea A. Lunsford. "Collaboration and Concepts of Authorship." *PMLA* 116.2 (2001): 354–69.

Egan, James. "Dark Apocalyptic: Lovecraft's Cthulhu Mythos as a Parody of Traditional Christianity." *Extrapolation* 23.4 (1982): 362–76.

Edgerton, Gary. *The Columbia History of American Television.* New York: Columbia University Press, 2007.

Farley, Christine Haight. "The Lingering Effects of Copyright's Response to the Invention of Photography." *University of Pittsburgh Law Review* 65 (2004): 385–456.

Feldman, David. "Finding a Home for Fictional Characters: A Proposal for Change in Copyright Protection." *California Law Review* 78 (1990): 687–720.

Fine, Richard. *James M. Cain and the American Authors' Authority.* Austin: University of Texas Press, 1992.

Finklestein, Herman. "The Copyright Law—A Reappraisal." *University of Pennsylvania Law Review* 104.8 (1956): 1045–49.

Finn, Mark. *Blood and Thunder: The Life and Art of Robert E. Howard.* Austin, TX: MonkeyBrain Books, 2006.

Fisk, Catherine. *Working Knowledge: Employee Innovation and the Rise of Corporate Intellectual Property, 1800–1930.* Chapel Hill: University of North Carolina Press, 2009.

Fisk, Catherine. *Writing for Hire: Unions, Hollywood, and Madison Avenue.* London: Harvard University Press, 2016.

Fleury, James, Bryan Hikari Hartzheim, and Stephen Mamber, eds. *The Franchise Era: Managing Media in the Digital Economy.* Edinburgh: Edindburgh University Press, 2019.

Flynn, Jacob, Rebecca Giblin, and François Petitjean. "What Happens When Books Enter the Public Domain? Testing Copyright's Underuse Hypothesis across Australia, New Zealand, the United States and Canada." *University of New South Wales Law Journal* 42.4 (2019): 1215–53.

Foley, Kathryn. "Protecting Fictional Characters: Defining the Elusive Trademark-Copyright Divide." *Connecticut Law Review* 41 (2009): 921–61.

Fortmueller, Kate. *Below the Stars: How the Labor of Working Actors and Extras Shapes Media Production.* Austin: University of Texas Press, 2021.

Friedman, Lawrence. *Contract Law in America: A Social and Economic Case Study.* Madison: University of Wisconsin Press, 1965.

Friedman, Lawrence. *A History of American Law.* New York: Simon and Schuster, 1974.

Fritz, Ben. *The Big Picture: The Fight for the Future of Movies.* New York: Houghton Mifflin Harcourt, 2018.

Frohlich, Louis, and Charles Schwartz. *The Law of Motion Pictures Including the Law of the Theatre.* New York: Baker, Voorhis and Company, 1918.

Fromer, Jeanne, and Christopher Sprigman. *Copyright Law: Cases and Materials v. 1.0.* N.p.: n.p., 2019.

Frymus, Agata. "Jetta Goudal Versus the Studio System: Star Labour in 1920s Hollywood." *Historical Journal of Film, Radio, and Television* 39.1 (2019): 36–53.

Fukumoto, Elton. "The Author Effect After the 'Death of the Author': Copyright in a Postmodern Age." *Washington Law Review* 72.3 (1997): 903–34.

Fuller, Ken. *Hardboiled Activist: The Work and Politics of Dashiell Hammett.* N.p.: Praxis Press, 2017.

Fulwiler, William. "Three Quotations and a Fabrication." *Crypt of Cthulhu* 46 (1987): 13–14.

Gabilliet, Jean-Paul. *Of Comics and Men: A Cultural History of American Comic Books.* Translated by Bart Beaty and Nick Nguyen. Jackson: University of Mississippi Press, 2010.

Gamer, Michael. *Romanticism and the Gothic: Genre, Reception, and Canon Formation.* New York: Cambridge University Press, 2000.

Gamwell, Annie. Last Will and Testament of Annie Gamwell [January 10, 1940], *Wikisource,* n.d., https://en.wikisource.org/wiki/Will_of_Annie_Gamwell,_January_10,_1940

Gao, Lulin. "Intellectual Property Rights in the Internet Era: The New Frontier." *John Marshall Review of Intellectual Property Law* 5 (2006): 589–95.

Gard, Ronald, and Elizabeth Townsend Gard. "The Present (User-Generated Crisis) Is the Past (1909 Copyright Act): An Essay Theorizing the 'Traditional Contours of Copyright' Language." *Cardozo Arts & Entertainment Law Journal* 28 (2011): 455–99.

Geertz, Clifford. "Thick Description: Toward an Interpretive Theory of Culture." In *The Cultural Geography Reader,* 310–23. New York: Routledge, 2008.

Giblin, Rebecca. "A New Copyright Bargain? Reclaiming Lost Culture and Getting Authors Paid." *Columbia Journal of Law and Arts* (2018): 369–411.

Giddens, Anthony. *The Constitution of Society: Outline of the Theory of Structuration.* Berkeley: University of California Press, 1986.

Gillespie, Tarleton. *Wired Shut: Copyright and the Shape of Digital Culture.* London: MIT Press, 2007.

Ginsburg, Jane. "The Author's Place in the Future of Copyright." *Willamette Law Review* 45 (2008–2009): 381–94.

Ginsburg, Jane. "The US Experience with Formalities: A Love/Hate Relationship." In *Global Copyright: Three Hundred Years Since the Statute of Anne, from 1709 to Cyberspace,* edited by Lionel Bently, Uma Suthersanen, and Paul Torremans, 425–59. Chelthenham, UK: Edward Elgar, 2010.

Goldman, Abe. "The History of U.S.A. Copyright Law Revision, 1901–1954." Washington, DC: United States Government Printing Office, 1955.

Goldstein, Patrick. "It's a Super Deal." *Los Angeles Times,* September 1, 2009. https://www.latimes.com/archives/la-xpm-2009-sep-01-et-bigpicture1-story.html

Gordon, Ian. "Comics, Creators, and Copyright: On the Ownership of Serial Narratives by Multiple Authors." In *A Companion to Media Authorship,* edited by Jonathan Gray and Derek Johnson, 221–36. New York: Wiley, 2013.

Gordon, Ian. *Superman: The Persistence of an American Icon.* New Brunswick, NJ: Rutgers University Press, 2017.

Gordon, Robert. "Macaulay, MacNeil, and the Discovery of Solidarity and Power in Contract Law." *Wisconsin Law Review* (1985): 565–80.

Gordon, Sanford, and Gregory Huber. "Accountability and Coercion: Is Justice Blind When It Runs for Office?" *American Journal of Political Science* 48 (2004): 247–63.

Gordon, Wendy. "Introduction: Ralph Sharp Brown, Intellectual Property, and the Public Interest." *Yale Law Journal* 108 (1999): 1611–17.

Goulart, Ron. *The Funnies: 100 Years of American Comic Strips.* New York: Adams Pub., 1995.

Gray, Jonathan, and Derek Johnson. "Introduction: The Problem of Media Authorship." In *A Companion to Media Authorship*, edited by Johnathan Gray and Derek Johnson, 1–19. Malden, MA: Wiley and Sons, 2013.

Greenberg, Marc. *Comic Art, Creativity and the Law*, 2nd ed. Northamption, MA: Edward Elgar, 2022.

Groffman, Elliot. "Divisibility of Copyright: Its Application and Effect." *Santa Clara Law Review* 19, no. 1 (1979): 171–94.

Groth, Gary. "Pushing Marvel into the '80's: An Interview with Jim Shooter." *Comics Journal* 60 (1980): 55–86.

Haefele, John. *A Look Behind the Derleth Mythos: Origins of the Cthulhu Mythos.* N.p.: Cimmerian Press, 2014.

Hamilton, Ian. *Writers in Hollywood 1915–1951.* New York: Harper, 1990.

Hammett, Dashiell. "From the Memoirs of a Private Detective." In *Crime Stories and Other Writings*, 905–9. New York: Library Classics of the United States, 2001.

Hammett, Dashiell. *The Maltese Falcon.* In *Complete Novels*, 387–586. New York: Library Classics of the United States, 1999.

Hammett, Dashiell. *Selected Letters of Dashiell Hammett: 1921–1960.* Washington, DC: Counterpoint, 2001.

Handel, Jonathan. *Hollywood on Strike! An Industry at War in the Internet Age.* Los Angeles: Hollywood Analytics, 2011.

"Harold H. Knerr, A Cartoonist, 66." *New York Times*, July 9, 1949, 13.

Harris, Bruce. "Final Appellate Courts Overruling Their Own 'Wrong' Precedents: The Ongoing Search for Principle." *Law Quarterly Review* 118 (2002): 408–27.

Harvey, Colin. *Fantastic Transmedia: Narrative, Play and Memory across Science Fiction and Fantasy Storyworlds.* New York: Palgrave Macmillan, 2015.

Harwood, Tracy, and Tony Garry. "Co-creation and Ambiguous Ownership within Virtual Communities: The Case of the Machinima Community." *Journal of Consumer Behavior* 13.2 (2014): 148–56.

Hays, H. R. "Superman on a Psychotic Bender." *New York Times Book Review*, September 29, 1946, 35.

Heald, Paul. "How Copyright Keeps Works Disappeared." *Journal of Empirical Legal Studies* 11.4 (2014): 829–66.

Heald, Paul, and Christopher Buccafusco. "Do Bad Things Happen When Works Fall into the Public Domain." *Berkeley Technology Law Journal* 28.1 (2013): 1–43.

Hemmingway, Emma. *Into the Newsroom: Exploring the Digital Production of Regional Television News.* London: Routledge, 2007.

Henn, Harry. "Magazine Rights: A Division of Indivisible Copyright." *Cornell Law Review* 40.3 (1955): 411–74.

Herron, Don. Acknowledgments. In *The Barbaric Triumph: A Critical Anthology on the Writings of Robert E. Howard*, edited by Don Herron, ix–x. N.p.: Wildside Press, 2004.

Herron, Don. *The Dashiell Hammett Tour: Thirtieth Anniversary Guidebook.* San Francisco: Vince Emery Productions, 2010.

Hill, Anne Marie. "Work for Hire Definition in the Copyright Act of 1976." *Cornell Law Review* 74.3 (1989): 559–86.

Hilmes, Michele. "Never Ending Story: Authorship, Seriality, and the Radio Writers Guild." In *A Companion to Media Authorship*, edited by Jonathan Gray and Derek Johnson, 181–99. Malden, MA: Wiley-Blackwell, 2013.

Hilmes, Michele. *Radio Voices: American Broadcasting 1922–1952*. Minneapolis: University of Minnesota Press, 1997.

House, Meredith Annan. "*Marvel v. Kirby*: A Clash of Comic Book Titans in the Work Made for Hire Arena." *Berkeley Technology Law Journal* (2015): 933–64.

Howard, Isaac. *The Collected Letters of Doctor Isaac M. Howard.* N.p.: Robert E. Howard Foundation Press, 2011.

Howard, Robert E. "Beyond the Black River [Part 1]." *Weird Tales,* May 1935, 591–608.

Howard, Robert E. "Beyond the Black River [Part 2]." *Weird Tales,* June 1935, 734–54.

Howard, Robert E. "The Black Stranger." In *The Conquering Sword of Conan,* 101–73. New York: Del Rey/Ballantine Books, 2005.

Howard, Robert E. "By This Axe I Rule!" In *Kull: Exile of Atlantis,* 155–80. New York: Del Rey/Ballantine Books, 2006.

Howard, Robert E. *The Collected Letters of Robert E. Howard,* vol. 2. Edited by Rob Roehm and John Bullard. N.p.: Robert E. Howard Foundation Press, 2007.

Howard, Robert E. "The Frost-Giant's Daughter." Edited by L. Sprague de Camp. *Fantasy Fiction,* August 1953, 78–85.

Howard, Robert E. "The God in the Bowl." In *The Coming of Conan,* 39–58. New York: Del Rey/Ballantine Books, 2005.

Howard, Robert E. "Hour of the Dragon [Part 1]." *Weird Tales,* December 1935, 658–84.

Howard, Robert E. "Hour of the Dragon [Part 2]." *Weird Tales,* January 1936, 72–105.

Howard, Robert E. "Hour of the Dragon [Part 3]." *Weird Tales,* February 1936, 72–105.

Howard, Robert E. "Hour of the Dragon [Part 4]." *Weird Tales,* March 1936, 323–44.

Howard, Robert E. "Hour of the Dragon [Part 5]." *Weird Tales,* April 1936, 450–71.

Howard, Robert E. *The Hyborian Age,* facsimile ed. Tallahassee, FL: Skelos Press, 2015.

Howard, Robert E. "Jewels of Gwahlur." *Weird Tales,* March 1935, 299–327.

Howard, Robert E. "Phoenix on the Sword." *Weird Tales,* December 1932, 769–84.

Howard, Robert E. "Pool of the Black One." *Weird Tales,* October 1933, 447–66.

Howard, Robert E. "Queen of the Black Coast." *Weird Tales,* May 1934, 530–49.

Howard, Robert E. "Red Nails [Part 1]." *Weird Tales,* July 1936, 16–35.

Howard, Robert E. "Red Nails [Part 2]." *Weird Tales,* August/September 1936, 205–21.

Howard, Robert E. "Red Nails [Part 3]." *Weird Tales,* October 1936, 334–53.

Howard, Robert E. "The Scarlet Citadel." *Weird Tales,* January 1933, 51–77.

Howard, Robert E. "The Tower of the Elephant." *Weird Tales,* March 1933, 306–22.

Howard, Robert E., and H. P. Lovecraft. *A Means to Freedom: The Letters of H. P. Lovecraft and Robert E. Howard,* vol. 1. Edited by S. T. Joshi, David E. Schultz, and Rusty Burke. New York: Hippocampus Press, 2009.

Howard, Robert E., and L. Sprague de Camp. *Conan the Adventurer.* New York: Lancer Books, 1966.

Howell, Dorothy. *Intellectual Properties and the Protection of Fictional Characters: Copyright, Trademark, or Unfair Competition?* New York: Quorum Books, 1990.

Hua, Jerry Jie. *Toward a More Balanced Approach: Rethinking and Readjusting Copyright Systems in the Digital Network Era.* Berlin: Springer, 2014.

Hughes, Justin. "The Personality Interest of Artists and Inventors in Intellectual Property." *Cardozo Arts and Entertainment Law Journal* 16 (1998): 81–181.

Hurd, Jud. "Rudolph Dirks." *Cartoonist Profiles,* September 1974, 40–47.

Hutchins, Edwin. *Cognition in the Wild.* London: MIT Press, 1995.

Iansiti, Marco, and Roy Levien. *The Keystone Advantage: What the New Dynamics of Busi-*

ness Ecosystems Mean for Strategy, Innovation, and Sustainability. Boston: Harvard Business School Press, 2004,

Indick, Ben. "The Sage of Sauk City." *Science Fiction Studies* 22.1 (1995): 134–36.

Jameson, Frederic. *Postmodernism, or, The Cultural Logic of Late Capitalism*. Durham: Duke University Press, 1992.

Jamison, Anne. "Copyright and Collaboration: Wordsworth, Coleridge, and the Debate over Literary Property." *Romanticism* 17.2 (2011): 209–21.

Janicker, Rebecca. "Conveying Cosmicism: Visual Interpretations of Lovecraft." In *The Medial Afterlives of H. P. Lovecraft: Comic, TV, Film, Podcast, Games*, edited by Tim Lanzendörfer and Max José Dreysse Passos de Carvalho, 63–75. New York: Palgrave, 2023.

Jaszi, Peter. "Is There Such a Thing as Postmodern Copyright?" *Tulane Journal of Technology and Intellectual Property* 12 (2009): 105–21.

Jaszi, Peter. "On the Author Effect: Contemporary Copyright and Collective Creativity." *Cardozo Arts and Entertainment Law Journal* 10 (1991–1992): 293–320.

Jaszi, Peter. "On the Author Effect: Contemporary Copyright and Collective Creativity." In *The Construction of Authorship*, edited by Martha Woodmansee and Peter Jaszi, 29–36. Durham: Duke University Press, 1994.

Jaszi, Peter. "Toward a Theory of Copyright: The Metamorphoses of 'Authorship.'" *Duke Law Journal* (1991): 455–502.

Jaszi, Peter, and Martha Woodmansee. "Copyright in Transition." In *A History of the Book in America*, vol. 4, edited By Carl Kaestle and Janice Radway, 90–101. Chapel Hill: University of North Carolina Press, 2009.

Jenkins, Henry. *Convergence Culture: Where Old and New Media Collide*. New York: New York University Press, 2006.

Jenkins, Henry. "Fandom, Negotiation, and Participatory Culture." In *A Companion to Media Fandom and Fan Studies*, edited by Paul Booth, 13–26. Oxford: Wiley Blackwell, 2018.

Johnson, Catherine. "The Authorial Function of the Television Channel: Augmentation and Identity." In *A Companion to Media Authorship*, edited by Johnathan Gray and Derek Johnson, 275–91. Malden, MA: Wiley and Sons, 2013.

Johnson, Derek. *Media Franchising: Creative License and Collaboration in the Culture Industries*. New York: New York University Press, 2013.

Joshi, S. T. Forward. In *New Critical Essays on H. P. Lovecraft*, edited by David Simmons, xi–xvi. New York: Palgrave Macmillan, 2013.

Joshi, S. T., ed. *H. P. Lovecraft: Four Decades of Criticism*. Athens: Ohio University Press, 1980.

Joshi, S. T. *I Am Providence: The Life and Times of H. P. Lovecraft*, vol. 2. New York: Hippocampus Press, 2013.

Joshi, S. T. *Lovecraft and a World in Transition: Collected Essays on H.P. Lovecraft*. New York: Hippocampus Press, 2014.

Joshi, S. T. *The Rise and Fall of the Cthulhu Mythos*. Poplar Bluff, MO: Mythos Books, 2008.

Joshi, S. T. *The Rise, Fall, and Rise of the Cthulhu Mythos*. New York: Hippocampus Press, 2015.

Joshi, S. T., and David E. Schultz. Introduction. In H. P. Lovecraft, *O Fortunate Floridian: H. P. Lovecraft's Letters to R. H. Barlow*, edited by S. T. Joshi and David Schultz, x–xiii. Tampa: University of Tampa Press, 2016.

Joyce, Craig, Tyler Ochoa, Marshall Leaffer, and Michael Carroll. *Copyright Law*, 10th ed. Durham: Carolina Academic Press, 2016.

Kaplan, Benjamin. *Study No. 17: The Registration of Copyright*. In *Copyright Law Revision Studies Prepared for the Subcommittee on Patents, Trademarks, and Copyrights of the Committee on the Judiciary Studies 17–19*, 1–105. Washington, DC: Government Printing Office, 1960.

Karr, Chris J. "The Black Seas of Copyright: Arkham House Publishers and the H. P. Lovecraft Copyrights." *Chris J. Karr*, n.d., https://www.aetherial.net/lovecraft/arkham.html

Karydes, Karen Huston. *Hard-Boiled Anxiety: The Freudian Desires of Dashiell Hammett, Raymond Chandler, Ross MacDonald, and Their Detectives*. Salisbury, UK: Secant, 2016.

Kellman, Leon. "Legal Protection of Fictional Characters." *Brooklyn Law Review* 25 (1958): 3–19.

Kemper, Tom. *Hidden Talent: The Emergence of Hollywood Agents*. Berkeley: University of California Press, 2009.

Kidman, Shawna. *Comic Books Incorporated: How the Business of Comics Became the Business of Hollywood*. Oakland: University of California Press, 2019.

Kirzner, Israel. *Discovery and the Capitalist Process*. Chicago: University of Chicago Press, 1985.

Kirzner, Israel. *Perception, Opportunity, and Profit: Studies in the Theory of Entrepreneurship*. Chicago: University of Chicago Press, 1979.

Knight, Damon. *The Futurians*. New York: John Day, 1977.

Knudsen, Kristen. "Tomorrow Never Dies: The Protection of James Bond and Other Fictional Characters under the Federal Trademark Dilution Act." *Vanderbilt Journal of Entertainment Law & Practice* 2 (2000): 13–28.

Kobak, James, Jr. "Totem and Taboo: Growth of a Common Law of Unfair Competition in New York with Some Notes on the Effect of the Lanham Act of 1946." *New York Law Forum* 17 (1972): 941–82.

Koblas, Jack. *The Lovecraft Circle and Others as I Remember Them*. Eugenia, Canada: Battered Silicon Dispatch Box, 2012.

Kohnen, Melanie. "'The Power of Geek': Fandom as Gendered Commodity at Comic-Con." *Creative Industries Journal* 7.1 (2014): 75–78.

Kretschmer, Martin. "Digital Copyright: The End of an Era." *European Intellectual Property Review* 25.8 (2003): 333–41.

Ladas, Stephen. *The International Protection of Literary and Artistic Property*, vol. 2. New York: Macmillan, 1938.

La Farge, Paul. "The Complicated Friendship of H. P. Lovecraft and Robert Barlow, One of His Biggest Fans." *The New Yorker*, March 9, 2017. https://www.newyorker.com/books/page-turner/the-complicated-friendship-of-h-p-lovecraft-and-robert-barlow-one-of-his-biggest-fans

Lam, Anita. *Making Crime Television: Producing Entertaining Representations of Crime for Television Broadcast*. London: Routledge, 2013.

Laney, Francis. "The Cthulhu Mythology: A Glossary." In H. P. Lovecraft, *Beyond the Wall of Sleep*, 415–23. Sauk City, WI: Arkham House, 1943.

Laskin, Franklin. "All Rights Unreserved—The Author's Lost Property in Publishing and Entertainment." *Copyright Law Symposium* 7 (1954): 91–138.

Latour, Bruno. *An Inquiry into Modes of Existence: An Anthropology of the Moderns*. Translated by Catherine Porter. Cambridge, MA: Harvard University Press, 2013.

Latour, Bruno. *The Making of Law: An Ethnography of the Conseil d'État.* Translated by Marina Brilman and Alain Pottage. Cambridge: Polity, 2010.

Latour, Bruno, *Reassembling the Social: An Introduction to Actor-Network Theory.* New York: Oxford University Press, 2005.

Latour, Bruno. *We Have Never Been Modern.* Translated by Catherine Porter. Cambridge, MA: Harvard University Press, 1993.

Law, John. *After Method: Mess in Social Science Research.* New York: Routledge, 2004.

Law, John, and John Hassard. *Actor Network Theory and After.* Oxford: Blackwell Publishers/The Sociological Review, 1999.

Layman, Richard. *Discovering the Maltese Falcon and Sam Spade*, rev. ed. San Francisco: Vince Emery Productions, 2005.

Layman, Richard. *Shadow Man: The Life of Dashiell Hammett.* New York: Harcourt Brace Jovanovich, 1981.

Lemley, Mark. "The Modern Lanham Act and the Death of Common Sense." *Yale Law Journal* (1999): 1687–1715.

Leonardi, Paul. *Car Crashes without Cars.* Cambridge, MA: MIT Press, 2012.

Lern, Lydia, and Joseph Miller. *Intellectual Property Law: Cases & Materials*, 7th ed. Oregon City: Semaphore Press, 2021.

"'Lettie Lynton' Movie Ruled a Plagiarism." *New York Times*, January 18, 1936, 19.

Leval, Pierre. "Nimmer Lecture: Fair Use Rescued." *UCLA Law Review* 44.5 (1997): 1449–66.

Leval, Pierre. "Toward a Fair Use Standard." *Harvard Law Review* 103 (1990): 1105–36.

Levine, Sondra. "The Origins of the Lanham Act." *Journal of Contemporary Legal Issues* 19 (2010): 22–27.

Lévy, Maurice. *Lovecraft: A Study in the Fantastic.* Translated by S. T. Joshi. Detroit: Wayne State University Press, 1988.

Lewellyn, Karl. *The Bramblebush: On Our Law and Its Study.* Dobbs Ferry, NY: Oceana Publications, 1960.

Lieber, Fritz, Jr. "A Literary Copernicus." In H. P. Lovecraft, *The Shuttered Room*, 290–303. Sauk City, WI: Arkham House, 1959.

Lim, Tze Ping. "Beyond Copyright: Applying a Radical Idea-Expression Dichotomy to the Ownership of Fictional Characters." *Vanderbilt Journal of Entertainment and Technology Law* 21 (2018): 95–144.

Litman, Jessica. "Copyright, Compromise and Legislative History." *Cornell Law Review* 72.5 (1987): 857–904.

Liu, Jiarui. "An Empirical Study of Transformative Use in Copyright Law." *Stanford Technology Law Review* 22 (2019): 163–241.

Liu, Wenqi. "Reform of China's Copyright Legislation." *Journal of the Copyright Society of the U.S.A.* 59 (2011): 843–63.

Llewellyn, Karl. *The Common Law Tradition: Deciding Appeals.* Boston: Little, Brown and Co., 1960.

Long, Doris Estelle. "Rebooting Trademarks for the Twenty-first Century." *University of Louisiana Law Review* 495 (2011): 517–54.

Long, Frank. *Rim of the Unknown.* Sauk City, WI: Arkham House, 1972.

Long, Frank Belknap. *Howard Phillips Lovecraft: Dreamer on the Night Side.* Sauk City, WI: Arkham House, 1975.

Lord, Glenn. "A Vulture Comes Up Snake Eyes." *The Cimmerian* 3.2 (February 2006): 24–26.

Lorna, Margolis. "Supplement 1: Divisibility in Relation to Income Tax." In Abraham

Kaminstein, *Study No. 11: Divisibility of Copyright,* 39–56. In *Copyright Law Revision Studies Prepared for the Subcommittee on Patents, Trademarks, and Copyrights of the Committee on the Judiciary Studies 11–13,* 1–81. Washington, DC: Government Printing Office, 1960.

Louinet, Patrice. "Hyborian Genesis." In Robert E. Howard, *The Coming of Conan the Cimmerian,* 429–52. New York: Random House, 2002.

Louinet, Patrice. "Hyborian Genesis, Part III." In *The Conquering Sword of Conan,* by Robert E. Howard, 369–86. New York: Del Rey/Ballantine Books, 2005.

Lovecraft, H. P. "The Haunter in the Dark." In *Lovecraft: Collected Fiction,* vol. 3, Variorum Edition, edited by S. T. Joshi, 451–77. New York: Hippocampus Press, 2017.

Lovecraft, H. P. "Instructions in Case of Decease." In H. P. Lovecraft, *Collected Essays,* vol. 5, edited by S. T. Joshi, 237–40. New York: Hippocampus Press, 2006.

Lovecraft, H. P. *Last Will and Testament of H.P. Lovecraft* [August 12, 1912]. *Wikisource.* N.d. https://en.wikisource.org/wiki/Will_of_H.P._Lovecraft,_August_12,_1912

Lovecraft, H. P. *Letters to Robert Bloch and Others.* Edited by David Schultz and S. T. Joshi. New York: Hippocampus Press, 2015.

Lovecraft, H. P. *O Fortunate Floridian: H. P. Lovecraft's Letters to R. H. Barlow.* Edited by S. T. Joshi and David Schultz. Tampa: University of Tampa Press, 2016.

Lovecraft, H. P. *Selected Letters,* vol. 2. Edited by August Derleth and Donald Wandrei. Sauk City, WI: Arkham House, 1968.

Lovecraft, H. P. *Selected Letters,* vol. 3. Edited by August Derleth and Donald Wandrei. Sauk City, WI: Arkham House, 1971.

Lovecraft, H. P., and August Derleth. *The Lurker at the Threshold.* Sauk City, WI: Arkham House, 1945.

Lovecraft, H. P., and August Derleth. *The Survivor and Others.* Sauk City, WI: Arkham House, 1957.

Lovecraft, H. P., and E. Hoffman Price. "Through the Gates of the Silver Key." In *Lovecraft: Collected Fiction,* vol. 3, Variorum Edition, edited by S. T. Joshi, 276–323. New York: Hippocampus Press, 2017.

Lowe, Jim. *The Katzenjammer Kids,* June 25, 1998, http://www.dumboozle.com/katzies/katzdex

Lowell, Mark. "Lovecraft's Cthulhu Mythos." *The Explicator* 63.1 (2004): 47–50.

Macaulay, Stewart. "Elegant Models, Empirical Pictures, and the Complexities of Contract." *Law & Society Review* 11.3 (1977): 507–28.

Macaulay, Stewart. "Non-Contractual Relations in Business: A Preliminary Study." *American Sociological Review* 28.1 (1963): 55–67.

MacCulloch, Simon. "Lovecraft Waits Dreaming." In *Dissecting Cthulhu: Essays on the Cthulhu Mythos,* edited by S. T. Joshi, 37–42. Lakeland, FL: Miskatonic River Press, 2011.

Manual of Classification of Subjects of Invention of the United States Patent Office. Washington, DC: U.S. Government Printing Office, 1912.

Margolies, Alan. "Fitzgerald and Hollywood." In *The Cambridge Companion to F. Scott Fitzgerald,* edited by Ruth Prigozy, 189–208. New York: Cambridge University Press, 2002.

Markstein, Don. "The Katzenjammer Kids." Toonopedia (website), n.d., http://www.toonopedia.com/katzen.htm, accessed July 15, 2022.

Maroney, Terry. "(What We Talk About When We Talk About) Judicial Temperament." *Boston College Law Review* 61 (2020): 2085–2153.

Marrisa, Joseph. "Enter the Middleman: Legitimisation of Literary Agents in the

British Victorian Publishing Industry, 1875–1900." *Business History* 62.6 (2020): 940–59.
Marshall, Lee. *Bootlegging: Romanticism and Copyright in the Music Industry*. London: Sage, 2005.
Matteson, Joel. "Unfair Misuse: How Section 512 of the DMCA Allows Abuse of the Copyright Fair Use Doctrine and How to Fix It." *Santa Clara High Technology Law Journal* 35.2 (2018): 1–22.
Mazurek, Carl. "Through the Looking Glass: Photography and the Idea/Expression Dichotomy." *NYU Journal of Intellectual Property and Entertainment Law* 6 (2016): 278–309.
McAdams, Richard, and Eric Rasmusen. "Norms and the Law." In *Handbook of Law and Economics*, vol. 2, edited by A Mitchell Polinsky and Steven Shavell, 1574–1618. Amsterdam: Elsevier, 2007.
McClure, Daniel. "Trademarks and Unfair Competition: A Critical History of Legal Thought." *Trademark Reporter* 69 (1979): 305–56.
McIntyre, Phillip. "Copyright and Creativity: Changing Paradigms and the Implications for Intellectual Property and the Music Industry." *Media International Australia* 123.1 (2007): 82–94.
McKenna, Mark. "The Normative Foundations of Trademark Law." *Notre Dame Law Review* 82.5 (2007): 1839–1916.
McLaughlin, Gary. "Oral Contracts in the Entertainment Industry." *Virginia Sports & Entertainment Law Journal* (2000): 101–34.
Meikle, Kyle. *Adaptations in the Franchise Era, 2001–16*. New York: Bloomsbury, 2019.
Menne, Jeff. *Post-Fordist Cinema: Hollywood Auteurs and the Corporate Counterculture*. New York: Columbia University Press, 2019.
Merges, Robert. *American Patent Law: A Business and Economic History*. New York: Cambridge University Press, 2022.
Meyer, Timothy. "Codifying Custom." *University of Pennsylvania Law Review* 160 (2012): 995–1069.
Michael, Mike. *Actor-Network Theory: Trials, Trails and Translations*. London: Sage, 2017.
Miller, Peter Schuyler, and John Clark. "A Probable Outline of Conan's Career." In *The Hyborian Age*, facsimile ed., by Robert E. Howard, 17–22. Tallahassee, FL: Skelos Press, 2015.
Mills, M. A. "The Protection of Titles." *Bulletin of the Authors' League of America* 1.4 (August 1913): 3–5.
Molloy, Tim. "Blacklight Does Transmedia: The Future of Storytelling—and End of Lame Movie Tie-Ins." *The Wrap*, April 22, 2011, https://www.thewrap.com/transmedia-death-lame-movie-tie-ins-26718/
Mooney, William. *Dashiell Hammett and the Movies*. New Brunswick, NJ: Rutgers University Press, 2014.
Mosig, Dirk. "H. P. Lovecraft: Myth-Maker." In *Dissecting Cthulhu: Essays on the Cthulhu Mythos*, edited by S. T. Joshi, 104–12. Lakeland, FL: Miskatonic River Press, 2011.
Moss, Scott. "Bad Briefs, Bad Law, Bad Markets: Documenting the Poor Quality of Plaintiffs' Briefs, Its Impact on the Law, and the Market Failure It Reflects." *Emory Law Journal* 63 (2013): 58–125.
Murray, Chris, and Kevin Corstorphine. "Co(s)mic Horror." In *New Essays on H. P. Lovecraft*, edited by David Simmons, 157–92. New York: Palgrave, 2013.
Myrick, Kim, Jean Helms Mills, and Albert Mills. "History-making and the Academy

of Management: An ANTi-History Perspective." *Management & Organizational History* 8.4 (2013): 345–70.

Ndalianis, Angela. "Female Fans, Female Creators, and Female Superheroes: The Semiotics of Changing Gender Dynamics." In *The Routledge Companion to Gender and Sexuality in Comic Book Studies,* edited by Frederick Luis Aldama, 310–28. New York: Routledge, 2020.

"Needs of Such an Organization." *Bulletin of the Authors' League of America* 1 (April 1913): 7.

Nicholson, Margaret. *A Manual of American Copyright Practice.* London: Oxford University Press, 1945.

Nicholson, Margaret. *A Manual of Copyright Practice: For Writers, Publishers, and Agents,* 2nd ed. New York: Oxford University Press, 1956.

Nimmer, Melville. "The Old Copyright Act as a Part of the New Act." *New York Law School Law Review* 22 (1976): 471–76.

Nimmer, Melville, Paul Marcus, David Myers, and David Nimmer. *Cases and Materials on Copyright and Other Aspects of Entertainment Litigation including Unfair Competition, Defamation, Privacy,* 7th ed. Newark, NJ: Lexis Nexis, 2006.

Nolan, William. *Hammett: A Life at the Edge.* New York: St. Martin's Press, 1983.

Ogilvie, John. "Defining Computer Program Parts under Learned Hand's Abstractions Test in Software Copyright Infringement Cases." *Michigan Law Review* 91 (1992): 526–70.

O'Hara, Nicole. "The Arc and Art of Protecting Fictional Characters." *Legal Intelligence,* April 2, 2018. https://perma.cc/YH49-VLAX

Olson, D. H. "Of Donald Wandrei, August Derleth, and H. P. Lovecraft." In Donald Wandrei, *Don't Dream: The Collected Horror and Fantasy Fiction of Donald Wandrei,* 367–91. Minneapolis: Fedogan & Bremer, 1997.

Orlikowski, Wanda. "Sociomaterial Practices: Exploring Technology at Work." *Organization Studies* 28.9 (2007): 1435–48.

Oxford English Dictionary (website). Accessed August 5, 2022. Oxford University Press.

Pappalardo, Kylie, and Patricia Aufderheide. "Romantic Remixers: Hidden Tropes of Romantic Authorship in Creators' Attitudes about Reuse." *Cultural Science Journal* 12.1 (2020): 1–12.

Parks, Lisa. "Infrastructure." In *Keywords for Media Studies,* edited by Laurie Ouellette and Jonathan Gray, 106–7. New York: New York University Press, 2017.

Peers, Martin. "Disney Marvels at Superhero Potential." *Wall Street Journal,* September 1, 2009, C10.

Perren, Alisa, and Gregory Steirer. *The American Comic Book Industry and Hollywood.* London: Bloomsbury, 2021.

Peterson, Theodore. *Magazines in the Twentieth Century.* Urbana: University of Illinois Press, 1964.

Ponterotto, Joseph. "Brief Note on the Origins, Evolution, and Meaning of the Qualitative Research Concept 'Thick Description.'" *Qualitative Reporter* 11.3 (2006): 538–49.

Port, Kenneth. "The Expansion Trajectory: Trademark Jurisprudence in the Modern Age." *Journal of the Patent and Trademark Office Society* 92.4 (2010): 474–97.

Port, Kenneth. "The Illegitimacy of Trademark Incontestability." *Indiana Law Review* 23 (1993): 519–87.

Pottage, Alain. *Figures of Invention: A History of Modern Patent Law.* Oxford: Oxford University Press, 2010.

Pound, Roscoe. "Theory of Judicial Decision III. A Theory of Judicial Decision for Today." *Harvard Law Review* 36.8 (1923): 940–59.

Price, E. Hoffmann. Introduction. In *The Last Celt: A Biobibliography of Robert E. Howard, the Creator of Conan*, edited by Glenn, Lord, 9–16. New York: Berkley Publishing, 1976.

Price, Robert M. "Lovecraft's 'Artificial Mythology.'" In *An Epicure in the Terrible: A Centennial Anthology of Essays in Honor of H. P. Lovecraft*, edited by David Schultz and S. T. Joshi, 247–56. London: Associated University Presses, 1991.

Price, Robert M. "The Revision Mythos." In *H. P. Lovecraft and the Cthulhu Mythos*, 103–12. San Bernardino, CA: Borgo Press, 1990.

"The Protection Afforded Literary and Cartoon Characters through Trademark, Unfair Competition, and Copyright." *Harvard Law Review* 68.2 (1954): 349–63.

Quinlan, Andrea. "Visions of Public Safety, Justice, and Healing: The Making of the Rape Kit Backlog in the United States." *Social & Legal Studies* 29.2 (2019): 225–45.

Rampant, James. "The Manga Polysystem: What Fans Want, Fans Get." In *Manga: An Anthology of Global and Cultural Perspectives*, edited by Toni Johnson-Woods, 221–32. London: Continuum, 2010.

Ransom, Harry. *The First Copyright Statute: An Essay on an Act for the Encouragement of Learning*. Austin: University of Texas Press, 1956.

"Recent Cases." *University of Pennsylvania Law Review* 73.1 (1924): 96–113.

Register of Copyrights. *Section 512 of Title 17*. Washington, DC: United States Copyright Office, 2020. https://www.copyright.gov/policy/section512/section-512-full-report.pdf

Reisman, Michael. "The Cult of Custom in the Late 20th Century." *California Western International Law Journal* 17.1 (1987): 133–45.

Reynolds, B. M. Untitled letter. *Weird Tales* 26.5 (November 1935): 652.

Rigamonti, Cyril. "Deconstructing Moral Rights." *Harvard International Law Journal* 47.2 (2006): 353–412.

Ringer, Barbara. "First Thoughts on the Copyright Act of 1976." *New York Law School Law Review* 22 (1976): 477–95.

Ringer, Barbara. *Study No. 31: Renewal of Copyright*. In *Copyright Law Revision Studies Prepared for the Subcommittee on Patents, Trademarks, and Copyrights of the Committee on the Judiciary Studies 29–31*, 105–224. Washington, DC: U.S. Government Printing Office, 1961.

Roark, Byron. "Vultures over Cross Plains." *REH: Lone Star Fictioneer* 1.3 (Fall 1975): 40–45.

Robert, Daphne. *The New Trade-Mark Manual: A Handbook on Protection of Trade-Marks in Interstate Commerce*. Washington, DC: Bureau of National Affairs, 1947.

Robin, Neal. "Hit Losers: The Good (Faith) Fight for Net-Profits Payments from Blockbuster Hollywood Productions." *Case Western Reserve Journal of Law, Technology, & The Internet* (2012–2013): 445–82.

Roehm, Rob. "The Legend of the Trunk." *REH: Two-Gun Raconteur*, January 14–April 17, 2014. http://www.rehtwogunraconteur.com/the-legend-of-the-trunk-part-1/

Rosen, Gary. *Adventures of a Jazz Age Lawyer: Nathan Burkan and the Making of American Popular Culture*. Berkeley: University of California Press, 2020.

Roussel, Violaine. *Representing Talent: Hollywood Agents and the Making of Movies*. Chicago: University of Chicago Press, 2017.

Ruber, Peter. "Introduction: The Un-Demonizing of August Derleth." In *Arkham's Masters of Horror: A 60th Anniversary Anthology Retrospective of the First 30 Years of Arkham House*, edited by Peter Ruber, 3–33. N.p.: Arkham House Publishers, 2000.

"Rudolph Dirks." Lambiek Comiclopedia (website), June 21, 2021. https://www.lambiek.net/artists/d/dirks_r.htm

"Rudolph Dirks." Wikipedia, n.d. https://en.wikipedia.org/wiki/Rudolph_Dirks, accessed July 18, 2022.

Rules and Regulations for the Registration of Claims to Copyright (Copyright Office Bulletin No. 15). Washington, DC: U.S. Government Printing Office, 1913.

Said, Zarh. "Fixing Copyright in Characters: Literary Perspectives on a Legal Problem." *Cardozo Law Review* 35 (2013): 769–829.

Saint-Amour, Paul. *The Copywrights: Intellectual Property and the Literary Imagination.* Ithaca: Cornell University Press, 2003.

Salter, Anastasia, and Mel Stanfill. *A Portrait of the Auteur as Fanboy: The Construction of Authorship in Transmedia Franchises.* Jackson: University Press of Mississippi, 2020.

Sammon, Paul. *Conan: The Phenomenon.* Milwaukie, OR: Dark Horse, 2013.

Sams, Ed. *Dashiell Hammett's San Francisco.* N.p.: CreateSpace, 2014.

Samuels, Edward. "The Idea-Expression Dichotomy in Copyright Law." *Tennessee Law Review* vol. 56 (1989): 321–463.

Samuelson, Pamela. "Copyright and Freedom of Expression in Historical Perspective." *Journal of Intellectual Property Law* 10.2 (2003): 319–44.

Sanders, Kurt. *Intellectual Property and the Law of Ideas.* London: Routledge, 2021.

Sanders, Peter, Rebecca Dana, and Sam Schechner. "Hollywood Is Going Off Script as Writers Gamble for Digital Pie." *Wall Street Journal,* November 6, 2007, B8.

Sarraute, Raymond. "Current Theory on the Moral Right of Authors and Artists under French Law." *American Journal of Comparative Law,* 16.4 (1968): 465–86.

Scafidi, Susan. "Intellectual Property and Cultural Products." *Boston University Law Review* 81 (2001): 793–842.

Scaggs, John. *Crime Fiction.* New York: Routledge, 2005.

Schatz, Thomas. *The Genius of the System: Hollywood Filmmaking in the Studio Era.* New York: Henry Holt and Company, 1986.

Schechter, Frank. *The Historical Foundations of the Law Relating to Trade-marks.* Clark, NJ: Lawbook Exchange, 2012.

Schechter, Roger, and John Thomas. *Intellectual Property: The Law of Copyrights, Patents and Trademarks.* St. Paul, MN: West Group, 2003.

Schienke, Gregory. "The Spawn of Learned Hand—A Reexamination of Copyright Protection and Fictional Characters: How Distinctly Delineated Must the Story Be Told?" *Marquette Intellectual Property Law Review* 9.1 (2005): 63–90.

Schultz, David. "The Origin of Lovecraft's 'Black Magic' Quote." In *Dissecting Cthulhu: Essays on the Cthulhu Mythos,* edited by S. T. Joshi, 216–23. Lakeland, FL: Miskatonic River Press, 2011.

Schweitzer, Darrell. *Conan's World and Robert E. Howard.* San Bernardino, CA: Borgo Press, 1978.

Scolari, Carlos, Paolo Bertteti, and Matthew Freeman. *Transmedia Archaeology: Storytelling in the Borderlines of Science Fiction, Comics and Pulp Magazines.* New York: Palgrave, 2014.

Scott, Geoffrey, and Karen Maul. "Kryptonite, Duff Beer and the Protection of Fictional Characters and Products in the Global Community." *Monash University Law Review* 38.1 (2012): 228–82.

Scott, Suzanne. "'Cosplay Is Serious Business': Gendering Material Fan Labor on *Heroes of Cosplay.*" *Cinema Journal* 54.3 (2015): 146–54.

Scott, Suzanne. "Who's Steering the Mothership? The Role of the Fanboy Auteur in Transmedia Storytelling." In *The Participatory Cultures Handbook,* edited by Aaron

Delwiche and Jennifer Jacobs Henderson, 43–52. London: Taylor and Francis, 2012.

Searcey, Dionne, and James Hagerty. "Lawyerese Goes Galactic as Contracts Try to Master the Universe." *Wall Street Journal*, October 29, 2009. https://www.wsj.com/articles/SB125658217507308619

Sederholm, Carl. "H. P. Lovecraft, Heavy Metal, and Cosmicism." *Rock Music Studies* 3.3 (2016): 266–80.

Sederholm, Carl, and Jeffrey Andrew Weinstock. *The Age of Lovecraft*. London: University of Minnesota Press, 2016.

Shanks, Jeffrey. "Introduction to the 2015 Fascimile Edition: Constructing an Age Undreamed Of." In *The Hyborian Age*, facsimile ed., by Robert E. Howard, iii–xii. Tallahassee, FL: Skelos Press, 2015.

Sheridan, Martin. *Comics and Their Creators: Life Stories of American Cartoonists*. N.p.: Hale, Cushman & Flint, 1942.

Sheridan, Martin. "The Kids that Never Grew Up." *The Quill*, October 1958, 11–12, 18.

Sherman, Brad, and Lionel Bently. *The Making of Intellectual Property Law: The British Experience, 1760–1911*. New York: Cambridge University Press, 1999.

Sherman, Philip. *Leo Marguiles: Giant of the Pulps*. N.p.: Altus Press, 2017.

Siegel, Jerry (writer), and Joe Shuster, Jack Burnley, and Wayne Boring (artists). *The Golden Age Superman Omnibus*, vol. 1. Burbank, CA: DC Comics, 2013.

Simmons, David, ed. *New Critical Essays on H. P. Lovecraft*. New York: Palgrave Macmillan, 2013.

Sisk, Gregory, and Michael Heise. "Ideology All the Way Down: An Empirical Study of Establishment Clause Decisions in the Federal Courts." *Michigan Law Review* 110 (2012): 1201–63.

Sites, Brian. "Fair Use and the New Transformative." *Columbia Journal of Law & Arts* 39 (2016): 513–50.

Sobel, Lionel. "The Law of Ideas, Revisited." *UCLA Entertainment Law Review* 1.1 (1994): 9–94.

Solberg, Thorvald. *Report on Copyright Legislation, by the Register of Copyrights*. Washington, DC: U.S. Government Printing Office, 1904.

Solomon, Stefan. *William Faulkner in Hollywood: Screenwriting for the Studios*. Athens: University of Georgia Press, 2017.

Sorenson, Olav, and David Waguespack. "Social Structure and Exchange: Self-confirming Dynamics in Hollywood." *Administrative Science Quarterly* 51.4 (2006): 560–89.

Sprigman, Christopher. "Reform(aliz)ing Copyright." *Stanford Law Review* 57.2 (2004): 485–568.

Spring, Samuel. *Risks and Rights in Publishing, Radio, Television, Motion Pictures, Advertising, and the Theater*. New York: W. W. Norton & Co., 1952.

Steirer, Gregory. "Narrative Worlds: A Provisional Definition." *Cultural Production* (blog), October 2, 2011, http://culturalproductionblog.com/?=480

Stendell, Leanne. "Fanfic and Fan Fact: How Current Copyright Law Ignores the Reality of Copyright Owner and Consumer Interests in Fan Fiction." *Sothern Methodist University Law Review* 58 (2005): 1551–82.

Stolte, Keith. "A Response to Jerome Gilson's Call for an Overhaul of the Lanham Act." *Trademark Reporter* 94 (2004): 1335–59.

Stone, Harlan. "The 'Mutuality' Rule in New York." *Columbia Law Review* 16.6 (1916): 443–64.

Stropper, Michael. "The Transition to Flexible Specialisation in the US Film Industry: External Economies, the Division of Labour, and the Crossing of Industrial Divides." *Cultural Journal of Economics* 13 (1989): 273–305.

Strum, Eric. "Hollywood Accounting: Profit Participation and the Use of Mediation as a Mode of Resolving These Disputes." *Cardozo Journal of Conflict Resolution* (2016–2017): 457–87.

Sumner, David. *The Magazine Century: American Magazines Since 1900.* New York: Peter Lang, 2010.

Tannenbaum, David. "Enforcement of Personal Service Contracts in the Entertainment Industry." *California Law Review* 42 (1954): 18–27.

Thompson, John. *Books in the Digital Age: The Transformation of Academic and Higher Education Publishing in Britain and the United States.* Malden, MA: Polity, 2005.

Thompson, John. *Merchants of Culture: The Publishing Business in the Twenty-First Century.* Malden, MA: Polity, 2010.

Thornham, Helen. *Ethnographies of the Videogame: Gender, Narrative, and Praxis.* London: Routledge, 2016.

"Thou art the Man!" *Ellery Queen's Mystery Magazine* 10.44 (July 1947): 4–5.

Threedy, Debora. "Legal Archaeology: Excavating Cases, Reconstructing Context." *Tulsa Law Review* (2006): 1197–1238.

Tibbets, John. *The Gothic Imagination: Conversations on Fantasy, Horror, and Science Fiction in the Media.* New York: Palgrave, 2011.

Train, Arthur. *My Day in Court.* New York: Charles Scribner's Sons, 1939.

Turan, Kenneth. "The Barbarian in Babylon: Conan's Greatest Challenge." *Savage Sword of Conan* no. 48 (January 1980): 55–66.

Tushnet, Rebecca. "Fixing Incontestability: The Next Frontier." *Boston University Journal of Science and Technology Law* 23 (2017): 434–55.

Ulin, Jeffrey. *The Business of Media Distribution: Monetizing Film, TV, and Video Content in an Online World*, 3rd ed. New York: Routledge, 2019.

Umbreit, Kenneth. "A Consideration of Copyright." *University of Pennsylvania Law Review* 87 (1939): 932–53.

Untitled article. *The Bulletin of the Authors' League of America* 1.1 (April 1913): 2.

Urban, Jennifer, Joe Karaganis, and Briana Schofield. *Notice and Takedown in Everyday Practice*, version 2. Berkeley: BerkeleyLaw, 2017. https://files.osf.io/v1/resources/59m86/providers/osfstorage/578939e6594d9001f1859ef7?action=download&direct&version=2

Urban, Jennifer, and Laura Quilter. "Efficient Process or Chilling Effects—Takedown Notices under Section 512 of the Digital Millennium Copyright Act." *Santa Clara High Technology Law Journal* 22.4 (2006): 621–93.

Vaidhyanathan, Siva. *Copyrights and Copywrongs: The Rise of Intellectual Property and How It Threatens Creativity.* New York: New York University Press, 2001.

van Hise, James. Untitled editorial. *Swords & Fantasy* no. 5 (January 2006): n.p.

van Oorschot, Irene. *The Law Multiple: Judgment and Knowledge in Practice.* Cambridge: Cambridge University Press, 2021.

Varmer, Borge. "Study No. 13: Works Made for Hire and On Commission." In *Copyright Law Revision: Studies Prepared for the Subcommittee on Patents, Trademarks, and Copyrights, 86th Congress, 2d session*, 123–55. Washington, DC: U.S. Government Printing Office, 1960.

Walsh, Jim. "Classics of the Comics: *The Katzenjammers*." *Hobbies—The Magazine for Collectors*, April 1953, 146–51, 163.

Walsh, Thomas. *Playwrights and Power: The Making of the Dramatists Guild.* Hanover, NH: Smith & Kraus, 2016.

Wandrei, Donald. Brief. *In the Manner of the Estate of August Derleth,* Sauk County, Wisconsin, County Court, Probate Branch, July 19, 1974.

Ward, Nathan. *The Lost Detective: Becoming Dashiell Hammett.* New York: Bloomsbury, 2015.

Warner, Harry. *All Our Yesterdays: An Informal History of Science Fiction Fandom in the Forties.* Chicago: Advent, 1969.

Wasserstrom, Alfred. "Magazine, Newspaper and Syndication Problems." In *1953 Copyright Problems Analyzed,* edited by Theodore Kupferman, 159–76. Chicago: Commerce Clearning House, 1953.

Wedgeworth, Robert, and Barbara Ringer. "The Library of Congress Advisory Committee on Copyright Registration and Deposit—Letter and Report of the Co-Chairs." *Columbia-VLA Journal of Law and the Arts* 17 (1993): 271–310.

Wetzel, George. "Copyright Problems of the Lovecraft Literary Estate." In *Collected Essays on H.P. Lovecraft and Others.* Cabin John, MD: Wildside Press, 2015. Kindle version.

Wetzel, George. "The Cthulhu Mythos: A Study." In *H. P. Lovecraft: Four Decades of Criticism,* edited by S. T. Joshi, 79–95. Athens: Ohio University Press, 1980.

Wetzel, George. *The Lovecraft Scholar.* Darien, CT: Hobgoblin Press, 1983.

Wetzel, George. "Lovecraft's Literary Executor." In *Collected Essays on H. P. Lovecraft and Others.* Cabin John, MD: Wildside Press, 2015. Kindle version.

"What Is Your Opinion of August Derleth?" *R/Lovecraft,* Reddit, 2010, https://www.reddit.com/r/Lovecraft/comments/gvmej/what_is_your_opinion_of_august_derleth/

"What Trademark Covers." *Digital Media Law Project,* September 10, 2022, https://www.dmlp.org/legal-guide/what-trademark-covers

Whiteside, Thomas. *The Blockbuster Complex: Conglomerates, Show Business, and Book Publishing.* Middletown, CT: Wesleyan University Press, 1981.

Winchester, Mark. "Litigation and Early Comic Strips: The Lawsuits of Outcault, Dirks and Fisher." *Inks,* May 1995, 16–25.

Woodmansee, Martha. "The Genius and the Copyright: Economic and Legal Conditions of the Emergence of the 'Author.'" *Eighteenth-Century Studies* 17.4 (1984): 425–48.

Woodmansee, Martha. "On the Author Effect: Recovering Collectivity." *Cardozo Arts and Entertainment Law Journal* 10 (1991–1992): 279–92.

Woodmansee, Martha, and Peter Jaszi, eds. *The Construction of Authorship: Textual Appropriation in Law and Literature.* Durham: Duke University Press, 1994.

Zafiarau, Stephen. "Reputation Work in Selling Film and Television: Life in the Hollywood Talent Industry." *Qualitative Sociology* 31 (2008): 99–127.

Zeitchik, Steven. "Can Corporate Hollywood Make Peace with Voice-Minded Directors? The Fight Continues with 'Star Wars.'" *Los Angeles Times,* June 21, 2017, https://www.latimes.com/entertainment/movies/la-et-mn-star-wars-lord-miller-20170621-story.html

Zemer, Lior. "'We-Intention' and the Limits of Copyright." *Cardozo Arts & Entertainment Law Journal* 24.1 (2006): 99–120.

Zimmerman, Diane. "The More Things Change the Less They Seem 'Transformed': Some Reflections on Fair Use." *Journal of the Copyright Society of the U.S.A.* 46 (1998): 251–69.

Legal Cases

Atlas Mfg. Co. v. Street and Smith, 204 Fed. 398 (C.C.A. 1913).
Baker v. Selden, 101 U.S. 99 (1880).
Bleistein v. Donaldson Lithographing Company, 188 U.S. 239 (1903), 250.
Burrows-Giles Lithographic Company v. Sarony, 111 U.S. 53 (1884).
Campbell v. Acuff-Rose Music, Inc., 510 U.S. 569 (1994).
Canal Co. v. Clark, 80 U.S. 311 (1872).
Cinema Corporation of America v. De Mille, 149 Misc. 358 (N.Y. 1933).
Clark Paper 7 Mfg. Co. v. Stenacher, 236 N.Y. 312 (1923).
Curwood v. Affiliated Distributors, 283 F. 219, 222–223 (S.D.N.Y. 1922).
Dam v. Kirk La Shelle Co., 175 F. 902 (2nd Cir. 1910).
Detective Comics v. Bruns Publications, 28 F. Supp. 399 (S.D.N.Y. 1939), *rev'd*, 111 F.2d 432 (2d Cir. 1940).
Dymow v. Bolton, 11. F.2d 690 (2nd Cir. 1926).
Ely-Norris Safe Co. v. Mosler Safe Co., 7 F.2d 603 (2d Cir. 1925).
Esquire, Inc. v. Varga Enterprises, Inc., 81 F. Supp. 306 (N.D. Ill. 1948).
Fairbanks v. Winik, 201 N.Y.S. 487 (1923).
Fendler v. Morosco, 253 N.Y. 281 (1930).
Fleischer Studios, Inc. v. Ralph A. Freundlich, Inc., 73 F. 2d 276 (2d Cir. 1934).
Fox Film Corp. v. Doyal, 286 U.S. 123 (1932).
Gaiman v. McFarlane, 360 F.3d 644 (7th Cir. 2004).
Hammett v. Warner Bros. Pictures, 84 F. Supp. 28 (S.D.N.Y. 1949), *aff'd* 176 F.2d 145 (2d Cir. 1949).
Hanover Star Milling Co. v. Metcalf, 240 U.S., 403 (1916).
Hart v. Community School Bd of Brooklyn, 383 F. Supp. 699 (E.D.N.Y. 1974).
Hart v. Fox, 166 N.Y. Supp. 793 (1917).
In re DC Comics, Inc., 689 F.2d 1042 (C.C.P.A. 1982).
International News Service v. Associated Press, 248 U.S. 215 (1918).
Jeweler's Circular Pub. Co. v. Keystone Pub. Co., 281 Fed. 83 (2d Cir. 1922).
Kalem Company v. Harper Brothers, 222 U.S. 55 (1911).
Kendall v. Winsor, 62 U.S. 322 (1858).
King Features Syndicate v. Fleischer, 299 F. 533 (2nd Cir. 1924).
Lumley v. Wagner, 42 Eng. Rep. 687 (1852).
Manners v. Morosco, 252 U.S. 317 (1920).
National Comics Publications v. Fawcett Publications, 93 F. Supp. 349 (S.D.N.Y. 1950), *rev'd* 191 F.2d 594 (2d Cir., 1951), petition for injunction denied 198 F.2d 927 (2d Cir., 1952).
New York Herald Co. v. Star Co., 146 F. 204 (C.C.S.D. 1906), *aff'd* 146 F. 1023 (2d Cir. 1906).
Nichols v. Universal Pictures Co., 45 F.2d 119 (2d Cir. 1930).
Olson v. National Broadcasting Company, 855 F.2d 1446 (9th Cir. 1988).
Peter Pan Fabrics, Inc. v. Martin Weiner Corp., 274 F.2d 487 (2nd Cir. 1960).
Photo Drama Motion Picture Co. v. Social Uplift Film Corp., 213 Fed. 374 (S.D.N.Y. 1914), *aff'd* 220 F. 448 (2d Cir., 1915).
Rogers v. Republic Prod., Inc., 213 F.2d 662 (9th Cir. 1954).
Royal Sales Co. v. Gaynor, 164 F. 207 (2d Cir. 1908).
Rush v. Oursler, 39 F.2d 468 (2d Cir. 1930).
Sheldon v. Metro-Goldwyn Pictures Corp., 7 F. Supp. 837 (S.D.N.Y. 1934), *rev'd* 81 F. 2d 49 (2d Cir. 1936).

Shipman v. R.K.O. Radio Pictures, 100 F.2d 533 (2nd Cir. 1938).
Sperry v. Florida, 373 U.S. 379 (1963).
Star Co. v. Press Publishing Co., 143 N.Y.S. 1144 (1913).
Star Co. v. Press Publishing Co., 162 App. Div. 486 (N.Y. 1914).
Stowe v. Thomas, 23. F. Cas. 201 (C.C.E.D. Pa. 1853).
Time, Inc. v. Life Television, 123 F. Supp. 470 (D. Minn. 1954).
Warner Bros. Pictures v. Columbia Broadcasting System, 216 F. 2d 945 (9th Cir. 1954).
Washingtonian Publishing Co. v. Pearson, 360 U.S. 30 (1939).
White Smith Music Publishing Co. v. Apollo Company, 209 U.S. 1 (1908).

Index

Printed and bound by CPI Group (UK) Ltd, Croydon, CR0 4YY
16/09/2026
14963489-0001